REAL WORLD
MACRO

THIRTY-FIFTH EDITION

EDITED BY LUIS ROSERO, NICK SERPE, BRYAN SNYDER, CHRIS STURR,

AND THE *DOLLARS & SENSE* COLLECTIVE

REAL WORLD MACRO, THIRTY-FIFTH EDITION

Published by:
Economic Affairs Bureau, Inc. d/b/a *Dollars & Sense*
89 South Street, Suite LL02, Boston, MA 02111
617-447-2177; dollars@dollarsandsense.org.
For order information, contact Economic Affairs Bureau or visit: www.dollarsandsense.org.

Real World Macro is edited by the *Dollars & Sense* Collective, which also publishes *Dollars & Sense* magazine and the classroom books *Real World Micro, Current Economic Issues, Real World Globalization, Labor and the Global Economy, Real World Latin America, Real World Labor, Real World Banking and Finance, The Wealth Inequality Reader, The Economics of the Environment, Introduction to Political Economy, Unlevel Playing Fields: Understanding Wage Inequality and Discrimination*, and *Our Economic Well-Being*.

The 2018 *Dollars & Sense* Collective:
Betsy Aron, Will Beaman, Autumn Beaudoin, Sarah Cannon, Peter Kolozi, Tom Louie, John Miller, Jawied Nawabi, Nick Serpe, Zoe Sherman, Bryan Snyder, Chris Sturr, De'En Tarkpor, Cadwell Turnbull, and Jeanne Winner.

Co-editors of this volume: Luis Rosero, Nick Serpe, Bryan Snyder, and Chris Sturr

Design and layout: Nick Serpe
Cover photo: Reduction gears on Pratt & Whitney Canada PT6 gas turbine engine, Flickr user Sparkignitor, Creative Commons Attribution 3.0 Unported license.

Printed in U.S.A.

CONTENTS

THE TWO ECONOMIES

I t sometimes seems that the United States has not one, but two economies. The first exists in economics textbooks and in the minds of many government policymakers. It is an economy in which no one is involuntarily unemployed for long, families are rewarded with an ever-improving standard of living, and anyone who works hard can live the American Dream. In this economy, people are free and roughly equal, and each individual carefully looks after him- or herself, making voluntary choices to advance his or her own economic interests. Government has some limited roles in this world, but it is increasingly marginal, since the macroeconomy is a self-regulating system of wealth generation.

The second features vast disparities of income, wealth, and power. It is an economy where economic instability and downward mobility are facts of life. Jobs disappear, workers suffer long spells of unemployment, and new jobs seldom afford the same standard of living as those lost. As for the government, it sometimes adopts policies that ameliorate the abuses of capitalism, and other times does just the opposite, but it is always an active and essential participant in economic life.

If you are reading this introduction, you are probably a student in an introductory college course in macroeconomics. Your textbook will introduce you to the first economy, the harmonious world of self-regulating and stable markets. *Real World Macro* will introduce you to the second.

Why "Real World" Macro?

A standard economics textbook is full of powerful concepts. It is also, by its nature, a limited window on the economy. What is taught in most introductory macroeconomics courses today is a relatively narrow set of concepts. Inspired by neoclassical economic theory, most textbooks depict an inherently stable economy in little need of government intervention. Fifty years ago, textbooks were very different. Keynesian economic theory, which holds that government action can and must stabilize modern monetized economies, occupied a central place in introductory textbooks. Even Marxist economics, with its piercing analysis of class structure and inherent instability in capitalism, appeared regularly on the pages of those textbooks. This contraction of economics education has turned some introductory courses into little more than celebrations of today's economy as "the best of all possible worlds."

Real World Macro, designed as a supplement to standard macroeconomics text-books, is dedicated to widening the scope of economic inquiry. Its articles confront mainstream theory with a more complex reality—providing vivid, real-world illustrations of economic concepts. And where most texts uncritically present the key assumptions and propositions of traditional macroeconomic theory, *Real World Macro* asks provocative questions: What are alternative propositions about how the economy operates and who it serves? What difference do such propositions make? If this is not the best of all possible macroeconomic worlds, what might make the actual world better?

For instance, *Real World Macro*'s authors question the conventional wisdom that economic growth "lifts all boats," or benefits all of us. While mainstream text-books readily allow that economic growth has not benefited us all to the same degree, we go further and ask: Who benefits from economic growth and how much? Who has been left behind by the economic growth of the last few decades? The answers are quite disturbing. Today, economic growth, when it occurs, benefits far fewer of us than it did just a few decades ago. Economic growth during the last business-cycle expansion did more to boost profits and less to lift wages than during any economic upswing since World War II. This pattern has continued during the current long but slow recovery following the Great Recession. Spreading the benefits of economic growth more widely, through public policies intended to improve the lot of most people in the work-a-day world, would not only make our economy more equitable, but would also go a long way toward restoring more robust growth in the U.S. economy.

Ten years later after the Great Recession, the effects of the worst crisis since the Great Depression linger. But you might not know that the day-to-day operation of the market economy—unregulated financial markets, the increasing concentration of power in the hands of business, and burgeoning inequality—caused the accumulation of debt that set the stage for the crisis. Explaining how and why that happened and what to do about it is every responsible economist's job.

Today, employment growth remains stubbornly sluggish, and the decline in the unemployment rate has been driven not just by people moving from unemployment into jobs, but also by people dropping out of the labor force altogether. That supports the argument that government needs to ensure sustained full employment. Similarly, to avoid another financial crisis, the government needs to properly regulate financial markets and institutions. Those two steps would go a long way toward improving the lot of those who have fallen on hard times. Genuine and sustained full employment, with unemployment rates as low as 2%, would lead to "a major reduction in the incidence of poverty, homelessness, sickness, and crime," as William Vickery, the Nobel Prize–winning economist, once argued. We think that policies like these, and the alternative perspectives that lie behind them, are worth debating—and that requires hearing a range of views.

What's in This Book

Real World Macro is organized to follow the outline of a standard economics text. Each chapter leads off with a brief introduction, including study questions for the chapter, and then provides several articles, mostly drawn from *Dollars & Sense* magazine, that illustrate the chapter's key concepts. Here is a quick walk through the contents.

Chapter 1, Perspectives on Macroeconomic Theory, introduces alternatives to neoclassical-inspired macroeconomic theory. The chapter explains in everyday language the roots of the economic crisis—the extreme inequality, elite power, and unregulated financial markets of today's economy. It looks at what's wrong with neoliberal policies that would turn the operation of the domestic and international economy over to unregulated markets. Finally, the chapter moves beyond Keynesianism, to include Marxist and environmentalist perspectives on the macroeconomy.

Chapter 2, Macroeconomic Measurement, takes a critical look at the standard measures of economic activity, such as GDP, the unemployment rate, the Consumer Price Index (and other price indices), and the official poverty rate. What do those measures actually tell us about the quality of life in today's economy, and what crucial aspects of economic life do they leave uncounted? This chapter underscores that economic measurement issues are not just dry, technical questions for economists to answer—they play a critical role in defining the economic problems that face us and the economic goals we aspire to reach.

Chapter 3, Economic Growth and Business Cycles, covers two of the most important issues in macroeconomics: the causes of cyclical fluctuations in economic activity—the boom-and-bust patterns of capitalist economies—and the factors determining long-term economic growth and development. This chapter includes articles analyzing the causes of the global "Great Recession," and the stagnation that has set in since then. It also addresses the challenges facing the developing world, such as transitioning away from dependence on resource extraction and commodities booms, developing domestic demand-driven approaches to growth and development, and avoiding debt traps. This chapter also explores the subject of environmental sustainability and the pairing of environmental goals and economic growth.

Chapter 4, Unemployment and Inflation, looks at the relationships between these two macroeconomic variables and addresses the causes of unemployment today. It continues with a discussion of the "natural rate of unemployment," offering an interpretation very different from that intended by its originators. Next, we find three articles on how unemployment is tabulated and the economic consequences of an increase in the minimum wage. The final article in this chapter covers an important part of Keynesian theory: "sticky wages" and their effect on labor markets.

Chapter 5, Wealth, Inequality, and Poverty, examines these three outcomes of economic activity and growth. *Dollars & Sense* authors show who is accumulating wealth and who isn't, both in the United States and worldwide. They examine the reasons for increasing inequality in the United States over the last several decades and argue that inequality is not a prerequisite for economic growth, but rather a major contributor to today's economic problems. The chapter concludes with a "Primer on Piketty," the French economist whose book *Capital in the Twenty-First Century* made a major impact on public discussions of inequality on both sides of the Atlantic.

Chapter 6, Fiscal Policy, Deficits, and Austerity, assesses government spending and tax policy. The chapter's authors examine the arguments made against fiscal stimulus in the face of the Great Recession and argue that the government could and should have done more. The next articles address recent U.S. tax legislation and its economic impact along with New York State's response to its punitive measures. We then move on to the effects of austerity policies on Greece and crushing debt and austerity on Puerto Rico. We finish this chapter with a timely essay on the macroeconomics of increased military spending.

Chapter 7, Money and Monetary Policy, looks at what money is, how money is created, and how the Federal Reserve ("the Fed") conducts monetary policy. After Doug Orr's seminal essay "What is Money?" we follow up with an article on Modern Monetary Theory. Following this are essays on banks, the Fed, and the limits of monetary policy as a stimulus for weak economies. The chapter ends with three articles on broader topics: John Maynard Keynes' views of monetary policy and its limitations, the question of what macroeconomic objectives monetary policy authorities should prioritize, and how the Fed actually changes interest rates.

Chapter 8, Savings, Investment, and Finance, peers inside the world of finance and comes up with some probing questions. What factors affect the pace of investment? What role did financial deregulation and exotic new financial instruments play in the economic crisis? What are the sources of financial "bubbles"? And what alternative public policies can promote stable investment and functional financial markets? Primers on financialization, stock buybacks, and Hyman Minsky's financial instability hypothesis all lend themselves to the analysis of the financial crisis of 2008 and the subsequent global meltdown.

Chapter 9, The Global Economy, assesses the prevailing neoliberal policy prescriptions for the global economy. The articles criticize globalization based on "free trade" and financial liberalization, looking closely at its effects on economic growth and development, as well as inequality, poverty, and labor conditions. They consider the changing place of the United States in the global economy, the role of the dollar, the promotion of new "trade and investment" agreements, and the impacts on businesses and households in the United States and worldwide. We have also included updates on Trump's trade wars and an analysis of the motivations behind Brexit.

Chapter 10, Resistance and Alternatives, returns to many of the issues covered in the course of the previous nine chapters, but with a special focus on challenges to prevailing economic policies and institutions. Among the issues addressed are employment, the environment, tax reform, financial regulation, labor conditions, and economic development. ❏

Chapter 1

PERSPECTIVES ON MACROECONOMIC THEORY

INTRODUCTION

Years ago, political economist Bob Sutcliffe developed a sure-fire economic indicator that he called the Marx/Keynes ratio—the ratio of references to Karl Marx to references to John Maynard Keynes in Paul Samuelson's *Economics*, the bestselling introductory economics textbook in the decades following World War II. During a recession or period of sluggish economic growth, the Marx/Keynes ratio would climb, as social commentators and even economists fretted over the future of capitalism. During economic booms, however, Marx's predictions of the collapse of capitalism disappeared from the pages of Samuelson's textbook, while the paeans to Keynesian demand-management policies multiplied.

Today, Sutcliffe's ratio wouldn't work very well. Marx has been pushed off the pages of most introductory macroeconomics textbooks altogether, and even Keynes has been left with only a minor role. Our authors don't agree that these important thinkers should be marginalized. In this chapter, they critically assess the classical-inspired mainstream models and reintroduce the dissident schools of thought that have been purged from economics textbooks in recent decades. And they offer a serious look at the forces that brought on the economic crisis and what to do about them.

Zoe Sherman (Article 1.1) turns Ronald Reagan's famous 1980 presidential debate question—"Are you better off than you were four years ago?"— into a look at the changes in the quality of life in the United States in recent decades. She asks whether we're better off as a society than we were 40 years ago. Certainly, per capita income is higher (what mainstream economists would define as being "better off"), but we also have rising inequality, increased burdens of work, greater insecurity, and serious problems of environmental sustainability.

Next, economist Robert Pollin (Article 1.2) tackles the underpinnings of neoliberal policy prescriptions for the global economy. As he sees it, unfettered globalization will be unable to resolve three basic problems: an ever-larger "reserve army of the unemployed" that reduces the bargaining power of workers in all countries (the "Marx problem"); the inherent instability and volatility of investment and financial markets (the "Keynes problem"); and the erosion of "fairness" and a sense of "the common good" that lend legitimacy to the state (the "Polanyi problem").

Economist Alejandro Reuss contributes a primer on Marxist economics (Article 1.3). Marx rejected the idea of a self-equilibrating economy and argued that capitalism was inherently dynamic and unstable. Reuss describes some of Marx's key ideas, including the nature of capitalist exploitation, and what Marx saw as two ingredients of an eventual crisis of capitalism: overproduction and the falling rate of profit.

Then, in "Sharing the Wealth of the Commons" (Article 1.4), Peter Barnes focuses our attention on the oft-ignored forms of wealth that we do not own privately, but are held in "commons." He challenges the way that conventional economists view the environment and other goods that are shared by many people.

Finally, we have an interview with economist William K. Tabb on "Transnational Capital and Transnational Labor" (Article 1.5), which looks at globalization through a "class" analysis.

Discussion Questions

1. (Article 1.1) What are the main ways that Sherman argues that well-being in the United States has deteriorated over the last 40 years? In what ways does she argue it has improved?

2. (Article 1.2) Summarize the Marx, Keynes, and Polanyi problems. Why does Pollin think that neoliberal globalization policies will be unable to resolve them?

3. (Article 1.3) What roles do a "falling rate of profit," a "reserve army of the unemployed," and "overproduction" play in Marx's theory of capitalist crisis? Do you think today's macroeconomy displays any of those tendencies?

4. (Article 1.4) What is a "commons"? According to Barnes, how has our common wealth been "given away"? What do you think of his plans on how to take it back?

5. (Article 1.5) How far do theories of a "transnational capitalist class" and "transnational capitalist state" get us in understanding the restructuring of the capitalist world economy in the late 20th century?

Article 1.1

WHAT DOES IT MEAN TO BE "BETTER OFF"?

Taking stock of how U.S. society has progressed or faltered over the last 40 years.

BY ZOE SHERMAN
November/December 2014

In 1980, Ronald Reagan, trying to defeat Jimmy Carter's bid for a second term as president, asked, "Are you better off than you were four years ago?" A conservative turn in American politics was already underway and, campaigning on that question, Reagan rode the wave into the presidency. Forty years into the political epoch he symbolizes, and 40 years into this magazine's history, we might well echo Reagan's question: Are you better off than you were 40 years ago?

It is a deceptively simple question. What would it mean to be better off? Probably a lot of good things and a lot of bad things have happened to you in forty years (or however many of those years you've been alive) and to decide whether you are better off you would have to do some weighing. For many of us the final answer would be, "well, yes and no..." For any one person many of the then-vs.-now differences are largely a matter of the life cycle—maybe you were a child decades ago and an adult now. It really makes more sense to ask whether we as a society are better off that we were forty years ago.

The well-being of a society cannot be measured in a single dimension any more than a single person's well-being can. Assessments of our national well-being often begin—and too often end—with gross domestic product (GDP). Per capita GDP basically answers the question, "Are we collectively, on average, richer, as measured by the dollar value of the things we produce and sell to one another?" (This includes the government's provision of goods and services, even if they are not really "sold.")

Not only is GDP limited to measuring just one dimension of well-being—it doesn't even measure that dimension all that well. It fails to count the work we do for one another at home or in other non-monetized ways. It gives us only an aggregate with no information about how access to all those goods and services is distributed. And goods and bads get added together so long as they cost money and therefore generate income for someone—that is, a thousand dollars spent on cigarettes and treatments for emphysema add just as much to GDP as a thousand dollars spent on healthy foods and preventive medicine.

We'll certainly want to go beyond just GDP per capita, as we take a tour through various dimensions of well-being and take stock of how we have progressed or faltered over the last 40 years.

Income and Stuff

Though we know from the outset that we will not stop here, we may as well start in the traditional starting place: Changes in our national income, taking into account population growth and inflation. Real per capita GDP was $25,427 in 1974 (in 2009 U.S. dollars) and now it is almost double that at $49,810. A lot of that GDP growth represents more of the good stuff we already had in 1974 or cool, well-being-enhancing new stuff that we have now but didn't have then. I really like having a dishwasher and enough dishes that we don't have to wash the plates and forks after every meal (more of the already-invented good stuff). I am also awfully fond of my computer, Internet service, DVDs, and streaming video (cool new stuff).

But some of the higher production/higher income measured by GDP represents not-so-great things. Longer car commutes, for example, are costly and contribute to GDP through spending on gasoline, car repairs and replacement, and purchases of more cars per household. But long car commutes add nothing and likely subtract from the commuters' well-being. They also add pollutants to the air that affect us all.

Even if we subtract out the bads, the goods themselves can get to be too much of a good thing. Plenty of people know the experience of feeling that they are choking on stuff, crowded out of their living spaces by their belongings. Self storage ranks as the fastest growing segment of the commercial real estate industry since 1975. Self-storage businesses brought in revenues of $24 billion dollars in 2013. Now, consider that the average size of a new single family home increased 57% from 1970 to the early 2000s. That means we spent $24 billion to store the things that we can't fit in our homes, even though many of our homes are bigger than ever!

Economic and Social Inequality

If the distribution of income had remained roughly the same over the last 40 years, then the fact that per capita GDP nearly doubled would mean that everyone's income had nearly doubled. That's not what happened. Instead, those at the top of the income distribution have vastly more income than 40 years ago while those at the bottom have less. The real income of a household at the 20th percentile (above 20% of all households in the income ranking) has scarcely budged since 1974—it was $20,000 and change then and is $20,000 and change now. For those below the 20th percentile, real income has fallen. The entire bottom 80% of households ranked by income now gets only 49% of the national pie, down from 57% in 1974. That means that the top 20% has gone from 43% to 51% of total income. Even within the top 20%, the distribution skews upward. Most of the income gains of the top 20% are concentrated in the top 5%; most of the gains of the top 5% are concentrated in the top 1%; most of the gains in the top 1% are concentrated in the top 0.1%.

By 1974, labor force participation rates were in the midst of a marked upward trend, driven largely by the entry of women into the paid labor force. Starting from a low of 59% in the early 1960s, the labor force participation rate passed 61% in 1974 and peaked at 67% in the late 1990s. Labor force participation has drifted back downward somewhat since then through a combination of baby boomer retirement and discouraged workers giving up on the labor force since the crisis that began in 2007, but it remains at 63%, still higher than in 1974. That means that even while more of us are participating in market work, the market is concentrating its rewards in a shrinking cabal of increasingly powerful hands.

More of us are working, but the share of national income that goes to ordinary workers is smaller. National income can be sorted into categories based on the route it takes to a person's pocket. One category of income—wages and salaries earned in return for work—is labor income. The other categories—profit, dividends, rent, interest—are all forms of income that result from owning. For many decades, the labor share of national income held fairly steady, but beginning in the mid-1970s it started falling. Economist James Heintz found that the share of the national income earned as private-business-sector wages (excluding executive compensation) fell from 58% in 1970 to 50% in 2010; the share that went to non-supervisory workers fell from 45% to 31%.

Even as hourly pay for a broad swath of people in the middle—between the 20th and 80th percentiles—has just about kept pace with inflation, the traditional tickets to the middle class have become more of a reach. Rising costs of higher education and housing have consigned many to a near-permanent state of debt peonage to maintain a tenuous grasp on middle-class social status, while others are blocked from access entirely.

While more employers now require a college degree before letting a job applicant set foot on the bottom rung of the career ladder, college tuitions have risen more than three times as fast as inflation since 1974. The total volume of outstanding student debt has passed $1 trillion—greater than even the volume of outstanding credit card debt.

Housing, too, has become more unaffordable. For white people who bought houses in the mid 20th century with the benefits of supportive government policies, a home was a secure form of both savings and shelter. (Discriminatory neighborhood redlining prevented most nonwhites from enjoying these benefits.) Within recent decades, however, home prices have risen faster than median incomes and deceptive lending practices trapped many home-buyers in unaffordable mortgages. For those who were lucky, and bought and sold at the right times, the housing bubble was a windfall. For many more, the home has become a millstone of debt, and the threat of foreclosure has rendered shelter uncertain.

The division of the national income pie may be more skewed, but do we all have an equal shot at finding our way into the charmed circle of plenty? The probability that a person who starts out in the bottom income quintile will make it into the top quintile has stayed remarkably constant since the mid 20th century. A child born in the bottom quintile in 1971 had an 8.4% chance of making it to the top quintile; for a child born in 1986, the probability is 9.0%. Our national mythology notwithstanding, mobility is lower in the United States than in other comparably developed economies.

Now for some good news: although wealth and income disparities have worsened, we have made real strides in reducing disparities based on race and gender. Long-standing identity-based hierarchies have weakened, though they certainly have not disappeared. The narrowing of race and gender gaps in economic well-being owes everything to the social movements of the 20th century. The gaps' persistence can be attributed both to differential impacts of ostensibly race- or gender-neutral policies and to our low levels of social mobility. The war on drugs and other "get tough on crime" polices really mean the mass incarceration of black men. "Welfare reform" withdrew much of whatever limited support there was for the intense labor—mostly women's—of raising children with minimal cash resources. Even as bigotry, in several forms, has lost explicit government sanction, the lack of social mobility casts the shadow of the more explicit inequities of the past longer and deeper.

Not only is income unequally distributed, it is also, for many, insecure. Having income is a good thing and helps to meet present needs. If there's some left over, present income might even help meet future needs. But confidence in future income

Narrowing Race and Gender Gaps

The Civil Rights Movement, which achieved many of its judicial and legislative successes between 1954 (*Brown v. Board of Education*) and 1965 (Voting Rights Act), and the Women's Movement, whose judicial and legislative successes followed soon after (Title IX in 1972; *Roe v. Wade* in 1973) have reduced the role of outright, explicit discrimination. This is no small matter. Yet there are still wide gaps between white and nonwhite, especially black Americans, in measures of economic well-being, and also gaps between men and women of all races.

	White Men	White Women	Black Men	Black Women
1974 Median Income (in 2013 dollars)	38,517	13,944	23,372	11,988
2013 Median Income (in 2013 dollars)	40,122	23,780	24,855	20,044
1974 Unemployment rate	3.5%	5.1%	7.4%	8.8%
2013 Unemployment rate	6.2%	5.7%	12.9%	11.3%

Sources: Median income: Census Bureau, Current Population Survey, Table P02 (census.gov); Unemployment: Bureau of Labor Statistics (bls.gov).

The resources that would close the racial income gap are hard for individuals and families to come by. There is a strong correlation between educational attainment and future earnings, but black children on average get less from their public schools than white children get. The racial income gap has narrowed slightly between

matters to us a lot. We worry about whether we will be able to meet our needs tomorrow—and we have more reasons to worry now than ever.

Employment is a sometime thing: Workers on short-term contracts—like the majority of undergraduate college instructors who work on an adjunct basis—and the self-employed, whose income is also unpredictable, add up to 30% of the U.S. work force with uncertain, episodic income. It is difficult to know exactly how the current level of job insecurity compares to 1974 because the Census Bureau only began systematic data collection on contingent labor in 1995. Median job tenure (years with one's current employer) has fallen for men over the past generation, though it has risen for women. Perhaps the feeling of greater insecurity is a result of men's paid work coming to resemble the precariousness of women's paid work, even while many families still think of a man's income as the mainstay.

The constant churn of a short-term-employment labor system means that for most who fall into poverty, poverty is not a permanent condition. By the mid-1970s, a decade into the War on Poverty, the poverty rate had fallen to 11%, but the reduction was not sustained. Since then, the poverty rate has fluctuated between 11% and 15% with no consistent long-term trend. Today, we are in a high-poverty phase: somewhere in the neighborhood of 15% of the population is living in poverty during any given month. While most spells of poverty last well under a year (6.6 months is the median), a large minority of the population cycles in and out of poverty. From

1974 and now, but the median white household still has more than six times the wealth of the median nonwhite or Hispanic household. Low wealth reduces nonwhite families' ability to buy housing in better-funded public school districts or invest in college education—or in private K-12 substitutes if the public schools available to them are subpar.

People with criminal convictions, once released, face enormous barriers to employment. For the more than one-in-six black men who have been incarcerated (a rate six times that for white men), a criminal record consigns them to the margins of the labor market. In some states, moreover, a felony conviction results in a permanent loss of voting rights and therefore the loss of one of the most powerful tools for political change.

The story for the gender gap in economic well-being is mixed. Women earn lower average incomes and suffer higher poverty rates than men (despite now graduating from college in greater numbers than men). But the female unemployment rate is, on average, lower than for men, and it has become less volatile; in the last few business-cycle downturns,hh men have been more at risk of job loss than women.

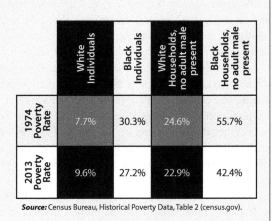

	White Individuals	Black Individuals	White Households, no adult male present	Black Households, no adult male present
1974 Poverty Rate	7.7%	30.3%	24.6%	55.7%
2013 Poverty Rate	9.6%	27.2%	22.9%	42.4%

Source: Census Bureau, Historical Poverty Data, Table 2 (census.gov).

January 2009 to December 2011, 31.6% of the population spent at least two consecutive months below the poverty line.

Families can fall into poverty for a number of reasons. Loss of employment, certainly, is a major cause. Another common precipitating event is the birth of a child—without guaranteed paid family leave, childbirth often means a simultaneous increase in household size (and expenses) and decrease in income. Health problems are another trigger for economic distress. Medical bills are the number-one cause of personal bankruptcy; even those who have health insurance may be unable to pay for their medical care. Insecurity is our constant companion.

What Money Can't Buy

Many measures of our well-being cannot be viewed through the lens of income and the consumer spending it enables. A full life is not just made of purchased goods. Some of the most important gains in well-being have to do witht the political and social gains achieved by social movements countering sexism and racism. The Civil Rights and Women's Liberation movements helped achieve an increase in economic well-being, sure, but also an increase in dignity and political power.

In the mid-1970s, marriage was still a strikingly unequal contract that subordinated wives to husbands. (Same-sex marriage was not permitted anywhere in the United

States. Though there were already legal cases on the issue in the early 1970s, the courts upheld same-sex marriage bans.) The criminal laws did not grant married women a right to sexual autonomy and did little to protect their physical or emotional safety; rape laws contained exemptions in the case of husbands, and domestic violence was largely hidden from view. But change was beginning. The Women's Movement brought attention to gender-based violence and built a network of support for survivors; the earliest rape crisis centers and emergency shelters are now marking their 40th anniversaries, taking stock of the considerable progress we've made, and pressing on with the work that still needs to be done. By 1993, all states had changed their rape laws, withdrawing a husband's unlimited sexual access to his wife's body. In 1994, President Clinton signed into law the Violence Against Women Act, which devotes federal resources to the investigation and prosecution of violent crimes targeting women. Indeed, marriage contracts are now legally symmetrical (even if marriage is not yet symmetrical in practice)—and 33 states license marriages between any two unrelated adults, regardless of sex.

Not only are women safer at home than we were 40 years ago, we have also claimed larger roles outside the home. Amendments made in 1972 to the Civil Rights Act expanded legal prohibitions on sex discrimination, including the Title IX provision prohibiting educational institutions receiving federal financial assistance from discriminating on the basis of sex. Protections against workplace discrimination are also stronger—the term "sexual harassment," unknown in 1974, is now recognized as describing a form of discrimination that can carry serious legal consequences. In the political arena, the number of women in Congress has more than tripled since the mid-seventies. Prior to 1974, only four women had ever served as state governors. Since then, 32 more women have held that office.

Important work combating racial discrimination was also underway 40 years ago. The Equal Employment Opportunity Commission, responsible for enforcing the Civil Rights Act in the workplace, was not yet a decade old in 1974, still early in the process of setting legal precedent for documenting and opposing workplace discrimination, including the disguised discrimination of disparate impact (when a seemingly neutral rule disproportionately affects members of a protected group). The battle to make banks' mortgage lending data public was won in the mid-1970s, which then allowed organized (and ongoing) opposition to the "redlining" that the publicized data revealed. Twenty years after *Brown v. Board of Education* prohibited explicit, legally mandated school segregation, education activists in the mid-1970s pushed governments to take a more proactive role in school integration, albeit with mixed and in many places only temporary results.

A Time for Every Matter

The good life for most of us means not just money to buy the stuff we need, but also plenty of time off the job to participate in social and civic life and to rest. The inequities of the labor market have divided us into two categories—the overworked and the underemployed. For those with consistent employment, the work is often too much work. Even as output per worker hour rises—meaning that, as a society we could increase our material standard of living while holding leisure time steady, or hold our material standard of living steady while increasing leisure time, we have instead increased average work hours per year. Hours of paid labor per employee were about the same in 2000 as in 1973, but since more people were in the paid labor force, the average number of hours per working age person rose from 1,217 to 1,396, equivalent to a full extra month of 40-hour workweeks.

One consequence is that we have a leisure shortage. Chronic sleep deprivation has become the norm. According to a study by the National Academy of Sciences, Americans' average amount of sleep fell by 20% over the course of the 20th century. Meanwhile, the unemployed and underemployed have hours on their hands that they either spend job hunting, in the endless sequence of bureaucratic tasks necessary to access the meager benefits available through the threadbare social safety net, or idle, their unclaimed hours more a burden than a gift. The supposed benefit of unemployment—leisure time to mitigate the loss of income—is not in evidence in the subjective well-being of the unemployed, who are more likely to suffer depression and family stress.

The time crunch resulting from more hours of paid work also squeezes our ability to keep up with the necessary unpaid work at home. Sociologist Arlie Hochschild was already noting in her research during the 1980s that dual-income households were giving up leisure or letting the standards of housework and at-home caregiving slip—often a mix of both. When a stay-at-home mother goes out to work for pay and reduces her hours of home production, the household's increase in cash income gets added to GDP but the household's loss of unpaid labor time is not subtracted. Or, if she hires a housecleaning service and a babysitter, the wages earned by the mother, the housecleaner, and the babysitter all get added to GDP, but the work done by the housecleaner and babysitter are substituting for unpaid work that was already being done. Correcting for the loss of home production that has accompanied the rise in female participation in the paid labor force requires us to revise downward the increase in output over the period 1959–2004—the largest hit came between 1959 and 1972 with the withdrawal of about 500 hours of household labor per year, a reduction of almost 20%.

Common Resources and Public Goods

Just as mothers' labor is treated by official measures as a freely available resource, so are the gifts of nature. Nature is the source of the resources our lives depend on—trace back any production process and the earth's resources are there at the origin. Nature is also the sink into which all the refuse and byproducts of our production get dumped. Environmental concerns were at the core of another one of the 1970s' mass social movements. The first Earth Day was celebrated in 1970, and the Environmental Protection Agency (EPA) was created that same year. Concerns and activism around air pollution, water pollution, and the loss of biodiversity led, over the course of the 1970s, to the Clean Air, Clean Water, and Endangered Species Acts. Since the 1970s, the harms of an automotive culture have been lessened with emissions standards, fuel-efficiency standards, and the ban on leaded gasoline. Municipal recycling programs now divert tons of materials back into the human production cycle, reducing the strains on the planet as both a source of materials and as a sink for waste products.

Over the past 40 years, we have made some important gains in how we make use of the gifts of nature, but our gains are nowhere near enough. Probably the most disastrous

---

Private Wealth, Public Squalor

Just as we are depleting the gifts of nature, we are depleting or withdrawing many of the gifts we have collectively bestowed on ourselves, our publicly provided goods. We are consuming our public infrastructure—as seen dramatically in the 2004 failure of the levies in New Orleans during Hurricane Katrina and in the 2007 collapse of a bridge in Minneapolis.

Public goods can only be sustained if we each contribute. If we don't trust one another to contribute, we each feel the need to hoard our resources privately. When we hoard our resources privately, we discourage others from contributing, and our public goods wither.

The hoarding is especially extreme at the top of the income distribution. The top marginal tax rate has fallen from 70% in the 1970s to less than 40% today. The money not put into the common kitty instead pays for private substitutes—private schools (instead of public), private clubs (instead of public parks), gated communities (instead of neighborhoods that welcome visitors), and private security to defend these private goods against the claims of those who are excluded.

---

shortcoming of all is our collective failure to maintain the atmospheric balance. Since the middle of the twentieth century, we have known that an increased concentration of carbon dioxide (CO_2) in the atmosphere will cause dangerous climate change. Despite that, we have continued to emit CO_2 at a staggering rate. Even if we were to stop tomorrow, the effects on the global climate would play out at an accelerating rate for centuries. Several of the destabilizing shifts—melting of the polar ice caps, thawing of the arctic permafrost—are only in the early stages of "positive feedback loops," in which the result of some warming triggers more warming. Rising sea levels threaten coastal cities around the world. Severe storms will continue to increase in frequency. Wider year-to-year variations in temperature and rainfall will disrupt food production.

Looking Backward, Looking Forward

When Reagan asked, "Are you better off than you were four years ago?" he predicted that many people would say "no" and that those who answered "no" would vote for change (not necessarily the kinds of change, as it turns out, that would solve their problems). We are still in the era that Reagan helped to usher in. How is it working for us? Are we better off now, or is it time for a change?

We have seen average income rise, though not as fast as it had in the post–World War II era. Many of the most important gains we have made, moreover, are not dependent on rising average income. The achievements of the Civil Rights and Women's Movements were about dismantling barriers to full participation in a society wealthy enough that it already could provide for all. Now rising income inequality is throwing up new barriers to inclusion.

There are enough ways in which we have lost ground that it must be time for a change. Not a change back—I would not trade the real gains we've made for a return to the so-called "Golden Age" of the 1940s–1970s—but a change that can carry us forward to a world we will still want to live in 40 years from now.

The environmental crisis means that continuing with business as usual would sink us soon. Salvation can only come with a turn away from the fetish of GDP growth. About 40 years ago, research began systematically documenting the failure of rising average income to keep delivering rising levels of happiness (a phenomenon known as the "Easterlin paradox," for researcher Richard Easterlin). Unorthodox economists rethought the growth imperative: E.F. Schumacher wrote *Small is Beautiful* and Herman Daly penned *Steady-State Economics*. The kingdom of Bhutan famously rejected GDP and instituted instead the measurement of Gross National Happiness. All urged a turn away from defining well-being according to money incomes.

Once a society reaches a level of income that overcomes deprivation—when nobody need go hungry or homeless, nor suffer or die from preventable disease—more income has little affect on the dimensions of well-being that have intrinsic value.

Instead we must turn toward maximizing equality. In their book *The Spirit Level*, Richard Wilkinson and Kate Pickett demonstrate how consistently the empirical evidence shows that more equal societies have better social outcomes in many dimensions, including longer life expectancy, better educational outcomes, stronger environmental protection, and lower rates of incarceration, obesity, and teen pregnancy. Perhaps—after 40 more years of trying and failing to find our way to well-being through more and more market activity, in a quest for more and more income, which has been distributed more and more unequally—we are finally ready to set our priorities straight. It is equality and environmental sustainability that will allow for human flourishing. ❑

Sources: Self Storage Association (selfstorage.org); Margot Adler, "Behind the Ever-Expanding American Dream House," National Public Radio (npr.org); U.S. Census Bureau, Current Population Survey, Tables H-1 and H-2 (census.gov); Bureau of Labor Statistics, CPI Detailed Report, Data for August 2014 (bls.gov); Case-Shiller Home Price Index (us.spindices.com); Census Bureau, Table H-8 (census.gov); Jim Tankersley, "Economic mobility hasn't changed in a half-century in America, economists declare," *Washington Post*, Jan. 23, 2014 (washingtonpost.com); The Equality of Opportunity Project (equality-of-opportunity.org); U.S. Census 2012 Statistical Abstract, Table 721 (census.gov); NAACP, Criminal Justice Fact Sheet (naacp.org); Ibby Caputo, "Paying the Bills One Gig at a Time," WGBH, Feb. 1, 2012 (wgbh.org); Bureau of Labor Statistics, "Employee Tenure in 2014" (bls.gov); Ashley N. Edwards, "Dynamics of Economic Well-Being: Poverty, 2009-2011," Report Number: P70-137, January 2014 (census.gov); Moms Rising, Maternity/Paternity Leave (momsrising.org); Dan Mangan, "Medical Bills Are the Biggest Cause of US Bankruptcies: Study," CNBC, June 25, 2013 (cnbc.com); Christina LaMontagne, "NerdWallet Health finds Medical Bankruptcy accounts for majority of personal bankruptcies," March 26, 2014 (nerdwallet.com); Juliet Schor, "Sustainable Consumption and Worktime Reduction," *Journal of Industrial Ecology*, 2005; Edward Wolff, Ajit Zacharias, and Thomas Masterson, "Long-Term Trends in the Levy Institute Measure of Economic Well-Being (LIMEW), United States, 1959-2004," Levy Economics Institute of Bard College (levyinstitute.org); Nancy Folbre, *The Invisible Heart*, Chapter 3: "Measuring Success" (New Press, 2001); Environmental Protection Agency, "Earth Day and EPA History" (epa.gov); Environmental Protection Agency, Laws and Executive Orders (epa.gov).

Article 1.2

WHAT'S WRONG WITH NEOLIBERALISM?
The Marx, Keynes, and Polanyi Problems

BY ROBERT POLLIN
May/June 2004

During the years of the Clinton administration, the term "Washington Consensus" began circulating to designate the common policy positions of the U.S. administration along with the International Monetary Fund (IMF) and World Bank. These positions, implemented in the United States and abroad, included free trade, a smaller government share of the economy, and the deregulation of financial markets. This policy approach has also become widely known as *neoliberalism*, a term which draws upon the classical meaning of the word *liberalism*.

Classical liberalism is the political philosophy that embraces the virtues of free-market capitalism and the corresponding minimal role for government interventions, especially as regards measures to promote economic equality within capitalist societies. Thus, a classical liberal would favor minimal levels of government spending and taxation, and minimal levels of government regulation over the economy, including financial and labor markets. According to the classical liberal view, businesses should be free to operate as they wish, and to succeed or fail as such in a competitive marketplace. Meanwhile, consumers rather than government should be responsible for deciding which businesses produce goods and services that are of sufficient quality as well as reasonably priced. Businesses that provide overexpensive or low-quality products will then be out-competed in the marketplace regardless of the regulatory standards established by governments. Similarly, if businesses offer workers a wage below what the worker is worth, then a competitor firm will offer this worker a higher wage. The firm unwilling to offer fair wages would not survive over time in the competitive marketplace.

This same reasoning also carries over to the international level. Classical liberals favor free trade between countries rather than countries operating with tariffs or other barriers to the free flow of goods and services between countries. They argue that restrictions on the free movement of products and money between countries only protects uncompetitive firms from market competition, and thus holds back the economic development of countries that choose to erect such barriers.

Neoliberalism and the Washington Consensus are contemporary variants of this longstanding political and economic philosophy. The major difference between classical liberalism as a philosophy and contemporary neoliberalism as a set of policy measures is with implementation. Washington Consensus policymakers are committed to free-market policies when they support the interests of big business, as, for example, with lowering regulations at the workplace. But these same policymakers become far less insistent on free-market principles when invoking such principles might damage big business interests. Federal Reserve and IMF interventions to bail out wealthy asset holders during the frequent global financial crises in the 1990s are obvious violations of free-market precepts.

Broadly speaking, the effects of neoliberalism in the less developed countries over the 1990s reflected the experience of the Clinton years in the United States. A high proportion of less developed countries were successful, just in the manner of the United States under Clinton, in reducing inflation and government budget deficits, and creating a more welcoming climate for foreign trade, multinational corporations, and financial market investors. At the same time, most of Latin America, Africa, and Asia—with China being the one major exception—experienced deepening problems of poverty and inequality in the 1990s, along with slower growth and frequent financial market crises, which in turn produced still more poverty and inequality.

If free-market capitalism is a powerful mechanism for creating wealth, why does a neoliberal policy approach, whether pursued by Clinton, Bush, or the IMF, produce severe difficulties in terms of inequality and financial instability, which in turn diminish the market mechanism's ability to even promote economic growth? It will be helpful to consider this in terms of three fundamental problems that result from a free-market system, which I term "the Marx Problem," "the Keynes problem," and "the Polanyi problem." Let us take these up in turn.

The Marx Problem

Does someone in your family have a job and, if so, how much does it pay? For the majority of the world's population, how one answers these two questions determines, more than anything else, what one's standard of living will be. But how is it decided whether a person has a job and what their pay will be? Getting down to the most immediate level of decision-making, this occurs through various types of bargaining in labor markets between workers and employers. Karl Marx argued that, in a free-market economy generally, workers have less power than employers in this bargaining process because workers cannot fall back on other means of staying alive if they fail to get hired into a job. Capitalists gain higher profits through having this relatively stronger bargaining position. But Marx also stressed that workers' bargaining power diminishes further when unemployment and underemployment are high, since that means that employed workers can be more readily replaced by what Marx called "the reserve army" of the unemployed outside the office, mine, or factory gates.

Neoliberalism has brought increasing integration of the world's labor markets through reducing barriers to international trade and investment by multinationals. For workers in high-wage countries such as the United States, this effectively means that the reserve army of workers willing to accept jobs at lower pay than U.S. workers expands to include workers in less developed countries. It isn't the case that businesses will always move to less developed countries or that domestically produced goods will necessarily be supplanted by imports from low-wage countries. The point is that U.S. workers face an increased *credible* threat that they can be supplanted. If everything else were to remain the same in the U.S. labor market, this would then mean that global integration would erode the bargaining power of U.S. workers and thus tend to bring lower wages.

But even if this is true for workers in the United States and other rich countries, shouldn't it also mean that workers in poor countries have greater job opportunities and better bargaining positions? In fact, there are areas where workers in poor countries are gaining enhanced job opportunities through international trade and multinational investments. But these gains are generally quite limited. This is because a long-term transition out of agriculture in poor countries continues to expand the reserve army of unemployed and underemployed workers in these countries as well. Moreover, when neoliberal governments in poor countries reduce their support for agriculture—through cuts in both tariffs on imported food products and subsidies for domestic farmers—this makes it more difficult for poor farmers to compete with multinational agribusiness firms. This is especially so when the rich countries maintain or increase their own agricultural supports, as has been done in the United States under Bush. In addition, much of the growth in the recently developed export-oriented manufacturing sectors of poor countries has failed to significantly increase jobs even in this sector. This is because the new export-oriented production sites frequently do not represent net additions to the country's total supply of manufacturing firms. They rather replace older firms that were focused on supplying goods to domestic markets. The net result is that the number of people looking for jobs in the developing countries grows faster than the employers seeking new workers. Here again, workers' bargaining power diminishes.

This does not mean that global integration of labor markets must necessarily bring weakened bargaining power and lower wages for workers. But it does mean that unless some non-market forces in the economy, such as government regulations or effective labor unions, are able to counteract these market processes, workers will indeed continue to experience weakened bargaining strength and eroding living standards.

The Keynes Problem

In a free-market economy, investment spending by businesses is the main driving force that produces economic growth, innovation, and jobs. But as John Maynard Keynes stressed, private investment decisions are also unavoidably risky ventures. Businesses have to put up money without knowing whether they will produce any profits in the future. As such, investment spending by business is likely to fluctuate far more than, say, decisions by households as to how much they will spend per week on groceries.

But investment fluctuations will also affect overall spending in the economy, including that of households. When investment spending declines, this means that businesses will hire fewer workers. Unemployment rises as a result, and this in turn will lead to cuts in household spending. Declines in business investment spending can therefore set off a vicious cycle: the investment decline leads to employment declines, then to cuts in household spending and corresponding increases in household financial problems, which then brings still more cuts in business investment and financial difficulties for the business sector. This is how capitalist economies produce mass unemployment, financial crises, and recessions.

Keynes also described a second major source of instability associated with private investment activity. Precisely because private investments are highly risky propositions, financial markets have evolved to make this risk more manageable for any given investor. Through financial markets, investors can sell off their investments if they need or want to, converting their office buildings, factories, and stock of machinery into cash much more readily than they could if they always had to find buyers on their own. But Keynes warned that when financial markets convert long-term assets into short-term commitments for investors, this also fosters a speculative mentality in the markets. What becomes central for investors is not whether a company's products will produce profits over the long term, but rather whether the short-term financial market investors *think* a company's fortunes will be strong enough in the present and immediate future to drive the stock price up. Or, to be more precise, what really matters for a speculative investor is not what they think about a given company's prospects per se, but rather what they think *other investors are thinking*, since that will be what determines where the stock price goes in the short term.

Because of this, the financial markets are highly susceptible to rumors, fads, and all sorts of deceptive accounting practices, since all of these can help drive the stock price up in the present, regardless of what they accomplish in the longer term. Thus, if U.S. stock traders are convinced that Alan Greenspan is a *maestro*, and if there is news that he is about to intervene with some kind of policy shift, then the rumor of Greenspan's policy shift can itself drive prices up, as the more nimble speculators try to keep one step ahead of the herd of Greenspan-philes.

Still, as with the Marx problem, it does not follow that the inherent instability of private investment and speculation in financial markets are uncontrollable, leading inevitably to persistent problems of mass unemployment and recession. But these social pathologies will become increasingly common through a neoliberal policy approach committed to minimizing government interventions to stabilize investment.

The Polanyi Problem

Karl Polanyi wrote his classic book *The Great Transformation* in the context of the 1930s depression, World War II, and the developing worldwide competition with Communist governments. He was also reflecting on the 1920s, dominated, as with our current epoch, by a free-market ethos. Polanyi wrote of the 1920s that "economic liberalism made a supreme bid to restore the self-regulation of the system by eliminating all interventionist policies which interfered with the freedom of markets."

Considering all of these experiences, Polanyi argued that for market economies to function with some modicum of fairness, they must be embedded in social norms and institutions that effectively promote broadly accepted notions of the common good. Otherwise, acquisitiveness and competition—the two driving forces of market economies—achieve overwhelming dominance as cultural forces, rendering life under capitalism a Hobbesian "war of all against all." This same idea is also central for Adam Smith. Smith showed how the invisible hand of self-interest and competition will yield higher levels of individual effort that increases the wealth of nations, but that it will also produce the corruption of our moral sentiments unless the market is itself governed at a fundamental level by norms of solidarity.

In the post–World War II period, various social democratic movements within the advanced capitalist economies adapted to the Polanyi perspective. They argued in favor of government interventions to achieve three basic ends: stabilizing overall demand in the economy at a level that will provide for full employment; creating a financial market environment that is stable and conducive to the effective allocation of investment funds; and distributing equitably the rewards from high employment and a stable investment process. There were two basic means of achieving equitable distribution: relatively rapid wage growth, promoted by labor laws that were supportive of unions, minimum wage standards, and similar interventions in labor markets; and welfare state policies, including progressive taxation and redistributive programs such as Social Security. The political ascendancy of these ideas was the basis for a dramatic increase in the role of government in the post–World War II capitalist economies. As one indicator of this, total government expenditures in the United States rose from 8% of GDP in 1913, to 21% in 1950, then to 38% by 1992. The IMF and World Bank were also formed in the mid-1940s to advance such policy ideas throughout the world—that is, to implement policies virtually the opposite of those they presently favor. John Maynard Keynes himself was a leading intellectual force contributing to the initial design of the IMF and World Bank.

From Social Democracy to Neoliberalism

But the implementation of a social democratic capitalism, guided by a commitment to full employment and the welfare state, did also face serious and persistent difficulties, and we need to recognize them as part of a consideration of the Marx, Keynes, and Polanyi problems. In particular, many sectors of business opposed efforts to sustain full employment because, following the logic of the Marx problem, full employment provides greater bargaining power for workers in labor markets, even if it also increases the economy's total production of goods and services. Greater worker bargaining power can also create inflationary pressures because businesses will try to absorb their higher wage costs by raising prices. In addition, market-inhibiting financial regulations limit the capacity of financial market players to diversify their risk and speculate.

Corporations in the United States and Western Europe were experiencing some combination of these problems associated with social democratic capitalism. In particular, they were faced with rising labor costs associated with low unemployment rates, which then led to either inflation, when corporations had the ability to pass on their higher labor costs to consumers, or to a squeeze on profits, when competitive pressures prevented corporations from raising their prices in response to the rising labor costs. These pressures were compounded by the two oil price "shocks" initiated by the Oil Producing Exporting Countries (OPEC)—an initial fourfold increase in the world price of oil in 1973, then a second fourfold price spike in 1979.

These were the conditions that by the end of the 1970s led to the decline of social democratic approaches to policymaking and the ascendancy of neoliberalism. The two leading signposts of this historic transition were the election in 1979 of Margaret Thatcher as prime minister of the United Kingdom and in 1980 of Ronald Reagan as the president of the United States. Indeed, it was at this point that Thatcher made her famous pronouncement that "there is no alternative" to neoliberalism.

This brings us to the contemporary era of smaller government, fiscal stringency, and deregulation, i.e., to neoliberalism under Clinton and Bush, and throughout the less-developed world. The issue is not a simple juxtaposition between either regulating or deregulating markets. Rather it is that markets have become deregulated to support the interests of business and financial markets, even as these same groups still benefit greatly from many forms of government support, including investment subsidies, tax concessions, and rescue operations when financial crises get out of hand. At the same time, the deregulation of markets that favors business and finance is correspondingly the most powerful regulatory mechanism limiting the demands of workers, in that deregulation has been congruent with the worldwide expansion of the reserve army of labor and the declining capacity of national governments to implement full-employment and macroeconomic policies. In other words, deregulation has exacerbated both the Marx and Keynes problems.

Given the ways in which neoliberalism worsens the Marx, Keynes, and Polanyi problems, we should not be surprised by the wreckage that it has wrought since the late 1970s, when it became the ascendant policy model. Over the past generation, with neoliberals in the saddle almost everywhere in the world, the results have been straightforward: worsening inequality and poverty, along with slower economic growth and far more unstable financial markets. While Margaret Thatcher famously declared that "there is no alternative" to neoliberalism, there are in fact alternatives. The experience over the past generation demonstrates how important it is to develop them in the most workable and coherent ways possible. ❑

Article 1.3

OPENING PANDORA'S BOX
The Basics of Marxist Economics

BY ALEJANDRO REUSS
February 2000

I n most universities, what is taught as "economics" is a particular brand of orthodox economic theory. The hallmark of this school is a belief in the optimal efficiency (and, it goes without saying, the equity) of "free markets."

The orthodox macroeconomists—who had denied the possibility of general economic slumps—were thrown for a loop by the Great Depression of the 1930s, and by
the challenge to their system of thought by John Maynard Keynes and others. Even so,
the orthodox system retains at its heart a view of capitalist society in which individuals,
each roughly equal to all others, undertake mutually beneficial transactions tending to a
socially optimal equilibrium. There is no power and no conflict. The model is a perfectly
bloodless abstraction, without all the clash and clamor of real life.

Karl Marx and the Critique of Capitalist Society

One way to pry open and criticize the orthodox model of economics is by returning to
the idiosyncracies of the real world. That's the approach of most of the articles in this
book, which describe real-world phenomena that the orthodox model ignores or ex-
cludes. These efforts may explain particular facts better than the orthodoxy, while not
necessarily offering an alternative general system of analysis. They punch holes in the
orthodox lines but, ultimately, leave the orthodox model in possession of the field.

This suggests the need for a different conceptual system that can supplant orthodox economics as a whole. Starting in the 1850s and continuing until his death in 1883,
the German philosopher and revolutionary Karl Marx dedicated himself to developing
a conceptual system for explaining the workings of capitalism. The system that Marx
developed and that bears his name emerged from his criticism of the classical political
economy developed by Adam Smith and David Ricardo. While Marx admired Smith
and Ricardo, and borrowed many of their concepts, he approached economics (or "political economy") from a very different standpoint. He had developed a powerful criticism
of capitalist society before undertaking his study of the economy. This criticism was inspired by French socialist ideas and focused on the oppression of the working class. Marx
argued that wage workers—those working for a paycheck—were "free" only in the sense
that they were not beholden to a single lord or master, as serfs had been under feudalism. But they did not own property, nor were they craftspeople working for themselves,
so they were compelled to sell themselves for a wage to one capitalist or another. Having
surrendered their freedom to the employer's authority, they were forced to work in the
way the employer told them while the latter pocketed the profit produced by their labor.

Marx believed, however, that by creating this oppressed and exploited class of
workers, capitalism was creating the seeds of its own destruction. Conflict between
the workers and the owners was an essential part of capitalism. But in Marx's view

of history, the workers could eventually overthrow the capitalist class, just as the capitalist class, or "bourgeoisie," had grown strong under feudalism, only to supplant the feudal aristocracy. The workers, however, would not simply substitute a new form of private property and class exploitation, as the bourgeoisie had done. Rather, they would bring about the organization of production on a cooperative basis, and an end to the domination of one class over another.

Marx was strongly influenced by the ideas of the day in German philosophy, which held that any new order grows in the womb of the old, and eventually bursts forth to replace it. Marx believed that the creation of the working class, or "proletariat," in the heart of capitalism was one of the system's main contradictions. Marx studied capitalist economics in order to explain the conditions under which it would be possible for the proletariat to overthrow capitalism and create a classless society. The orthodox view depicts capitalism as tending toward equilibrium (without dynamism or crises), serving everyone's best interests, and lasting forever. Marx saw capitalism as crisis-ridden, full of conflict, operating to the advantage of some and detriment of others, and far from eternal.

Class and Exploitation

Looking at economic systems historically, Marx saw capitalism as only the latest in a succession of societies based on exploitation. When people are only able to produce the bare minimum needed to live, he wrote, there is no room for a class of people to take a portion of society's production without contributing to it. But as soon as productivity exceeds this subsistence level, it becomes possible for a class of people who do not contribute to production to live by appropriating the surplus for themselves. These are the masters in slave societies, the lords in feudal societies, and the property owners in capitalist society.

Marx believed that the owners of businesses and property—the capitalists— take part of the wealth produced by the workers, but that this appropriation is hidden by the appearance of an equal exchange, or "a fair day's work for a fair day's pay."

Those who live from the ownership of property—businesses, stocks, land, etc.—were then a small minority and now are less than 5% of the population in countries like the United States. (Marx wrote before the rise of massive corporations and bureaucracies, and did not classify managers and administrators who don't own their own businesses as part of the bourgeoisie.) The exploited class, meanwhile, is the vast majority who live by earning a wage or salary—not just "blue collar" or industrial workers but other workers as well.

Marx's view of how exploitation happened in capitalist society depended on an idea, which he borrowed from Smith and Ricardo, called the labor theory of value. The premise of this theory, which is neither easily proved nor easily rejected, is that labor alone creates the value that is embodied in commodities and that creates profit for owners who sell the goods. The workers do not receive the full value created by their labor and so they are exploited.

Students are likely to hear in economics classes that profits are a reward for the "abstinence" or "risk" of a businessperson—implying that profits are their just deserts. Marx would argue that profits are a reward obtained through the exercise of power—the power owners have over those who own little but their ability to work and so must sell this ability for a wage. That power, and the tribute it allows owners of capital to extract from workers, is no more legitimate in Marx's analysis than the power of a slaveowner over a slave. A slaveowner may exhibit thrift and take risks, after all, but is the wealth of the slaveowner the just reward for these virtues, or a pure and simple theft from the slave?

Joan Robinson, an important 20th-century critic and admirer of Marx, noted that mainstream economists, "by treating capital as productive, used to insinuate the suggestion that capitalists deserve well by society and are fully justified in drawing income from their property." In her view, however, "What is important is that *owning* capital is not a productive activity" [emphasis added].

The Falling Rate of Profit

Marx believed that his theory had major implications for the crises that engulf capitalist economies. In Marx's system, the raw materials and machinery used in the manufacture of a product do not create the extra value that allows the business owner to profit from its production. That additional value is created by labor alone.

Marx recognized that owners could directly extract more value out of workers in three ways: cutting their wages, lengthening their working day, or increasing the intensity of their labor. This need not be done by a direct assault on the workers. Capitalists can achieve the same goal by employing more easily exploited groups or by moving their operations where labor is not as powerful. Both of these trends can be seen in capitalism today, and can be understood as part of capital's intrinsic thirst for more value and increased exploitation.

With the mechanization of large-scale production under capitalism, machines and other inanimate elements of production form a larger and larger share of the inputs to production. Marx believed this would result in a long-term trend of the rate of profit to fall, as the enriching contribution of human labor declined (relative to the inert contribution of these other inputs). This, he believed, would make capitalism increasingly vulnerable to economic crises.

This chain of reasoning depends, of course, on seeing workers as the source of the surplus value created in the production process, and can be avoided by rejecting this view outright. Orthodox economics has not only rejected the labor theory of value, but abandoned the issue of "value" altogether. Value analysis in the spirit of Ricardo and Marx was revived during the 1960s by a number of unorthodox economists, including the Italian economist Piero Sraffa. Marx did not get the last word on the subject.

Unemployment, Part I: The "Reserve Army of the Unemployed"

Marx is often raked over the coals for arguing that workers, under capitalism, were destined to be ground into ever-more-desperate poverty. That living standards improved in rich capitalist countries is offered as proof that his system is fatally flawed. While Marx was not optimistic about the prospect of workers raising their standard of living very far under capitalism, he was critical of proponents of the "iron law of wages," such as Malthus, who held that any increase in wages above the minimum necessary for survival would simply provoke population growth and a decline in wages back to subsistence level. Marx emphasized that political and historical factors influencing the relative power of the major social classes, rather than simple demographics, determined the distribution of income.

One economic factor to which Marx attributed great importance in the class struggle was the size of the "reserve army of the unemployed." Marx identified unemployment as the major factor pushing wages down—the larger the "reserve" of unemployed workers clamoring for jobs, the greater the downward pressure on wages. This was an influence, Marx believed, that the workers would never be able to fully escape under capitalism. If the workers' bargaining power rose enough to raise wages and eat into profits, he argued, capitalists would merely substitute labor-saving technology for living labor, recreating the "reserve army" and reasserting the downward pressure on wages.

Though this has not, perhaps, retarded long-term wage growth to the degree that Marx expected, his basic analysis was visionary at a time when the Malthusian (population) theory of wages was the prevailing view. Anyone reading the business press these days—which is constantly worrying that workers might gain some bargaining power in a "tight" (low unemployment) labor market, and that their wage demands will provoke inflation—will recognize its basic insight.

Unemployment, Part II: The Crisis of Overproduction

Marx never developed a single definitive version of his theory of economic crises (recessions) under capitalism. Nonetheless, his thinking on this issue is some of his most visionary. Marx was the first major economic thinker to break with the orthodoxy of "Say's Law." Named after the French philosopher Jean-Baptiste Say, this theory held that each industry generated income equal to the output it created. In other words, "supply creates its own demand." Say's conclusion, in which he was followed by orthodox economists up through the Great Depression, was that while a particular industry could overproduce, no generalized overproduction was possible. In this respect, orthodox economics flew in the face of all the evidence. In his analysis of overproduction, Marx focused on what he considered the basic contradiction of capitalism—and, in microcosm, of the commodity itself: the contradiction between "use value" and "exchange value." The idea is that a commodity both satisfies a specific need (it has "use value") and can be exchanged for other articles (it has "exchange value"). This distinction was not invented by Marx; it can be found in the work of Smith. Unlike Smith, however, Marx emphasized the way exchange value—what something is worth in the market—overwhelms the use value of a commodity. Unless a commodity can be sold, the useful labor embodied in it is wasted (and the product is useless to those in need). Vast real needs remain unsatisfied for the majority of people, doubly so when—during crises of overproduction—vast quantities of goods remain unsold because there is not enough "effective demand."

It is during these crises that capitalism's unlimited drive to develop society's productive capacity clashes most sharply with the constraints it places on the real incomes of the majority to buy the goods they need. Marx developed this notion of a demand crisis over 75 years before the so-called "Keynesian revolution" in economic thought (whose key insights were actually developed before Keynes by the Polish economist Michal Kalecki on the foundations of Marx's analysis).

Marx expected that these crises of overproduction and demand would worsen as capitalism developed, and that the crises would slow the development of society's productive capacities (what Marx called the "forces of production"). Ultimately, he believed, these crises would be capitalism's undoing. He also pointed to them as evidence of the basic depravity of capitalism. "In these crises," Marx writes in the *Communist Manifesto*,

> there breaks out an epidemic that, in all earlier epochs would have seemed an absurdity, the epidemic of overproduction. ... [I]t appears as if a famine, a universal war of devastation had cut off the supply of every means of subsistence; industry and commerce seem to be destroyed; and why? Because there is ... too much industry, too much commerce ....

This kind of crisis came so close to bringing down capitalism during the Great Depression that preventing them became a central aim of government policy. While government intervention has managed to smooth out the business cycle, especially in the wealthiest countries, capitalism has hardly become crisis-free.

Marx as Prophet

Marx got a great deal about capitalism just right—its incessant, shark-like forward movement; its internal chaos, bursting forth periodically in crisis; its concentration of economic power in ever fewer hands. Judged on these core insights, the Marxist system can easily stand toe-to-toe with the orthodox model. Which comes closer to reality? The capitalism that incessantly bursts forth over new horizons, or the one that constantly gravitates towards comfortable equilibrium? The one where crisis is impossible, or the one that lurches from boom to bust to boom again? The one where perfect competition reigns, or the one where a handful of giants tower over every industry? In all these respects, Marx's system captures the thundering dynamics of capitalism much better than the orthodox system does. As aesthetically appealing as the clockwork harmony of the orthodox model may be, this is precisely its failing. Capitalism is anything but harmonious.

There was also a lot that Marx, like any other complex thinker, predicted incorrectly, or did not foresee. In this respect, he was not a prophet. His work should be read critically, and not, as it has been by some, as divine revelation. Marx, rather, was the prophet of a radical approach to reality. In an age when the "free market" rides high, and its apologists claim smugly that "there is no alternative," Joan Robinson's praise of Marx is apt: "[T]he nightmare quality of Marx's thought gives it ... an air of greater reality than the gentle complacency of the orthodox academics. Yet he, at the same time, is more encouraging than they, for he releases hope as well as terror from Pandora's box, while they preach only the gloomy doctrine that all is for the best in the best of all *possible* worlds." ❑

Sources: Joan Robinson, *An Essay on Marxian Economics* (Macmillan, 1952); "Manifesto of the Community Party," and "Crisis Theory (from Theories of Surplus Value)," in Robert C. Tucker, ed., *The Marx-Engels Reader* (W.W. Norton, 1978); Roman Rosdolsky, *The Making of Marx's 'Capital'* (Pluto Press, 1989); Ernest Mandel, "Karl Heinrich Marx"; Luigi L. Pasinetti, "Joan Violet Robinson"; and John Eatwell and Carlo Panico, "Piero Sraffa"; in John Eatwell, Murray Milgate, and Peter Newman, eds., *The New Palgrave: A Dictionary of Economics* (Macmillan, 1987).

Article 1.4

SHARING THE WEALTH OF THE COMMONS

BY PETER BARNES
November/December 2004

We're all familiar with private wealth, even if we don't have much. Economists and the media celebrate it every day. But there's another trove of wealth we barely notice: our common wealth.

Each of us is the beneficiary of a vast inheritance. This common wealth includes our air and water, habitats and ecosystems, languages and cultures, science and technologies, political and monetary systems, and quite a bit more. To say we share this inheritance doesn't mean we can call a broker and sell our shares tomorrow. It does mean we're responsible for the commons and entitled to any income it generates. Both the responsibility and the entitlement are ours by birth. They're part of the obligation each generation owes to the next, and each living human owes to other beings.

At present, however, our economic system scarcely recognizes the commons. This omission causes two major tragedies: ceaseless destruction of nature and widening inequality among humans. Nature gets destroyed because no one's unequivocally responsible for protecting it. Inequality widens because private wealth concentrates while common wealth shrinks.

The great challenges for the 21st century are, first of all, to make the commons visible; second, to give it proper reverence; and third, to translate that reverence into property rights and legal institutions that are on a par with those supporting private property. If we do this, we can avert the twin tragedies currently built into our market-driven system.

Defining the Commons

What exactly is the commons? Here is a workable definition: The commons includes all the assets we inherit together and are morally obligated to pass on, undiminished, to future generations.

This definition is a practical one. It designates a set of assets that have three specific characteristics: they're (1) inherited, (2) shared, and (3) worthy of long-term preservation. Usually it's obvious whether an asset has these characteristics or not.

At the same time, the definition is broad. It encompasses assets that are natural as well as social, intangible as well as tangible, small as well as large. It also introduces a moral factor that is absent from other economic definitions: it requires us to consider whether an asset is worthy of long-term preservation. At present, capitalism has no interest in this question. If an asset is likely to yield a competitive return to capital, it's kept alive; if not, it's destroyed or allowed to run down. Assets in the commons, by contrast, are meant to be preserved regardless of their return.

This definition sorts all economic assets into two baskets, the market and the commons. In the market basket are those assets we want to own privately and manage for profit. In the commons basket are the assets we want to hold in common and manage for long-term preservation. These baskets then are, or ought to be, the yin and yang of economic activity; each should enhance and contain the other. The role of the state should be to maintain a healthy balance between them.

The Value of the Commons

For most of human existence, the commons supplied everyone's food, water, fuel, and medicines. People hunted, fished, gathered fruits and herbs, collected firewood and building materials, and grazed their animals in common lands and waters. In other words, the commons was the source of basic sustenance. This is still true today in many parts of the world, and even in San Francisco, where I live, cash-poor people fish in the bay not for sport, but for food.

Though sustenance in the industrialized world now flows mostly through markets, the commons remains hugely valuable. It's the source of all natural resources and nature's many replenishing services. Water, air, DNA, seeds, topsoil, minerals, the protective ozone layer, the atmosphere's climate regulation, and much more are gifts of nature to us all.

Just as crucially, the commons is our ultimate waste sink. It recycles water, oxygen, carbon, and everything else we excrete, exhale, or throw away. It's the place we store, or try to store, the residues of our industrial system.

The commons also holds humanity's vast accumulation of knowledge, art, and thought. As Isaac Newton said, "If I have seen further it is by standing on the shoulders of giants." So, too, the legal, political, and economic institutions we inherit—even the market itself—were built by the efforts of millions. Without these gifts we'd be hugely poorer than we are today.

To be sure, thinking of these natural and social inheritances primarily as economic assets is a limited way of viewing them. I deeply believe they are much more than that. But if treating portions of the commons as economic assets can help us conserve them, it's surely worth doing so.

How much might the commons be worth in monetary terms? It's relatively easy to put a dollar value on private assets. Accountants and appraisers do it every day, aided by the fact that private assets are regularly traded for money.

This isn't the case with most shared assets. How much is clean air, an intact wetlands,

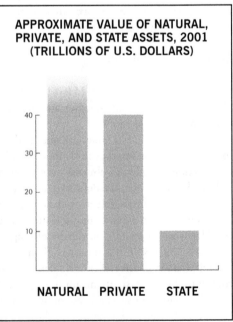

APPROXIMATE VALUE OF NATURAL, PRIVATE, AND STATE ASSETS, 2001 (TRILLIONS OF U.S. DOLLARS)

NATURAL   PRIVATE   STATE

or Darwin's theory of evolution worth in dollar terms? Clearly, many shared inheritances are simply priceless. Others are potentially quantifiable, but there's no current market for them. Fortunately, economists have developed methods to quantify the value of things that aren't traded, so it's possible to estimate the value of the "priceable" part of the commons within an order of magnitude. The surprising conclusion that emerges from numerous studies is that the wealth we share is worth more than the wealth we own privately.

This fact bears repeating. Even though much of the commons can't be valued in monetary terms, the parts that can be valued are worth more than all private assets combined.

It's worth noting that these estimates understate the gap between common and private assets because a significant portion of the value attributed to private wealth is in fact an appropriation of common wealth. If this mislabeled portion was subtracted from private wealth and added to common wealth, the gap between the two would widen further.

Two examples will make this point clear. Suppose you buy a house for $200,000 and, without improving it, sell it a few years later for $300,000. You pay off the mortgage and walk away with a pile of cash. But what caused the house to rise in value? It wasn't anything you did. Rather, it was the fact that your neighborhood became more popular, likely a result of the efforts of community members, improvements in public services, and similar factors.

Or consider another fount of private wealth, the social invention and public expansion of the stock market. Suppose you start a business that goes "public" through an offering of stock. Within a few years, you're able to sell your stock for a spectacular capital gain.

Much of this gain is a social creation, the result of centuries of monetary-system evolution, laws and regulations, and whole industries devoted to accounting, sharing information, and trading stocks. What's more, there's a direct correlation between the scale and quality of the stock market as an institution and the size of the private gain. You'll fetch a higher price if you sell into a market of millions than into a market of two. Similarly, you'll gain more if transaction costs are low and trust in public information is high. Thus, stock that's traded on a regulated exchange sells for a higher multiple of earnings than unlisted stock. This socially created premium can account for 30% of the stock's value. If you're the lucky seller, you'll reap that extra cash—in no way thanks to anything you did as an individual.

Real estate gains and the stock market's social premium are just two instances of common assets contributing to private gain. Still, most rich people would like us to think it's their extraordinary talent, hard work, and risk-taking that create their well-deserved wealth. That's like saying a flower's beauty is due solely to its own efforts, owing nothing to nutrients in the soil, energy from the sun, water from the aquifer, or the activity of bees.

The Great Commons Giveaway

That we inherit a trove of common wealth is the good news. The bad news, alas, is that our inheritance is being grossly mismanaged. As a recent report by the advocacy group Friends of the Commons concludes, "Maintenance of the commons is terrible, theft is rampant, and rents often aren't collected. To put it bluntly, our common wealth—and our children's—is being squandered. We are all poorer as a result."

Examples of commons mismanagement include the handout of broadcast spectrum to media conglomerates, the giveaway of pollution rights to polluters, the extension of copyrights to entertainment companies, the patenting of seeds and genes, the privatization of water, and the relentless destruction of habitat, wildlife, and ecosystems.

This mismanagement, though currently extreme, is not new. For over 200 years, the market has been devouring the commons in two ways. With one hand, the market takes valuable stuff from the commons and privatizes it. This is called "enclosure." With the other hand, the market dumps bad stuff into the commons and says, "It's your problem." This is called "externalizing." Much that is called economic growth today is actually a form of cannibalization in which the market diminishes the commons that ultimately sustains it.

Enclosure—the taking of good stuff from the commons—at first meant privatization of land by the gentry. Today it means privatization of many common assets by corporations. Either way, it means that what once belonged to everyone now belongs to a few.

Enclosure is usually justified in the name of efficiency. And sometimes, though not always, it does result in efficiency gains. But what also results from enclosure is the impoverishment of those who lose access to the commons, and the enrichment of those who take title to it. In other words, enclosure widens the gap between those with income-producing property and those without.

Externalizing—the dumping of bad stuff into the commons—is an automatic behavior pattern of profit-maximizing corporations: if they can avoid any out-of-pocket costs, they will. If workers, taxpayers, anyone downwind, future generations, or nature have to absorb added costs, so be it.

For decades, economists have agreed we'd be better served if businesses "internalized" their externalities—that is, paid in real time the costs they now shift to the commons. The reason this doesn't happen is that there's no one to set prices and collect them. Unlike private wealth, the commons lacks property rights and institutions to represent it in the marketplace.

The seeds of such institutions, however, are starting to emerge. Consider one of the environmental protection tools the U.S. currently uses, pollution trading. So-called cap-and-trade programs put a cap on total pollution, then grant portions of the total, via permits, to each polluting firm. Companies may buy other firms' permits if they want to pollute more than their allotment allows, or sell unused permits if they manage to pollute less. Such programs are generally supported by business because they allow polluters to find the cheapest ways to reduce pollution.

Public discussion of cap-and-trade programs has focused exclusively on their trading features. What's been overlooked is how they give away common wealth to polluters.

To date, all cap-and-trade programs have begun by giving pollution rights to existing polluters for free. This treats polluters as if they own our sky and rivers. It means that future polluters will have to pay old polluters for the scarce—hence valuable—right to dump wastes into nature. Imagine that: Because a corporation polluted in the past, it gets free income forever! And, because ultimately we'll all pay for limited pollution via higher prices, this amounts to an enormous transfer of wealth—trillions of dollars—to shareholders of historically polluting corporations.

In theory, though, there is no reason that the initial pollution rights should not reside with the public. Clean air and the atmosphere's capacity to absorb pollutants are "wealth" that belongs to everyone. Hence, when polluters use up these parts of the commons, they should pay the public—not the other way around.

Taking the Commons Back

How can we correct the system omission that permits, and indeed promotes, destruction of nature and ever-widening inequality among humans? The answer lies in building a new sector of the economy whose clear legal mission is to preserve shared inheritances for everyone. Just as the market is populated by profit-maximizing corporations, so this new sector would be populated by asset-preserving trusts.

Here a brief description of trusts may be helpful. The trust is a private institution that's even older than the corporation. The essence of a trust is a fiduciary relationship. A trust holds and manages property for another person or for many other people. A simple example is a trust set up by a grandparent to pay for a grandchild's education. Other trusts include pension funds, charitable foundations, and university endowments. There are also hundreds of trusts in America, like the Nature Conservancy and the Trust for Public Land, that own land or conservation easements in perpetuity.

If we were to design an institution to protect pieces of the commons, we couldn't do much better than a trust. The goal of commons management, after all, is to preserve assets and deliver benefits to broad classes of beneficiaries. That's what trusts do, and it's not rocket science.

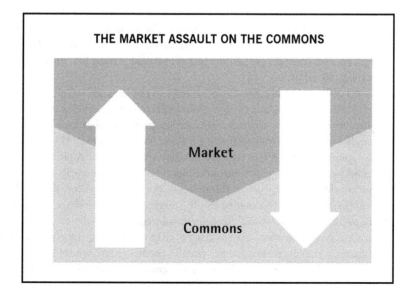

THE MARKET ASSAULT ON THE COMMONS

Market

Commons

Over centuries, several principles of trust management have evolved. These include:

- Trustees have a fiduciary responsibility to beneficiaries. If a trustee fails in this obligation, he or she can be removed and penalized.
- Trustees must preserve the original asset. It's okay to spend income, but don't invade the principal.
- Trustees must assure transparency. Information about money flows should be readily available to beneficiaries.

Trusts in the new commons sector would be endowed with rights comparable to those of corporations. Their trustees would take binding oaths of office and, like judges, serve long terms. Though protecting common assets would be their primary job, they would also distribute income from those assets to beneficiaries. These beneficiaries would include all citizens within a jurisdiction, large classes of citizens (children, the elderly), and/or agencies serving common purposes such as public transit or ecological restoration. When distributing income to individuals, the allocation formula would be one person, one share. The right to receive commons income would be a nontransferable birthright, not a property right that could be traded.

Fortuitously, a working model of such a trust already exists: the Alaska Permanent Fund. When oil drilling on the North Slope began in the 1970s, Gov. Jay Hammond, a Republican, proposed that 25% of the state's royalties be placed in a mutual fund to be invested on behalf of Alaska's citizens. Voters approved in a referendum. Since then, the Alaska Permanent Fund has grown to over $28 billion, and Alaskans have received roughly $22,000 apiece in dividends. In 2003 the per capita dividend was $1,107; a family of four received $4,428.

What Alaska did with its oil can be replicated for other gifts of nature. For example, we could create a nationwide Sky Trust to stabilize the climate for future generations. The trust would restrict emissions of heat-trapping gases and sell a declining number of emission permits to polluters. The income would be returned to U.S. residents in equal yearly dividends, thus reversing the wealth transfer built into current cap-and-trade programs. Instead of everyone paying historic polluters, polluters would pay all of us.

Just as a Sky Trust could represent our equity in the natural commons, a Public Stock Trust could embody our equity in the social commons. Such a trust would capture some of the socially created stock-market premium that currently flows only to shareholders and their investment bankers. As noted earlier, this premium is sizeable—roughly 30% of the value of publicly traded stock. A simple way to share it would be to create a giant mutual fund—call it the American Permanent Fund—that would hold, say, 10% of the shares of publicly traded companies. This mutual fund, in turn, would be owned by all Americans on a one share per person basis (perhaps linked to their Social Security accounts).

To build up the fund without precipitating a fall in share prices, companies would contribute shares at the rate of, say, 1% per year. The contributions would be the price companies pay for the benefits they derive from a commons asset, the large, trusted market for stock—a small price, indeed, for the hefty benefits. Over time, the mutual fund would assure that when the economy grows, everyone benefits. The top 5% would still own more than the bottom 90%, but at least every American would have some property income, and a slightly larger slice of our economic pie.

Sharing the Wealth

The perpetuation of inequality is built into the current design of capitalism. Because of the skewed distribution of private wealth, a small self-perpetuating minority receives a disproportionate share of America's nonlabor income.

Tom Paine had something to say about this. In his essay "Agrarian Justice," written in 1790, he argued that, because enclosure of the commons had separated so many people from their primary source of sustenance, it was necessary to create a functional equivalent of the commons in the form of a National Fund. Here is how he put it:

> There are two kinds of property. Firstly, natural property, or that which comes to us from the Creator of the universe—such as the earth, air, water. Secondly, artificial or acquired property—the invention of men. In the latter, equality is impossible; for to distribute it equally, it would be necessary that all should have contributed in the same proportion, which can never be the case .... Equality of natural property is different. Every individual in the world is born with legitimate claims on this property, or its equivalent.

Enclosure of the commons, he went on, was necessary to improve the efficiency of cultivation. But:

> The landed monopoly that began with [enclosure] has produced the greatest evil. It has dispossessed more than half the inhabitants of every nation of their natural inheritance, without providing for them, as ought to have been done, an indemnification for that loss, and has thereby created a species of poverty and wretchedness that did not exist before.

The appropriate compensation for loss of the commons, Paine said, was a national fund financed by rents paid by land owners. Out of this fund, every person reaching age 21 would get 15 pounds a year, and every person over 50 would receive an additional 10 pounds. (Think of Social Security, financed by commons rents instead of payroll taxes.)

A Progressive Offensive

Paine's vision, allowing for inflation and new forms of enclosure, could not be more timely today. Surely from our vast common inheritance—not just the land, but the atmosphere, the broadcast spectrum, our mineral resources, our threatened habitats and water supplies—enough rent can be collected to pay every American over age 21 a modest annual dividend, and every person reaching 21 a small start-up inheritance.

Such a proposal may seem utopian. In today's political climate, perhaps it is. But consider this. About 20 years ago, right-wing think tanks laid out a bold agenda. They called for lowering taxes on private wealth, privatizing much of government, and de-regulating industry. Amazingly, this radical agenda has largely been achieved.

It's time for progressives to mount an equally bold offensive. The old shibbo-leths—let's gin up the economy, create jobs, and expand government programs—no longer excite. We need to talk about fixing the economy, not just growing it; about income for everyone, not just jobs; about nurturing ecosystems, cultures, and communities, not just our individual selves. More broadly, we need to celebrate the commons as an essential counterpoise to the market.

Unfortunately, many progressives have viewed the state as the only possible coun-terpoise to the market. The trouble is, the state has been captured by corporations. This capture isn't accidental or temporary; it's structural and long-term.

This doesn't mean progressives can't occasionally recapture the state. We've done so before and will do so again. It does mean that progressive control of the state is the exception, not the norm; in due course, corporate capture will resume. It follows that if we want lasting fixes to capitalism's tragic flaws, we must use our brief moments of political ascendancy to build institutions that endure.

Programs that rely on taxes, appropriations, or regulations are inherently transitory; they get weakened or repealed when political power shifts. By contrast, institutions that are self-perpetuating and have broad constituencies are likely to last. (It also helps if they mail out checks periodically.) This was the genius of So-cial Security, which has survived—indeed grown—through numerous Republi-can administrations.

If progressives are smart, we'll use our next New Deal to create common prop-erty trusts that include all Americans as beneficiaries. These trusts will then be to the 21st century what social insurance was to the 20th: sturdy pillars of shared responsi-bility and entitlement. Through them, the commons will be a source of sustenance for all, as it was before enclosure. Life-long income will be linked to generations-long ecological health. Isn't that a future most Americans would welcome? ❏

Article 1.5

TRANSNATIONAL CAPITAL AND TRANSNATIONAL LABOR

AN INTERVIEW with WILLIAM K. TABB
November/December 2017

William K. Tabb *is an economist and author of* The Restructuring of Capitalism in Our Time *(2012),* Economic Governance in the Age of Globalization *(2004), and* The Amoral Elephant: Globalization and the Struggle for Social Justice in the Twenty-First Century *(2001). He spoke with* Dollars & Sense *in July 2017 on the global economic crisis, its causes and consequences; the transnational capitalist class and neoliberal globalization; and the prospects for resistance and alternatives to capitalism now and in the future.*

Dollars & Sense: If we look at a world map showing GDP growth rates in 2009 or 2010, during the Great Recession, we see most of the high-income countries of North America, Europe, and East Asia with negative growth rates. Meanwhile, we see some of South America, much of Africa, and most of South Asia and East Asia still with positive economic growth. Why would the wealthiest and most powerful countries be at the epicenter of a global economic crisis?

William Tabb: The crisis was triggered in the financial sector, and while that didn't *cause* the problem, it brought the economy down. The financial crisis itself was created by the over-indebtedness in the richer countries and the extent of leverage, that is of borrowing, mostly by the private sector, actually, and the slow rate of growth in their economies. They dealt with the slow rate of growth in the economy by offering people the chance to borrow more money. And they did. As they borrowed more and more, they reached the point that they couldn't pay it back, especially the mortgages and, within that, the subprime mortgage in the United States. But that same property crash happened in a number of other advanced countries.

The other thing that was behind the borrowing was the stagnation of income for working classes across the advanced capitalist world. Slowing growth in the real economy and rapid growth in the financial economy came from increased unequal distribution of income, where the 1%—in Occupy Wall Street's terms—accrued more and more of the surplus created. They put it into finance because there was no point in producing more goods and services, investing in the real economy, because most people didn't have the money because of the stagnation of incomes. So you had the slowing down leading to the financialization.

The other piece of that was the globalization of the economy, in which industry or deindustrialization had killed so many of the good and many unionized jobs, which added to the stagnation pressures.

D&S: Just to follow up on that, do you think it's useful to talk about a possibility where—even if the crisis detonated in the higher-income countries—they might have offloaded more of the fallout onto other countries? People talk about Germany "exporting unemployment" to other countries, but these were mostly countries in the European periphery. Is it possible to imagine the high-income countries doing something similar on a global scale?

WT: To begin with the German case which you raise: It's an important one, because what the Germans succeeded in doing was holding down the wages in their own country, so that they could continue to export. The rest of Europe became less competitive, with the euro, since they were all tied to the same currency. The German economy grew basically by exploiting their neighbors in Europe. As far as the developing countries are concerned: Many were commodity producers, and with the downturn, commodity prices fell and they were damaged heavily through that.

I also wanted to go back to the way that finance hurt Latin America and Asia in earlier crises, where the same form of borrowing was interrupted by U.S. monetary policy. The countries that had borrowed first in the Latin American debt crisis of the 1980s and then in the Asian crisis of the '90s, suddenly had to pay back debt that they couldn't pay back because of the suddenness of the change.

In the current period, or the period since 2007–2008 with the downturn, something similar happened, in which the developing countries did suffer the consequences of the slowdown in the core. The extent to which this was the higher-income countries "putting it on them" rather than merely co-suffering—it's a harder one for me to answer.

D&S: You mentioned the Latin American debt crisis, which served as the lance point, in many countries, for the imposition of "neoliberal" economic policies. The United States government was certainly in the forefront of spreading this "free market" or "neoliberal" economic policy paradigm to other parts of the world, in Latin America and elsewhere, and giant U.S. corporations have certainly been major beneficiaries. Is the hegemonic position of the United States in the capitalist world economy dependent on the continuation of this paradigm?

WT: It certainly is important to transnational capital, and especially to U.S.-based transnational capital. But one of the things to think about is that the nationality of capital has become more internationalized. For many major U.S. corporations, or major German or French corporations, the stock is owned much more widely, so that their headquarters may still be in the country of origin but capital has become more internationalized in terms of ownership and control. So, yes, for American corporations it is very important, but it is important for all transnational capital.

What neoliberalism does is force the countries of Latin America or other developing countries to hold their own wages down in order to be competitive in the global marketplace. Capital is mobile, and transnational capital will buy from the lowest-cost sources, given that their supply chains can alter where production is taking place. It gives them bargaining power for lower taxes in the countries of the Third World, lower wages for the workers in those countries, and incentives to in fact locate there. So a great deal of the profitability of transnational capital comes from this greater bargaining power over both the workers of the world and the coun-

---

The Evolution of Imperialism

A century ago, it was clear that the division of labor was the Global South producing raw materials and the "core" countries of the world system producing industrial goods. The peripheral countries produced raw materials, which were sold at low prices because of the lower cost of reproducing labor power in those countries as well as the military stranglehold the colonial power had, and their ability to appropriate land and labor from the peoples of the Global South. That was first called "colonialism," later "imperialism." Some of these countries got their independence—became formally independent—but the economic relationship continued, and the countries of the core continued to exploit them basically in the same manner.

You did have a period of national development, of autocentric development, at the end of World War II. This was a strategy where national elites, pushed by progressive movements in these countries, tried to pursue a different form of development. Even groups like OPEC [the Organization of the Petroleum Exporting Countries] trying to raise the price of oil by coming together. The Bandung Conference of 1954 of progressive Third World leaders—called the "Third" World between the Soviet system and the Western capitalist system—tried to negotiate a better deal for their countries.

Neoliberalism basically undid that. So we move from the earlier period, of 100 years ago, of straight, exploitative, military, violent control, to informal control. When the colonial powers left a particular country, they tried to leave in place leaders who had been educated in the colonial country, chosen by the foreign ministries of the colonial powers, to be cooperative in a period when the former colony had become formally independent. That was challenged by some of the important leaders in the postwar period—Nehru in India, Sukarno in Indonesia, and others—who tried to negotiate in a very meaningful sense for the Global South. They were succeeded, unfortunately, by leaders who were more in favor of the later development of transnational control. —WT

---

tries of the world, especially the less powerful countries that are more dependent on transnational capital.

D&S: How far do theories of a "transnational capitalist class" and "transnational capitalist state" get us in understanding the restructuring of the capitalist world economy in the late 20th century? Do those ideas help us explain the transition from the clashing colonial empires of a century ago (each seeking to carve out exclusive access for their own capitalist companies) to today's global regime maintaining global access (to markets, natural resources, labor, etc.) for transnational capital?

WT: I had earlier been skeptical of the theory, because all of the actions of local capitalist classes—in terms of protecting their interests—were strong going into the 1980s and the 1990s. But we did see a major change, a change that actually originated earlier, as national development strategies gave way—with elites, instead of trying to follow autonomous development and trying to protect themselves from foreign capital, becoming instead junior partners of foreign capital and giving up national independence and autonomous development.

When that happened, they became junior partners for transnational capital and to a much greater extent were integrated into the global capitalist class. This was a significant change from the era of national Keynesianism of the postwar period into global neoliberalism, where transnational capital is able not only to penetrate these countries, but the elites of these countries see their interests in working as part of a global capitalist class. I think that the theory, as it has been developed, is now much more convincing and the evidence for it is much greater.

D&S: How do you see the prospects for a new anti-capitalist politics, meaning a politics that aims at the replacement of the capitalist system with a new form of economic organization on a world scale? Does the globalization of capital undermine the viability of the "working class" as a driving force of social change, or could it foster (as one of its contradictions) a truly "transnational working class" that could be an agent of a global economic transformation?

WT: One of the things Karl Marx saw in the 1840s, when he and Friedrich Engels were writing the *Communist Manifesto*, was that capitalism was a world system (which was a pretty impressive insight back then) and that the global working class had nothing to lose and much to gain by uniting against capital. The idea that this might happen was dismissed by many people, but Marx just keeps coming back. In the current period, as global capital gets more and more control, it becomes clearer what is really going on. So in the United States, we have a situation where a little over half of young people are anti-capitalist and prefer socialism. This is a major change. The other change, speaking for the moment about the United States, is that surveys are showing that people identify not as middle class (because they are being pushed out of the middle class and people who are coming into the economy have not been given a chance for a middle-class standard of living) but as working class.

The rise of the right is the same thing as we saw in the 1930s: When the left becomes stronger—the progressive movement, the workers movement becomes stronger—it's only a violent, racist, xenophobic, Trump-like administration that can try to contain what in our country would be the base of the Democratic Party, the trade union movement, young people, Black Lives Matter, the fight for the $15 an hour minimum wage. These movements are getting stronger, and organizing at the local level is important. We're seeing the same trends, not only in the other advanced countries—in England especially, with [Jeremy] Corbyn—but in the countries that have been hardest hit by the crisis. We're seeing strong left-wing movements in Greece and Spain. Latin America has become more complex, as the left-wing governments that came in had trouble delivering on what they wished to deliver, given that they were part of a global system. They were unable on their own, even though they were able to improve conditions, to fundamentally challenge capitalism.

I think the idea that capitalism will be challenged—it will be challenged in the advanced countries and perhaps in China, where the number of strikes and the extent of unrest is really quite substantial, although the Communist Party power remains very strong. As the Chinese economy slows down—and their financial system, the overextension of debt, their banks getting in trouble—I would not rule out a serious change there as well. It is true, in the short run, that neoliberalism and transnational capital have restructured the economy, but it is not a sustainable model. The model cannot produce growth that is ecologically sensible in this period, which becomes much more of a challenge, and people around the world are much more aware of that. So I am actually encouraged that—maybe not tomorrow—but that we're moving into an era where class analysis becomes more important. Where resistance to capitalism, which 10, 20, or 30 years ago would've been considered beyond the conversation, now becomes part of the conversation. ❏

Chapter 2

MACROECONOMIC MEASUREMENT

INTRODUCTION

Most macroeconomics textbooks begin with a snapshot of today's economy as seen through the standard measures of economic performance. This chapter provides a different view of today's economy, one far more critical of current economic policy and performance, one that asks what the standard measures of economic performance really tell us and what they might be missing.

Increases in real gross domestic product (GDP) define economic growth and, for most economists, rising real GDP per capita shows that a nation's standard of living is improving. But our authors are not convinced. The first four articles in this chapter focus on critiques of GDP.

Environmentalist Jonathan Rowe offers a green perspective on the economy. He is critical of economists' worship of economic growth, and their use of measures (like GDP) that count environmental destruction, worsening health, and ruinous overconsumption as contributions to economic growth. These, he argues, have misled economists, policymakers, and the public about the goals we should be pursuing (Article 2.1). Feminist economist Nancy Folbre zeroes in on the exclusion of household labor and production from official government economic accounts, and how this distorts both our understanding of the economy and the policies governing it (Article 2.2). Alejandro Reuss summarizes three key lines of criticism against the use of GDP to measure economic well-being, focusing on the failure of GDP to take into account income distribution, environmental quality, and non-market production (Article 2.3).

The next article focuses on an alternative way to measure economic performance, by considering the economy a means of achieving social goals rather than treating economic activity as an end in itself. Reuss (Article 2.4) describes the ins and outs of the Human Development Index (HDI), the United Nations Development Programme's alternative to GDP as a single-number measure of economic well-being.

Next is a short article on regional inequality in the United States by Gerald Friedman (Article 2.5). Regional growth disparities have led to polarization politically and socially.

The differences between different price indices—whose rates of change we use as measures of inflation—may not seem like burning issues of our times. The Center for Economic and Policy Research, however, shows us the importance of price indices when used to "deflate" money figures that people really care about—like the real value of the minimum wage (Article 2.6).

Finally, economist Jeannette Wicks-Lim tackles another measurement issue that directly addresses social well-being (Article 2.7). She analyzes an alternate way of calculating the official "poverty line"—the income threshold below which people are deemed "poor" for purposes of government statistics. The traditional poverty line, she argues, is both misdefined and too low, and the new one does not go far enough to correct these shortcomings.

Discussion Questions

1. (Article 2.1) Why does Rowe argue that more economic growth and rising GDP are not necessarily desirable? How would he change the ground rules of the economy to produce more genuine economic growth?

2. (Article 2.2) In Folbre's view, how has the failure to count household labor and production in official economic data had negative consequences, both on our economic understanding and economic policies?

3. (Article 2.3) How is GDP measured, and what does it represent? What are the three main criticisms of GDP described by Reuss? Do you find them convincing?

4. (Articles 2.4) How does the HDI differ from GDP per capita? What problems of GDP as a measure of well-being does the HDI attempt to overcome? How successful do you think the HDI is in overcoming these problems?

5. (Article 2.5) Why does Gerald Friedman say that "Wall Street favors the urban coasts"? What economic policies over the past 30 years reflect Wall Street's interests and how has that affected regional disparities in growth?

6. (Article 2.6) Why do economists disagree about whether the increase of the minimum wage has kept pace with inflation over time? Is there any argument that the minimum wage should increase faster than the rate of inflation?

7. (Article 2.7) How is the federal poverty line calculated? How does the new Supplemental Poverty Measure differ, and why does Wicks-Lim consider the changes inadequate?

Article 2.1

THE GROWTH CONSENSUS UNRAVELS

BY JONATHAN ROWE
July/August 1999

Economics has been called the dismal science, but beneath its gray exterior is a system of belief worthy of Pollyanna. Yes, economists manage to see a dark cloud in every silver lining. Downturn follows uptick, and inflation rears its ugly head. But there's a story within that story—a gauzy romance, a lyric ode to Stuff. It's built into the language. A thing produced is called a "good," for example, no questions asked. The word is more than just a term of art. It suggests the automatic benediction that economics bestows upon commodities of any kind.

By the same token, an activity for sale is called a "service." In conventional economics there are no "dis-services," no actions that might be better left undone. The bank that gouges you with ATM fees, the lawyer who runs up the bill—such things are "services" so long as someone pays. If a friend or neighbor fixes your plumbing for free, it's not a "service" and so it doesn't count.

The sum total of these products and activities is called the Gross Domestic Product, or GDP. If the GDP is greater this year than last, then the result is called "growth." There is no bad GDP and no bad growth; economics does not even have a word for such a thing. It does have a word for less growth. In such a case, economists say growth is "sluggish" and the economy is in "recession." No matter what is growing—more payments to doctors because of worsening health, more toxic cleanup—so long as there is more of it, then the economic mind declares it good.

This purports to be "objective science." In reality it is a rhetorical construct with the value judgments built in, and this rhetoric has been the basis of economic debate in the United States for the last half century at least. True, people have disagreed over how best to promote a rising GDP. Liberals generally wanted to use government more, conservatives less. But regarding the beneficence of a rising GDP, there has been little debate at all.

If anything, the left traditionally has believed in growth with even greater fervor than the right. It was John Maynard Keynes, after all, who devised the growth-boosting mechanisms of macroeconomic policy to combat the Depression of the 1930s; it was Keynesians who embraced these strategies after the war and turned the GDP into a totem. There's no point in seeking a bigger pie to redistribute to the poor, if you don't believe the expanding pie is desirable in the first place.

Today, however, the growth consensus is starting to unravel across the political spectrum and in ways that are both obvious and subtle. The issue is no longer just the impact of growth upon the environment—the toxic impacts of industry and the like. It now goes deeper, to what growth actually consists of and what it means in people's lives. The things economists call "goods" and "services" increasingly don't strike people as such. There is a growing disconnect between the way people experience growth and the way the policy establishment talks about it, and this gap is becoming an unspoken subtext to much of American political life.

The group most commonly associated with an antigrowth stance is environmentalists, of course. To be sure, one faction, the environmental economists, is trying to put green new wine into the old bottles of economic thought. If we would just make people pay the "true" cost of, say, the gasoline they burn, through the tax system for example, then the market would do the rest. We'd have benign, less-polluting growth, they say, perhaps even more than now. But the core of the environmental movement remains deeply suspicious of the growth ethos, and probably would be even if the environmental impacts somehow could be lessened.

In the middle are suburbanites who applaud growth in the abstract, but oppose the particular manifestations they see around them—the traffic, sprawl, and crowded schools. On the right, meanwhile, an anti-growth politics is arising practically unnoticed. When social conservatives denounce gambling, pornography, or sex and violence in the media, they are talking about specific instances of the growth that their political leaders rhapsodize on other days.

Environmentalists have been like social conservatives in one key respect. They have been moralistic regarding growth, often scolding people for enjoying themselves at the expense of future generations and the earth. Their concern is valid, up to a point—the consumer culture does promote the time horizon of a five year old. But politically it is not the most promising line of attack, and conceptually it concedes too much ground. To moralize about consumption as they do is to accept the conventional premise that it really is something chosen—an enjoyable form of self-indulgence that has unfortunate consequences for the earth.

That's "consumption" in the common parlance—the sport utility vehicle loading up at Wal-Mart, the stuff piling up in the basement and garage. But increasingly that's not what people actually experience, nor is it what the term really means. In economics, consumption means everything people spend money on, pleasurable or not. Wal-Mart is just one dimension of a much larger and increasingly unpleasant whole. The lawyers' fees for the house settlement or divorce; the repair work on the car after it was rear-ended; the cancer treatments for the uncle who was a three-pack-a-day smoker; the stress medications and weight-loss regimens—all these and more are "consumption." They all go into the GDP.

Cancer treatments and lawyer's fees are not what come to mind when environmentalists lament the nation's excess consumption, or for that matter when economists applaud America's "consumers" for keeping the world economy afloat. Yet increasingly such things are what consumption actually consists of in the economy today. More and more, it consists not of pleasurable things that people choose, but rather of things that most people would gladly do without.

Much consumption today is addictive, for example. Millions of Americans are engaged in a grim daily struggle with themselves to do less of it. They want to eat less, drink less, smoke less, gamble less, talk less on the telephone—do less buying, period. Yet economic reasoning declares as growth and progress that which people themselves regard as a tyrannical affliction.

Economists resist this reality of a divided self, because it would complicate their models beyond repair. They cling instead to an 18th-century model of human psychology—the "rational" and self-interested man—which assumes those complexities away. As David McClelland, the Harvard psychologist, once put it, economists "haven't even discovered Freud, let alone Abraham Maslow." (They also haven't discovered the Apostle Paul, who lamented that "the good that I would I do not, but the evil that I would not, that I do.")

Then too there's the mounting expenditure that sellers foist upon people through machination and deceit. People don't choose to pay for the corrupt campaign finance system or for bloated executive pay packages. The cost of these is hidden in the prices that we pay at the store. *The Washington Post* recently reported that Microsoft hired Ralph Reed, former head of the Christian Coalition, and Grover Norquist, a right-wing polemicist, as lobbyists in Washington. When I bought this computer with Windows 95, Bill Gates never asked me whether I wanted to help support a bunch of Beltway operators like these.

This is compulsory consumption, not choice, and the economy is rife with it today. People don't choose to pay some $40 billion a year in telemarketing fraud. They don't choose to pay 32% more for prescription drugs than do people in Canada. ("Free trade" means that corporations are free to buy their labor and materials in other countries, but ordinary Americans aren't equally free to do their shopping there.) For that matter, people don't choose to spend $25 and up for inkjet printer cartridges. The manufacturers design the printers to make money on the cartridges because, as the *Wall Street Journal* put it, that's "where the big profit margins are."

Yet another category of consumption that most people would gladly do without arises from the need to deal with the offshoots and implications of growth. Bottled water has become a multibillion dollar business in the United States because people don't trust what comes from the tap. There's a growing market for sound insulation and double-pane windows because the economy produces so much noise. A wide array of physical and social stresses arise from the activities that get lumped into the euphemistic term "growth."

The economy in such cases doesn't solve problems so much as create new problems that require more expenditure to solve. Food is supposed to sustain people, for example. But today the dis-economies of eating sustain the GDP instead. The food industry spends some $21 billion a year on advertising to entice people to eat food they don't need. Not coincidentally there's now a $32 billion diet and weight-loss industry to help people take off the pounds that inevitably result. When that doesn't work, which is often, there is always the vacuum pump or knife. There were some 110,000 liposuctions in the United States last year; at five pounds each that's some 275 tons of flab up the tube.

It is a grueling cycle of indulgence and repentance, binge and purge. Yet each stage of this miserable experience, viewed through the Pollyannish lens of economics, becomes growth and therefore good. The problem here goes far beyond the old critique of how the consumer culture cultivates feelings of inadequacy, lack, and need so people will buy and buy again. Now this culture actually makes life worse, in order to sell solutions that purport to make it better.

Traffic shows this syndrome in a finely developed form. First we build sprawling suburbs so people need a car to go almost anywhere. The resulting long commutes are daily torture but help build up the GDP. Americans spend some $5 billion a year in gasoline alone while they sit in traffic and go nowhere. As the price of gas increases this growth sector will expand.

Commerce deplores a vacuum, and the exasperating hours in the car have spawned a booming subeconomy of relaxation tapes, cell phones, even special bibs. Billboards have 1-800 numbers so commuters can shop while they stew. Talk radio thrives on traffic-bound commuters, which accounts for some of the contentious, get-out-of-my-face tone. The traffic also helps sustain a $130 billion a year car wreck industry; and if Gates succeeds in getting computers into cars, that sector should get a major boost.

The health implications also are good for growth. Los Angeles, which has the worst traffic in the nation, also leads—if that's the word—in hospital admissions due to respiratory ailments. The resulting medical bills go into the GDP. And while Americans sit in traffic they aren't walking or getting exercise. More likely they are entertaining themselves orally with a glazed donut or a Big Mac, which helps explain why the portion of middle-aged Americans who are clinically obese has doubled since the 1960s.

C. Everett Koop, the former Surgeon General, estimates that some 70% of the nation's medical expenses are lifestyle induced. Yet the same lifestyle that promotes disease also produces a rising GDP. (Keynes observed that traditional virtues like thrift are bad for growth; now it appears that health is bad for growth too.) We literally are growing ourselves sick, and this puts a grim new twist on the economic doctrine of "complementary goods," which describes the way new products tend to spawn a host of others. The automobile gave rise to car wash franchises, drive-in restaurants, fuzz busters, tire dumps, and so forth. Television produced an antenna industry, VCRs, soap magazines, ad infinitum. The texts present this phenomenon as the wondrous perpetual motion machine of the market— goods beget more goods. But now the machine is producing complementary ills and collateral damages instead.

Suggestive of this new dynamic is a pesticide plant in Richmond, California, which is owned by a transnational corporation that also makes the breast cancer drug tamoxifen. Many researchers believe that pesticides, and the toxins created in the production of them, play a role in breast cancer. "It's a pretty good deal," a local physician told the *East Bay Express*, a Bay Area weekly. "First you cause the cancer, then you profit from curing it." Both the alleged cause and cure make the GDP go up, and this syndrome has become a central dynamic of growth in the U.S. today.

Mainstream economists would argue that this is all beside the point. If people didn't have to spend money on such things as commuting or medical costs, they'd simply spend it on something else, they say. Growth would be the same or even greater, so the actual content of growth should be of little concern to those who promote it. That view holds sway in the nation's policy councils; as a result we try continually to grow our way out of problems, when increasingly we are growing our way in.

To the extent conventional economics has raised an eyebrow at growth, it has done so mainly through the concept of "externalities." These are negative side effects suffered by those not party to a transaction between a buyer and a seller. Man buys car, car pollutes air, others suffer that "externality." As the language implies, anything outside the original transaction is deemed secondary, a subordinate reality, and therefore easily overlooked. More, the effects upon buyer and seller—the "internalities," one might say—are assumed to be good.

Today, however, that mental schema is collapsing. Externalities are starting to overwhelm internalities. A single jet ski can cause more misery for the people who reside by a lake than it gives pleasure to the person riding it.

More important, and as just discussed, internalities themselves are coming into question, and with them the assumption of choice, which is the moral linchpin of market thought.

If people choose what they buy, as market theory posits, then—externalities aside—the sum total of all their buying must be the greatest good of all. That's the ideology behind the GDP. But if people don't always choose, then the model starts to fall apart, which is what is happening today. The practical implications are obvious. If growth consists increasingly of problems rather than solutions, then scolding people for consuming too much is barking up the wrong tree. It is possible to talk instead about ridding our lives of what we don't want as well as forsaking what we do want—or think we want.

Politically this is a more promising path. But to where? The economy may be turning into a kind of round robin of difficulty and affliction, but we are all tied to the game. The sickness industry employs a lot of people, as do ad agencies and trash haulers. The fastest-growing occupations in the country include debt collectors and prison guards. What would we do without our problems and dysfunctions?

The problem is especially acute for those at the bottom of the income scale who have not shared much in the apparent prosperity. For them, a bigger piece of a bad pie might be better than none.

This is the economic conundrum of our age. No one has more than pieces of an answer, but it helps to see that much growth today is really an optical illusion created by accounting tricks. The official tally ignores totally the cost side of the growth ledger—the toll of traffic upon our time and health for example. In fact, it actually counts such costs as growth and gain. By the same token, the official tally ignores the economic contributions of the natural environment and the social structure; the more the economy destroys these, and puts commoditized substitutes in their places, the more the experts say the economy has "grown."

Pollute the lakes and oceans so that people have to join private swim clubs and the economy grows. Erode the social infrastructure of community so people have to buy services from the market instead of getting help from their neighbors, and it grows some more. The real economy—the one that sustains us—has diminished. All that has grown is the need to buy commoditized substitutes for things we used to have for free.

So one might rephrase the question thus: how do we achieve real growth, as opposed to the statistical illusion that passes for growth today? Four decades ago, John

Kenneth Galbraith argued in *The Affluent Society* that conventional economic reasoning is rapidly becoming obsolete. An economics based upon scarcity simply doesn't work in an economy of hyper-abundance, he said. If it takes a $200 billion advertising industry to maintain what economists quaintly call "demand," then perhaps that demand isn't as urgent as conventional theory posits. Perhaps it's not even demand in any sane meaning of the word.

Galbraith argued that genuine economy called for shifting some resources from consumption that needs to be prodded, to needs that are indisputably great: schools, parks, older people, the inner cities, and the like. For this he was skewered as a proto-socialist. Yet today the case is even stronger, as advertisers worm into virtually every waking moment in a desperate effort to keep the growth machine on track.

Galbraith was arguing for a larger public sector. But that brings dysfunctions of its own, such as bureaucracy; and it depends upon an enlarging private sector as a fiscal base to begin with. Today we need to go further and establish new ground rules for the economy, so that it produces more genuine growth on its own. We also need to find ways to revive the nonmarket economy of informal community exchange, so that people do not need money to meet every single life need.

In the first category, environmental fiscal policy can help. While the corporate world has flogged workers to be more productive, resources such as petroleum have been in effect loafing on the job. If we used these more efficiently the result could be jobs and growth, even in conventional terms, with less environmental pollution. If we used land more efficiently—that is, reduced urban sprawl—the social and environmental gains would be great.

Another ground rule is the corporate charter laws. We need to restore these to their original purpose: to keep large business organizations within the compass of the common good. But such shifts can do only so much. More efficient cars might simply encourage more traffic, for example. Cheap renewable power for electronic devices could encourage more noise. In other words, the answer won't just be a more efficient version of what we do now. Sooner or later we'll need different ways of thinking about work and growth and how we allocate the means of life.

This is where the social economy comes in, the informal exchange between neighbors and friends. There are some promising trends. One is the return to the traditional village model in housing. Structure does affect content. When houses are close together, and people can walk to stores and work, it encourages the spontaneous social interaction that nurtures real community. New local currencies, such as Time Dollars, provide a kind of latticework upon which informal nonmarket exchange can take root and grow.

Changes like these are off the grid of economics as conventionally defined. It took centuries for the market to emerge from the stagnation of feudalism. The next organizing principle, whatever it is, most likely will emerge slowly as well. This much we can say with certainty. As the market hurtles towards multiple implosions, social and environmental as well as financial, it is just possible that the economics profession is going to have to do what it constantly lectures the rest of us to do: adjust to new realities and show a willingness to change. ❏

Article 2.2

HOUSEHOLD LABOR, CARING LABOR, UNPAID LABOR

AN INTERVIEW with NANCY FOLBRE
September/October 2015

Nancy Folbre is a professor emerita of economics at the University of Massachusetts-Amherst. She is the author of numerous books, including Who Pays for the Kids? Gender and the Structures of Constraint *(1994)*, The Invisible Heart: Economics and Family Values *(2001)*, and Valuing Children: Rethinking the Economics of the Family *(2008)*, related to household and caring labor.

Dollars & Sense: You've written about the tendency in economics to view household labor (and especially women's labor) as "unproductive." Can you explain how this is reflected in conventional macroeconomic measures?

Nancy Folbre: Non-market household services such as meal preparation and childcare are not considered part of what we call "the economy." This means they literally don't count as part of Gross Domestic Product, household income, or household consumption.

This is pretty crazy, since we know that these services contribute to our living standards and also to the development of human capabilities. They are all at least partially fungible: time and money may not be perfect substitutes, but there is clearly a tradeoff. You can, in principle, pay someone to prepare your meals (as you do in a restaurant), or to look after your kids.

If you or someone else in your household provides these services for no charge (even if they expect something in return, such as a share of household earnings), that leaves more earnings available to buy other things. In fact, you could think of household income after taxes and after needs for domestic services have been met as a more meaningful definition of "disposable income" than the conventional definition, which is simply market income after taxes.

D&S: What is the practical consequence of not measuring household labor and production? Are economic policies and institutions different, especially in their impact on women, than what they would be if household labor were fully reflected in statistics on total employment or output?

NF: One macroeconomic consequence is a tendency to overstate economic growth when activities shift from an arena in which they are unpaid to one in which they are paid (all else equal). When mothers of young children enter paid employment, for instance, they reduce the amount of time they engage in unpaid work, but that reduction goes unmeasured. All that is counted is the increase in earnings that results, along with the increase in expenditures on services such as paid childcare.

As a result, rapid increases in women's labor force participation, such as those typical in the United States between about 1960 and the mid-1990s, tend to boost the rate of growth of GDP. When women's labor force participation levels out, as it has in the United States since the mid 1990s, the rate of growth of GDP slows down. At least some part of the difference in growth rates over these two periods simply reflects the increased "countability" of women's work.

Consideration of the microeconomic consequences helps explain this phenomenon. When households collectively supply more labor hours to the market, their market incomes go up. But they have to use a substantial portion of those incomes to purchase substitutes for services they once provided on their own—spending more money on meals away from home (or pre-prepared foods), and child care. So, the increase in their money incomes overstates the improvement in their genuinely disposable income.

A disturbing example of policy relevance emerges from consideration of the changes in public assistance to single mothers implemented in the United States in 1996, which put increased pressure on these mothers to engage in paid employment. Many studies proclaimed the success because market income in many of these families went up. But much of that market income had to be spent paying for services such as child care, because public provision and subsidies fell short.

D&S: You've also written extensively about "caring labor"? What is caring labor? To what extent is this labor (and the output of services associated with it) directly or indirectly captured by conventional measures like GDP?

NF: Everything I've discussed above is about quantity. But quality is also important. I define caring labor as labor where the quality of the services provided is likely to be affected by concern for the well-being of the care recipient. Love, affection, and commitment almost always enhance the care of dependents, and this is a big reason why market-provided services are not always perfect substitutes for those provided by family members and friends.

On the other hand, many people—especially women—work in occupations like child care, elder care, education, medicine, or social services where they genuinely care about their clients or "consumers." The market value of this work is counted as part of Gross Domestic Product and household income. But in many cases, the wage paid is considerably less than the value of the services provided. Workers in these jobs often give more in the way of quality than they are actually paid for.

D&S: As a practical matter, how could one go about measuring the value of services currently provided by unpaid household labor? In your estimation, how would our picture of economic life change if we did?

NF: It is pretty easy to estimate a lower-bound for the value of unpaid work by counting the number of hours that people spend engaging in it (which in the United States adds up to almost exactly the same total as hours of market work), and multiplying those hours times the hourly wage one would pay for a replacement.

Measures of hours worked in different activities such as meal preparation, child care, cleaning, shopping, and so on are typically based on a nationally representative survey of individuals who report all of their activities on the preceding day. The American Time Use Survey, administered since 2003 on an annual basis as a supplement to the Current Population Survey, provides reliable, high-quality data on time use.

Several studies have used these data to assign a dollar value to non-market work in what is called a "satellite" national income account (because it revolves around, rather than replacing the conventional account). Obviously, including this value in a measure of "extended GDP" makes the economy look bigger. More importantly, it revises estimates of how the economy has grown over time—in the downward direction.

Counting the value of non-market work has an equalizing effect on measures of household income, not because low-income households do a lot more of it, but because most households of similar size and composition do about the same amount. Here again, the trends are more interesting than the levels: since the relative importance of non-market work has declined over time, its equalizing effect has probably also declined. ❑

Article 2.3

GDP AND ITS DISCONTENTS

BY ALEJANDRO REUSS
April 2013

Economists have been thinking for a long time about what it means for a country or its people to be rich or poor. That was one of the main questions Adam Smith, the British philosopher often described as the "father of modern economics," took on in his most famous book *The Wealth of Nations* (1776). At the very outset, Smith made a point of defining the "real wealth" of a country as consisting in the "annual produce of the land and labour of the society." (Note that Smith was using the word "wealth" in a way that is closer to the colloquial meaning of the word than to its current technical meaning in economics. He was actually defining a country's income rather than its wealth.) That definition might seem uncontroversial now. Many economists would certainly respond that *of course* it's the production of goods and services that makes a country wealthy. But Smith had an important axe to grind. He was arguing against the view, widespread in his day, that a country's wealth consisted in the accumulation of gold and silver—an aim that led to a set of policies (especially promoting exports and suppressing imports) known as "mercantilism." In his own time, Smith was a maverick.

The kind of approach that Smith advocated, of counting up the total quantities of goods and services produced in a country in a year, is now a central part of macroeconomic measurement. When economists tabulate a country's gross domestic product (GDP), they're trying to measure the "annual produce ... of the society" more or less as Smith proposed. GDP attempts to add up the total value, counted in money units, of the goods and services produced within a country in the course of a year. This approach, while a big advance over the view that a country's wealth consisted primarily of its hoards of precious metals, however, is more problematic and controversial than it might appear at first glance. Economists and other social scientists have, in various ways, criticized the ways that GDP is counted and used as a measure of a country's "wealth" or "development." Here, we'll focus on three key critiques: 1) the distributional critique, 2) the feminist critique, and 3) the environmental critique. The first is really a criticism of the approach of looking at the total (or average) production of goods and services for a society as a whole, and ignoring the distribution of access among its members. The other two argue that GDP is misleading because it fails to count all goods and services (focusing narrowly on those that are easiest to put prices on).

What is GDP Per Capita?

Gross domestic product (GDP) per capita is the standard measure of average income used by mainstream economists, and it has become widely used as a measure of economic well-being. Gross domestic product is a measure of the total value of all the goods and services produced in a country in a year, which we can also think of as the total incomes of all the people in that country. A country's total GDP is a very poor measure of how "rich" or "poor" its people are. A country can have a very high total income, even if the average income is low, just because it has a very high population. China, for example, now has the highest total income of any country in the world, even the United States. Its average income, however, is about one-sixth that of the United States, in terms of real purchasing power. China ranks so high in total income because it is the largest country (by population) in the world. By the same token, a country can have a very large average income, but have a low total income, because it has small population. Developed countries have relatively high levels of income per capita. The top twenty countries, by this measure, include thirteen European countries, the United States and two other British offshoots (Australia and Canada), and Japan. Two of the remaining three members of this exclusive list, Qatar and United Arab Emirates, are small, oil-rich countries.

This problem, unlike those spotlighted in the three critiques we'll discuss below, is easy to solve. Instead of stopping at total GDP, we can calculate a country's GDP per capita. The phrase "per capita" simply means per person. ("Capita" comes from the Latin word meaning "head," so "per capita" means "per head.") To get GDP per capita, we just divide a country's GDP by its population. This gives us the average GDP for that country, or a measure of the average income. (Other measures of a country's total income, such as Gross National Product or Gross National Income are similar to GDP, so GNP per capita or GNI per capita are similar to GDP per capita.) Income per capita gives us a better picture of the standards of living in a country than total income.

What's Wrong with GDP Per Capita?

Mainstream economists and policymakers have treated increasing GDP per capita as virtually synonymous with development, so it's important to discuss GDP in more detail. Here, we will focus on three major criticisms of GDP per capita as a measure of well-being or "development":

The Distributional Critique
Average income can be misleading. Average (mean) income is one estimate of the "middle" of the distribution of income in a country. Most people, however, do not get the average income. Most get less than the average, some get more (and a few get much, much more). A relatively small number of people with very high incomes can pull the average up by a great deal, making the average less representative of most people's standard of living.

Figure 1, for example, shows the income distribution for Brazil in 2007. The population has been ranked by income, and then divided into five equal parts (or quintiles). Each bar represents the difference between the average income for one of these quintiles and the average income for the country as a whole. The bar furthest to the left represents the difference between the average income of the lowest-income quintile and the overall average. The next bar represents this difference for the next-lowest-income quintile, and so on, all the way up to the bar at the far right, which represents this difference for the highest-income quintile. (The lowest-income quintile is called the "first" quintile, the next-to-lowest is called the "second" quintile, and so on, up to the highest-income, or "fifth," quintile.) The GDP per capita for Brazil in 2007 was about $9800. Notice that the average income for each of the bottom four quintiles is less than the GDP per capita

INCOME DISTRIBUTION, BRAZIL, 2007 (DIFFERENCE BETWEEN EACH QUINTILE'S AVERAGE INCOME AND OVERALL AVERAGE INCOME)

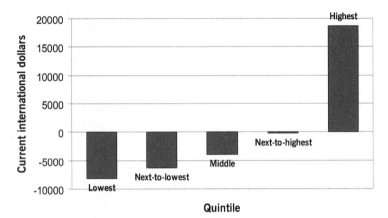

Source: World Bank, World Development Indicators: Income share held by lowest 20%, second 20%, third 20%, fourth 20%, highest 20%; GDP per capita, PPP (constant 2005 international $); GDP, PPP (constant 2005 international $) (data.worldbank.org/indicator).

(or average income) for the society as a whole, as indicated by the bars extending down. The average income for Brazil as a whole is more than six times as much as the average income for the first (lowest-income) quintile, almost three times as much as the average income for the second quintile, and more than one-and-a-half times as much as the average income for the third quintile. Even the average income for the fourth quintile is a little less than the average income for the whole country (so many people in the fourth quintile have incomes below the national average, though some have incomes above it.)

More than two-thirds of Brazil's population, then, have incomes below the country's per capita income—many of them, far below it. The reason GDP per capita for Brazil is so much higher than the incomes of most Brazilians is that the income distribution is so unequal. The average income for the fifth (highest-income) quintile is almost three times the average income for Brazil as a whole.

The Feminist Critique

GDP only counts part of the goods and services produced in a country. Earlier, we said that GDP was "a measure of the total value of goods and services" produced in a country. This is true, but it is a very flawed measure. GDP only includes the value of goods that are produced for sale in markets, ignoring goods and services that people produce for their own consumption, for the consumption of family members, and so on. In developed economies, most individuals or households have money incomes that allow them to buy most of the things they need to live. They also, however, produce goods and services for themselves, family members, and others. For example, people care for and educate their children, cook meals for themselves and other members of their family, clean their own homes, drive themselves and family members to work, school, and errands, and so on. These kinds of goods and services count as part of GDP when someone is paid to do them (for example, when we pay tuition to a school, the bill at a restaurant, the fee to a professional cleaning crew, or the fare to a taxi driver), but not when people do it for themselves, family members, or others free of charge. One could add many other examples, but the first lesson here is that GDP undercounts the total output of goods and services. Since so much of the labor that produces these uncounted goods and services is done by women, feminist economists have been in the forefront of this critique of GDP as a measure of economic development or well-being. (See Marilyn Waring, *If Women Counted: A New Feminist Economics* (Harper & Row, 1988).)

In some developing economies, the uncounted goods and services may form a larg-er part of the overall economy than in developed countries. Many people may have small farms and grow their own food. Some people weave their own cloth and make their own clothes. Some people build their own shelters. As economies "develop" economically, they may become more "monetized." This means that people produce fewer goods for their own consumption, for their families, or to trade for other goods (barter), relative to the total amount of goods and services. Instead, they start selling either goods they pro-duce or selling their own labor for money, and buying the things they need. An increase in GDP over time may, in part, reflect an increasing output of goods and services. But it may also reflect, in part, that some goods went uncounted before (because they were not produced for sale in markets) and are now being counted. This means that GDP (or GDP per capita) may exaggerate the growth of economies over time.

The Environmental Critique

GDP does not account for changes in the natural environment. We can think of parts of the natural environment as providing people with valuable "natural servic-es." Until recently, economic measurement has almost completely ignored natural services. Once we start thinking about the environment serieous, it becomes obvi-ous how critical they are for our well-being. A forest, for example, absorbs carbon dioxide from and provides oxygen to the atmosphere, provides flood control, re-duces soil erosion, provides habitat for wildlife, offers natural beauty and outdoor recreation, provides some people with sources of food and fuel (especially in lower-income countries), and so on.

If GDP only counts human-produced goods and services, then, it is undercount-ing the total goods and services. If a forest is cut down for timber, and the wood is sold in a market, this adds to GDP. However, the value of the services the forest provided are not deducted from GDP as conventionally measured, since these are not sold in markets and do not have prices. Cutting down a forest may both add something (har-vested wood, which can be used, for example, to build houses or make furniture) and subtract something (natural services) from the well-being of society. There is no way to say, in general, whether what it gained is greater or less than what is lost. However, as long as we think that the services the forest provided were worth *something*, we can say for certain that what GDP measures as being gained is greater than what it is really gained—since GDP only counts what is gained and ignores what is lost.

If Not GDP, then What?

Part of the power of GDP per capita is that it boils everything down to one easy-to-digest number. It is easy to create a table comparing the GDPs of many countries.

(Obviously, it would be harder to compare many countries in more complex ways, including a bunch of descriptive numbers for each.) This is also at the core of the weaknesses of GDP per capita. When we calculate a total or average of anything, we are, in effect, throwing out the information we have about variation between different individuals. This problem is at the heart of the first critique: Calculating total GDP or GDP per capita means excluding information about income distribution. In addition, calculating the total output of goods and services, when a modern economy includes thousands and thousands of different kinds of goods, requires some unit in which we can measure these output of each one. (We can't add together pounds of potatoes and pounds of steel, much less goods and services that can't be measured in pounds at all, like electricity or haircuts.) GDP has accomplished this by measuring everything in terms of monetary units. This leads to the second and third critiques. Monetary measurement has led to a blind spot for goods and services that do not have market prices (household production, environmental services) and are not easy to measure in money terms.

There are three major possibilities. One is to go on calculating GDP per capita, but to do a better job at capturing what GDP misses. For example, some scholars have tried to put a dollar values on non-market production (like subsistence farming or household production) and add these to GDP to get a more accurate estimate.

Another is to come up with an alternative one-number measure to compete with GDP. Two important ones are the genuine progress indicator (GPI) and the human development index (HDI). The GPI incorporates, in addition to market production, measures of both nonmarket production and environmental destruction into a single summary figure (in money terms). It does not address the distributional critique. Calculated by the United Nations Development Programme (UNDP), the HDI combines GDP per capita, average educational attainment, and average life expectancy into a single numerical index. It addresses neither the feminist nor the environmental critique, and it does not explicitly address the distributional critique. However, more equal societies tend to rank better on HDI than on GDP per capita, because they tend to achieve higher average education and life expectancy. (The UNDP also calculates an inequality-adjusted HDI, which explicitly penalizes inequality.)

Finally, a third approach is to abandon the quest for a single summary measurement. Some environmental economists oppose attempts to incorporate environmental changes into GDP or other monetary measures, which requires reducing environmental services to money values. This implies, they argue, that some quantity of produced goods can substitute for any environmental good, which is not true. They propose instead "satellite accounts" that measure environmental changes alongside GDP. Widely used measures of income inequality also exist, and can enhance our picture of an economy. Measurements of median income, access to basic goods (like health and education), economic inequality, nonmarket production, environmental quality, and other factors all should figure, in some way, into our understanding of economic life. We may just have to accept that we need to take into account multiple measures, and that no single-number "bottom line" will do. ❏

Article 2.4

MEASURING ECONOMIC DEVELOPMENT
The "Human Development" Approach

BY ALEJANDRO REUSS
April 2012

Some development economists have proposed abandoning GDP per capita, the dominant single-number measure of economic development, in favor of the "human development" approach—which focuses less on changes in average income and more on widespread access to basic goods.

Advocates of this approach to the measurement of development, notably Nobel Prize-winning economist Amartya Sen, aim to focus attention directly on the *ends* (goals) of economic development. Higher incomes, Sen notes, are *means* people use to get the things that they want. The human development approach shifts the focus away from the means and toward ends like a long life, good health, freedom from hunger, the opportunity to get an education, and the ability to take part in community and civic life. Sen has argued that these basic "capabilities" or "freedoms"—the kinds of things almost everyone wants no matter what their goals in life may be— are the highest development priorities and should, therefore, be the primary focus of our development measures.

If a rising average income guaranteed that everyone, or almost everyone, in a society would be better able to reach these goals, we might as well use average income (GDP per capita) to measure development. Increases in GDP per capita, however, do not always deliver longer life, better health, more education, or other basic capabilities to most people In particular, if these income increases go primarily to those who are already better-off (and already enjoy a long life-expectancy, good health, access to education, and so on), they probably will not have much effect on people's access to basic capabilities.

Sen and others have shown that, in "developing" countries, increased average income by itself is not associated with higher life expectancy or better health. In countries where average income was increasing, but public spending on food security, healthcare, education, and similar programs did not increase along with it, they have found, the increase in average income did not appear to improve access to basic capabilities. If spending on these "public supports" increased, on the other hand, access to basic capabilities tended to improve, whether average income was increasing or not. Sen emphasizes two main lessons based on these observations: 1) A country cannot count on economic growth alone to improve access to basic capabilities. Increased average income appears to deliver "human development" largely by *increasing the wealth a society has available for public supports*, and not in other ways. 2) A country does not have to prioritize economic growth—*does not have to "wait" until it grows richer*—to make basic capabilities like long life, good health, and a decent education available to all.

The Human Development Index (HDI)

The "human development" approach has led to a series of annual reports from the United Nations Development Programme (UNDP) ranking countries according to a "human development index" (HDI). The HDI includes measures of three things: 1) health, measured by average life expectancy, 2) education, measured by average years of schooling and expected years of schooling, and 3) income, measured by GDP per capita. The three categories are then combined, each counting equally, into a single index. The HDI has become the most influential alternative to GDP per capita as a single-number development measure.

Looking at the HDI rankings, many of the results are not surprising. The HDI top 20 is dominated by very high-income countries, including thirteen Western European countries, four "offshoots" of Great Britain (Australia, Canada, New Zealand, and the United States), and two high-income East Asian countries (Japan and South Korea). Most of the next 20 or so are Western or Eastern European, plus a few small oil-rich states in the Middle East. The next 50 or so include most of Latin America and the Caribbean, much of the Middle East, and a good deal of Eastern Europe (including Russia and several former Soviet republics). The next 50 or so are a mix of Latin American, Middle Eastern, South and Southeast Asian, and African countries. The world's poorest continent, Africa, accounts for almost all of the last 30, including the bottom 24.

TABLE 1: HDI RANKS COMPARED TO INCOME PER CAPITA RANKS (2010)

Highest HDI ranks compared to income per capita ranks (difference in parentheses)*	Lowest HDI ranks compared to income per capita ranks (difference in parentheses)
New Zealand (+30)	Equatorial Guinea (-78)
Georgia (+26)	Angola (-47)
Tonga (+23)	Kuwait (-42)
Tajikistan (+22)	Botswana (-38)
Madagascar (+22)	South Africa (-37)
Togo (+22)	Qatar (-35)
Fiji (+22)	Brunei (-30)
Ireland (+20)	Gabon (-29)
Iceland (+20)	United Arab Emirates (-28)
Ukraine (+20)	Turkey (-26)

* The numbers in parentheses represent a country's GDP-per-capita rank minus its HDI rank. Remember that in a ranking system, a "higher" (better) rank is indicated by a lower number. If a country is ranked, say, 50th in GDP per capita and 20th in HDI, its number would be 50 – 20 = +30. The positive number indicates that the country had a "higher" HDI rank than GDP per capita rank. If a country is ranked, say, 10th in GDP per capita and 35th in HDI, its number would be 10 – 35 = -25. The negative number indicates that the country had a "lower" HDI rank than GDP per capita rank.

Source: United Nations Development Programme, Indices, Getting and using data, 2010 Report—Table 1: Human Development Index and its components (hdr.undp.org/en/statistics/data/).

It is not surprising that higher GDP per capita is associated with a higher HDI score. After all, GDP per capita counts for one third of the HDI score itself. The relationship between the two, however, is not perfect. Some countries have a higher HDI rank than GDP per capita rank. These countries are "over-performing," getting more human development from their incomes, compared to other countries. Meanwhile, some countries have a lower HDI rank than GDP per capita rank. These countries are "under-performing," not getting as much human development from their incomes, compared to other countries. The list of top "over-performing" countries includes three very high-income countries that had still higher HDI ranks (Iceland, Ireland, and New Zealand), three former Soviet republics (Georgia, Tajikistan, and Ukraine), two small South Pacific island nations (Fiji, Tonga), and two African countries (Madagascar, Togo). The list of top "under-performing" countries includes four small oil-rich countries (Brunei, Kuwait, Qatar, and United Arab Emirates) and five African countries (Angola, Botswana, Equatorial Guinea, Gabon, and South Africa).

The UNDP also calculates an inequality-adjusted HDI. Note that, for all the measures included in the HDI, there is inequality within countries. The inequality-adjusted HDI is calculated so that, the greater the inequality for any measure included in the HDI (for health, education, or income), the lower the country's score. Since all countries have some inequality, the inequality-adjusted HDI for any country is always lower than the regular HDI. However, the scores for countries with greater inequality drop more than for those with less inequality. That pushes some countries up in the rankings, when inequality is penalized, and others down. Among the thirteen countries moving up the most, five are former Soviet republics. Among the ten mov-

TABLE 1: INEQUALITY-ADJUSTED HDI RANKS
COMPARED UNADJUSTED HDI RANKS

Highest inequality-adjusted HDI ranks compared unadjusted HDI ranks (difference in parentheses)	Lowest inequality-adjusted HDI ranks compared unadjusted HDI ranks (difference in parentheses)
Uzbekistan (+17)	Peru (-26)
Mongolia (+16)	Panama (-20)
Moldova (+16)	Colombia (-18)
Kyrgystan (+15)	South Korea (-18)
Maldives (+14)	Bolivia (-17)
Ukraine (+14)	Belize (-16)
Philippines (+11)	Brazil (-15)
Sri Lanka (+11)	Namibia (-15)
Tanzania, Viet Nam, Indonesia, Jamaica, Belarus (+9)	El Salvador (-14)
	Turkmenistan (-12)

Source: United Nations Development Programme, 2010 Report, Table 3: Inequality-adjusted Human Development Index (hdr. undp.org/en/media/HDR_2010_EN_Table3_reprint.pdf).

ing down the most, seven are Latin American countries. The United States narrowly misses the list of those moving down the most, with its rank dropping by nine places when inequality is taken into account.

GDP Per Capita and HDI

The relationship between income per capita and the HDI is shown in the "scatterplot" graph below. (Instead of GDP per capita, the graph uses a closely related measure called Gross National Income (GNI) per capita.) Each point represents a country, with its income per capita represented on the horizontal scale and its HDI score represented on the vertical scale. The further to the right a point is, the higher the country's per capita income. The higher up a point is, the higher the country's HDI score. As we can see, the cloud of points forms a curve, rising up as income per capita increases from a very low level, and then flattening out. This means that a change in GDP per capita from a very low level to a moderate level of around $8000 per year is associated with large gains in human development. Above that, we see,

RELATIONSHIP BETWEEN HDI AND INCOME PER CAPITA (2010)

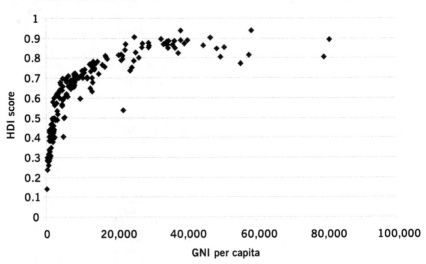

Source: United Nations Development Programme, Indices, 2010 Report - Table 1 Human Development Index and its components (hdr.undp.org/en/statistics/data/).

the curve flattens out dramatically. A change in income per capita from this moderate level to a high level of around $25,000 is associated with smaller gains in human development. Further increases in income per capita are associated with little or no gain in human development.

This relationship suggests two major conclusions, both related to greater economic equality.

First, achieving greater equality in incomes between countries, including by redistributing income from high-income countries to low-income countries, could result in increased human development. Over the highest per capita income range, from about $25,000 on up, increases in income are not associated with higher human development. Decreases in income above this threshold, by the same token, need not mean lower human development. On the other hand, over the lowest income range, below $8000, increases in income are associated with dramatic gains in HDI (largely due to increased public supports). Therefore, the redistribution of incomes from high-income countries to low-income countries could increase human development in the latter a great deal, while not diminishing human development in the former by very much (if at all)—resulting in a net gain in human development.

Second, high-income countries might make greater gains in HDI, as their incomes continued to increase, if a larger share of income went to low-income people or to public supports. Part of the reason that the relationship between per capita income and HDI flattens out at high income levels may be that there are inherent limits to variables like life expectancy (perhaps 90-100 years) or educational attainment (perhaps 20 years). These "saturation" levels, however, have clearly not been reached by all individuals, even in very high-income countries. In the United States, as of 2008, the infant mortality rate for African-Americans was more than double that for whites. The life expectancy at birth for white females was more than three years greater than that of African-American females; for white males, more than five years greater than for African-American males. As of 2010, over 40% of individuals over 25 years old have no education above high school. Over 60% have no degree from a two- or four-year college. It is little wonder that higher income would not bring about greatly increased human development, considering that, over the last 30 years, many public supports have faced sustained attack and most income growth has gone to people already at the top. ❑

Sources: Amartya Sen, *Development as Freedom* (New York: Oxford University Press, 1999); United Nations Development Programme, Indices, Getting and using data, *2010 Report*, Table 1 Human Development Index and its components (hdr.undp.org/en/statistics/data/); United Nations Development Programme, *2010 Report*, Table 3: Inequality-adjusted Human Development Index (hdr.undp.org/en/media/HDR_2010_EN_Table3_reprint.pdf); U.S. Census Bureau, The 2012 Statistical Abstract, Births, Deaths, Marriages, & Divorces: Life Expectancy, Table 107: Expectation of Life and Expected Deaths by Race, Sex, and Age: 2008; Educational Attainment, Population 25 Years and Over, U.S. Census Bureau, Selected Social Characteristics in the United States, 2010 American Community Survey, 1-Year Estimates.

Article 2.5

GROWING TOGETHER, FLYING APART

Regional Disparities in American Politics and Economics

BY GERALD FRIEDMAN
March/April 2018

For decades after the New Deal of the 1930s, the different states and regions of the United States grew together. As different regions—North and South, East and West—became more alike in their economies, they also came to resemble each other more in their politics and social attitudes. The Civil Rights revolution, of course, contributed to this by ending the South's peculiar system of *de jure* segregation. Also important in spreading economic development throughout the United States, however, were New Deal programs, including welfare spending, progressive taxation, and programs to promote development in rural and mountain areas. (These include the placing of military bases in southern and western states.)

During the post-World War II era, the New Deal continued to shape federal programs, raising income in poorer states, in rural regions, the South, and in the mountain West, and equalizing living standards throughout the United States. Beginning in the late 1970s, however, cutbacks in government social spending, changes in tax policy, and deregulation, including the opening of markets to foreign competition, reversed the narrowing of regional disparities. In recent decades, while goods-producing interior regions including southern states have suffered from foreign competition in manufacturing and other areas, richer coastal regions have benefited from deregulation, stronger protection of intellectual property, and the expansion of foreign trade in entertainment and in financial and business services. These economic changes have contributed to a political upheaval where industrial regions in the South and Midwest have abandoned their traditional loyalty to the Democratic Party even while Democrats have gained in prosperous, export-oriented coastal regions.

THE REGIONS

Coastal: CA, CO, DE, DC, FL, HI, MD, MA, ME, NH, NJ, NY, OR, PA, RI, VT, VA, WA.
Deep South: AL, GA, LA, MS, SC.
Border South: AR, KY, MO, OK, TN, TX, WV.
Midwest: IL, IN, MI, OH, WI.
Farm: IA, KS, MN, NE, ND, SD.

Regional growth disparities have increased (see Figure 1). Starting in the 1970s, a larger share of economic growth began to go to export-oriented economies on the coasts and in the farm belt, less to other rural areas in the South and West and to the industrial Midwest. Before 2000, income generally grew faster in the poorer regions of the South than in the coastal regions. But since 2000, coastal entertainment, high tech, and financial centers like Los Angeles, New York, and San Francisco have boomed while income growth in the South has slowed and the industrial Midwest and the mountain West continued to lag. Between 1963 and 2000, per capita income differentials narrowed. In 1963, for example, per capita income in coastal states was 48% above that of the Deep South and the differential fell to 34% by 2000. By 2016, however, the gap had grown to 55% and per capita income in the coastal states rose to 28% above the industrial Midwest in 2016, up from -3% in 1963, to 46% relative to the Border South states, up from 33% in 2000, and up to 33% relative to the Mountain states in 2016 compared to 15% in 2000. Only the export-oriented farm belt increased its relative income compared with the coastal states.

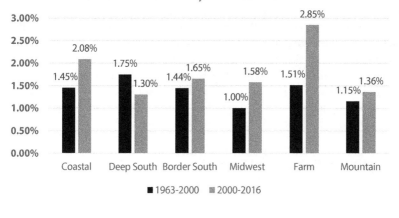

FIGURE 1: PER CAPITA INCOME GROWTH, 1968–2000, 2000–2016

Wall Street favors the urban coasts (see Figure 2). Economic policies favoring Wall Street (as well as entertainment and other professional employments) over Main Street favor residents of coastal states over the nation's interior. Different regions have been affected differently by economic policies benefiting the export of financial and professional services in exchange for imports of manufacturing goods. Regions with goods-producing industry, like manufacturing, have suffered from import competition, while the affluent coastal regions with fewer workers in manufacturing and mining, have benefited from the export of financial and business services, and maintained employment-producing and hard-to-import services such as education, entertainment, and healthcare.

FIGURE 2: EMPLOYMENT MIX BY INDUSTRY AND REGION

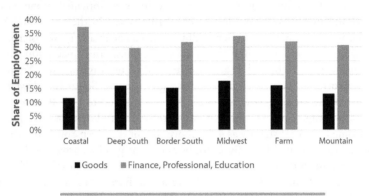

Economic policies since the early 1970s have accelerated the decline of American unions (see Figure 3). While the share of workers belonging to unions has declined in every state, the greatest absolute decline has been in the industrial Midwest, where the share of workers belonging to unions has fallen by nearly 14 percentage points, and the Deep South, where the union membership share has fallen by nearly 7 percentage points or 60%. By contrast, unions have fared better in the affluent coastal regions where total membership has been sustained by the growth of public-sector unions. Indeed, the coastal states are now the most unionized part of the United States. While national policies of free trade and industrial deregulation, and the hostility of economic and political elites to public-sector organization, have decimated unions throughout the rest of the United States, unions, especially public-sector unions, have fared better in affluent coastal states than elsewhere.

FIGURE 3: UNION SURVIVAL RATE
UNION MEMBERSHIP RATE 2016 COMPARED WITH 1983

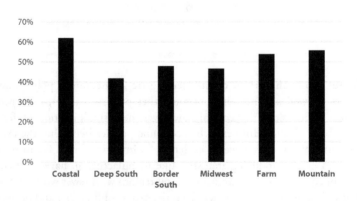

Regional economics affects politics (see Figure 4). Through the 1980s, the Democratic Party represented poorer parts of the country and campaigned for broad-based economic growth with industrial policy, business regulations, and income redistribution. Since the economic turmoil of the 1970s, however, and with the Democrats' embrace of the Civil Rights movement and the Republicans' embrace of Nixon's "Southern Strategy," the two parties have shifted. The Democrats now represent the more prosperous and cosmopolitan regions while Republicans represent the regions left behind by economic growth. The new (and influential) affluent component of the Democrats' base has pulled them away from policies to promote shared regional growth, such as support for managed trade or industrial policy, even while Republicans remain tied to neoliberal policies of fiscal austerity and industrial deregulation that hurt many of their own supporters. While the Democrats continue to support elements of the social safety net, such as Social Security, their support for income redistribution has been softened, as when Democrat Bill Clinton supported repeal of the Aid to Families with Dependent Children. ❑

FIGURE 4: DEMOCRATIC VOTE SHARE BY REGION, 1976–2016

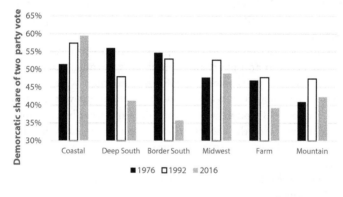

Sources: Figure 1: Spreadsheet "State exports" Tab "State GDP 1999–2016." Per capita income (PCY) from state GDP (from Bureau of Economic Analysis) divided by population (from the Census). The change in PCY is the 2016 level divided by the relative price increase 1978-2016, total divided by the 1978 level. The price level is from the BLS in tab CPI in the "State exports" spreadsheet. Annual change is the log of the change divided by the number of years.

Figure 2: Total Employment and employment by industry in 2016 is from the Bureau of Labor Statistics, ESTABLISHMENT DATA, STATE EMPLOYMENT, SEASONALLY ADJUSTED, Table D1. Data are in spreadsheet "State Exports" tab "Employment Mix."

Figure 3: Union decline uses data from Union Stats. It is in spreadsheet "State exports" Tab "2017."

Figure 4: Spreadsheet "State Exports" Tab "Elections". Results for 1976 and 1992 are from U.S. Election Atlas. Results for 2016 are from the *New York Times*.

Article 2.6

DEFLATORS AND THE PURCHASING POWER OF THE MINIMUM WAGE

BY THE CENTER FOR ECONOMIC AND POLICY RESEARCH
February 2014

Recently some opponents of an increase in the minimum wage have argued that we are using an inaccurate measure of inflation when we say the 1968 minimum wage would be equal to about $10.00 an hour in today's prices. They argue that if we use the Personal Consumption Expenditures Deflator (PCE) to measure inflation—instead of the Consumer Price Index (CPI-U, modified slightly to reflect current methods back as far as 1968—we would need a minimum wage of just $8.50 an hour to have the same purchasing power as in 1968. Furthermore, if we take the average value of the minimum wage over the years 1960–1980, the current minimum wage of $7.25 would already be roughly equivalent in purchasing power.

This argument raises several interesting points about the measure of inflation. It also calls attention to an important point about government policy toward the minimum wage. In the years prior to 1968, the minimum wage was deliberately raised by more than enough to keep pace with purchasing power. In the three decades from 1938 to 1968 Congress raises the minimum wage by enough to keep in step with productivity growth. The intention was to ensure that even workers at the bottom shared in the benefits of economic growth. This issue is worth noting in the current debate.

First, there are three important points about the measure of inflation used to assess the minimum wage:

Unlike the Bureau of Labor Statistics' Consumer Price Index (CPI-U-RS, the version of the CPI that approximates the current method of measuring inflation to earlier years), the PCE is not designed as a deflator of cash income.

There are difficult issues about assessing the cost-of-living over time that have been debated by economists and policy makers. It is not clear that the PCE comes closer to a "true" measure than the CPI-U-RS.

Congress has not used the PCE for other purposes. For example, if the PCE were applied consistently, the cutoff for income tax brackets would all be around 10% lower than is currently the case, raising tax rates relative to the current brackets, which are based on the CPI-U.

Taking these in turn, the CPI-U-RS that economists use to measure the rate of inflation seen by consumers is intended to reflect the portion of their income devoted to the various items they consume. By contrast, the PCE is intended as a price index to assess prices changes for everything that falls into the consumption component of GDP. This leads to some important differences.

For example, the PCE includes a component to measure the portion of consumer expenditures that are covered either by employer-provided health insurance or government provided health insurance, like Medicare. The CPI medical spending component only picks up expenses that are paid by individuals either as directly purchased insurance, premiums on an employer or government plan, or out of pocket expenses.

The PCE also includes many expenses related to the operation of home businesses. For example, the weight of computer in the PCE (0.87%) is more than three times larger than its weight in the CPI (0.26%). The PCE also includes items that are not a visible part of consumers' market basket. For example, it includes the value of financial services provided without payment, like free checking accounts for people who maintain a certain minimum deposit. These services accounted for 2.3% of the PCE in 2013. The PCE also includes expenditures made by non-profit organizations like private universities or charities. In short, the PCE is not designed to be a measure of the rate of inflation seen by consumers, so its use for this purpose has to be questioned.

There is a second issue as to whether the PCE may still more accurately reflect the rate of inflation experienced by consumers even if it was not designed for this purpose. The biggest methodological difference is that the PCE takes account of the substitutions in consumption, as consumers shift away from items that see rapid rises in price to ones that see less rapid rises in price. This means that if people shift from consuming apples to oranges, because the price of apples rose, then the PCE would decrease the weight of apples and increase the weight of oranges. By contrast, CPI-U-RS would hold the weight of apples and oranges fixed.

Clearly consumers can and do shift their consumption to some extent to protect themselves against price increases. However, it is not clear that all consumers are capable of substituting to the same extent. Research by the Bureau of Labor Statistics indicated that lower income consumers may be able to substitute less than higher income consumers. (It is worth noting that the CPI-U-RS already assumes substantial substitution at lower levels, for example between types of apples or types of oranges.)

The issue of how substitution should be treated in a price index and whether it is the same for all groups is an important one. It certainly has not yet been resolved. While inadequately capturing substitution may lead to an overstatement of inflation, it is also worth noting that there are reasons that the CPI-U-RS may understate the rate of inflation seen by consumers.

For example, people need items in their normal basket of consumption goods, like cell phones, computers, and Internet access, that they would not have needed 30 years ago. All of these items provide enormous benefits, but they also come with additional cost. A person without Internet access in 1980 would not have suffered any hardship; however a person without Internet access in 2014 is cut off from a major means of social communication. It is not clear exactly how new needs should be captured in the CPI, but by missing these items the CPI is almost certainly understating the true increase in the cost of living.

Finally, in using the CPI-U-RS to adjust the minimum wage, President Obama is following the general practice for other items that are indexed, most importantly income-tax brackets. If the PCE had been used to adjust income-tax brackets since indexation first went into effect in 1983, the bracket cutoffs would be close to 10%

lower than they are today. This means that most people would be paying higher taxes since more of their income would be taxed at a higher rate. If we really believe that the PCE is a better measure for inflation, we should be using it to adjust the income tax brackets as well, not just the minimum wage.

The last point, that taking the whole period 1960–1980 as a basis of comparison, rather than just the peak year of 1968 brings up the important point that the minimum wage used to be increased in step with productivity growth, not just the cost-of-living. In other words, prior to 1968 Congress quite deliberately chose to increase the minimum wage by more than the rate of inflation to ensure that workers at the bottom of the wage distribution got their share of the benefits of economic growth.

If we had continued to increase the minimum wage in step with productivity growth its current value would be close to $17 an hour. While it would not be plausible to imagine the government could raise the minimum wage to this amount quickly without having a big impact on employment, there is no obvious reason that we could not over time develop an economy that could support employment at these wages. In any case, it is important to remember that we had once been on path that would have led to a minimum wage that is well more than twice the minimum wage we have today. ❑

Article 2.7

UNDERCOUNTING THE POOR

BY JEANNETTE WICKS-LIM

May/June 2013

In 1995, a blue-ribbon panel of poverty experts selected by the National Academy of the Sciences (NAS) told us that the "current U.S. measure of poverty is demonstrably flawed judged by today's knowledge; it needs to be replaced." Critics have long pointed out shortcomings including the failure to adequately account for the effects of "safety net" programs and insensitivity to differences in the cost of living between different places.

The Census Bureau, the federal agency charged with publishing the official poverty numbers, has yet to replace the poverty line. However, in the last couple years it has published an alternative, the Supplemental Poverty Measure (SPM). The SPM is the product of over two decades of work to fix problems in the federal poverty line (FPL).

This new measure takes us one step forward, two steps back. On the one hand, it has some genuine improvements: The new measure makes clearer how the social safety net protects people from economic destitution. It adds basic living costs missing from the old measure. On the other hand, it does little to address the most important criticism of the poverty line: it is just too damned low. The fact that the poverty line has only now been subject to revision—50 years after the release of the first official poverty statistic—likely means that the SPM has effectively entrenched this major weakness of the official measure for another 50 years.

The 2011 official poverty rate is 15.1%. The new poverty measure presented—and missed by a wide margin—the opportunity to bring into public view how widespread the problem of poverty is for American families. If what we mean by poverty is the inability to meet one's basic needs a more reasonable poverty line would tell us that 34% of Americans—more than one in three—are poor.

What's in a Number?

The unemployment rate illustrates the power of official statistics. In the depths of the Great Recession, a new official statistic—the rate of underemployment, counting people working part time who want full-time work and those who have just given up on looking for work—became part of every conversation about the economy. One in six workers (17%) counted as underemployed in December 2009, a much higher number than the 9.6% unemployment rate. The public had not been confronted with an employment shortage that large in recent memory; it made political leaders stand up and pay attention.

The supplemental poverty measure had the potential to do the same: a more reasonable poverty line—the bottom line level of income a household needs to avoid poverty—would uncover how endemic the problem of economic deprivation is here in the United States. That could shake up policymakers and get them to prioritize anti-poverty policies in their political agendas. Just as important, a more accurate count of the poor would acknowledge the experience of those struggling mightily to put food on the table or to keep the lights on. No one wants to be treated like "just a number," but not being counted at all is surely worse.

With a couple of years of data now available, the SPM has begun to enter into anti-poverty policy debates. Now is a good time to take a closer look at what this measure is all about. The supplemental measure makes three major improvements to the official poverty line. It accounts for differences in the cost of living between different regions. It changes the way it calculates the standard of living necessary to avoid poverty. And it accounts more fully for benefits from safety net programs.

Different Poverty Lines for Cost-of-Living Differences

Everyone knows that $10,000 in a small city like Utica, New York, can stretch a lot farther than in New York City. In Utica, the typical monthly cost of rent for a two-bedroom apartment, including utilities, was about $650 during 2008–2011. The figure for New York City? Nearly double that at $1,100. Despite this, the official poverty line has been the same regardless of geographic location.The supplemental poverty measure adjusts the poverty income threshold by differences in housing costs in metropolitan and rural areas in each state—a step entirely missing in the old measure.

We can see how these adjustments make a real difference by simply comparing the official poverty and SPM rates by region. In 2011, according to the official poverty line, the Northeast had the lowest poverty rate (13.2%), the South had the highest (16.1%), and the Midwest and the West fell in between (14.1% and 15.9%, respectively). With cost-of-living differences factored in, the regions shuffled ranks. The SPM poverty rates of the Northeast and South look a lot more alike (15.0% and 16.0%, respectively). The Midwest's cheaper living expenses pushed its SPM rate to the lowest among the four regions (12.8%). The West, on the other hand, had an SPM rate of 20.0%, making it the highest-poverty region.

Updating Today's Living Costs

Obviously, household expenses have changed a lot over the last half-century. The original formula used to construct the official poverty line used a straightforward rule-of-thumb calculation: minimal food expenses time three. It's been well-documented since then that food makes up a much smaller proportion of households' budgets, something closer to one-fifth, as new living expenses have been added (e.g., childcare, as women entered the paid workforce in droves) and the costs of other expenses ballooned (e.g., transportation and medical care).

The new poverty measure takes these other critical expenses into account by doing the following. First, the SPM income threshold tallies up necessary spending on food, clothing, shelter and utilities. The other necessary expenses like work-related child care and medical bills are deducted from a household's resources to meet the SPM income threshold. A household is then called poor if its resources fall below the threshold.

These non-discretionary expenses clearly take a real bite out of family budgets. For example, the "costs of working" cause the SPM poverty rate to rise to nearly doubles that of the official poverty rate among full-time year-round workers from less than 3% to over 5%. Bringing the Social Safety Net into Focus

Today's largest national anti-poverty programs operate in the blind spot of the official poverty line. These include programs like Supplemental Nutrition Assistance Program (SNAP) and the Earned Income Tax credit (EITC). The supplemental measure does us a major service by showing in no uncertain terms how our current social safety net protects people from economic destitution. The reason for this is that the official poverty measure only counts cash income and pre-tax cash benefits (e.g., Social Security, Unemployment Insurance, and Temporary Assistance to Needy Families (TANF)) towards a household's resources to get over the poverty line. The supplemental poverty measure, on the other hand, adds to a household's resources near-cash government subsidies—programs that help families cover their expenditures on food (e.g. SNAP and the National School Lunch program), shelter (housing assistance from HUD) and utilities (Low Income Home Energy Assistance Program (LIHEAP))—as well as after-tax income subsidies (e.g., EITC). This update is long overdue since the 1996 Personal Responsibility and Work Opportunity Reconciliation Act (a.k.a., the Welfare Reform Act) largely replaced the traditional cash assistance program AFDC with after-tax and in-kind assistance.

Here are some figures for 2011 that illustrate the impact of each of twelve different economic assistance programs. Social Security, refundable tax credits (largely EITC but also the Child Tax Credit (CTC)), and SNAP benefits do the most to reduce poverty. In the absence of Social Security, the supplemental poverty rate would be 8.3 percentage points higher, shooting up from 16.1% to over 23.8%. Without refundable tax credits, the supplemental poverty rate would rise 2.8 percentage points, up to nearly 19%, with much of the difference being in child poverty. Finally, SNAP benefits prevent poverty across households from rising 1.5 percentage points. The SPM gives us the statistical ruler by which to measure the impact of the major anti-poverty programs of the day. This is crucial information for current political feuds about falling over fiscal cliffs and hitting debt ceilings.

A Meager Supplement

Unfortunately, the new poverty measure adds all these important details to a fundamentally flawed picture of poverty.

In November 2012, the Census Bureau published, for only the second time, a national poverty rate based on the Supplemental Poverty Measure: it stood at 16.1% (for 2011), just one percentage point higher than the official poverty rate of 15.1%. Why such a small difference? The fundamental problem is that the supplementary poverty measure, in defining the poverty line, builds from basically the same level of extreme economic deprivation as the old measure.

In an apples-to-apples comparison (see sidebar), the new supplemental measure effectively represents a poverty line roughly 30% higher than the official poverty income threshold for a family of four. For 2011, the official four-person poverty line was $22,800, an adjusted SPM income threshold—one that can be directly

---

Federal Poverty Line vs. Supplemental Poverty Measure

The new supplemental measure (SPM) modestly bumps up the federal poverty line (FPL). Let's start with the published measures of the two thresholds. When you compare these, for a family of four (two adults, two children) the SPM is only 11% more than the official poverty line: $22,800 versus $25,200. But this isn't an apples-to-apples comparison. The official income poverty threshold is supposed to represent the income a family needs to cover all the expenses they have to support a minimal standard of living. The SPM income threshold on the other hand represents only the income a family needs to cover necessary food, clothing, shelter, and utility expenses (FCSU). "Nondiscretionary spending"—money spent on things like work-related expenses (transportation, childcare, and taxes) don't get counted in the income threshold. Instead, the SPM deducts these from what they call the "economic resources" a household has to cover their FCSU expenses. This way of accounting for such work-related expenses has the effect of making the SPM threshold look lower than it is actually is relative to the official poverty line. In order to make an apples-to-apples comparison, we have to adjust the SPM income threshold upward so that it includes the income needed to cover "nondiscretionary spending" the way the official poverty line does. This adds about 20% to the SPM income threshold, so that the supplementary poverty measure actually stands about 30% higher than the FPL.

---

compared to the FPL—is about $30,500. Unfortunately, the NAS panel of poverty experts appears to have taken an arbitrarily conservative approach to setting poverty income threshold. Reasonably enough, NAS panel uses as their starting point how much households spend on the four essential items: food, clothing, shelter, and utilities. A self-proclaimed "judgment call," they choose what they call a "reasonable range" of expenditures to mark poverty. What's odd is that their judgment leans back toward the official poverty line—the measure they referred to as "demonstrably flawed."

To justify this amount they show how their spending levels fall within the range of two other "expert budgets" (i.e., poverty income thresholds) in the poverty research. What they do not explain is why, among the ten alternative income thresholds they review in detail, they focus on two of the lower ones. In fact, one of these two income thresholds they describe as an "outlier at the low end." The range of the ten thresholds actually spans between 9% and 53% more than the official poverty line; their recommended range for the threshold falls between 14% and 33% above the official poverty line.

Regardless of the NAS panel's intention, the Inter-agency Technical Working group (ITWG) tasked with the job of producing the new poverty measure adopted the middle point of this "reasonable range" to establish the initial threshold for the revised poverty line. This conflicts with what we know about the level of economic deprivation that households experience in the range of the federal poverty line. In a 1999 book *Hardship in America*, researchers Heather Boushey, Chauna Brocht, Bethney Gunderson, and Jared Bernstein examined the rates and levels of economic hardship among officially poor households (with incomes less than the poverty line), near-poor households (with incomes between the poverty line and twice the poverty line), and not poor households (with incomes more than twice the poverty line).

As expected, they found high rates of economic distress among households classified as "officially poor." For example, in 1996, 29% of poor households experienced one or more "critical" hardships such as missing meals, not getting necessary medical care, and having their utilities disconnected. Near-poor households experienced these types of economic crises only a little less frequently (25%). Only when households achieved incomes above twice the poverty line did the incidence of these economic problems fall substantially—down to 11%. (Unfortunately, the survey data on which the study was based have been discontinued, so more up-to-date figures are unavailable.) This pattern repeats for "serious" hardships that include being worried about having enough food, using the ER for healthcare due to lack of alternatives, and falling behind on housing payments. So if what we mean by poverty is the inability to meet one's basic needs, then twice the poverty line—rather than the SPM's 1.3 times—appears to be an excellent marker.

Let's consider what the implied new poverty income threshold of $30,500 feels like for a family of four. (This, by the way, is about what a household would take in with two full-time minimum-wage jobs.)

This annual figure comes out to $585 per week. Consider a family living in a relatively low-cost area like rural Sandusky, Michigan. Based on the basic-family-budget details provided by the Economic Policy Institute, such a family typically needs to spend about $175 on food (this assumes they have a nearby grocery store, a stove at home, and the time to cook all their meals) and another $165 on rent for a two-bedroom apartment each week. This eats up 60% of their budget, leaving only about $245 to cover all other expenses. If they need childcare to work ($180), then this plus the taxes they have to pay on their earnings ($60) pretty much wipes out the rest. In other words, they have nothing left for such basic needs as telephone service, clothes, personal care products like soap and toilet paper, school supplies, out of pocket medical expenses, and transportation they may need to get to work. Would getting above this income threshold seem like escaping poverty to you?

For many federal subsidy programs this doesn't seem like escaping poverty either. That's why major anti-poverty programs like that National School Lunch program, Low Income Home Energy Assistance Program (LIHEAP), State Children's Health Insurance Program (SCHIP) step in to help families with incomes up to twice the poverty line.

If the supplementary poverty measure tackled the fundamental problem of a much-too-low poverty line then it would likely draw an income threshold closer to 200% of the official poverty line (or for an apples-to-apples comparison, about 150% of the SPM income threshold). This would shift the landscape of poverty statistics and produce a poverty rate of an astounding one in three Americans.

Now What?

The Census Bureau's supplemental measure doesn't do what the underemployment rate did for the unemployment rate—that is, fill in the gap between the headline number and how many of us are actually falling through the cracks.

The poverty line does a poor job of telling us how many Americans are struggling to meet their basic needs. For those of us who fall into the "not poor" category but get struck with panic from time to time that we may not be able to make ends meet—with one bad medical emergency, one unexpected car repair, one unforeseen cutback in work hours—it makes us wonder, if we're not poor or even near poor, why are we struggling so much? The official statistics betray this experience. The fact is that so many Americans are struggling because many more of us are poor or near-poor than the official statistics lead us to believe.

The official poverty line has only been changed—supplemented, that is—once since its establishment in 1963. What can we do to turn this potentially once-in-a-century reform into something more meaningful? One possibility: we should simply rename the supplemental poverty rates as the severe poverty rate. Households with economic resources below 150% of the new poverty line then can be counted as "poor." By doing so, politicians and government officials would start to recognize what Americans have been struggling with: One-third of us are poor. ❑

Sources: Kathleen Short, "The Research Supplemental Poverty Measure: 2011," *Current Population Report*, U.S. Bureau of the Census, November 2012 (census.gov); Constance F. Citro and Robert T. Michael (eds.), *Measuring Poverty: A New Approach*, Washington D.C.: National Academy Press, 1995; Trudi Renwick, "Geographic Adjustments of Supplemental Poverty Measure Thresholds: Using the American Community Survey Five-Year Data on Housing Costs," U.S. Bureau of the Census, January 2011 (census.gov).

Chapter 3

ECONOMIC GROWTH AND BUSINESS CYCLES

INTRODUCTION

Economic growth and business cycles could hardly be a more pertinent topic than they are today—with the world having recently gone through the deepest economic crisis since the Great Depression, and experiencing sluggish growth and persistent economic fragility since then.

Arthur MacEwan and John Miller take a close look at the current U.S. economic expansion, which the business press has taken to calling a "Goldilocks economy" (Article 3.1). The expansion began with the official end of Great Recession in June 2009, and as of June 2018 the economy had grown continuously for nine years, making it the second longest economic expansion on record. But despite the length of the expansion and low unemployment rates, today's economy is far from "just right." Economic growth in this expansion has been slower than in any other economic expansion since World War II. MacEwan and Miller argue that different public policies, from serious public investment to support for unions and more equitable labor relations, would go a long way toward restoring more robust economic growth and undoing the ever-worsening inequality of today's economy.

Next, Gerald Friedman addresses long-running debates about the reasons for the slowdown in growth of economic output and standards of living (Article 3.2). He disputes the view that "supply-side" factors, like the exhaustion of technological innovation, are the root problem. Rather, he points to economic policies that have stifled the growth in demand, as well as the growing power imbalance between employers and owners (which has stuck workers with a shrinking share of the slow-growing economic pie).

In Article 3.3, Arthur MacEwan takes on this question: Are economic growth and environmental sustainability compatible? For the economic growth of the last 200 years, the answer is surely no. But MacEwan reminds us that technology and the carbon intensity of production are not givens but subject to social control. While he sees formidable obstacles to slowing global economic growth, he remains hopeful that the large-scale adoption of alternative technologies will be able to make economic growth and environmental sustainability compatible.

Finally, Jayati Ghosh offers an overview of the linkages between the high-income countries, "emerging" manufacturing economies like China, and raw-material and intermediate input producers (Article 3.4). She argues that slow economic growth in high-income countries has caused a slowdown in the emerging economies and an end to the commodity boom that fueled growth for raw-materials exporters. In her view, however, economic growth should not be the goal, and developing countries can do much better at improving the standards of living of the majority if they cast off the focus on maximizing GDP growth.

Discussion Questions

1. (Article 3.1) What do MacEwan and Miller mean when they write that the current U.S. economic expansion has been so long because it has been so slow? What evidence do they present to support their argument?

2. (Article 3.2) Why does Friedman disagree with the view that stagnant growth in output and standards of living are due to the exhaustion of technological innovation? What alternate explanation does he offer?

3. (Article 3.3) According to MacEwan, what are the obstacles to slowing global economic growth and what would it take to make economic growth compatible with a sustainable environment?

4. (Article 3.4) Are rising wages a good thing or a bad thing for developing economies? Why have policymakers seen them as a bad thing? Why does Ghosh see them as a good thing?

Article 3.1

THE U.S. ECONOMY: WHAT IS GOING ON?

BY ARTHUR MacEWAN AND JOHN MILLER

May 2018, New Labor Forum; *updated June 2018*

As 2017 came to an end, the popular story was that the U.S. economy was doing very well. On December 9, the *New York Times*, under the headline, "Sizzling Economy Heightens Fears of Overheating," told its readers that "The economy's vital signs are stronger than they have been in years." And in its December 14 edition, the *Economist* reported that "America's economy is in good shape."

These stories had some empirical foundation. The unemployment rate was down to 4.1%. The stock market and corporate profits were soaring to record heights. Family incomes, including those of low-income families, were increasing sharply. In the second quarter of 2017, Gross Domestic Product (GDP) had grown by 3.1%, and then by 3.2% in the third quarter. Neither the *Times* nor the *Economist* attributed the favorable conditions of 2017 to the ascension of Donald Trump to the presidency, seeing the year's economic record as a continuation of the trend well established in the Obama years.

"Good" and "well," however, are relative concepts. Seen against the backdrop of the Great Recession and the slow economic recovery of subsequent years, a GDP growth rate of just over 3% does look good, if not great. By other standards, this is not so good, even if sustained for more than those two quarters of 2017. During the decade-long economic expansion of the 1990s, the average annual growth rate of GDP was 3.6%. And in the nine-year expansion of the 1960s, the annual rate was 4.6%. Indeed, even with the growth in 2017, the economic expansion since 2009 has been slower than in any other expansion since World War II.

Still, as of the end of 2017, the expansion had been going on for 102 months, the third longest expansion on record—exceeded in length only by those expansions in the 1990s (120 months) and the 1960s (106 months). Given the severity of the economic downturn in 2008 and 2009—when it appeared that the economy was about to implode—and the limited fiscal stimulus that was provided by the federal government to restart the economy, it is reasonable to ask, "Why has the economy done as well as it has? Why has the debacle of the Great Recession been, at least to a degree, overcome?"

Why Has the Recovery Continued So Long?

Part of the answer, ironically, is that the expansion has continued for so long because it has been so slow. U.S. expansions have generally been driven by rising demand, often supplied by the government through tax cuts or increased spending. Government spending, though insufficient to stimulate a strong recovery (as we will explain), did contribute significantly to the initiation of recovery in late 2009 and 2010. But as this stimulus ebbed, continuing expansion relied on low costs.

With slow growth, there has been minimal upward pressure on labor costs. Even with the unemployment rate close to 4% at the end of 2017, wages are only rising slowly. As has become increasingly evident, however, the unemployment rate is not such a good measure of labor market conditions. The unemployment rate measures the people who do not have jobs and are looking for jobs as a percentage of the labor force, and the labor force is defined as people who have jobs plus those who are looking for jobs. In the Great Recession, many people simply gave up looking for jobs and are not counted as in the labor force. The percentage of people 16 years and older in the labor force—the labor force participation rate—dropped from a pre-recession peak of 66.4% (December 2006) to 62.5% in late 2015 and stood at only 62.7% in October and November of 2017. Although there are reports of "discouraged workers" reentering the labor force as the economy has expanded, these data suggest that there are still many capable people who are not looking for employment.

If the labor force participation rate had remained at its December 2006 level, then, with the number of jobs that existed in November 2017, the unemployment rate would have been over 9%. Under these conditions, workers' bargaining power and ability to push up wages are less than that indicated by the official unemployment rate. And the slow growth of wages has probably been one of the most important factors contributing to the length of the expansion. (The sharp rise in family incomes, mentioned previously, has been primarily a result of more people working, not the result of higher wages.)

Another part of the answer as to why economic growth in the United States has continued so long is that commodity prices fell and remained low—that is, prices of basic raw materials, everything from copper and oil to soy beans and corn. Low commodity prices, like low labor prices, contribute to low costs of production. In 2017, the Bloomberg index of commodity prices was about 50% lower than it was in 2011, just after it had recovered from the Great Recession. Slow growth in the United States, while not the main factor, has contributed to keeping down the price of commodities. Also, similarly slow growth in Europe has been a factor. But perhaps the most important factor has been the slowdown of economic growth in China. GDP in China grew at 9.4% in 2008 and 2009, rose to 10.6% in 2010, but has since dropped in each year and was down to 6.7% in 2016.

One commodity price, the price of oil, has been especially important. Before the Great Recession, the per barrel price of oil had risen to $100 in 2008; it fell during the recession, recovered briefly, and then plummeted to $43 in 2016. As with commodities in general, the low oil price has allowed firms to grow. A major factor pushing oil prices lower was the great increase of oil production (supply) in the United States, which rose by almost 90% between 2006 and 2016. In addition, the rapid increase in production of natural gas, rising by close to 50% in the 2006 to 2016 decade (fracking) put downward pressure on the price of energy.

And then there are interest rates. Responding to the emergence of the Great Recession, the Federal Reserve, using its authority to control the money supply and interest rates, began to push down interest rates. The federal funds rate is the rate at which banks borrow short-term from each other and is the rate most directly affected by the Fed. This rate, in turn, affects interest rates throughout the economy. The federal funds rate dropped from about 5.25% in the middle of 2007 to 2% by the middle of 2008 and was virtually zero by the beginning of 2009. The Fed only began raising the rate in small increments at the end of 2015, and it remained below 2% in late 2017. When inflation is factored in, through most of the period since early 2009, the "real" federal funds rate has been zero or negative, so the cost of borrowing was very low throughout the economy.

Interest rates, like wages and commodity prices, are part of the cost of production. This collection of cost factors has been sufficient to keep the economy growing—though growing slowly.

It is somewhat surprising, however, that the uncertainty created by the Trump presidency and the threatened disruption of economic conditions has not had visible negative impacts on the growth of GDP. At this point, it is only possible to speculate as to why the uncertainty surrounding the Trump presidency has not brought about a negative economic impact. It is likely, however, that the negative impact has been tempered by two factors. First, while concerned about the uncertainty, most business officials have long railed against taxes and regulations. On these two important issues, the uncertainty has been largely over the extent of reductions, and any reduction would be positive in the minds of business officials. With passage of the tax bill and the record on deregulation, their hopes have been realized. Second, on some other aspects of uncertainty—particularly surrounding international trade agreements—it is likely that business officials did not believe that Trump would bring about changes to the extent he threatened during the campaign.

Why Has the Recovery Been So Slow?

Although the economy has grown, it has grown remarkably slowly. This slow growth has been in large part a consequence of government actions.

As the Great Recession emerged in the United States at the end of 2007 and beginning of 2008, the political choice of Congress and President Bush was to do virtually nothing to provide a fiscal stimulus—that is, to boost total spending in the economy by raising government spending or lowering taxes or both. Treating the crisis primarily as a financial crisis and fearing that the financial system would collapse, government officials focused on providing loans to bail out financial institutions. By late 2008, the financial system was saved (with the important exceptions of Bear Stearns, Lehman Brothers, and some relatively small banks). But by this point, the declines in production and employment were in full swing.

Within a month of taking office in January 2009, President Obama's American Recovery and Reinvestment Act (ARRA) was enacted (with support of only three Republicans in the Senate and none in the House). The Act, though providing $787 billion in new spending, was too little to provide the sort of stimulus that was needed. Although the ARRA did contribute to the cessation of economic decline by the middle of 2009, recovery was slower than it would have been with a larger stimulus. Not only were private firms cutting their workforces and holding off on new investment and employment, but across the country, state and local governments, experiencing sharp drop-offs in revenue, were eliminating jobs. The depth and breadth of the recession suggest that a federal stimulus some 50% larger than the ARRA would have been needed to set the economy on course for an effective recovery.

FIGURE 1: NET FIXED PRIVATE INVESTMENT, 2004–2016, BILLIONS OF 2009 DOLLARS

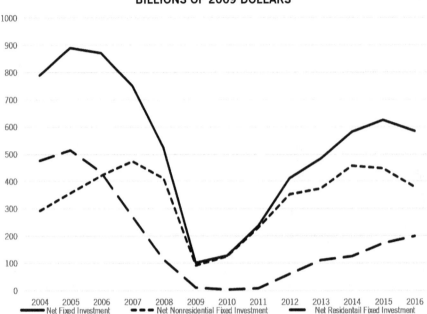

Source: U.S. Department of Commerce, Bureau of Economic Analysis: National Data, Table 5.2.6.

The Federal Reserve, as noted earlier, provided more support for economic growth by lowering interest rates to historically unprecedented levels. But this had limited impact. Low interest rates are supposed to spur investment and economic growth, as the lower cost of credit is expected to lead firms to borrow, invest, and generate expansion. Following 2009, net private investment (i.e., investment other than replacement of old capital equipment and facilities) did grow, but only slowly—as shown in Figure 1. By 2015, net private investment (inflation adjusted) was still 20% below the 2006 level and fell off 14% between 2015 and 2016. In the wake of the mortgage crisis of the last decade, residential investment has been especially weak. However, nonresidential investment (new machinery and buildings) also has not risen to pre-recession levels, and the 2016 fall-off was all in nonresidential investment.

The experience since the Great Recession indicates that lower financing costs, even when combined with other low production costs, are insufficient to generate a strong surge of investment when total spending or aggregate demand is weak. Economists sometimes liken the situation to pushing on a string: if you push on the back end of the string without anyone pulling on the front end, the string will not move forward. Demand is what pulls the economy forward.

The large and rising amount of cash and liquid assets that U.S. firms are holding provides further evidence that investment, nonresidential investment in particular, is not constrained by a lack of funds. In May of 2017, the rating agency Standard and Poor's (S&P) reported that cash and liquid investments held by U.S. firms "rose by 10% to $1.9 trillion in 2016 as the rich got richer." S&P goes on to say that $1.1 trillion of this is held overseas, with the remaining $800 billion held in the United

States. Other sources indicate that in total U.S. firms were holding $2.6 trillion overseas. Stronger demand would surely have led firms to use these assets—certainly a share of the $800 billion held in the country—for more real investments that would boost economic growth and create jobs.

Government investment—in particular, in infrastructure—has also been weak. During the recovery from the Great Recession, public investments by federal, state, and local governments have declined substantially. In 2013, 2014, and 2015, the levels of public investment (inflation adjusted) were 14% to 15% below their 2009 peak, and were lower than in any year since 2001. Combined with the weakness of private investment, these figures show that investment was not driving growth of the economy—to say nothing of failing to provide a strong foundation for long-term growth.

Moreover, after 2010, when the ARRA had had most of its impact, total government spending (inflation adjusted) fell continuously to 2014. Although this spending rose slightly in 2015 and 2016, it remained below pre-recession levels. In almost all post–World War II recoveries, government expenditures have increased. Also, since 2012, with weak government spending, the federal budget deficit as a percent of GDP (one measure of federal stimulus) dropped to levels similar to those of the mid-1980s and early 1990s—about 4% or a little less. As expressed in the *Economic Report of the President* in January 2017 (the last report of the Obama years), "Fiscal restraint in the United States continued in fiscal year 2016."

"Fiscal restraint," under the existing circumstances, is simply a euphemism for austerity. Slow economic growth, a continuing weak labor market, relatively stagnant wages, and growing inequality are all signs that the federal stimulus at the time of the Great Recession should have been greater and continuing stimulus should have been the order of the day in subsequent years.

Furthermore, the shift of government's role in public investment is not simply a phenomenon of recent years, but is evident in a comparison of the current period with earlier decades. For example, gross government investment (federal, state, and local) in the 2010 to 2016 period averaged 3.7% of GDP; in the 1950s and 1960s, the figure was greater than 6%, close to 5% in the 1970s and 1980s, and just over 4% in the 1990s and 2000s18 (see Figure 2). While the decline has thus been long term, regarding the most recent period, the *Financial Times* commented in a 2013 article: "Public investment in the U.S. has hit its lowest level since demobilisation after the Second World War because of Republican success in stymieing President Barack Obama's push for more spending on infrastructure, science and education."

All this is to say that the growth of the economy over the past nine years did not have to be so slow. *The recovery was kept weak by political choices*, choices about government stimulus and government investment, and about a variety of policies that limited wage growth and exacerbated economic inequality.

Inequality and Economic Growth

The expansion of the economy (GDP), whether slow or fast, does not tell us much about people's actual economic conditions. As is well known, economic inequality has been increasing in the United States for decades. The economic conditions of

FIGURE 2: GROSS AND NET GOVERNMENT INVESTMENT
AS A PERCENT OF GDP, 1950s TO 2010–16

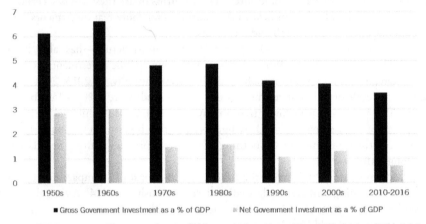

Source: U.S. Department of Commerce, Bureau of Economic Analysis: National Data. Table 1.1.5. and Table 5.2.5.

people in the bottom half of the income distribution have stagnated, or even declined. At the same time, the material conditions of the top 1% have skyrocketed. In 1975, the bottom 50% received 20.2% of pre-tax income, while the top 1% obtained 10.5%. By 2006, with inequality rising almost steadily, the share of the bottom 50% was only 13.5% and the top 1% was getting 20.1%. According to French economist Thomas Piketty and his colleagues, government redistributive actions have offset only a small fraction of the increase in pre-tax inequality.

The long-term trend of rising economic inequality has continued in recent years. Between 2008 and 2016, the household Gini ratio (a standard measure of inequality) rose from 0.466 to 0.481 (an annual rate of increase only slightly lower than the rate of increase since 1975). Slow economic growth has maintained a weak labor market, which tends to undermine workers' bargaining power and limit wage growth. Thus, the slow growth in the recovery has certainly been a major factor contributing to rising inequality.

The ethical and social problems of such a high degree of inequality are myriad. Here, however, we want to emphasize that just as slow growth of GDP has contributed to inequality, inequality tends to undermine the growth of GDP. With the publication of their 2014 study, the International Monetary Fund (IMF) joined the growing consensus among economists that inequality tends to have a negative impact on economic growth. Central points of the IMF study explaining this negative impact can be summarized as follows:

- Highly unequal societies tend to produce highly unequal health and education systems, which leads to lower rates of productivity increases. In addition, great inequality generates high levels of stress, which is detrimental to health outcomes across society.
- Great economic inequality generally yields political polarization, which, in turn, creates a degree of instability and uncertainty in political affairs (as witness the situation in Washington, D.C., in re-

cent decades). This uncertainty—having its practical manifestation in tax policy, regulations, and other aspects of economic policy—weakens investment.

- This political polarization, which has its roots in the breakdown of social solidarity associated with extreme economic inequality, makes it difficult for the political authorities at all levels to respond to economic shocks—most important, the emergence of recessionary indications.

Beyond these growth-inhibiting forces mentioned by the authors of the IMF study, additional factors include the weakness of consumer demand resulting from inequality, as higher income people tend to spend a lower share of their income than do people with low incomes, and the increasing political power of the rich, who tend to support the financial excesses (e.g., the deregulation of banking) that can lead into growth-disrupting crises.

Globalization and technological change, often cited as causes of rising inequality, have played their roles. In today's world, when workers demand higher wages, they can often be replaced by lower wage workers abroad or by machines (including robots). Yet, it is clear that more is involved. European countries have been exposed to the same global and technological forces. Yet, they have generally experienced a significantly lesser increase of inequality. Indeed, by way of example, as Thomas Piketty and his co-authors have pointed out, in the years of the twenty-first century, "The bottom 50 percent of income earners makes more in France than in the United States even though average income per adult is still 35 percent lower in France than in the United States . . ."

Important for our story here, it is apparent that political actions have played a substantial role in bringing about rising inequality. Globalization and technological change are relevant, but to an extent, these forces are shaped by political decisions—the particular structure of international trade and investment regulations in particular. Also, and essential, the government has shaped many markets in ways that exacerbate inequality. Examples include the strengthening of patents and copyrights, limiting financial regulations, and limiting the enactment and enforcement of regulations on business (now exacerbated by the Trump administration).

And, especially important from our perspective is the way the government has affected the labor market. At several points in recent decades, the federal and state governments have taken actions that have weakened unions and contributed to their declining membership. Under Republican administrations, appointees to the National Labor Relations Board (NLRB) have undermined unionization. As a result, for example, with weak enforcement of labor law by the NLRB, the likelihood that workers attempting to organize unions in their workplaces would be illegally fired rose substantially in the period since 1980.

At the state level, direct actions to weaken unions and prevent wage increases have been widespread. Several southern states have had "right to work" laws in place for decades, and recently, other states have enacted such laws. In 2011, the attacks on unions in Wisconsin highlighted this trend. In many cases, where authorities in cities and towns have enacted pro-labor regulations, state governments have overridden ("pre-empted") those local regulations. On issues ranging from raising minimum wages to mandating paid leave to establishing fair scheduling, since 1997, twenty-six state governments have overridden local actions a total of 67 times, with 55 of these pre-emptions coming since 2011.

Political actions, by increasing inequality, have in this way weakened the foundations of economic growth. Furthermore, an important aspect of these inequality-exacerbating actions has been the weakening of unions. The relationship between union strength and the distribution of income is illustrated in Figure 3. Over the last century, when union membership as a percentage of the labor force is high, income inequality is relatively low. And low union membership is associated with high inequality.

This connection between union membership and income inequality is partially direct, as unions are able to gain a larger share of income for their members and also as unions tend to promote government policies that support low-wage workers— for example, a higher minimum wage. Rising inequality, however, also has other causes—slow growth in itself, as we have pointed out, tends to weaken workers' bargaining power regardless of unionization and thus exacerbates inequality. Also, the decline in union membership since the 1960s has had some other causes beyond political decisions (e.g., the decline of manufacturing, which has been in part due to globalization and technological change). Nonetheless, the connection from political actions to weakening unions to greater inequality is clear.

The Economy and Political Choices

Capitalist economies, and the U.S. economy in particular, have a strong capacity for economic growth. What has been unusual about the expansion that has taken place

FIGURE 3: UNION MEMBERSHIP AS SHARE OF LABOR FORCE AND SHARE OF INCOME GOING TO THE TOP 10%, 1917–2014

Source: Will Kimball and Lawrence Mishel, "Unions' Decline and the Rise of the Top 10 Percent's Share of Income," Economic Policy Institute, February 3, 2015 (epi.org).

since the Great Recession of 2008 and 2009 is not that growth has taken place, but that it has been so slow. Indeed, as we have pointed out, this expansion has been slower than any other in the post–World War II era. On the other hand, although slow, the expansion has been relatively long, and at this writing, substantial signs of an end to the expansion have not yet appeared.

For us, the lesson that comes out of a review of economic experience since the severe 2008-2009 recession is that political choices play a major role in determining the course of the economy. These choices operate through policies explicitly directed at economic growth and through policies that affect growth by their impact on economic inequality. Forces beyond direct political control—the long-run integration of the world economy and aspects of technological change—are also relevant, but they do not remove the role of political choices. Which is to say: there are alternatives.

Update: June 2018

Little has changed since this article was originally written at the end of 2017. As of June 2018, the economic expansion, measured in terms of continually rising real GDP, had continued for 108 months. It is already the second-longest expansion of the U.S. economy since World War II, surpassed only by the 120-month expansion of the 1990s. Furthermore, the unemployment rate dropped to 3.9% in April of this year.

Yet, contrary to the narrative popular in the media, the U.S. economy is not doing so well. The expansion, while long, has been slow. As was the case at the end of 2017, it remains the slowest expansion since World War II. Moreover, while the unemployment rate has fallen, the percentage of the population participating in the labor force has been stable and well below the participation rate in the period preceding the Great Recession, indicating the labor market is not as "tight" as the low unemployment rate would suggest. Indeed, real wages rose just 0.5% per year from the official end of the Great Recession in June 2009 to June 2017, and have been virtually stagnant in the last year.

Most important, there is no reason to believe that economic inequality has abated in recent months. Low unemployment may have led to a small increase in the position of those near the bottom; even with stagnant wages, a person earns more being employed than unemployed. Yet the tax legislation enacted at the end of 2017 will make inequality even worse.

Moreover, as we emphasized in the article, political decisions have played an important role affecting both economic growth and economic inequality. Although a recession does not appear likely to emerge in the immediate future, the weight of political decisions in recent months have little likelihood of improving the economic record on either growth or economic inequality, and if those political decisions ignite a trade war, they could bring the economic expansion to an end. ❑

Sources: Sources: Ben Casselman, "After 7 Years of Job Growth, Room for More, or Danger Ahead?" *The New York Times*, December 9, 2017 (nytimes.com); "Can the Trump Boom Last? America's Long Running Economic Expansion," *The Economist*, December 14, 2017 (economist. com); "National Data, Table 1.1.6," U.S. Bureau of Economic Analysis (bea.gov); "US Business

Cycle Expansions and Contractions," National Bureau of Economic Research (nber.org); Labor Force Statistics from the Current Population Survey, Bureau of Labor Statistics (data.bls. gov); "Historical Income Tables: Households, Table H-6," U.S. Census Bureau (census.gov); "Bloomberg Commodity Index," *Financial Times* (markets.ft.com/data); "GDP Growth," World Bank Open Data (data.worldbank.org); *BP Statistical Review of World Energy 2017* (bp.com); "Effective Federal Funds Rate," Federal Reserve Bank of St. Louis (fred.stlouisfed.org); Arthur MacEwan and John Miller, *Economic Collapse, Economic Change: Getting to the Roots of the Crisis*, Chapter 9, "Palliative Care" (Routledge, 2011); "National Data, Table 1.1.5," "National Data, Table 3.1," "National Data, Table 3.9.3," "National Data, Table 5.2.5," and "National Data, Table 5.2.6," Bureau of Economic Analysis (bea.gov); Andrew Chang et al., "U.S. Corporate Cash Reaches $1.9 Trillion But Rising Debt and Tax Reform Pose Risk S&P Global Ratings," S&P Global, May 25, 2017 (spglobal.com); "Fortune 500 Companies Hold a Record $2.6 Trillion Offshore," Institute on Taxation and Economic Policy, March 2017 (itep.org); Robert E. Scott, "Worst Recovery in Postwar Era Largely Explained by Cuts in Government Spending," Economic Policy Institute, August 2, 2016 (epi.org); "10 Year Budget Projections," Congressional Budget Office, June 2017 (cbo.gov); *2017 Economic Report of the President*, Council of Economic Advisers (govinfo.gov); Robin Harding, Richard McGregor, and Gabriel Muller, "US public investment falls to lowest level since war," *Financial Times*, November 2, 2013 (ft.com); Lawrence Summers, "The Age of Secular Stagnation: What It Is and What to Do About It," *Foreign Affairs*, March/April 2016 (foreignaffairs.com); Thomas Piketty, Emmanuel Saez, and Gabriel Zucman, "Distributional National Accounts: Methods and Estimates for the United States, Data Appendix," December 15, 2016 (piketty.pse.ens.fr); Thomas Piketty, Emmanuel Saez, and Gabriel Zucman, "Economic Growth in the United States: A Tale of Two Countries," Washington Center for Equitable Growth, December 6, 2016 (equitablegrowth.org); "Table H-4," *Historical Income Tables: Households*, U.S. Bureau of the Census (census.gov); Jonathan D. Ostry, Andrew Berg, and Charalambos G. Tsangarides, "Redistribution, Inequality, and Growth," IMF Staff Discussion Note, February 2014 (imf.org); Richard Wilkinson and Kate Pickett, *The Spirit Level: Why Greater Equality Makes Societies Stronger* (Bloomsbury Press, 2009); Joseph Stiglitz, *The Price of Inequality: How Today's Divided Society Endangers Our Future* (W.W. Norton, 2012); John Schmitt and Ben Zipperer, "Dropping the Ax: Illegal Firings During Union Election Campaigns, 1951-2007," Center for Economic and Policy Research, March 2009 (cepr.net); "Worker Rights Preemption in the US: A Map of the Campaign to Suppress Worker Rights in the States," Economic Policy Institute, November 2017 (epi.org).

Article 3.2

A FUTURE FOR GROWTH—IF WE CHOOSE IT?

BY GERALD FRIEDMAN
July/August 2017

Defenders of capitalism argue that the hierarchy and inequality of the system are worth it because, as Austrian economist Ludwig von Mises put it, capitalism "delivers the goods"—high and rising living standards. The long-term slowdown of wage growth in advanced capitalist economies, then, poses a challenge the system's defenders. If capitalism is not only hierarchical and unequal, but increasingly does not "deliver the goods" to most, might we be better off replacing it with a different form of economic organization?

To the extent that wage stagnation is due to the changing balance of power between labor and capital, this reflects the unfairness of capitalism and its unequal distribution of wealth and power. From this perspective, the "Golden Age" of the post–World War II decades, with rising wages and steady improvements in working-class living standards, reflected that period's strong unions and progressive politics. Meanwhile, the stagnant wages and living standards since the 1970s are the result of union weakness and the growing dominance of conservative politics since the collapse of the New Deal coalition in the 1970s. On the other hand, to the extent wages have stagnated for reasons unrelated to the capitalist system, wage stagnation may be regrettable—but does not reflect on the political question of whether we might be better off replacing capitalism with a different economic system.

Economist and Northwestern University professor Robert Gordon has been a leading advocate of the view that wage stagnation is largely an unfortunate result of circumstances beyond anyone's control or political remedy. In his recent masterpiece, *The Rise and Fall of American Growth*, Gordon pulls together his analysis of earlier economic growth, driven by important innovations such as water supply networks, electricity, and the internal combustion engine, which he argues have had a vastly greater impact on economic growth than anything developed over the past 50 years. Because of the exhaustion of technological progress, growth in productivity (output per hour of work) and in overall output have slowed, and brought down the rate of growth in wages and living standards. It is all unfortunate, in Gordon's view, but beyond the power of either the state or organized labor to change.

Gordon is wrong on both counts: the slowdown in productivity is not "exogenous" it is not due to causes outside the capitalist economy, nor does it explain the slowdown in wage growth. Instead, both the productivity slowdown and wage stagnation are due to the go-slow economic policies followed by the United States and its major trading partners since the 1970s, policies intended to fight inflation even at the cost of higher unemployment rates and slower economic growth, policies chosen because economic elites gain by hoarding a larger share of even a slower-growing pie.

How much has economic growth slowed? Gordon's argument rests on familiar grounds: the relatively rapid growth in the American economy (and other affluent capitalist economies) from the end of World War II through the early 1970s has not been matched in the nearly half-century since. Between 1947 and 1972, per capita income in the United States increased at a rate of 2.4% per year. This slowed to 2.0% per year for 1972–96, and then to only 1.3% per year since. The slowdown after 1972 means a reduction in per capita income of over 25% by 2017: Instead of nearly $70,000 that it would have been in 2017 at the 1947–1972 growth rate, it is only about $52,000.

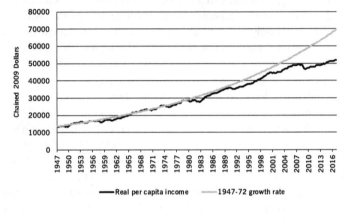

PER CAPITA INCOME, 1947–2017

What accounts for the slowdown in growth? Gordon attributes the slowdown to various "headwinds," with a focus on a fall in technological progress after the 1960s. In the 1972–96 period, rising employment, especially of women, compensated somewhat for falling productivity. More total hours of work counteracted low growth in output per hour worked, and buoyed up the growth in total output. In the tech boom of the 1990s, computerization boosted productivity growth enough to get per capita income rising at the old rate, though only briefly. Since 2004, demographic conditions, Gordon argues, have led Americans to drop out of the labor force, and productivity has fallen off due to declining technological innovation.

Gordon's main mistake is that he does not take account of changing macroeconomic conditions or total ("aggregate") demand. While focusing on the growth in the supply of inputs, workers, machines, and innovative ideas, Gordon ignores the other side of markets, the demand for output. Rather than a slowdown in supply, slow growth since the 1970s reflects a shortfall in aggregate demand because governments and monetary authorities have slowed economic growth in order to restrain inflation. Slow growth in aggregate demand has meant that workers face higher unemployment and shorter hours, and companies reduce investment in physical plant and in research and development— leading to slower growth in productivity. The long-term slowdown in growth coincides with a rise in unemployment, mostly due to deficiency of demand, except in the 1996–2004 period. During those years, booming demand drove job creation, technological progress, and overall growth back up to their earlier levels.

GROWTH RATES SINCE 1972

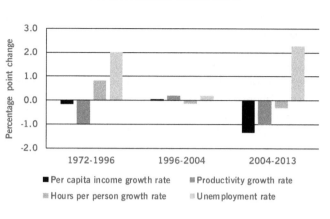

Why has productivity fallen? Loss of creativity or declining demand? Gordon's claim that technological progress has slowed for "exogenous" reasons—factors outside the economic system, such as an exhaustion of ideas—is crucial to the argument that political decisions and the power of capital are not responsible for the slowdown in income and wage growth. The relationship between productivity growth and overall economic growth runs in both directions. Faster productivity growth may increase GDP growth, especially when falling costs may increase a country's exports. But faster overall economic growth, fueled by rising demand, also generates faster productivity growth by incentivizing productivity-enhancing investment and innovation. The relationship between productivity and GDP growth is strong enough to explain 60% of the decline in productivity between the 1947–72 period and 1973–96, and all of the decline in productivity since.

PRODUCTIVITY GROWTH AND GDP GROWTH, 1947–2017

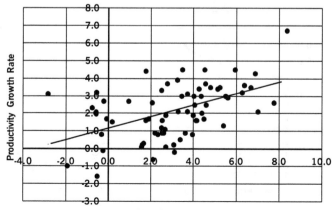

Since the 1970s, however, government macroeconomic policy has emphasized "inflation targeting"—achieving very low inflation rates—at the expense of growth in incomes and employment. Slower growth in demand, meanwhile, contributes to slower productivity growth by discouraging new investment—in physical plant, research and development, and worker training. In addition, when demand is weak, labor markets are "slack," and workers have little bargaining power. Lower wage pressure, in turn, means lower investment in labor-saving technologies. Capitalists have favored such policies for a simple reason—they have undermined workers' bargaining power and therefore tilted the distribution of income in the capitalists' favor.

Why don't Americans work as much as they used to? In addition to the decline in productivity, Gordon attributes the decline in output to falling employment, caused by the aging of the U.S. population. But an aging population is only part of the explanation. Into the 1990s, compared with other capitalist economies, the United States had high and rising employment rates with a rapidly increasing share of women in the paid labor force. This began to change after 1990, and changed more dramatically after 2000. Women's employment peaked in 2000 and has fallen since then, and men's employment and labor force participation have fallen sharply since around 1970. The United States' paid labor force has gotten dramatically smaller compared to its potential because of falling demand for goods and services, and therefore falling demand for workers. As a result, a significant share of the American population has given up looking for work. The problem originates from a drop in demand, not a fall in supply. An aggressive fiscal policy, as was proposed by Senator Sanders in his campaign for President in 2016, could help to bring more people into the workforce and into employment; and policies, like those in some Scandinavian countries, to help parents with childcare costs could, especially, help to promote women's employment.

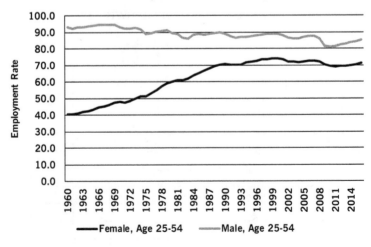

EMPLOYMENT RATES, FEMALE AND MALE, AGED 25–54

What about the distribution of income? Rising productivity is crucial for increasing national income but it does not necessarily determine the path of real wages. While for most of American history down to the mid-1960s, productivity and real wages grew together, since then they have diverged. From the mid-1960s through the mid 1970s, real wages grew by 1.5% a year but productivity grew nearly 1% a year faster.

For the next 20 years, however, real wages fell by around 0.5% a year even though productivity grew by over 1.7% a year; the slowdown in productivity growth of less than 1% a year was less than half the slowdown in wage growth of 2% a year. While wages have been rising since the mid-1990s, they have continued to grow at a much slower rate than productivity. Instead of leading to higher wages, rising productivity has fed growing corporate profits with a declining share of income going to labor. ❏

HOURLY EARNINGS VS. PRODUCTIVITY, 1964–2016

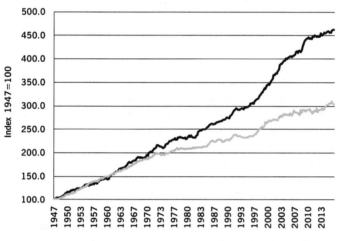

Sources: Llewellyn Rockwell, ed., *The Free Market Reader* (Ludwig von Mises Institute, n.d.); Jacob S. Hacker and Paul Pierson, *Winner-Take-All Politics* (Simon & Schuster, 2010); Robert B Reich, *Beyond Outrage* (Vintage Books, 2012); Richard D Wolff, *Capitalism Hits the Fan* (Olive Branch Press, 2010); David M. Kotz, *The Rise and Fall of Neoliberal Capitalism* (Harvard University Press, 2015); Robert Solow, "We'd Better Watch Out," *New York Times Book Review,* July 12, 1987; Robert J. Gordon, "Does the 'New Economy' Measure Up to the Great Inventions of the Past?," *Journal of Economic Perspectives* (December 2000); Robert J. Gordon, "Is U.S. Economic Growth Over?" Working Paper, National Bureau of Economic Research, August 2012 (nber.org); Robert J. Gordon, *The Rise and Fall of American Growth* (Princeton University Press, 2016); Nicholas Kaldor, *Causes of the Slow Rate of Economic Growth of the United Kingdom* (Cambridge University Press, 1966); R. Dixon and A. P. Thirlwall, "A Model of Regional Growth-Rate Differences on Kaldorian Lines," *Oxford Economic Papers* (1975); P. J. Verdoorn, "Verdoorn's Law in Retrospect: A Comment," *The Economic Journal* (1980); St. Louis Federal Reserve, Real gross domestic product per capita (fred.stlouisfed.org); Robert J. Gordon, "The Demise of U.S. Economic Growth: Restatement, Rebuttal, and Reflection," Working Paper, National Bureau of Economic Research, February 2014 (nber.org); Bureau of Labor Statistics, Nonfarm Business, Labor productivity (output per hour) (bls.gov); St. Louis Federal Reserve, Employment Rate: Aged 25-54: Males, Females for the United States (fred.stlouisfed.org).

Article 3.3

IS ECONOMIC GROWTH ENVIRONMENTALLY SUSTAINABLE?

BY ARTHUR MacEWAN
January/February 2018

> Dear Dr. Dollar:
> *I keep hearing progressive economists talking about environmental sustainabil-*
> *ity, in particular in the context of the looming catastrophe of global climate*
> *change. But when it comes to macroeconomics, they seem to switch to talking*
> *"growth, growth, growth." Aren't the two contradictory?*
> —Anonymous, Washington, D.C.

"The first law of ecology is that everything is related to everything else."
    —Barry Commoner

As is the case with many questions, the answer is "yes and no."
    Economic growth of the kind we have had for the last two hundred years—or longer—is in conflict with environmental sustainability. More growth has meant the use of more carbon-based fuels, so this growth has spewed more and more carbon dioxide into the atmosphere—and thus global warming. (Global warming is not the only environmental issue, but it is the danger that threatens the existence of human society as we know it. So let's focus on it here.)

Yet, the carbon intensity of economic growth is not something beyond social control. There are ways to grow—meeting human needs and desires—that greatly reduce, if not eliminate, the global warming impact. Most macroeconomic analyses, however, focus simply on growth without consideration of how this growth would affect the environment. There are two reasons for this error, one bad and one good.

The bad reason is that most economist take the basic arrangements of society for granted. They take the nature of technology as "given," and do not question either the technology itself or the social and political forces that maintain the existing path of technology.

The good reason is that we have more than one problem, and growth can provide positive social outcomes—reducing unemployment, general economic insecurity, and absolute poverty. None of this does any good if we are all soon washed away by rising tides, but it is a good reason that economic growth cannot be jettisoned out of hand.

Some Context

The environmental impact of human activity can be understood in terms of three factors:

- how many of us there are on the planet (population),

- the amount of output of goods and services produced per person (affluence), and
- the amount of environmental impact per unit of output (technology)

Over time, in terms of environmental impact, all three components of this relationship have gotten worse: population has grown and grown, the world as a whole has become more affluent, and technology has become more carbon intensive (more negative impact per unit of output). To halt global warming, it is necessary to pay attention to each of these factors.

What Can Change?

Population growth, at least in the long-run, can be reduced. Making contraception safe and widely available can help. Also, increased educational and employment opportunities for women tend to reduce fertility. But many people, especially in the agricultural sectors of low-income economies, choose to have several children. Children are their security, providing more hands to do a family's work and providing support for aging parents. Without greater affluence—hard to attain without economic growth—population will continue to grow. (That the most rapid population growth in the world is centered in African countries, which are among the least prosperous, illustrates the point.)

Curtailing economic growth as a means to contain environmental destruction has at least two main problems. First, unless it involves a massive, global redistribution of income and wealth, it condemns those at the bottom (countries and people) to their current economic level—both morally reprehensible and probably politically impossible. It is also probably politically impossible to overcome the obstacles to a massive redistribution. There are about 7.5 billion people in the world and total production is about $125 trillion, which means that average income is about $16,667. With no growth and redistribution getting everyone to this level, it would be necessary to reduce average income in the United States by over 70%, and in the Euro area and Japan by over 60%.

The second barrier to curtailing growth is that capitalism, which is pretty much the operating system of the whole world these days, is like a bicycle: If it stops, it (and the rider) falls over. The system depends on profits, and profits depend on either growth or redistributing income upward, and the latter has its limits. Getting rid of capitalism, running the world economy a different way, could have salutary results—though other social systems can do, and have done, substantial damage to the environment. Certainly, the political problems of getting rid of capitalism and insuring that its replacement would be environmentally friendly is a politically daunting tasks.

The Technology Option

Dealing with global warming needs to involve inhibiting population growth and curtailing economic growth—which means at least sharply constraining capitalism. But that's not enough. There need to be dramatic changes in the technology. At the present

time, the most promising energy production technologies are wind power and pho-
tovoltaics. Also, energy conservation has great potential for reducing the emissions of
greenhouse gases.

The effectiveness of the technology option has been demonstrated in other countries. As Frank Ackerman pointed out in the May/June 2017 issue of *Dollars & Sense*,
renewable electricity generation expanded from 5% of total German power consumption in 1999 to over 30% in 2015. Over the same period, Ackerman concludes, "there
has been no increase in [carbon] emissions from the electric sector ... [and] the reliabil-
ity of the German electric system has continued to improve."

The problem, then, is not so much technical (i.e., developing ways to reduce
emissions). The problem is political. Halting subsidies to the fossil fuel industries and providing support for environmentally friendly technological change
would be good beginnings. Also, a great deal could be accomplished through en-
couragement of energy conservation programs. Further steps will require major
limitations on firms' operations, limitations that prevent them from ignoring the
health, safety, and, ultimately, the survival of the populations. A difficult task, of
course, but we really have no choice. ❑

Article 3.4

THE "EMERGING ECONOMIES" TODAY

AN INTERVIEW WITH JAYATI GHOSH
May/June 2016

The terms "emerging markets" and "emerging economies" have come into fashion, especially to refer to countries supposedly poised to make the leap from "developing" to "developed" economies. There's no definitive list, but Brazil, India, Indonesia, Mexico, Russia, South Africa, Turkey, and China are among the large countries that often headline articles on "emerging economies." Economic growth rates—as well as the drop-off in growth during the global Great Recession and the recovery since—vary widely between countries typically placed in this group.

China is by far the most prominent of the emerging economies—the most populous country in the world, with an extraordinary period of industrial growth since the 1980s, and with an enormous impact (not only as an exporter of manufactured goods but also as an importer of raw-material and intermediate inputs to manufacturing) on the world economy. The "secular stagnation" of the high-income capitalist economies and resulting growth slowdown in China, therefore, has much wider implications for the developing world. In this interview, economist Jayati Ghosh addresses the current challenges for China and other countries—and possible paths toward inclusive and sustainable development. – Eds.

Dollars & Sense: You've written about the "retreat" of emerging-market economies, which until recently had been held up as examples of robust growth, in contrast to the stagnant economies of the so-called capitalist "core." What's driving the slowdown of economic growth in the emerging economies today?

Jayati Ghosh: The emerging economies are really those that have integrated much more into the global financial system, not just the global trade system. And I think what happened during the period of the economic boom is that many people forgot that their growth was still ultimately driven by what was happening in the North. That is, the engine of demand was still the northern economies. So whether you're talking about China in particular or the range of emerging economies that was seen as more prominent in the first half of the 2000s, all of them depended on exports to the North and particularly to the United States.

It was the U.S. boom that drew in more and more of the exports from developing countries. When it came to an end—as it inevitably had to—these economies had to look for other sources of demand. There are two ways of doing this. One is to try and do a domestic demand-driven expansion based on higher domestic incomes because of wage and employment growth. And the other is the model which unfortunately seems to be the more popular one, which is to have a debt-driven kind of growth, based on both consumption and accumulation that is essentially led by taking on more and more debt. This is, of course, also what the U.S. did in the 2000s, which unraveled in 2007 and 2008. But it's also what a number of European economies did, and they're paying the price now.

Remarkably, developing countries that don't need to take this path, and can see all the problems associated with it, also took this path in the wake of the global financial crisis. In China there was a doubling of the debt-to-GDP ratio between 2007 and 2014. This reflected increases in debt to every single sector, but it was dominantly for investment. In a range of other important developing countries, from Mexico to Indonesia, Malaysia, South Korea, etc., there was a dramatic expansion of household debt, particularly real estate and housing debt. We all know that these real-estate and housing bubbles that are led by taking on more debt, these end in tears. And that's really what has been happening.

In these "emerging" economies, financial integration allowed them to break the link between productive investment and growth. It fueled a debt-driven pattern of expansion, which inevitably has to end. It's ending now. The problem is that it's ending at a time when demand from the North is slowing dramatically. So there is a double whammy for these emerging economies. The slowdown in northern markets means that China—which had become the major driver of expansion—can no longer continue to export at the same rate. That means its imports have also come down. In the past year, China's exports fell by 5%, but its imports fell by 20%. That has affected all the other developing countries. And that's in combination with this end of the debt-driven expansion model.

D&S: A number of economists have argued for quite some time that China's export-oriented growth model would inevitably reach its limits. Are we seeing it finally reach an impasse now, and if so, is there a prospect for China to make a transition from a low-wage export-oriented model to a domestic demand-driven model that would necessarily require higher wages?

JG: I think it's indisputable that the export-driven model is over for the time being, for sure, certainly for the next five years, probably the next decade. That's not a bad thing, because one of the problems with that export-driven model is that it persists in seeing wages as costs rather than as a source of internal demand that you can use to your benefit. It encourages massive degradation of nature and taking on environmental costs that are now recognized to be completely unsustainable and socially undesirable. And, overall, we know that these can't last—these export-driven models can't last.

So, yes, it has ended. It does mean that the Chinese government and authorities have to look for an alternative. Many of us have been arguing that the alternative necessarily requires much more emphasis on increasing consumption, not through debt, but by increasing real incomes. And that means encouraging more employment of a desirable type—"decent work" as it's been called—and increasing wages. Now, this doesn't mean that the rates of growth will continue as high as they have been, but that doesn't matter.

In fact, the obsession with GDP growth is becoming a real negative now in the search for alternatives. The Chinese authorities, like all the financial analysts across the world who are constantly looking at China, are obsessed with GDP: Is it going to be 6.5% annual growth? Is it going to be 6.1%? Is it going to fall below 6%? As if that's all that matters. What they should really be looking at is the incomes of, let us say, the bottom 50 or 60%. Are these growing? If these are growing at about 4 or 5%, that's fantastic. That's wonderful. And that's really what the economy needs in a sustainable way. If these are growing in combination with patterns of production and consumption that are more sustainable, that are environmentally friendly, that are less carbon-emitting, then that is of course even more desirable.

But that means the focus has to shift away from GDP growth, and away from just pushing up GDP by any means whatsoever—to one which looks at how to improve the real incomes and the quality of life of the majority of the citizens. Unfortunately, the Chinese government doesn't seem to be choosing that path just yet. There have been some moves—in terms of increasing health spending, in terms of some attempts to increase wages and social protection for some workers—but overall the focus is still once again on more accumulation, on more investment, usually driven by more debt.

D&S: When you say the export-oriented model is "over," does that mean you think sticking to this approach will no longer deliver what policymakers and elites are aiming for, in terms of growth and accumulation? (And perhaps that this will lead to an elite-driven restructuring in the near term?) Or is it that this approach just cannot plausibly deliver in terms of inclusive development—the improvement in the quality of life for the majority?

JG: Both, really. The conditions of the global economy at present are such that an economy as large as that of China (and many other smaller economies as well) cannot expect much stimulus from external demand Significant increases in exports would only be possible by increasing markets share; that is, eating into some other country's exports. So the past pattern of accumulation based on external demand is unlikely to work in the near future.

But in addition, this approach has not delivered in terms of inclusive growth over the past decade except to some extent in China, which has been able to use it to generate a "Lewisian" process (theorized by economist Arthur Lewis in the 1950s) of shifting labor out of lower productivity activities. Even in China it was successful because wages increased much less than productivity and so export prices could fall or remain low. In many other countries, export-led expansion has actually been associated stagnant or lower wages and greater fragility of incomes, along with very substantial environmental costs that are typically not factored in.

D&S: Is it possible that that kind of transition is not going to happen in China until we see the development of a robust labor movement that's capable of winning a higher share of the national income in the form of wages, and pushing up mass consumption in that way?

JG: There is probably much greater public concern about all this in China than is often depicted in the media, certainly in the Chinese media, but even abroad. We know that there are thousands, literally, tens of thousands of protests in China—often about land grabs and so on in the peasantry, but also many, many workers' protests, and many other protests by citizens about environmental conditions. They have mostly been suppressed, but I don't think you can keep on suppressing these.

I do believe the Chinese elite has recognized that there are a couple of things that are becoming very important for them to maintain their political legitimacy. One is, of course, inequality and, associated with that, corruption. That is why the anti-corruption drive of President Xi Jinping retains a lot of popularity. Then there is the fact of the environmental unsustainability. Both India and China have created monstrosities in urban areas, in terms of the pollution, congestion, degradation, which are really making many of our cities and towns unlivable. There is widespread protest about that, and about the pollution of water sources, of the atmosphere, of land quality. And there is real concern that ordinary Chinese citizens are not continuously experiencing the better life that they have grown accustomed to expect.

So I think, even without a very large-scale social mobilization, there is growing awareness in China—among officialdom, as well—that they can't carry on as before. It is likely that there's a tussle at the very higher echelons of the leadership and in the Communist Party, between those who are arguing for the slower but more sustainable and more wage-led path, and those who just want to keep propping up growth by more financial liberalization, by encouraging investors to jump in and invest even in projects that are unlikely to continue, and somehow keep that GDP growth going. It's a political tussle but of course that will determine the direction of the economy as well.

D&S: In the midst of this period of stagnation of the very high-income capitalist economies, and a resulting slowdown of growth in the so-called emerging economies, we also have an effect on countries that had primarily remained raw-material (or "primary-product") exporters. Is that boom in commodities exports now also over for the foreseeable future, and do you see those countries as now reinventing their economic development models?

JG: I think that the period of the boom was really a bit of an aberration. Since the early 20th century, these periods of relatively high commodity prices have always been outliers, and they don't last very long. They last for about five, six, maybe eight years at most, and then they you come back to this more depressed situation relative to other prices. I have a feeling this is now going to continue, and that boom is, for the time being, over. It definitely means that the manna from heaven that many countries experienced has reduced, and therefore you have to think of other ways of diversifying your economies.

Many countries actually tried to do this but, you know, when you're getting so much income from the primary product exports it's very hard to diversify. It's actually easier to diversify when primary product prices are lower. So, once again, I think it's important for these countries to stop thinking of this as a huge loss, and start thinking of it as an opportunity—as an opportunity to use cheap primary commodities as a means of industrializing for domestic and regional markets. So it means a different strategy. The export-led obsession has to end. Without that, we're not going to get viable and sustainable strategies.

I'd like to make one other point, though, about the slowdown in China and the impact on developing countries, which is that it's also going to affect manufacturing exporters. China had become the center of a global production chain that was heavily exporting to the North but was drawing in more and more raw material and intermediate products from other developing countries. So almost every country had China become their main trade partner in both imports and exports. Many of these manufacturing economies are now going to face, once again, a double whammy. They will face a reduction, from China, in terms of lower Chinese imports of raw materials and intermediate goods for final export, and they're going to face greater competition from China in terms of their own export markets and their own domestic markets. Because China is now devaluing its currency, even though thus far it has been minor. It is looking to cheapen its exports even further, and this will definitely impact on both export markets and internal markets in developing countries.

So I think both primary exporters and manufacturing exporters are in for a bit of a bad time. They need to think of creative ways of dealing with the situation. It is not helped by believing that integration into global value chains is the only option, because these global value chains basically reduce the incomes of the actual producers. If you look at it, the emergence of global value chains and the associated trade treaties—not just the World Trade Organization (WTO) but the proliferation of regional trading agreements and things like the Trans-Pacific Partnership (TPP)—increase competition and reduce the value of the actual production stage of all commodities and goods. And they simultaneously increase the pre-production and post-production value. That is, all of the aspects that are driven by intellectual property monopolies—their values increase. So whether it is design elements or it is the marketing and branding and all of that—the intellectual property rights over which are retained by companies in the North—all of those are getting more and more value. And the actual production is getting less value because of the greater competitive pressure unleashed by these various trade agreements.

Developing countries that are seeking to get out of this really have to think of alternative arrangements—possibly regional arrangements, more reliance on domestic demand and South-South trade, which is more possible today than it has ever been—and moving away from a system that allows global and northern-led multinationals to capture all the rents and most of the profits of production everywhere.

D&S: So, in the course of this discussion, I think two major questions emerge about the way forward in so-called developing economies. One is how to square economic development—in terms of raising the quality of life for the majority—with environmental sustainability. The other is how to ensure the economic development of some countries isn't at odds with development in others. Are there ways of mutually fostering development—and in particular sustainable development—across the developing economies?

JG: Yes, I think we need to really move away from the traditional way of looking at growth and development, which is ultimately still based on GDP. As long as we keep doing that, we're going to be caught in this trap. We have to be focusing much more on quality of life and ensuring what we would call the basic needs or minimum requirements for a civilized life among all the citizenry. If we do that, then we're less in competition with one another and we're less obsessed with having to be the cheapest show in town. We then see wages and employment growth as a means of expansion of economic activity. We will see social policies as delivering not just better welfare for the people but also more employment, and therefore a better quality of life.

If we look for regional trading arrangements that recognize this, if we look to increase the value of domestic economic activity by encouraging the things that matter for ordinary people (especially, let's say, the bottom half of the population), if we focus on new technologies that are adapted to specific local requirements—in terms of being more green, more environmentally sustainable, as well as recognizing the specific availability of labor in these economies—I think we can do a lot more. It may be slower in terms of GDP growth, but really that doesn't mean anything. So we have to move away from GDP growth as the basic indicator of what is desirable. I think that's the ultimate and most essential issue. ❏

Chapter 4

UNEMPLOYMENT
AND INFLATION

INTRODUCTION

In an introductory macroeconomics course, students are likely to hear that two key macroeconomic outcomes are the rates of unemployment and inflation, and that there is a tradeoff between the two. In recent years, we have seen the seesaw of unemployment and inflation tilt very heavily in one direction. Unemployment in the United States and other countries reached rates not seen since the Great Depression, while many countries experienced not only very low inflation but even deflation for the first time in living memory. Unemployment has gradually come down over years of slow economic "recovery," but job growth remains sluggish and inflation very low.

To start, it is necessary to understand the tradeoff between inflation and unemployment described by the "Phillips curve." Economist Ramaa Vasudevan takes a careful look at the relationship between inflation and unemployment and how that tradeoff changed during two historical periods: the stagflation of the 1970s and the productivity boom of the 1990s. She attributes the sustained low inflation during the 1990s, despite low unemployment, to the relatively weak bargaining position of workers (Article 4.1).

Economist Robert Pollin delves into why the textbook tradeoff between inflation and unemployment affects the returns of stockholders and other investors. The answer, Pollin points out, is "all about class conflict" (Article 4.2). Higher unemployment rates and fewer jobs eat away at the bargaining power of workers, keeping wage growth and inflation in check and corporate profit margins wide. As Pollin sees it, the unemployment rate consistent with price stability—the so-called "natural rate"—declined dramatically in the 1990s because workers' economic power eroded during the decade.

Dean Baker argues the massive jump in the federal budget deficit caused by the 2018 budget agreement will create an economic experiment testing how low the unemployment rate can go (Article 4.3). Economists have long argued that there is a floor (5.5% according to the Congressional Budget Office) for how low the unemployment rate can fall without a jump in inflation. With the 2018 budget deficit, Baker expects the unemployment rate to fall well below 4.0%. That should answer the question of just how low the unemployment rate can go without a spike in inflation.

In the following article, Arthur MacEwan argues that boosting the minimum wage to $15 an hour over time would do much to improve the economic position of low-wage workers and their families (Article 4.4). MacEwan also takes on the argument that increasing the minimum wage would cost workers their jobs. For MacEwan, the argument doesn't hold up because it ignores the positive effect that higher wages have on worker productivity and fails to take into account the ability of employers to pass on all or some of their increased labor costs to customers in the form of higher prices.

John Miller turns our attention to the measurement of unemployment, showing how the official (or "headline") unemployment rate understates the extent of unemployment. Correcting the headline rate for underemployed workers and discouraged job-seekers, unemployment has remained unusually high even years after the beginning of the current "recovery" (Article 4.5).

Finally, in "Keynes, Wage and Price 'Stickiness,' and Deflation" (Article 4.6), Alejandro Reuss turns to the writings of John Maynard Keynes and arguments about whether declining wages are the cure for unemployment. He outlines Keynes' classic arguments—against conservative economists who believed that wage declines were part of the economy's "self-correction" during a depression—that depression conditions worsen when wages drop.

Discussion Questions

1. (Article 4.1) Why is there a "tradeoff" between unemployment and inflation?

2. (Article 4.2) The economists who first posited the idea of a "natural rate or unemployment" certainly did not think they were devising a class-conflict theory. Yet Pollin says the "natural rate" is "all about class conflict." Why?

3. (Article 4.3) Why are economists convinced that there is a floor to how low the unemployment rate can go without setting off economic problems? For Baker, what is an honest answer to the question of how low the unemployment rate can go?

4. (Article 4.4) According to MacEwan, how does the effect of increasing the price of labor differ from the effect of increasing the price of cars or tomatoes?

5. (Article 4.5) Is the overall unemployment rate a deceptive measure of economic hardship? What would be a better measure?

6. (Article 4.6) Deflation means a decrease in the overall price level. Lower prices sound good to most people. So what's not to like about deflation?

Article 4.1

THE RELATIONSHIP OF UNEMPLOYMENT AND INFLATION

BY RAMAA VASUDEVAN
September/October 2006

> Dear Dr. Dollar:
> *Back in first-year economics we learned that there is a tradeoff between un-*
> *employment and inflation, so you can't really have both low inflation and low*
> *unemployment at the same time. Do economists still consider that to be true?*
> —Edith Bross, Cambridge, Mass.

The tradeoff between inflation and unemployment was first reported by A. W. Phillips in 1958—and so has been christened the Phillips curve. The simple intuition behind this tradeoff is that as unemployment falls, workers are empowered to push for higher wages. Firms try to pass these higher wage costs on to consumers, resulting in higher prices and an inflationary buildup in the economy. The tradeoff suggested by the Phillips curve implies that policymakers can target low inflation rates or low unemployment, but not both. During the 1960s, monetarists emphasized price stability (low inflation), while Keynesians more often emphasized job creation.

The experience of so-called stagflation in the 1970s, with simultaneously high rates of both inflation and unemployment, began to discredit the idea of a stable tradeoff between the two. In place of the Phillips curve, many economists began to posit a "natural rate of unemployment." If unemployment were to fall below this "natural" rate, however slightly, inflation would begin to accelerate. Under the "natural rate of unemployment" theory (also called the Non-Accelerating Inflation Rate of Unemployment, or NAIRU), instead of choosing between higher unemployment and higher inflation, policymakers were told to focus on ensuring that the economy remained at its "natural" rate: the challenge was to accurately estimate its level and to steer the economy toward growth rates that maintain price stability, no matter what the corresponding level of unemployment.

The NAIRU has been extremely difficult to pin down in practice. Not only are estimates of it notoriously imprecise, the rate itself evidently changes over time. In the United States, estimates of the NAIRU rose from about 4.4% in the 1960s, to 6.2% in the 1970s, and further to 7.2% in the 1980s. This trend reversed itself in the 1990s, as officially reported unemployment fell. In the latter half of the 1990s, U.S. inflation remained nearly dormant at around 3%, while unemployment fell to around 4.6%. In the later Clinton years many economists warned that if unemployment was brought any lower, inflationary pressures might spin out of control. But growth in these years did not spill over into accelerating inflation. The United States, apparently, had achieved the Goldilocks state—everything just right!

What sustained this combination of low inflation and low unemployment? Explanations abound: a productivity boom, the high rates of incarceration of those who would otherwise fall within the ranks of the unemployed, the openness of the U.S. economy to world trade and competition, among others.

The full story, however, has to do with class conflict and the relatively weak position of workers in the 1990s. Both the breakdown of the Phillips curve in the 1970s and the recent "disappearance" of the natural rate of unemployment are in essence a reflection of institutional and political changes that affect the bargaining strength of working people—in other words, their ability to organize effective unions and establish a decent living wage.

Following the Reagan offensive against trade unions, workers' power fell dramatically. Consequently, unionization rates and the real value of the minimum wage each fell precipitously between the late 1970s and the 1990s. The period of stagflation, in contrast, had been one of labor militancy and rising wages. (Although "stagflation" has a negative ring, by many measures nonsupervisory workers—i.e., the vast majority of the U.S. labor force—fared better in the economy of the early-to mid-1970s than they do today, even after the long 1990s economic expansion.) Labor's weaker position in the 1990s meant that despite low unemployment, workers were not able to win higher wages that would have spurred inflation.

The long period of stable prices and low interest rates in the United States now seems to be coming to a close. The cost of the Iraq War and rising oil prices, among other factors, have fueled expectations of a resurgence of inflation. At the same time, the near jobless recovery from the last recession might suggest that the "natural rate" of unemployment is on the rise again—and that we are witnessing yet another twist in the strange history of the Phillips curve!

With inflation rising (albeit slowly, and still relatively mild at around 4.2%), some business sectors will no doubt begin clamoring for tighter monetary policies that sacrifice job-creation and wage growth by slowing the economy growth. But these fears of inflation are probably misplaced. A moderate rate of inflation is conducive to the growth of real investment, and in the context of a decades-long squeeze on workers' wage share, there is room to expand employment without setting off a wage-price spiral. What workers need is not greater fiscal and monetary austerity, but rather a revival of a Keynesian program of "employment targeting" that would sustain full employment and empower workers to push for higher wages. It's not likely, however, that the owners of capital and their political allies would sit idly by were such a program to be enacted. ❏

Article 4.2

THE "NATURAL RATE" OF UNEMPLOYMENT
It's all about class conflict.

BY ROBERT POLLIN
September/October 1998

In 1997, the official U.S. unemployment rate fell to a 27-year low of 4.9%. Most orthodox economists had long predicted that a rate this low would lead to uncontrollable inflation. So they argued that maintaining a higher unemployment rate—perhaps as high as 6%—was crucial for keeping the economy stable. But there is a hitch: last year the inflation rate was 2.3%, the lowest figure in a decade and the second lowest in 32 years. What then are we to make of these economists' theories, much less their policy proposals?

Nobel prize-winning economist Milton Friedman gets credit for originating the argument that low rates of unemployment would lead to accelerating inflation. His 1968 theory of the so-called "natural rate of unemployment" was subsequently developed by many mainstream economists under the term "Non-Accelerating Inflation Rate of Unemployment," or NAIRU, a remarkably clumsy term for expressing the simple concept of a threshold unemployment rate below which inflation begins to rise.

According to both Friedman and expositors of NAIRU, inflation should accelerate at low rates of unemployment because low unemployment gives workers excessive bargaining power. This allows the workers to demand higher wages. Capitalists then try to pass along these increased wage costs by raising prices on the products they sell. An inflationary spiral thus ensues as long as unemployment remains below its "natural rate."

Based on this theory, Friedman and others have long argued that governments should never actively intervene in the economy to promote full employment or better jobs for workers, since it will be a futile exercise, whose end result will only be higher inflation and no improvement in job opportunities. Over the past generation, this conclusion has had far-reaching influence throughout the world. In the United States and Western Europe, it has provided a stamp of scientific respectability to a whole range of policies through which governments abandoned even modest commitments to full employment and workers' rights.

This emerged most sharply through the Reaganite and Thatcherite programs in the United States and United Kingdom in the 1980s. But even into the 1990s, as the Democrats took power in the United States, the Labour Party won office in Britain, and Social Democrats won elections throughout Europe, governments remained committed to stringent fiscal and monetary policies, whose primary goal is to prevent inflation. In Western Europe this produced an average unemployment rate of over 10% from 1990-97. In the United States, unemployment rates have fallen sharply in the 1990s, but as an alternative symptom of stringent fiscal and monetary policies, real wages for U.S. workers also declined dramatically over the past generation. As of 1997, the average real wage for nonsupervisory workers in the United States was 14% below its peak in 1973, even though average worker productivity rose between 1973 and 1997 by 34%.

Why have governments in the United States and Europe remained committed to the idea of fiscal and monetary stringency, if the natural rate theory on which such policies are based is so obviously flawed? The explanation is that the natural rate theory is really not just about predicting a precise unemployment rate figure below which inflation must inexorably accelerate, even though many mainstream economists have presented the natural rate theory in this way. At a deeper level, the natural rate theory is bound up with the inherent conflicts between workers and capitalists over jobs, wages, and working conditions. As such, the natural rate theory actually contains a legitimate foundation in truth amid a welter of sloppy and even silly predictions.

The "Natural Rate" Theory Is About Class Conflict

In his 1967 American Economic Association presidential address in which he introduced the natural rate theory, Milton Friedman made clear that there was really nothing "natural" about the theory. Friedman rather emphasized that: "by using the term 'natural' rate of unemployment, I do not mean to suggest that it is immutable and unchangeable. On the contrary, many of the market characteristics that determine its level are man-made and policy-made. In the United States, for example, legal minimum wage rates … and the strength of labor unions all make the natural rate of unemployment higher than it would otherwise be."

In other words, according to Friedman, what he terms the "natural rate" is really a social phenomenon measuring the class strength of working people, as indicated by their ability to organize effective unions and establish a livable minimum wage.

Friedman's perspective is supported in a widely-read 1997 paper by Robert Gordon of Northwestern University on what he terms the "time-varying NAIRU." What makes the NAIRU vary over time? Gordon explains that, since the early 1960s, "The two especially large changes in the NAIRU… are the increase between the early and late 1960s and the decrease in the 1990s. The late 1960s were a time of labor militancy, relatively strong unions, a relatively high minimum wage and a marked increase in labor's share in national income. The 1990s have been a time of labor peace, relatively weak unions, a relatively low minimum wage and a slight decline in labor's income share."

In short, class conflict is the spectre haunting the analysis of the natural rate and NAIRU: this is the consistent message stretching from Milton Friedman in the 1960s to Robert Gordon in the 1990s.

Stated in this way, the "Natural Rate" idea does, ironically, bear a close family resemblance to the ideas of two of the greatest economic thinkers of the left, Karl Marx and Michal Kalecki, on a parallel concept—the so-called "Reserve Army of Unemployed." In his justly famous Chapter 25 of Volume I of *Capital*, "The General Law of Capitalist Accumulation," Marx argued forcefully that unemployment serves an important function in capitalist economies. That is, when a capitalist economy is growing rapidly enough so that the reserve army of unemployed is depleted, workers will then utilize their increased bargaining power to raise wages. Profits are correspondingly squeezed as workers get a larger share of the country's total income. As a result, capitalists anticipate further declines in profitability and they therefore reduce their investment spending. This then leads to a fall in job creation, higher unemployment, and a replenishment of the reserve army. In other words, the reserve army of the unemployed is the instrument capitalists use to prevent significant wage increases and thereby maintain profitability.

Kalecki, a Polish economist of the Great Depression era, makes parallel though distinct arguments in his also justly famous essay, "The Political Aspects of Full Employment." Kalecki wrote in 1943, shortly after the 1930s Depression had ended and governments had begun planning a postwar world in which they would deploy aggressive policies to avoid another calamity of mass unemployment. Kalecki held, contrary to Marx, that full employment can be beneficial to the profitability of businesses. True, capitalists may get a smaller share of the total economic pie as workers gain bargaining power to win higher wages. But capitalists can still benefit because the size of the pie is growing far more rapidly, since more goods and services can be produced when everyone is working, as opposed to some significant share of workers being left idle.

But capitalists still won't support full employment, in Kalecki's view, because it will threaten their control over the workplace, the pace and direction of economic activity, and even political institutions. Kalecki thus concluded that full employment could be sustainable under capitalism, but only if these challenges to capitalists' social and political power could be contained. This is why he held that fascist social and political institutions, such as those that existed in Nazi Germany when he was writing, could well provide one "solution" to capitalism's unemployment problem, precisely because they were so brutal. Workers would have jobs, but they would never be permitted to exercise the political and economic power that would otherwise accrue to them in a full-employment economy.

Broadly speaking, Marx and Kalecki do then share a common conclusion with natural rate proponents, in that they would all agree that positive unemployment rates are the outgrowth of class conflict over the distribution of income and political power. Of course, Friedman and other mainstream economists reach this conclusion via analytic and political perspectives that are diametrically opposite to those of Marx and Kalecki. To put it in a nutshell, in the Friedmanite view mass unemployment results when workers demand more than they deserve, while for Marx and Kalecki, capitalists use the weapon of unemployment to prevent workers from getting their just due.

From Natural Rate to Egalitarian Policy

Once the analysis of unemployment in capitalist economies is properly understood within the framework of class conflict, several important issues in our contemporary economic situation become much more clear. Let me raise just a few:

1. Mainstream economists have long studied how workers' wage demands cause inflation as unemployment falls. However, such wage demands never directly cause inflation, since inflation refers to a general rise in prices of goods and services sold in the market, not a rise in wages. Workers, by definition, do not have the power to raise prices. Capitalists raise prices on the products they sell. At low unemployment, inflation occurs when capitalists respond to workers' increasingly successful wage demands by raising prices so that they can maintain profitability. If workers were simply to receive a higher share of national income, then lower unemployment and higher wages need not cause inflation at all.

2. There is little mystery as to why, at present, the so-called "time-varying" NAIRU has diminished to a near vanishing point, with unemployment at a 25-year low while inflation remains dormant. The main explanation is the one stated by Robert Gordon—that workers' economic power has been eroding dramatically through the 1990s. Workers have been almost completely unable to win wage increases over the course of the economic expansion that by now is seven years old.

3. This experience over the past seven years, with unemployment falling but workers showing almost no income gains, demonstrates dramatically the crucial point that full employment can never stand alone as an adequate measure of workers' well-being. This was conveyed vividly to me when I was working in Bolivia in 1990 as part of an economic advising team led by Keith Griffin of the University of California-Riverside. Professor Griffin asked me to examine employment policies.

I began by paying a visit to the economists at the Ministry of Planning. When I requested that we discuss the country's employment problems, they explained, to my surprise, that the country *had no employment problems*. When I suggested we consider the situation of the people begging, shining shoes, or hawking batteries and Chiclets in the street just below the window where we stood, their response was that these people *were* employed. And of course they were, in that they were actively trying to scratch out a living. It was clear that I had to specify the problem at hand far more precisely. Similarly, in the United States today, we have to be much more specific as to what workers should be getting in a fair economy: jobs, of course, but also living wages, benefits, reasonable job security, and a healthy work environment.

4. In our current low-unemployment economy, should workers, at long last, succeed in winning higher wages and better benefits, some inflationary pressures are likely to emerge. But if inflation does not accelerate after wage increases are won, this would mean that businesses are not able to pass along their higher wage costs to their customers. Profits would therefore be squeezed. In any case, in response to *either* inflationary pressures or a squeeze in profitability, we should expect that many, if not most, segments of the business community will welcome a Federal Reserve policy that would slow the economy and raise the unemployment rate.

Does this mean that, as long as we live in a capitalist society, the control by capitalists over the reserve army of labor must remain the dominant force establishing the limits of workers' strivings for jobs, security, and living wages? The challenge for the progressive movement in the United States today is to think through a set of policy ideas through which full employment at living wages can be achieved and sustained.

Especially given the dismal trajectory of real wage decline over the past generation, workers should of course continue to push for wage increases. But it will also be crucial to advance these demands within a broader framework of proposals. One important component of a broader package would be policies through which labor and capital bargain openly over growth of wages and profits after full employment is achieved. Without such an open bargaining environment, workers, with reason, will push for higher wages once full employment is achieved, but capitalists will then respond by either raising prices or favoring high unemployment. Such open bargaining policies were conducted with considerable success in Sweden and other Nordic countries from the 1950s to the 1980s, and as a result, wages there continued to rise at full employment, while both accelerating inflation and a return to high unemployment were prevented.

Such policies obviously represent a form of class compromise. This is intrinsically neither good nor bad. The question is the terms under which the compromise is achieved. Wages have fallen dramatically over the past generation, so workers deserve substantial raises as a matter of simple fairness. But workers should also be willing to link their wage increases to improvements in productivity growth, i.e., the rate at which workers produce new goods and services. After all, if the average wage had just risen at exactly the rate of productivity growth since 1973 and not a penny more, the average hourly wage today for nonsupervisory workers would be $19.07 rather than $12.24.

But linking wages to improvements in productivity then also raises the question of who controls the decisions that determine the rate of productivity growth. In fact, substantial productivity gains are attainable through operating a less hierarchical workplace and building strong democratic unions through which workers can defend their rights on the job. Less hierarchy and increased workplace democracy creates higher morale on the job, which in turn increases workers' effort and opportunities to be inventive, while decreasing turnover and absenteeism. The late David Gordon of the New School for Social Research was among the leading analysts demonstrating how economies could operate more productively through greater workplace democracy.

But improvements in productivity also result from both the public and private sector investing in new and better machines that workers put to use every day, with the additional benefit that it means more jobs for people who produce those machines. A pro-worker economic policy will therefore also have to be concerned with increasing investments to improve the stock of machines that workers have at their disposal on the job.

In proposing such a policy approach, have I forgotten the lesson that Marx and Kalecki taught us, that unemployment serves a purpose in capitalism? Given that this lesson has become part of the standard mode of thinking among mainstream economists ranging from Milton Friedman to Robert Gordon, I would hope that I haven't let it slip from view. My point nevertheless is that through changing power relationships at the workplace and the decision-making process through which investment decisions get made, labor and the left can then also achieve a more egalitarian economy, one in which capitalists' power to brandish the weapon of unemployment is greatly circumscribed. If the labor movement and the left neglect issues of control over investment and the workplace, we will continue to live amid a Bolivian solution to the unemployment problem, where full employment is the by-product of workers' vulnerability, not their strength. ❑

Sources: A longer version of this article appears as "The 'Reserve Army of Labor' and the 'Natural Rate of Unemployment': Can Marx, Kalecki, Friedman, and Wall Street All Be Wrong?," *Review of Radical Political Economics*, Fall 1998. Both articles derive from a paper originally presented as the David Gordon Memorial Lecture at the 1997 Summer Conference of the Union for Radical Political Economics. See also Robert Pollin and Stephanie Luce, *The Living Wage: Building a Fair Economy*, 1998; David Gordon, *Fat and Mean*, 1997; David Gordon, "Generating Affluence: Productivity Gains Require Worker Support," *Real World Macro*, 15th ed., 1998.

Article 4.3

LET'S SEE HOW LOW THE UNEMPLOYMENT RATE CAN GO

BY DEAN BAKER
February 2018, Center for Economic and Policy Research

The new budget agreement crafted by Congress is projected to raise budget deficits by $150 billion annually over the next two years, an increase of a bit more than 0.7% of GDP. This follows the passage of the tax cuts, which are projected to increase the deficit by an average of more than 1% of GDP over the next five years.

This should settle one point beyond any dispute. Republicans do not give a damn about budget deficits. All the sanctimonious whining we heard when President Obama was trying to push his stimulus package as the economy was collapsing back in 2009, and when it was still languishing in 2011 as the Republicans regained control of Congress and demanded austerity, was crap.

The Republicans were trying to obstruct anything Obama proposed. There was no principle at play here, it was just a story where if Obama was for it, they were against it. The consequences for the economy—millions of people needlessly being unemployed, losing their homes, children going homeless—those didn't matter. Paul Ryan and Mitch McConnell's agenda is winning at politics, not being do-gooders for the country.

Most of us recognize politicians as being politically motivated, except of course for the people who get paid to tell us what they are doing. We heard and read endless pieces on National Public Radio, the *New York Times*, and other mainstream news outlets telling us how Republicans believe in balanced budgets, that they were concerned about debts and deficits, etc.

Don't tell us politicians' beliefs and concerns; just tell us what they say and do, full stop.

OK, but beyond Republicans being incredible liars and hypocrites, the big jump in the deficit will allow for an important economic experiment. We will get to test how far we can push the economy and how low we can get the unemployment rate before seeing serious problems with inflation.

The reality is that economists haven't a clue as to how far we can push the economy. Just four years ago the Congressional Budget Office put the floor of the unemployment rate at 5.5%. This estimate implied that if the unemployment rate fell below this level that the inflation rate would begin to spiral upwards.

The unemployment rate has now been well below this level for more than two-and-a-half years, and there is still no evidence of an inflationary spiral. In fact, the inflation rate remains well below the Federal Reserve's 2% target.

If the Fed and Congress had tried to craft monetary and fiscal policy around this 5.5% figure, as many economists advocated, millions of workers would have been needlessly denied the opportunity to get jobs. Tens of millions would be looking at lower wages, as the tighter labor market has finally allowing workers at the middle- and bottom-end of the labor market to finally share in the gains of economic growth.

We should be grateful that the Fed, under previous head Janet Yellen, held off on excessive rate hikes that would have substantially slowed growth, but the new tax cuts and spending pushed through by the Republican Congress take stimulus to another level. The additional demand resulting from the larger deficits should provide a considerable near-term boost to growth.

We are likely to see the unemployment rate fall well below 4%, reaching levels not seen since the height of the Vietnam War half a century ago. This will give many of the least advantaged in society—less-educated workers, formerly incarcerated individuals and the disabled—opportunities for work that they would never otherwise realize. It should also give tens of millions of workers additional bargaining power to secure larger wage gains.

Will the boost to the economy lead to serious problems with inflation? I'll give the honest economist's answer: I don't know. But this is an experiment worth performing. We should look to push the economy to its limits. We have repeatedly erred with excessive fiscal and monetary restraint, needlessly keeping millions unemployed. It's worth putting the foot on the accelerator and seeing how far we can go.

It is incredibly ironic that we need a Republican in the White House and a Republican Congress to perform this test. The Republicans did everything they could to make sure that we never tested the economy's limits under President Obama. The fact that many of his top advisers also had no interest in such a test also didn't help.

But the constraints are off now. Let's see how low the unemployment rate can go. ❑

Article 4.4

WHAT ARE THE EFFECTS OF A $15 PER HOUR MINIMUM WAGE?

BY ARTHUR MacEWAN
May/June 2018

> Dear Dr. Dollar:
> *While I am all for raising wages of low-income workers, it seems that there are some problems with setting the minimum wage at $15 per hour. Wouldn't pushing up the minimum wage lead to less employment for low-wage workers, as employers find it more profitable to use more machinery in place of workers and some employers actually shut down their operations, maybe moving offshore? And does it make sense to have the same minimum throughout the country, when income levels are so different in different states—West Virginia and Massachusetts, for example?*
> —Rebecca G., Hagerstown, W. Va.

Although Bernie Sanders and others have called for raising the national minimum wage to $15 per hour, this is not going to happen as long as Republicans control Congress and Donald Trump is in the White House. The national minimum wage remains at $7.25 per hour, where it has been since 2010. Real action, however, is taking place at the state and local level.

Seattle paved the way with 2014 legislation that is slated to raise the city's minimum wage to $15 an hour by 2021. Since then, there have been efforts in many cities and states to follow Seattle's lead. Under the "Fight for $15" banner, a national movement has emerged. In California, San Francisco will have a $15 minimum this year, Los Angeles by 2020, and the whole state by 2022.

New York's minimum wage will reach $15 at different times in different regions, with New York City's hitting the mark at the end of this year for large employers and at the end of 2019 for small employers (less than 10 employees); the phase-in will be slower in other regions of the state. In Washington, DC, the minimum wage will rise to $15 per hour in 2020.

In 2017, either by legislatures' actions or by the ballot box, 19 states raised their minimum wage. While none moved immediately to $15, and in some states the increases were very small, these changes illustrate the extent to which minimum wage action has moved out of Washington.

Not a Lot of Money, But...

Fifteen dollars an hour is not a lot of money. Forty hours a week for 52 weeks a year at this rate yields an annual income of $31,200, roughly half the median household income in the country. By 2021, when the $15 rate will be reality in some states and cities, inflation will have reduced the figure to less than $14 in current dollars (perhaps lower).

Still, the increase of the minimum wage to $15 could make a real difference for low-income workers and their families. In Massachusetts, for example, an increase of the minimum to $15 is under consideration by the legislature, and, if the legislature does not act favorably, the increase will be on the ballot in November. The Massachusetts law would raise the minimum wage from its current $11 per hour in $1 increments over the next four years. This increase would improve the economic well-being of over a million workers, close to 30% of the state's workforce. Fully 91% of affected workers are age 20 or older. Over half are women. Fifty-eight percent work full-time. Some 400,000 children (28% of all Massachusetts children) have at least one working parent who would get a raise.

At the current $11 per hour minimum in Massachusetts, even with more than one person working, a family with kids can make it only with several public supports, such as housing and daycare vouchers, food stamps, and MassHealth (a program that combines Medicaid and the Children's Health Insurance Program). Fifteen dollars an hour won't solve all this family's economic problems, but it will help.

Opposition and Response

Nonetheless, there are opponents of the new minimum wage laws. They argue that if the minimum wage is raised, the level of employment will fall—especially for low-wage workers. So instead of being helped, they claim, many low-wage workers would lose their jobs. It is a simple—and, unfortunately, a simplistic—argument. It is true that if the prices of tomatoes, cars, or many other items rise, people will buy less of those items. So, the argument goes, the same is true for low-wage workers. Employers, for example, will find ways, perhaps by using more equipment or cutting back services, to hire fewer employees.

But labor is different than tomatoes or cars. If a higher price is paid for the same tomato, that doesn't mean the tomato will become tastier. The same with the car; paying more for the same car won't make it run any better. But pay the same worker more and things change.

Workers who are paid better tend to be more productive, either because they feel better about their jobs or they now have a greater desire to keep that job, or both. Greater productivity lowers costs per unit of output. Also, better pay means less turnover, which can also lower employers' costs. While these cost reductions may not outweigh the higher wage, they certainly reduce the negative impact of the higher wage on employers' bottom lines.

Also, insofar as the higher costs are a burden on employers, much of that burden can be passed on to customers with relatively little impact on purchases. In Massachusetts, for example, even ignoring cost savings from higher productivity and lower turnover, McDonald's could fully cover the costs of raising the minimum wage from $11 to $15 by raising prices by 1.3% per year for four years.

Furthermore, when a city or state raises its minimum wage, low-wage firms are unlikely to move away. A large share of the low-wage labor force is employed in fast food sites and retail stores. Their very nature ties them to the location of their clientele. Very few low-wage workers are in manufacturing firms that might flee abroad.

It should be no surprise, then, that many economic studies have shown that in various states negative employment impacts of increases in the minimum wage have been either non-existent or trivial. To again use the Massachusetts example: As the state's minimum wage was raised over three years from $8 per hour to its current $11 per hour in recent years, there was no apparent negative impact on employment. To be sure, some studies of minimum wage increases show negative employment impacts. But, on balance, the increasing number of studies that show no negative impacts are more convincing. (See box.)

Variations

There are major differences among the states in the minimum wage, income levels, and the cost of living. States like Maryland, New Jersey, and Massachusetts have median household incomes about 70% higher than states like Mississippi, West Virginia, and Louisiana. In the lowest-income states, the cost of living is also quite low, so people in those states are not worse off to the degree that the income difference would imply. However, in the lowest-income states, in which the minimum wage is only the federal minimum of $7.25, a jump to $15 could be very disruptive to local firms and damaging to employment.

Seattle: A Tale of Two Studies

In June 2017, two papers were released evaluating the impact on employment of the increase of the minimum wage in Seattle. At that time, the minimum had increased to $13 an hour.

The first study, "Seattle's Minimum Wage Experience 2015–6," written by a group at the University of California Berkeley, found that there was no significant impact on employment of the move toward the $15 minimum wage.

The second study, "Minimum Wage Increases, Wages, and Low-Wage Employment: Evidence from Seattle," by a group at the University of Washington yielded, a very different result—that the impact on employment of low-wage workers was large and negative. This second study has been widely touted by opponents of increasing the minimum wage.

But in spite of the attention it received, the second study was unconvincing, in part because the large negative impact it found was very much larger than had been found in similar studies of minimum wage increase elsewhere by researchers critical of minimum wage increases. Also, this study excluded data from multi-site firms, which included most fast food and many retails sales operations. Further, it failed to effectively take account of the rapid growth of the Seattle economy, which appears to have moved many low-wage workers into higher-higher wage categories.

The Berkeley study focused on the Seattle food service industry, which is an intense user of minimum wage workers. If employment impacts resulted from the increase of the minimum wage, they should show up in this industry. As a control group, this study used cities elsewhere in the country which had economic experiences similar to Seattle over the years leading into the Seattle wage increase. Its methodology makes its result—no negative impact on employment—more convincing..

Yet there are also major differences within states in the minimum wage, income levels, and the cost of living. New York, as noted above, has taken at least some of this intra-state difference into account by setting different schedules for the establishment of the $15 minimum wage in different regions. If a $15 minimum were established nationally, means could be developed to ease the adjustment in areas where this would be an especially large increase. The New York procedure is one option, but others could be developed.

In whatever manner the introduction would be handled, there would be considerable value in moving toward economic equality among the states. Until the late 1970s, there was a general convergence among income levels across different states. In the 1930s, Mississippi had had a per capita income level about 30% as high as in Massachusetts, and by the late 1970s, that figure was almost 70%. But today, Mississippi is down to 55% of Massachusetts. (See Gerald Friedman, "Growing Together, Flying Apart," *D&S*, March/April 2018.)

This shift from convergence to divergence has been associated with the general rise of economic inequality in the country and surely has been driven by some of the same factors. Regional inequality is a problem in itself, but it is not unreasonable to see it as associated with the political and cultural polarization in the United States. Establishing a much higher national minimum wage, which would have its greatest impact in low-income regions, would be one step in reducing this undesirable—indeed, poisonous—inequality and polarization. ❏

Sources: Bill Kramer, "Minimum Wages Rise in 19 States," MultiState Insider, January 4, 2017 (multistate.us); "City Minimum Wage Laws: Recent Trends and Economic Evidence," National Employment Law Project, April 2016 (nelp.org); "New York State $15 Minimum Wage and Paid Family Leave," GovDocs (govdocs.com) Aaron C. Davis, "D.C. gives final approval to $15 minimum wage," *Washington Post*, June 21, 2016 (washingtonpost.com); "Personal Income Per Capita," Federal Reserve Bank of St. Louis (fred.stlouisfed.org); "Median Household Income," Federal Reserve Bank of St. Louis (fred.stlouisfed.org); Nicole Rodriguez, "Frequently Asked Questions Related to the $15 Minimum Wage," Massachusetts Budget and Policy Center, January 24, 2018 (massbudget.org); David Cooper, "Raising the minimum wage to $15 an hour would lift wages for 41 million American workers," Economic Policy Institute, April 26, 2017 (epi.org); Robert Pollin and Jeannette Wicks-Lim, "A $15 U.S. Minimum Wage: How the Fast-Food Industry Could Adjust Without Shedding Jobs," *Journal of Economic Issues*, Vol. 5 Issue 3, 2016; Arindrajit Dube, T. William Lester, and Michael Reich, "Minimum Wage Effects Across State Borders: Estimates Using Contiguous Counties," *Review of Economics and Statistics*, Vol. 92 Issue 4, November 2010; Michael Reich, Sylvia Allegretto, and Anna Godoey, "Seattle's Minimum Wage Experience 2015-16," Center for Wage and Employment Dynamics, Institute for Research on Labor and Employment, University of California Berkeley, June 2017 (irle.berkeley.edu); Ekaterina Jardim et al., "Minimum Wage Increases, Wages, and Low-Wage Employment: Evidence from Seattle," National Bureau of Economic Research, June 2017, Revised in October 2017 (nber.org); Ben Zipperer and John Schmitt, "The 'high road' Seattle labor market and the effects of the minimum wage increase," Economic Policy Institute (epi.org)

Article 4.5

THE *REAL* UNEMPLOYMENT RATE

BY JOHN MILLER

July/August 2009; updated June 2018

Since the Great Recession, the U.S. economy has grown more slowly and taken longer to replace the jobs lost during a recession than any economic recovery in the last seven decades. Nonetheless, by May 2018, after nearly nine years of economic recovery, the official unemployment rate had fallen from its October 2009 peak of 10.1% during the Great Recession to 3.8%, the lowest unemployment rate in 18 years (since April 2000).

Some groups of workers faced higher official unemployment rates, but even those rates were record or near-record lows. In May 2018, unemployment rates for black workers was 5.9%, the lowest rate on record (with data back to 1973); the unemployment rate for Hispanic workers was 4.9%, the lowest since 1973 when records began (except for the 4.8% rate posted the previous month); and the unemployment rate for adult workers without a high school diploma was 5.4%, the lowest rate on record (with data available since 1992). Teenage workers faced a yet higher official unemployment rate of 12.8%, but that rate was still the lowest in 18 years (since May 2000).

Other telltale signs, however, suggested that the unemployment picture was less rosy than those official rates indicate. To begin with, near-record low unemployment rates have done little to improve wages. Average hourly wages corrected for inflation rose just 0.5% per year from the official end of the Great Recession in June 2009 to June 2017, and have been virtually stagnant in the last year. On top of that, the proportion of workers employed part-time who would prefer to work full-time remained at historically high levels. For Janet Yellen, the chair of the Federal Reserve Board during most of the recovery, signs like those "underscore[d] the importance of considering more than the unemployment rate when evaluating the condition of the U.S. labor market."

Yellen was right. The official figures dramatically understate the true extent of unemployment. First, they exclude anyone without a job who is ready to work

THE MAY 2018 UNEMPLOYMENT PICTURE (DATA IN THOUSANDS, SEASONALLY ADJUSTED)	
Civilian Labor Force	161,539
Employed	155,474
Unemployed	6,065
Marginally Attached Workers	1,455
Discouraged workers	378
Reasons other than discouragement	1,077
Part-time for Economic Reasons	4,948
Slack work or business conditions	3,004
Could only find part-time work	1,480

Sources: Bureau of Labor Statistics, Employment Situation Summary A, Household data, seasonally adjusted, Economic News Release, June 1, 2018.

U3= headline unemployment rate
U6= actual U.S. rate
CHAPTER 4: UNEMPLOYMENT AND INFLATION | 117

but has not actively looked for a job in the previous four weeks. The Bureau of Labor Statistics (BLS) classifies such workers as "marginally attached to the labor force" so long as they have looked for work within the last year. Marginally attached workers include so-called discouraged workers who have given up looking because repeated job searches were unsuccessful, plus others who have given up for reasons such as school and family responsibilities, ill health, or transportation problems.

That workers who still want a job go unaccounted for helps to explain why wage growth has been so sluggish despite record low unemployment rates. Those workers can be hired from the sidelines of the labor market to relieve any upward pressure on wages from the shortage of idle workers indicated by low official unemployment rates.

Second, the official unemployment rate leaves out part-time workers looking for full-time work: part-time workers are "employed" even if they work as little as one hour a week. Most people working part-time involuntarily have had their hours cut due to slack or unfavorable business conditions. The rest are working part-time because they could only find part-time work.

To its credit, the BLS has developed alternative unemployment measures that go a long way toward correcting the shortcomings of the official rate. The broadest alternative measure, called the U-6, counts as unemployed "marginally attached workers" as well as those employed "part time for economic reasons." And even the business press, including the *Wall Street Journal*, has taken to reporting this more comprehensive measure of unemployment along with the official unemployment rate.

In May 2018, the broader measure of the unemployment rate was 7.6%, exactly double the official, or U-3, rate. That's lower than U-6 rate in 2007 prior to the onset of the Great Recession, but still greater than the 6.8% figure at the end of the ten-year 1990s expansion.

Why is the real unemployment rate, even after a long economic expansion, so much higher than the official rate? First, during the Great Recession forced part-time work reached higher levels than any time since 1956. In May 2018, 4.9 million workers were still forced to work part-time for economic reasons, more than any time since January 1994. Forced part-timers are concentrated in wholesale and retail trade, leisure and hospitality, and education and health service; they are nearly equally men and women but disproportionately younger workers (20 to 24 years old) and older workers (over 55 years old). The number of discouraged workers is also quite high today. The BLS counted 1.5 million "marginally attached" workers in May 2018. That figure exceeds the number of marginally attached workers in the months prior to the onset of the Great Recession, and in the eighth and ninth year of the long economic expansion during the 1990s.

Today U.S. labor markets continue to impose devastating costs on society, and much of the burden goes unaccounted for by a traditional unemployment rate. For instance, a recent study conducted by economists Alex Hollingsworth, Christopher Ruhm, and Kosali Simon found that each one percentage point uptick in the unemployment rate is associated with a 3.6% increase in opioid-involved drug deaths and 7% increase in emergency department visits linked to opioid overdose in the period from 1999 to 2014. In addition, of those who are counted as unemployed by the traditional measure, one quarter had gone more than 27 weeks without work.

Calculating the Real Unemployment Rate

The BLS calculates the official unemployment rate, U-3, as the number of unemployed as a percentage of the civilian labor force. The civilian labor force consists of employed workers plus the officially unemployed, those without jobs who are available to work and have looked for a job in the last 4 weeks. In May 2018, this calculation gave an official unemployment rate of 3.8%.

The comprehensive U-6 unemployment rate adjusts the official rate by adding marginally attached workers and part-time workers who would rather be working full time (known as "part-time for economic reasons" or "involuntary part-time") to the officially unemployed. To find the U-6 rate, the BLS takes that higher unemployment count and divides it by the official civilian labor force plus the number of marginally attached workers. (No adjustment is necessary for involuntary part-time workers since they are already counted in the official labor force as employed workers.)

Accounting for the large number of marginally attached workers and those working part-time for economic reasons raises the count of unemployed from 6.1 million to 12.5 million workers for May 2018. Those numbers push up the U-6 unemployment rate to 7.6%.

The persistence of such high levels of long-term unemployment are sure to sever further the connection of those without work to the labor force. After many months of looking for work, some of the long-term unemployed are likely to give up the search, falling into the category of marginally attached and disappearing from the official measure of unemployment. And victims of a malfunctioning U.S. labor market will continue to go uncounted by the traditional unemployment rate in the month and years ahead. ❏

Sources: U.S. Dept. of Labor, "The Unemployment Rate and Beyond: Alternative Measures of Labor Underutilization," *Issues in Labor Statistics*, June 2008; Jon Hilsenrath and Victoria McGrane, "Fed's Yellen Sets Course for Steady Bond-Buy Cuts," *Wall Street Journal*, February 11, 2014; Phil Izzo, "Don't Sweat the Rise in the Unemployment Rate," *Wall Street Journal*, March 7, 2014; "Are Opioid Deaths Affected by Macroeconomic Conditions?" *The National Bureau of Economics Research's Bulletin on Aging and Health*, 2017, No. 3..

Article 4.6

KEYNES, WAGE AND PRICE "STICKINESS," AND DEFLATION

BY ALEJANDRO REUSS

August 2009

Most people are accustomed to worrying about inflation, which has been a durable fact of life in the United States for half a century. The overall price level in the U.S. economy (a sort of average of prices across the economy), as measured by the Consumer Price Index, has increased every calendar year since 1957. Or, rather, had increased every year since 1957, until 2008. Last year, as the U.S. economy went into its most severe recession since the Great Depression, the CPI declined by 0.2%. For the first time in decades, there is reason in the United States to worry about the dangers of deflation.

Deflation: What's Not to Like?

Lower prices may sound appealing, but deflation can make a bad recession worse. Deflation can bring down overall demand. If individuals and firms expect prices to decline, they may postpone purchases. Why buy today, if the price will be lower tomorrow? Declining prices and wages can exacerbate firms' negative expectations about future sales and profits, discouraging current investment. If a firm does not think it will be able to sell future output at a sufficient profit, it will not make purchases of new plant and equipment now. Deflation can also make the cost of borrowing higher, and increase the burden of past debt. This can ruin debtors and bankrupt firms, as each dollar owed becomes harder to come by as prices drop. Over the three years with the sharpest drop in output and employment during the Great Depression, 1930–1933, the Consumer Price Index dropped by over 25%. More broadly, a study by economists Michael Bruno and William Easterly of over 100 countries from the 1960s to 1990s showed that rates of deflation between 0% and 20% were associated with lower rates of economic growth than low to moderate rates of inflation (up to 30%) were.

Such concerns about deflation run sharply counter to the "mainstream" or neoclassical view of recessions. Neoclassical economists argue that the economy is "self-correcting," and that if it dips into recession it will quickly return itself to "full employment" without any need for deliberate government action. One of their main arguments for this view is that prices—including wages (the price of labor) and interest rates (the price of money)—are flexible. If there is excess supply of labor (unemployment), workers will reduce their wage demands, causing employers to want to hire more labor and workers to offer less labor for sale, until the surplus is eliminated. Likewise, if there is excess saving, the interest rate will decline, causing people to save less and borrow more, until that surplus is eliminated. In this view, a recovery (from a period of low employment and output) involves a decrease in the price level. Deflation, in other words, is the cure for what ails us.

What Is Price "Stickiness"?

One response to the neoclassical argument is that, in fact, prices are not perfectly flexible (they exhibit "stickiness"). For this reason, the economy is not self-correcting, at least not in the short run. Wages and prices may be "too high" (and, therefore, result in suppliers offering larger quantities for sale than demanders are able and willing to buy), but not come down quickly and eliminate the market surplus. This view has been widely attributed to John Maynard Keynes, and is, in fact, a key argument in what is known as "New Keynesian" economic theory. But this was not Keynes' argument.

Keynes expressed, in numerous passages in *The General Theory,* the view that wages were "sticky" in terms of money. He noted, for example, that workers and unions tended to fight tooth-and-nail against any attempts by employers to reduce money wages (the actual sum of money workers receive, as opposed to the real purchasing power of these wages, taking account of changes in the cost of living), even by a little bit, in a way they did not fight for increases in wages every time there was a small rise in the cost of living eroding their "real wages." Keynes argued emphatically, however, against the idea that the stickiness of money wages was the cause of unemployment, or that full flexibility of money wages (in particular, a decline in money wages) was likely to be a cure for depressions.

Is Wage Flexibility the Solution?

Keynes was careful to describe many different possible effects of declining money wages, some pointing towards increased consumption or investment (and therefore an increase in total output and incomes), and some pointing in the opposite direction. He pointed out two fundamental errors in the conventional view that lower money wages would necessarily result in increased employment. First, he noted that, while one worker could gain employment (at the expense of someone else) by accepting a lower wage, this did not automatically mean that lower money wages across the board would cause overall employment to increase. Second, he argued that, while decreased money wages would result in increased employment if total ("aggregate") demand were unchanged, there was no reason to believe that would be the case.

Keynes made at least four major arguments that declining money wages were not the cure for unemployment (and depressions) that classical economists thought.

1. Workers do not decide their level of real wages, and so cannot reduce these to a level that will ensure full employment. Keynes pointed out that particular workers (or groups of workers) and employers bargained not over real wages, but money wages. Real wages depended not only on these money-wage bargains but also on the overall price level. The price level, in turn, depended on money-wage bargains made between many different groups of workers and employers across the economy as a whole. Keynes argued that, if workers in general were to accept lower money wages, the overall price level could not possibly remain unchanged. The price level, instead, would decline by a similar proportion, so real wages might not change very much at all. In that case, employers would not have an incentive to hire more workers, and overall employment would change very little.

2. Reductions in workers' money wages may result in decreased consumption, and therefore can result in lower incomes and output. Keynes argued that declines in money wages change the distribution of income—increasing the incomes of owners of other factors of production (capitalists and landowners) at the expense of workers, and those of rentiers (owners of money capital) at the expense of entrepreneurs (owners of businesses). These changes in distribution could result in a decrease in the "marginal propensity to consume" (the amount spent on consumption out of each additional dollar of income). Declining money wages (and the resulting decline in the price level) would tend to redistribute income from lower-income individuals (who tend to consume a very large proportion of their incomes) to higher-income individuals (who tend to consume lower proportions of their incomes, and to save higher proportions).

3. Declining wages can create incentives for employers to postpone purchases of durable equipment. Keynes argued that the effects of the reduction in money wages on the incentive for capitalists to invest (purchase durable equipment) depended on the expectations of future changes in money wages. If money wages declined, but capitalists expected them to go up in the immediate future (that is, money wages were thought to have "bottomed out"), Keynes argued, the effect on investment would be positive, since the cost of producing durable equipment now would be lower than in the future. However, if the decline in money wages made capitalists expect continued future declines, the effect on investment would be negative. Durable equipment purchased in the current period would, in Keynes' words, have to "compete ... with the output from equipment produced [in the future] ... at a lower labor cost." Owners of the more expensive equipment would have to cut their prices and accept lower profits to match the prices that owners of the less expensive equipment would be willing to accept (having the advantage of lower costs). This would produce an incentive to put off purchases of such equipment into the future.

4. A decline in the price level creates increased real burdens for debtors. When the price level goes down, the purchasing power of the currency increases. We would say, "A dollar becomes more valuable." Since most debts take the form of a specific sum of money owed, and the real purchasing power of this sum increases as the price level decreases, the real purchasing power that the debtor has to hand over also increase. Looked at another way, across-the-board deflation means that the debtor cannot charge as much for whatever she sells, but the amount of money she has to pay to the creditor does not change. Therefore, she now has to sell more units (of whatever it is she sells) to pay back the debt. Debt service will swallow up an increasing proportion of her gross income. "If the fall of wages and prices goes far ... those entrepreneurs who are heavily indebted," Keynes argues, "may soon reach the point of insolvency." That is, deflation can result in an epidemic of bankruptcies.

Keynes' arguments on the effects of declining wages and prices during a recession were part of his case, contrary to the mainstream economics of his time (and ours), that capitalist economies were not inherently "self-correcting." Depression conditions, Keynes argued, would not necessarily set off a chain of events pulling the economy back to its "full employment" level of output. Declining money wages and prices could, in fact, lead to a downward spiral deeper into recession. Capitalist economies could get stuck in a low-output, high-unemployment condition. Keynes believed that government action was necessary to guarantee a return to and maintenance of full employment. For this reason, he argued that the complacent attitude of conventional economists toward economic crises—that, eventually, the problem would solve itself—was not of much use. "Economists set them too easy, too useless a task," he wrote, "if in tempestuous seasons they can only tell us that when the storm is over the ocean is flat again." ❑

Sources: John Maynard Keynes, *The General Theory of Employment, Interest, and Money* (New York: Harcourt, Inc., 1964); John Maynard Keynes, *A Tract on Monetary Reform* (London: MacMillan, 1923); Consumer Price Index, All Urban Consumers (CPI-U), Economagic; Michael Bruno and William Easterly, "Inflation Crises and Long-Run Growth," Policy Research Working Paper, World Bank, September 1995.

Chapter 5

WEALTH, INEQUALITY, AND POVERTY

INTRODUCTION

Wealth and inequality are both end products of today's patterns of economic growth. But while all macroeconomics textbooks investigate wealth accumulation, most give less attention to wealth disparities. The authors in this chapter fill in the gap by looking at who makes out, and who doesn't, in the accumulation of wealth.

Economist Chris Tilly debunks the myth that today's inequality is inevitable or (as many mainstream economists would have it) actually desirable (Article 5.1). He argues that rampant inequality is not necessary for economic growth, showing that among both developing and industrial economies and across individual countries' distinct regions, there is no correlation between higher inequality and faster economic growth. He argues that greater equality actually supports economic growth by bolstering spending, raising productivity, and reducing social conflict.

A modest increase in wages in the beginning of 2018 was followed by an outbreak of stock market instability. In Article 5.2, John Miller asks why. His answer is that the interests of workers and stockholders are diametrically opposed. Higher wages drive up costs that either diminish profits or increase inflation. Either way, the returns of stockholders suffer.

The next article focuses on changes in inequality, rooted in changes in labor relations, between the mid 20th century and the present. As Arthur MacEwan points out, the income share of the richest 1% rose when the share of workers who were union members fell. To MacEwan it seems clear that restoring union size and strength would go a long way toward reducing inequality (Article 5.3).

One of the most perplexing problems of the current economic expansion is why wages have remained stagnant despite lower and lower official unemployment rates. In Article 5.4, Arthur MacEwan explains why: Workers' compensation and productivity gains no longer move together; actual unemployment rates are higher than the official unemployment rates suggest; government policies and private employers have blocked workers' attempts to unionize; and globalization has increased the ability of corporations to move their operations offshore.

Three authors from the Economic Policy Institute track how the position of African Americans has changed since the Kerner Commission report of 1968 documented the pervasive racial discrimination in U.S. society (Article 5.5). They find that compared to 1968, African Americans today are much better educated, are healthier, and have higher incomes and are less often poor in absolute terms. At the same time, they find that large gaps between the economic, health, and educational outcomes of African Americans and whites still persist.

What has happened to world income inequality is a matter of intense debate. Many analysts claim that globally, incomes have converged, leading to a sharp reduction in world inequality in the second half of the 20th century. Many others report that the gaps between the poorest and the richest people and between countries have continued to widen over the last two decades. Arthur MacEwan (Article 5.6) unpacks the trends, both in terms of rising inequality within most large economies and some reduction of the income gaps between different countries.

Rounding out the chapter, Steven Pressman (Article 5.7) analyzes the celebrated work of French economist Thomas Piketty on the growth of income inequality over the history of capitalism. Pressman summarizes Piketty's arguments that rising inequality is not a short-term anomaly, but a deep long-term trend in capitalist societies, then turns to a thoughtful discussion of Piketty's proposed policy responses

■ Discussion Questions

1. (General) The authors of this chapter believe that income and wealth distribution is as important as income and wealth creation, and consider greater economic equality an important macroeconomic goal. What are some arguments for and against this position? Where do you come down in the debate?

2. (General) "A rising tide lifts all boats," proclaimed John F. Kennedy as he lobbied for pro-business tax cuts in the early 1960s. Have recent periods of economic growth (or "booms") lifted all boats? How have stockholders fared versus wage earners? How has the distribution of income and wealth by income group and by race changed?

3. (Article 5.1) Why do conservatives argue that inequality is good for economic growth? What counterarguments does Tilly use to challenge this traditional view of the "tradeoff" between inequality and growth? What evidence convinces Tilly that equality is good for economic growth? Does that evidence convince you?

4. (Article 5.2) What evidence convinces Miller that there is a fundamental conflict between the interest of workers and the interest of stockholders?

5. (Article 5.3) MacEwan shows that union strength and economic inequality are negatively associated (when one is high, the other is low). What possible explanations does MacEwan offer? Is there good reason to believe that higher union-

ization was the cause of greater equality in the past, and the decline of unions explains increased inequality in recent years?

6. (Article 5.4) Describe the evidence MacEwan uses to support one of the reasons why wages have grown so slowly.

7. (Article 5.5) In Table 1, which data indicate that since 1968 the position of African Americans has improved? In which areas do they still lag behind the position of whites? Which data indicate that the position of African Americans has gotten worse?

8. (Article 5.6) MacEwan argues that income inequality within most large countries has widened in recent decades, while income inequality between countries has narrowed somewhat. Which of these trends would you consider more significant?

9. (Article 5.7) Economist Thomas Piketty proposes a global tax on wealth as a response to rising inequality. Do you think that his solution is feasible? Is it desirable?

Article 5.1

GEESE, GOLDEN EGGS, AND TRAPS
Why inequality is bad for the economy.

BY CHRIS TILLY
July/August 2004

Whenever progressives propose ways to redistribute wealth from the rich to those with low and moderate incomes, conservative politicians and economists accuse them of trying to kill the goose that lays the golden egg. The advocates of unfettered capitalism proclaim that inequality is good for the economy because it promotes economic growth. Unequal incomes, they say, provide the incentives necessary to guide productive economic decisions by businesses and individuals. Try to reduce inequality, and you'll sap growth. Furthermore, the conservatives argue, growth actually promotes equality by boosting the have-nots more than the haves. So instead of fiddling with who gets how much, the best way to help those at the bottom is to pump up growth.

But these conservative prescriptions are absolutely, dangerously wrong. Instead of the goose-killer, equality turns out to be the goose. Inequality stifles growth; equality gooses it up. Moreover, economic expansion does not necessarily promote equality—instead, it is the types of jobs and the rules of the economic game that matter most.

Inequality: Goose or Goose-Killer?

The conservative argument may be wrong, but it's straightforward. Inequality is good for the economy, conservatives say, because it provides the right incentives for innovation and economic growth. First of all, people will only have the motivation to work hard, innovate, and invest wisely if the economic system rewards them for good economic choices and penalizes bad ones. Robin Hood–style policies that collect from the wealthy and help those who are worse off violate this principle. They reduce the payoff to smart decisions and lessen the sting of dumb ones. The result: people and companies are bound to make less efficient decisions. "We must allow [individuals] to fail, as well as succeed, and we must replace the nanny state with a regime of self-reliance and self-respect," writes conservative lawyer Stephen Kinsella in *The Freeman: Ideas on Liberty* (not clear how the free woman fits in). To prove their point, conservatives point to the former state socialist countries, whose economies had become stagnant and inefficient by the time they fell at the end of the 1980s.

If you don't buy this incentive story, there's always the well-worn trickle-down theory. To grow, the economy needs productive investments: new offices, factories, computers, and machines. To finance such investments takes a pool of savings. The rich save a larger fraction of their incomes than those less well-off. So to spur growth, give more to the well-heeled (or at least take less away from them in the form of taxes), and give less to the down-and-out. The rich will save their money and then invest it, promoting growth that's good for everyone.

Unfortunately for trickle-down, the brilliant economist John Maynard Keynes debunked the theory in his *General Theory of Employment, Interest, and Money* in

1936. Keynes, whose precepts guided liberal U.S. economic policy from the 1940s through the 1970s, agreed that investments must be financed out of savings. But he showed that most often it's changes in investment that drive savings, rather than the other way around. When businesses are optimistic about the future and invest in building and retooling, the economy booms, all of us make more money, and we put some of it in banks, 401(k)s, stocks, and so on. That is, saving grows to match investment. When companies are glum, the process runs in reverse, and savings shrink to equal investment. This leads to the "paradox of thrift": if people try to save too much, businesses will see less consumer spending, will invest less, and total savings will end up diminishing rather than growing as the economy spirals downward. A number of Keynes's followers added the next logical step: shifting money from the high-saving rich to the high-spending rest of us, and not the other way around, will spur investment and growth.

Of the two conservative arguments in favor of inequality, the incentive argument is a little weightier. Keynes himself agreed that people needed financial consequences to steer their actions, but questioned whether the differences in payoffs needed to be so huge. Certainly state socialist countries' attempts to replace material incentives with moral exhortation have often fallen short. In 1970, the Cuban government launched the Gran Zafra (Great Harvest), an attempt to reap 10 million tons of sugar cane with (strongly encouraged) volunteer labor. Originally inspired by Che Guevara's ideal of the New Socialist Man (not clear how the New Socialist Woman fit in), the effort ended with Fidel Castro tearfully apologizing to the Cuban people in a nationally broadcast speech for letting wishful thinking guide economic policy.

But before conceding this point to the conservatives, let's look at the evidence about the connection between equality and growth. Economists William Easterly of New York University and Gary Fields of Cornell University have recently summarized this evidence:

- Countries, and regions within countries, with more equal incomes grow faster. (These growth figures do not include environmental destruction or improvement. If they knocked off points for environmental destruction and added points for environmental improvement, the correlation between equality and growth would be even stronger, since desperation drives poor people to adopt environmentally destructive practices such as rapid deforestation.)
- Countries with more equally distributed land grow faster.
- Somewhat disturbingly, more ethnically homogeneous countries and regions grow faster—presumably because there are fewer ethnically based inequalities.
- In addition, more worker rights are associated with higher rates of economic growth, according to Josh Bivens and Christian Weller, economists at two Washington think tanks, the Economic Policy Institute and the Center for American Progress.

These patterns recommend a second look at the incentive question. In fact, more equality can actually strengthen incentives and opportunities to produce.

Equality as the Goose

Equality can boost growth in several ways. Perhaps the simplest is that study after study has shown that farmland is more productive when cultivated in small plots. So organizations promoting more equal distribution of land, like Brazil's Landless Workers' Movement, are not just helping the landless poor—they're contributing to agricultural productivity!

Another reason for the link between equality and growth is what Easterly calls "match effects," which have been highlighted in research by Stanford's Paul Roemer and others in recent years. One example of a match effect is the fact that well-educated people are most productive when working with others who have lots of schooling. Likewise, people working with computers are more productive when many others have computers (so that, for example, e-mail communication is widespread, and know-how about computer repair and software is easy to come by). In very unequal societies, highly educated, computer-using elites are surrounded by majorities with little education and no computer access, dragging down their productivity. This decreases young people's incentive to get more education and businesses' incentive to invest in computers, since the payoff will be smaller.

Match effects can even matter at the level of a metropolitan area. Urban economist Larry Ledebur looked at income and employment growth in 85 U.S. cities and their neighboring suburbs. He found that where the income gap between those in the suburbs and those in the city was largest, income and job growth was slower for everyone.

"Pressure effects" also help explain why equality sparks growth. Policies that close off the low-road strategy of exploiting poor and working people create pressure effects, driving economic elites to search for investment opportunities that pay off by boosting productivity rather than squeezing the have-nots harder. For example, where workers have more rights, they will place greater demands on businesses. Business owners will respond by trying to increase productivity, both to remain profitable even after paying higher wages, and to find ways to produce with fewer workers. The CIO union drives in U.S. mass production industries in the 1930s and 1940s provide much of the explanation for the superb productivity growth of the 1950s and 1960s. (The absence of pressure effects may help explain why many past and present state socialist countries have seen slow growth, since they tend to offer numerous protections for workers but no right to organize independent unions.) Similarly, if a government buys out large land-holdings in order to break them up, wealthy families who simply kept their fortunes tied up in land for generations will look for new, productive investments. Industrialization in Asian "tigers" South Korea and Taiwan took off in the 1950s on the wings of funds freed up in exactly this way.

Inequality, Conflict, and Growth

Inequality hinders growth in another important way: it fuels social conflict. Stark inequality in countries such as Bolivia and Haiti has led to chronic conflict that hobbles economic growth. Moreover, inequality ties up resources in unproductive uses such as paying for large numbers of police and security guards—attempts to prevent individuals from redistributing resources through theft.

Ethnic variety is connected to slower growth because, on the average, more ethnically diverse countries are also more likely to be ethnically divided. In other words, the problem isn't ethnic variety itself, but racism and ethnic conflict that can exist among diverse populations. In nations like Guatemala, Congo, and Nigeria, ethnic strife has crippled growth—a problem alien to ethnically uniform Japan and South Korea. The reasons are similar to some of the reasons that large class divides hurt growth. Where ethnic divisions (which can take tribal, language, religious, racial, or regional forms) loom large, dominant ethnic groups seek to use government power to better themselves at the expense of other groups, rather than making broad-based investments in education and infrastructure. This can involve keeping down the underdogs—slower growth in the U.S. South for much of the country's history was linked to the Southern system of white supremacy. Or it can involve seizing the surplus of ethnic groups perceived as better off—in the extreme, Nazi Germany's expropriation and genocide of the Jews, who often held professional and commercial jobs.

Of course, the solution to such divisions is not "ethnic cleansing" so that each country has only one ethnic group—in addition to being morally abhorrent, this is simply impossible in a world with 191 countries and 5,000 ethnic groups. Rather, the solution is to diminish ethnic inequalities. Once the 1964 Civil Rights Act forced the South to drop racist laws, the New South's economic growth spurt began. Easterly reports that in countries with strong rule of law, professional bureaucracies, protection of contracts, and freedom from expropriation—all rules that make it harder for one ethnic group to economically oppress another—ethnic diversity has no negative impact on growth.

If more equality leads to faster growth so everybody benefits, why do the rich typically resist redistribution? Looking at the ways that equity seeds growth helps us understand why. The importance of pressure effects tells us that the wealthy often don't think about more productive ways to invest or reorganize their businesses until they are forced to. But also, if a country becomes very unequal, it can get stuck in an "inequality trap." Any redistribution involves a tradeoff for the rich. They lose by giving up part of their wealth, but they gain a share in increased economic growth. The bigger the disparity between the rich and the rest, the more the rich have to lose, and the less likely that the equal share of boosted growth they'll get will make up for their loss. Once the gap goes beyond a certain point, the wealthy have a strong incentive to restrict democracy, and to block spending on education which might lead the poor to challenge economic injustice—making reform that much harder.

Does Economic Growth Reduce Inequality?

If inequality isn't actually good for the economy, what about the second part of the conservatives' argument—that growth itself promotes equality? According to the conservatives, those who care about equality should simply pursue growth and wait for equality to follow.

"A rising tide lifts all boats," President John F. Kennedy famously declared. But he said nothing about which boats will rise fastest when the economic tide comes in.

Growth does typically reduce poverty, according to studies reviewed by economist Gary Fields, though some "boats"—especially families with strong barriers to participating in the labor force—stay "stuck in the mud." But inequality can increase at the same time that poverty falls, if the rich gain even faster than the poor do. True, sustained periods of low unemployment, like that in the late 1990s United States, do tend to raise wages at the bottom even faster than salaries at the top. But growth after the recessions of 1991 and 2001 began with years of "jobless recoveries"— growth with inequality.

For decades the prevailing view about growth and inequality within countries was that expressed by Simon Kuznets in his 1955 presidential address to the American Economic Association. Kuznets argued that as countries grew, inequality would first increase, then decrease. The reason is that people will gradually move from the low-income agricultural sector to higher-income industrial jobs—with inequality peaking when the workforce is equally divided between low- and high-income sectors. For mature industrial economies, Kuznets's proposition counsels focusing on growth, assuming that it will bring equity. In developing countries, it calls for enduring current inequality for the sake of future equity and prosperity.

But economic growth doesn't automatically fuel equality. In 1998, economists Klaus Deininger and Lyn Squire traced inequality and growth over time in 48 countries. Five followed the Kuznets pattern, four followed the reverse pattern (decreasing inequality followed by an increase), and the rest showed no systematic pattern. In the United States, for example:

- incomes became more equal during the 1930s through 1940s New Deal period (a time that included economic decline followed by growth);
- from the 1950s through the 1970s, income gaps lessened during booms and expanded during slumps;
- from the late 1970s forward, income inequality worsened fairly consistently, whether the economy was stagnating or growing.

The reasons are not hard to guess. The New Deal introduced widespread unionization, a minimum wage, social security, unemployment insurance, and welfare. Since the late 1970s, unions have declined, the inflation-adjusted value of the minimum wage has fallen, and the social safety net has been shredded. In the United States, as elsewhere, growth only promotes equality if policies and institutions to support equity are in place.

Trapped?

Let's revisit the idea of an inequality trap. The notion is that as the gap between the rich and everybody else grows wider, the wealthy become more willing to give up overall growth in return for the larger share they're getting for themselves. The "haves" back policies to control the "have-nots," instead of devoting social resources to educating the poor so they'll be more productive.

Sound familiar? It should. After two decades of widening inequality, the last few years have brought us massive tax cuts that primarily benefit the wealthiest, at the expense of investment in infrastructure and the education, child care, and income supports that would help raise less well-off kids to be productive adults. Federal and state governments have cranked up expenditures on prisons, police, and "homeland security," and Republican campaign organizations have devoted major resources to keeping blacks and the poor away from the polls. If the economic patterns of the past are any indication, we're going to pay for these policies in slower growth and stagnation unless we can find our way out of this inequality trap. ❏

Sources: William Easterly, *The Elusive Quest for Growth*, MIT Press 2001; Gary S. Fields, *Distribution and Development*, MIT Press 2001; Josh Bivens and Christian Weller, "Rights make might: Ensuring workers' rights as a strategy for economic growth," Economic Policy Institute 2003.

THE STOCK MARKET AND CLASS CONFLICT
Trump's State of the Union Message and the Economy

BY JOHN MILLER
March/April 2018

Since the election, we have created 2.4 million new jobs. After years of wage stagnation, we are finally seeing rising wages.

Unemployment claims have hit a 45-year low. African-American unemployment stands at the lowest rate ever recorded.

The stock market has smashed one record after another, gaining $8 trillion in value.

—President Donald Trump's State of the Union address as prepared for delivery and released by the White House, January 30, 2018.

Jay Powell started work as Federal Reserve chairman on Monday, and stocks promptly fell by the largest single-session point decline on record.

The paradox of the equity-market correction is that it's taking place even as the real economy looks stronger than it's been since at least 2005 and maybe 1999.

—"The Return to Normal Risk," by the Editorial Board, *Wall Street Journal*, February 5, 2018.

"**N**ever mind!" That's how Gilda Radner's character Emily Litella ended each of her error-filled commentaries on the *Saturday Night Live* news report. "Never mind!" would have been a fitting close to the economic news in President Trump's first State of the Union address.

Just three days after his speech, volatility had returned to Trump's record-breaking stock market, at one point wiping out the euphoria-fueled gains made since the passage of the Republican tax cut for the wealthy in late December. And the Bureau of Labor Statistics reported that the record low African-American unemployment rate, which Trump's policies had done little to bring about, was a full percentage point higher in January 2018.

Nor was it the case that job growth had accelerated during Trump's first year in office. Counting from the first of the year, instead of from Trump's election, the economy added 2.1 million jobs during 2017, fewer jobs than the economy had added in any of Obama's last six years in office.

Wages and the Stock Market

The one bit of news that had staying power was Trump's claim that, "we are finally seeing rising wages." Average hourly wages for private-sector (nonfarm) employees rose 2.9% from January 2017 to January 2018, the highest rate since 2008. That was good news, a pick-up from the 2.3% rate during the second term of the Obama administration. But it was a far from a harbinger of the arrival of widespread economic prosperity in the ninth year of the long but slow economic expansion since the end of the Great Recession. To begin with, adjusted for inflation, average hourly earnings increased just 0.8%. What's more, the gains in earnings were concentrated among managerial workers, and were highest in the financial sector. Wages of non-supervisory workers, who hold about four-fifths of private sector jobs, rose just 2.4%, and only 0.1% after adjusting for inflation. On top of that, without the increase in the minimum wage in 18 states that went into effect on the first of the year, those numbers would have been lower. Finally, 2.4% is well below the 3.8% increase in hourly wages of non-supervisory personnel during the last three years of the long economic expansion in the 1990s.

Nonetheless, the pick-up in wage growth was enough to send the stock market into paroxysms of volatility. In one way, the *Wall Street Journal* editors were right, the stock market volatility was a return to normal. The Standard & Poor's index of the price of 500 stocks, the benchmark used by most professional investors, had almost tripled in value from a low in March 2009 near the end of the Great Recession, with only four corrections, defined as a 10% or greater decline in stock prices. That track record, and 15 straight months without a market decline, fueled a growing sense that stock prices only went up. The 10.2% decline in stock prices (measured by the S&P 500) in early February was a harsh reminder of the risks inherent in stock investment, or what the editors call "normal risk."

In another way, however, the stock market has been operating in its normal way all along: Good news for investors on Wall Street came at the expense of bad news for workers on Main Street. As the stock market soared since March 2009, wage growth was kept in check. But when Wall Street was coming out on top, the conflict between wage growth and stock returns was of little concern to the editors. Only when the cumulative effects of over eight years of economic growth began to pay off in wage gains for workers and volatility returned to the stock market did the *WSJ* editors find it paradoxical that the interests of workers on Main Street and investors on Wall Street were not aligned.

It's No Paradox; It's Class Conflict.

But that conflict is hardly surprising. The stock market boom did little to make most workers better off. Stock returns go overwhelmingly to the wealthy. Economist Edward Wolff reports that in 2016 some 84% of stocks are owned by the wealthiest 10% of households. The richest 1% of households alone own two-fifths (40.3%) of stocks, more than twice the share of the bottom 90% of households. Fully one-half of households own no stock. Just 13.9% of households directly own stocks, and another 35.4% of households own stock indirectly (e.g., through retirement funds).

What wealth most workers have is in their homes. While national housing prices increased 43.7% from their December 2011 low to November 2017, that was just one-seventh of the threefold rise in stocks prices.

So it remains that most workers depend on wage growth, not the stock market gains or appreciating housing values, to improve their economic position. And contrary to most mainstream economics reporting, we are not all—workers and investors alike—on the same elevator, moving up or down in concert.

While the *WSJ* editors are rather puzzled by the adverse effects of wages increases on stock market returns, the conflict is not mysterious. Here's why.

Economic growth creates jobs, lowering unemployment. Low unemployment gives workers greater bargaining power to press for higher wages and benefits. Businesses can either absorb these higher labor costs by cutting profits, or pass them along by raising prices.

Either way, investors lose out. If their profits decline, corporations may pay their stockholders less in dividends and/or see their share prices fall. If prices rise, that inflation cuts into the real value of investor assets and may provoke the Federal Reserve to hike interest rates, dampening economic growth.

Concerns that the Fed might press harder on the economic brakes contributed to the February stock sell off. Higher interest rates make it harder to borrow, which would likely reduce the money going into the stock market. In addition, higher interest rates increase the rate of return on bonds, one of the chief alternatives to purchasing stocks. For instance, by mid-February the yield for holding a nearly risk-free ten-year Treasury bond had increased to 2.9% from its 2.3% interest rate a year earlier. Both these effects—higher costs of borrowing and higher yields on bonds—dampen the demand for stocks and lower stock prices.

On the other hand, when wage gains are kept in check and the Fed delivers rock-bottom interest rates, as was the case in the first eight years of the economic recovery, profits soar and Wall Street investors prosper, while those on Main Street flounder.

The Markets Protest Too Much

But are investors' fears of higher costs and inflation justified? Labor compensation does make up the largest chunk of business costs and rising labor costs can eat into business profits. And labor compensation (wages and benefits) as a share of the output of the non-farm sector did improve somewhat from its low point in 2011. But the labor share remains lower than any time before the 2008 onset of the Great Recession, and corporate profits as a share of national income continue at near record levels.

Also, "unit labor costs," which measure the actual dollar costs firms pay for employees to make a unit of output, have shown less upward pressure on costs than the wage increases that have rendered investors apoplectic. Despite a sizeable increase in the fourth quarter of 2017, unit labor costs remain below their levels in the second half of 2016.

These numbers reveal the unwillingness of the financial powers to share with workers the gains of economic growth even when increases in labor costs are modest and profit rates continue to outdistanced those of earlier periods.

But that's hardly new. In the midst of the Great Depression, Woody Guthrie said Wall Street was "the street that keeps the rest of us off Easy Street." It still is. ❑

Sources: "Employment Situation Summary," Bureau of Labor Statistics, Feb. 2, 2018; "Productivity and Costs," Bureau of Labor Statistics, Feb. 1, 2018; Chuck Jones, "Trump's Economic Scorecard:

One Year Since Inauguration," *Forbes*, Jan. 18, 2018; Julien Ponthus and Ritvik Carvalho, "Explainer: Why higher wages are whacking global stock markets," Reuters, Feb. 5, 2018; Edward Wolff, "The Asset Price Meltdown and the Wealth of the Middle Class," National Bureau of Economic Research Working Paper, No.18559.

Article 5.3

UNIONS AND INCOME INEQUALITY

BY ARTHUR MacEWAN
November/December 2011

> Dear Dr. Dollar:
> *I know unions have shrunk in the United States, but by how much? And how best to respond to my right-wing friends who claim that unions are bad for the economy?* —Rich Sanford, Hardwick, Mass.

Take a look at the graph below. The two lines on the graph show for the period 1917 through 2007 (1) labor union membership as a percentage of the total U.S. work force and (2) the percentage of all income obtained by the highest 1% of income recipients. So the lines show, roughly, the strength of unions and the distribution of income for the past century. (John Miller and I developed this graph for our book *Economic Collapse, Economic Change*.)

The picture is pretty clear. In periods when unions have been strong, income distribution has been less unequal. In periods when unions have been weak, income distribution has been more unequal. In the post–World War II era, union members were about 25% of the labor force; today the figure is about 10%. In those postwar years, the highest-income 1% got 10% to 12% of all income; today they get about 25%.

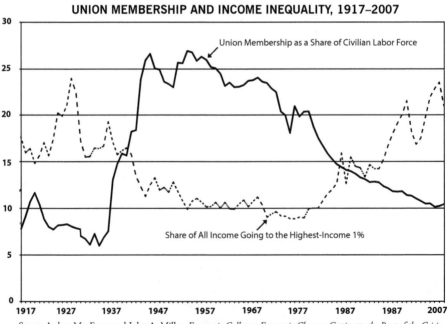

UNION MEMBERSHIP AND INCOME INEQUALITY, 1917–2007

Union Membership as a Share of Civilian Labor Force

Share of All Income Going to the Highest-Income 1%

Source: Arthur MacEwan and John A. Miller, *Economic Collapse, Economic Change: Getting to the Root of the Crisis* (M.E. Sharpe, 2011).

The causation between union strength and income distribution is not simple. Nonetheless, there are some fairly direct connections. For example, when unions are strong, they can push for higher wages and thus we see a more equal distribution of income. Also, strong unions can have an impact on the political process, bringing about policies that are more favorable to workers.

But causation can work in the other direction as well. Great income inequality puts more power in the hands of the rich, and they can use that power to get policies put in place that weaken unions—for example, getting people who are hostile to unions appointed to the National Labor Relations Board.

And then there are other factors that affect both union strength and income distribution—for example, the changing structure of the global economy, which places U.S. workers in competition with poorly paid workers elsewhere. Yet the structure of the global economy is itself affected by the distribution of political power. For example, the "free trade" agreements that the United States has established with other countries generally ignore workers' rights (to say nothing of the environment) and go to great lengths to protect the rights of corporations. So, again, causation works in complex ways, and there are certainly other factors that need to be taken account of to explain the relationship shown in the graph.

However one explains the relationship, it is hard to imagine that we can return to a more equal distribution of income while unions remain weak. This means, at the very least, that the interests of unions and of people at the bottom of the income distribution are bound up with one another. Building stronger unions is an important part of fighting poverty—and the hunger and homelessness that are the clear manifestations of poverty.

One important thing to notice in the graph: In the post–World War II years, economic growth was the best we have seen. Certainly no one can claim that it is impossible for strong unions and a more equal distribution of income to co-exist with fairly rapid economic growth. Indeed, we might even argue that strong unions and a more equal distribution of income create favorable conditions for economic growth!

Stronger unions, it turns out, could be good preventive medicine for much of what ails our economy. ❑

Article 5.4

WHY ARE WAGES GROWING SO SLOWLY?

BY ARTHUR MacEWAN
September/October 2017

> Dear Dr. Dollar:
> *With such low unemployment these days, why are wages growing so slowly?*
> —Anonymous, via email

In June 1973, the average hourly wage of production and non-supervisory workers was $4.12. In terms of June 2017 purchasing power, this 1973 wage was $22.72. In June 2017, the actual average wage for this group of workers was $22.03. For no year in this 44 year period was the wage higher in terms of purchasing power (i.e., inflation adjusted) than in 1973. (For someone working full time, 2000 hours, for a whole year, $22.03 yields an annual income of $44,060, 66% above the poverty line for a family of four but about 20% below the median family income.)

In other words, on average, wages have stagnated for almost half a century. The slow growth of wages in recent years should, then, be viewed in this longer context.

Not So Good but Not So Bad

In recent years, as the unemployment rate has fallen, average wages have slowly increased, rising by 4.7% in the five years from June 2012 to June 2017. Not great. But compared to what happened to wages in similar periods following the three previous recessions, this

FIGURE 1: DISCONNECT BETWEEN PRODUCTIVITY AND TYPICAL WORKER'S COMPENSATION, 1948–2013

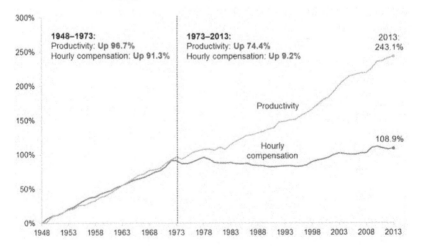

Source: Economic Policy Institute (EPI), *Raising America's Pay: Why It's Our Central Economic Policy Challenge*; Bureau of Labor Statistics (LCS) and Bureau or Economic Analysis (BEA) data; figure reproduced here courtesy of EPI.

is not so bad: following the recession of the early 1980s, wages simply did not rise; after the early 1990s recession, the increase was also about 4.7%; and in the years following the early 2000s recession, the increase was only 2.5%.

There has been a connection between the unemployment rate and the wages in each of these periods. After the early 1980s recession, the unemployment rate never fell below 5%; after the early 2000s recession, the rate did fall below 5%, but not as low as after the early 1990s recession or after the Great Recession. So these experiences fit roughly with the pattern that low unemployment increases workers' bargaining power and makes it possible for them to push up their wages. When workers have more options, they have more power.

But bargaining power is not so simple—it does not depend on the unemployment rate alone—and wage increases do not follow automatically from a drop in the unemployment rate. First of all, there is a lag between the time unemployment drops and the time workers are able to push up their wages, and that lag time can be especially long following a severely disruptive recession, like the Great Recession. Also, there is a measurement problem: The official unemployment rate does not take into account the number of people who have given up looking for jobs during the downturn, but who would be ready to re-enter the labor force as things improve. (The official unemployment rate is defined as the number of people employed as a percent of the labor force; the labor force, in turn, is defined as the number of people employed plus the number of people *actively* looking for jobs.)

Perhaps a better measure of the labor-market situation would be the labor force participation rate (LFPR, the percent of people 16 and over employed working or ac-

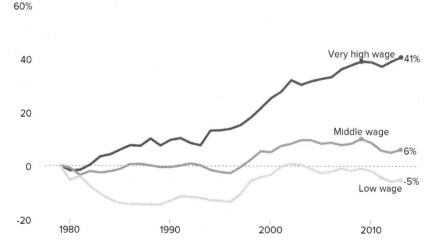

FIGURE 2: CUMULATIVE CHANGE IN REAL HOURLY WAGE OF ALL WORKERS, BY WAGE PERCENTILE, 1979–2013

*Low wage is 10th percentile, middle wage is 50th percentile, very high wage is 95th percentile.

Source: Economic Policy Institute (EPI), *Why America's Workers Need Faster Wagre Growth And What We Can Do About It*; Current Population Survey (CPS) Outgoing Rotation Group microdata; figure reproduced here courtesy of EPI.

tively looking for jobs). Leading into the Great Recession, in June 2008, the LFPR was 66.1%. In June of 2017, this rate was down to 62.8%. While part of this decline might be explained by the aging of the population (more people who have no intention of re-entering the labor force), part of it is surely a result of people giving up but who would be ready to take jobs again if more jobs were available. So the official unemployment rate makes it look as if the labor market is "tighter" than it really is. And a less-tight labor market tends to mean less power for workers.

The Important Reasons

There are, however, more important reasons that the relatively low unemployment rate does not readily translate into a strong upsurge of wages. These reasons are "more important" because they lie in long-term phenomena that help explain the several decades of wage stagnation. Foremost among these reasons is the decline of labor unions. Union membership in the private sector has fallen dramatically, from 24.2% in 1973 to 6.4% in 2016. (See table.) Bargaining on their own, workers are much less powerful and much less effective than when they bargain as a group—i.e., as a union. Furthermore, while workers have become less powerful, employers have become more powerful as business has become increasingly concentrated in a smaller number of firms. It is, for example, one thing to bargain with a local store, even a local chain, and quite another to bargain with a behemoth like Amazon or Walmart.

Explanations sometimes advanced for the decline of unions include globalization and the smaller share of the workforce in large factories (e.g., auto and steel). These phenomena are not irrelevant, but much of the decline is explained by political factors. For one, Republic administrations have been able to shape the National Labor Relations Board (NLRB) in ways that make its rulings anti-union (and Democratic administrations have not wholly reversed the situation). For example, without effective NLRB protection during the Reagan administration, workers leading attempts to organize unions in their work places faced a 20% to 25% chance of being fired, and the odds were similar in the administrations of George H.W. Bush and George W. Bush. Another factor weakening unions' and workers' ability to push up wages has been the erosion of the minimum wage as Washington has declined to increase the minimum to keep up with inflation. The current federal minimum wage of $7.25 is 18% below the 1973 minimum wage, in terms of real buying power. (The 1973 federal minimum wage was $1.60, which is equivalent to $8.84 in terms of 2017 prices—a July to July comparison.)

On top of government actions, employers have taken increasingly aggressive anti-union efforts in recent decades. A whole industry has arisen to guide employers in preventing success of union-organizing campaigns. Anti-union consulting firms have certainly contributed to the union membership decline. On the other side, some established unions have been excessively timid in developing new organizing drives.

And then there is globalization—but this too has been, in part, a political phenomenon. Global trade and investment agreements have been designed to bring about greater mobility for firms—to give them more options, which translates into greater power in their relations with workers. The mobility of firms has led to more movement of plants to low-wage sites outside the United States. As Kate Brofenbrenner of Cornell University's School of Industrial and Labor Relations has pointed out in a study related to the North American Free Trade Agreement (NAFTA), the threat of plant movement has become increasingly credible, significantly weakening the effectiveness of union organizing drives. What is true in the context of NAFTA is also true with regard to the reduction of U.S. trade restrictions with other low-wage countries. It is only somewhat of an exaggeration to say the labor market has now become global, and the unemployment rate in the United States is only a minor indicator of the "tightness" of the labor market. It is hard for workers in the U.S. to push up their wages when they can be replaced by workers, in many parts of the world, who will accept much lower wages and who often face more severe repression of their right to unionize.

But what about workers in the public sector, where the percentage who are in unions has increased substantially over recent decades? (See Table.) They too have been affected by the larger economic and political situation, in spite of their higher rate of unionization. While union membership has helped, it is difficult for public-sector workers to improve their positions when private-sectors workers—the people who pay the taxes that provide the wages for the public-sector workers—are experiencing wage stagnation. Also, the anti-tax political climate, including of course the unwillingness of governments at all levels to raise taxes on the rich (quite the opposite, in fact), has put stress on public budgets. (On top of this, it appears likely that coming Supreme Court rulings will apply "right to work" regulations on public-sector workers, severely undermining their unions' operations.)

Measurement and Other Factors

Many other reasons have been offered in the media (just take a look on the web) as to why wages have been slow to rise in recent years as the unemployment rate has fallen. One explanation involves a measurement problem. As relatively high-wage workers (including many prime-age workers) retire or are pushed out, they are replaced with new, low-wage entrants to the labor market. Thus, even if the wages of all other workers remain the same, the average falls. This probably does make wage increases appear lower than they really are.

Another explanation for poor wage growth—put forth, for example, in a recent *New York Times* article—is that wage increases have been limited because productivity (output per worker) has grown so slowly since the Great Recession. The problem with this argument is that it assumes a link between productivity growth and

LABOR UNION MEMBERSHIP AS A PERCENT OF WAGE AND SALARY WORKERS 1973 AND 2016

Year	All Workers	Private Sector	Public Sector
1973	24.0%	24.2%	23.0%
2016	10.7%	6.4%	34.4%

Source: unionstats.com.

wage growth. Clearly, however, that link has been broken since the 1970s; from then onward, wages have stagnated as productivity has risen right along.

When all is said and done, even under the best of circumstances, it takes time for a strong job market—i.e., low unemployment—to lead to significant wage increases. It is certainly possible that the coming years will see some more meaningful improvement. Don't hold your breath, but it might happen. ❏

Sources: All data used in this article, unless otherwise indicated are from the Bureau of Labor Statistics (BLS), either directly or via the Economic Report of the President, 2017, and the Census Bureau's American Community Survey. In some cases—e.g., to determine the buying power in 2017 of wages in earlier years—the BLS Consumer Price Index Calculator was used (bls.gov). Also: Neil Irwin, "The Question Isn't Why Wage Growth Is So Low. It's Why It's So High," *New York Times*, May 26, 2017; John Schmitt and Ben Zipperer, *Dropping the Ax: Illegal Firings During Union Elections, 1951-2007*, Center for Economic and Policy Research, Washington, DC, March 2009; Kate Brofenbrenner, "Organizing in the NAFTA Environment: How Companies Use 'Free Trade' to Stop Unions" (digitalcommons.ilr.cornell.edu).

Article 5.5

FIFTY YEARS AFTER THE KERNER COMMISSION

African Americans are better off in many ways but are still disadvantaged by racial inequality.

BY JANELLE JONES, JOHN SCHMITT, AND VALERIE WILSON

February 2018, Economic Policy Institute

The year 1968 was a watershed in American history and black America's ongoing fight for equality. In April of that year, Martin Luther King Jr. was assassinated in Memphis and riots broke out in cities around the country. Rising against this tragedy, the Civil Rights Act of 1968 outlawing housing discrimination was signed into law. Tommie Smith and John Carlos raised their fists in a black power salute as they received their medals at the 1968 Summer Olympics in Mexico City. Arthur Ashe became the first African American to win the U.S. Open singles title, and Shirley Chisholm became the first African American woman elected to the House of Representatives.

The same year, the National Advisory Commission on Civil Disorders, better known as the Kerner Commission, delivered a report to President Johnson examining the causes of civil unrest in African American communities. The report named "white racism"—leading to "pervasive discrimination in employment, education and housing"—as the culprit, and the report's authors called for a commitment to "the realization of common opportunities for all within a single [racially undivided] society." The Kerner Commission report pulled together a comprehensive array of data to assess the specific economic and social inequities confronting African Americans in 1968.

Where do we stand as a society today? In this brief report, we compare the state of black workers and their families in 1968 with the circumstances of their descendants today, 50 years after the Kerner report was released. We find both good news and bad news. While African Americans are in many ways better off in absolute terms than they were in 1968, they are still disadvantaged in important ways relative to whites. In several important respects, African Americans have actually lost ground relative to whites, and, in a few cases, even relative to African Americans in 1968.

The following are some of the key findings:

- African Americans today are much better educated than they were in 1968 but still lag behind whites in overall educational attainment. More than 90% of younger African Americans (ages 25 to 29) have graduated from high school, compared with just over half in 1968— which means they've nearly closed the gap with white high school graduation rates. They are also more than twice as likely to have a college degree as in 1968 but are still half as likely as young whites to have a college degree.

- The substantial progress in educational attainment of African Americans has been accompanied by significant absolute improvements in wages, incomes, wealth, and health since 1968. But black workers still make only 82.5 cents on every dollar earned by white workers, African Americans are 2.5 times as likely to be in poverty as whites, and the median white family has almost 10 times as much wealth as the median black family.

- With respect to homeownership, unemployment, and incarceration, America has failed to deliver any progress for African Americans over the last five decades. In these areas, their situation has either failed to improve relative to whites or has worsened. In 2017 the black unemployment rate was 7.5%, up from 6.7% in 1968, and is still roughly twice the white unemployment rate. In 2015, the black homeownership rate was just over 40%, virtually unchanged since 1968, and trailing a full 30 points behind the white homeownership rate, which

TABLE 1: SOCIAL AND ECONOMIC CIRCUMSTANCES OF AFRICAN AMERICAN AND WHITE FAMILIES, C. 1968 AND C. 2018

	c. 1968	c. 2018 (most recent available data)	Change
High school graduate rate, adults ages 25–29 (%)			
Black	54.4%	92.3%	37.9 ppt.
White	75.0%	95.6%	20.6 ppt.
Gap (black as % of white)	72.6%	96.5%	
College graduate rate, adults ages 25–29 (%)			
Black	9.1%	22.8%	13.7 ppt.
White	16.2%	42.1%	25.9 ppt.
Gap (black as % of white)	56.0%	54.2%	
Unemployment rate (%)			
Black	6.7%	7.5%	0.8 ppt.
White	3.2%	3.8%	0.6 ppt.
Gap (ratio black to white)	2.1	2.0	
Median hourly wage (2016$)			
Black	$12.16	$15.87	30.5%
White	$17.06	$19.23	12.7%
Gap (black as % of white)	71.3%	82.5%	
Median household income (2016$)			
Black	$28,066	$40,065	42.8%
White	$47,596	$65,041	36.7%
Gap (black as % of white)	59.0%	61.6%	
Poverty rate (%)			
Black	34.7%	21.8%	-12.9 ppt.
White	10.0%	8.8%	-1.2 ppt.
Gap (ratio black to white)	3.5	2.5	

saw modest gains over the same period. And the share of African Americans in prison or jail almost tripled between 1968 and 2016 and is currently more than six times the white incarceration rate.

Educational Attainment

The most important development since 1968 is that African Americans today are much better educated than they were in 1968. These absolute improvements in educational attainment—including substantial increases in both high school and college completion rates—have opened important doors for black workers compared with their counterparts 50 years ago. In relative terms, African Americans today are almost as likely as whites to have completed high school. But even though the share of younger African Americans with a college degree has more than doubled, African Americans today are still only about half as likely to have a college degree as whites of the same age.

	c.1968	c. 2018 (most recent available data)	Change
Median household wealth (2016$)			
Black	$2,467	$17,409	605.7%
White	$47,655	$171,000	258.8%
Gap (black as % of white)	5.2%	10.2%	
Homeownership rate (%)			
Black	41.1%	41.2%	0.1 ppt.
White	65.9%	71.1%	5.2 ppt.
Gap (black as % of white)	62.4%	57.9%	
Infant mortality (per 1,000 births)			
Black	34.9	11.4	-67.4%
White	18.8	4.9	-74.0%
Gap (ratio black to white)	1.9	2.3	
Life expectancy at birth (years)			
Black	64.0 yrs.	75.5 yrs.	11.5 yrs.
White	71.5 yrs.	79.0 yrs.	7.5 yrs.
Gap (black as % of white)	89.5%	95.6%	
Incarcerated population (per 100,000)			
Black	604	1,730	286.3%
White	111	270	242.7%
Gap (ratio black to white)	5.4	6.4	

Notes: In the "Change" column, "ppt." indicates percentage point change—that is, the point difference (absolute difference) between two percentages; percentage (%) change indicates the relative difference between two numbers.

High School Graduation Rates

Over the last five decades, African Americans have seen substantial gains in high school completion rates. In 1968, just over half (54.4%) of 25- to 29-year-old African Americans had a high school diploma. Today, more than nine out of 10 African Americans (92.3%) in the same age range had a high school diploma. (See Table 1 for all data presented in this report.)

The large increase in high school completion rates helped to close the gap relative to whites. In 1968, African Americans trailed whites by more than 20 percentage points (75.0% of whites had completed high school, compared with 54.4% of blacks). In the most recent data, the gap is just 3.3 percentage points (95.6% for whites versus 92.3% for African Americans).

College Graduation Rates

College graduation rates have also improved for African Americans. Among 25- to 29-year-olds, less than one in 10 (9.1%) had a college degree in 1968, a figure that has climbed to almost one in four (22.8%) today.

Over the same period, however, college completion expanded for whites at a similar pace, rising from 16.2% in 1968 to 42.1% today, leaving the relative situation of African Americans basically unchanged: In 1968 blacks were just over half (56.0%) as likely as whites to have a college degree, a situation that is essentially the same today (54.2%).

We would expect that these kinds of increases in the absolute levels of formal education would translate into large improvements in economic and related outcomes for African Americans. The rest of our indicators test the validity of this assumption.

Unemployment

The unemployment rate for African Americans in 2017 (the last full year of data) was 7.5%, 0.8% points higher than it was in 1968 (6.7%). The unemployment rate for whites was 3.8% in 2017 and 3.2% in 1968.

The unemployment data for these two years, almost 50 years apart, demonstrate a longstanding and unfortunate economic regularity: The unemployment rate for black workers is consistently about twice as high as it is for white workers.

Wages and Income

Hourly Wages

The inflation-adjusted hourly wage of the typical black worker rose 30.5% between 1968 and 2016, or about 0.6% per year. This slow rate of growth is particularly disappointing given the large increase in educational attainment among African Americans over these decades.

Even slower real wage growth (about 0.2% per year) for the typical white worker—albeit starting from a higher initial wage—meant that African Americans did modestly close the racial wage gap over the last five decades. But, in 2016, by the hourly wage measure used here, the typical black worker still only made 82.5 cents on every dollar earned by the typical white worker.

Household Income

The inflation-adjusted annual income of the typical African American household increased 42.8% between 1968 and 2016, slightly outpacing income growth for the typical white household (36.7%). But the typical black household today still receives only 61.6% of the annual income received by the typical white household.

Poverty Rates

The share of African Americans living in poverty has declined substantially in the last five decades. Using the official federal poverty measure as a benchmark, over one-third (34.7%) of African Americans were in poverty in 1968. Today, the share in poverty is just over one in five (21.4%). For whites, the decline in the poverty rate was much smaller, from 10.0% in 1968 to 8.8% in 2016. In the most recent data, African Americans are about 2.5 times as likely to be in poverty as whites. (In 1968, they were 3.5 times as likely to be in poverty.)

Family Wealth

The typical black family had almost no wealth in 1968 ($2,467; data refer to 1963). Today, that figure is about six times larger ($17,409), but it is still not that far from zero when you consider that families typically draw on their wealth for larger expenses, such as meeting basic needs over the course of retirement, paying for their children's college education, putting a down payment on a house, or coping with a job loss or medical crisis.

Over the same period, the wealth of the typical white family almost tripled, from a much higher initial level. In 2016, the median African-American family had only 10.2% of the wealth of the median white family ($17,409 versus $171,000).

Homeownership

One of the most important forms of wealth for working and middle-class families is home equity. Yet, the share of black households that owned their own home remained virtually unchanged between 1968 (41.1%) and today (41.2%). Over the same period, homeownership for white households increased 5.2 percentage points to 71.1%, about 30 percentage points higher than the ownership rate for black households.

Health

Infant Mortality

Over the last five decades, African Americans have experienced enormous improvements in infant mortality rates. The number of deaths per 1,000 live births has fallen from 34.9 in 1968 to 11.4 in the most recent data. Over the same period, whites have also seen dramatic reductions in infant mortality, with rates falling from 18.8 to 4.9 by the same measure.

In relative terms, however, African Americans have fallen behind. In 1968, black infants were about 1.9 times as likely to die as white infants. Today, the rate is 2.3 times higher for African Americans.

Life Expectancy

African Americans' life expectancy at birth has also increased substantially (up 11.5 years) between 1968 and today, outpacing the increase for whites (up 7.5 years). But an African American born today can, on average, still expect to live about 3.5 fewer years than a white person born on the same day.

Incarceration

The share of African Americans in prison or jail almost tripled between 1968 (604 of every 100,000 in the total population) and 2016 (1,730 per 100,000).

The share of whites in prison or jail has also increased dramatically, but from a much lower base. In 1968, about 111 of every 100,000 whites were incarcerated. In the most recent data, the share has increased to 270 per 100,000.

In 1968, African Americans were about 5.4 times as likely as whites to be in prison or jail. Today, African Americans are 6.4 times as likely as whites to be incarcerated, which is especially troubling given that whites are also much more likely to be incarcerated now than they were in 1968.

Appendix: Data Notes

Making comparisons over five decades is challenging. Data sources collected across so many years are not always directly comparable. One issue is that most government data in the 1960s grouped the population into only two groups: "white" and "nonwhite." Following the Kerner Commission and other researchers, our figures here use the "nonwhite" data as a proxy for the circumstances of African Americans at the time. We are confident that the "nonwhite" data do a reasonably good job capturing the experience of African Americans. The 1970 census, which included more detailed information on race than most government data in the 1960s, estimates that people from races other than white and African American (primarily Native Americans and Asians) constituted only about 1.4% of the U.S. population at the time. The 1980 census allowed respondents of any race to identify themselves as Hispanic, and in that year only about 7% did so.

A second issue is that data specifically for 1968 are not always available. In these cases, we either use data for the closest available year, or we use data for years before and after 1968 (usually 1960 and 1970) and interpolate. Our data for "2018" are the most recent data available for each of the indicators we examine, typically either 2015, 2016, or 2017 data. ❑

Sources: *Report of the National Advisory Commission on Civil Disorders: Summary of Report*, National Advisory Commission on Civil Disorders, 1968 (hsdl.org); "Table 104.20. Percentage of Persons 25 to 29 Years Old with Selected Levels of Educational Attainment, by Race/Ethnicity and Sex: Selected Years, 1920 through 2017," *2017 Tables and Figures*, National Center for Education Statistics, 2017 (nces.ed.gov); "Table B-43. Civilian Unemployment Rate by Demographic Characteristic, 1968–2009," *Economic Report of the President 2010* (gpo.gov); Bureau of Labor Statistics, , series ID LNU04000003 and LNU04000006 (bls.gov/data/#unemployment); "Current Population Survey," U.S. Census Bureau and the U.S. Bureau of Labor Statistics (census.

gov); "Table H-5. Race and Hispanic Origin of Householder—Households by Median and Mean Income: 1967 to 2016," *Historical Income Tables*, U.S. Census Bureau (census.gov); "Table 2. Poverty Status of People by Family Relationship, Race, and Hispanic Origin: 1959 to 2016," *Historical Poverty Tables*, U.S. Census Bureau (census.gov); "Chart 3: Average Family Wealth by Race/Ethnicity, 1963–2016," *Nine Charts about Wealth Inequality in America, Urban Institute* (urban.org); Laurie Goodman, Jun Zhu, and Rolf Pendall, "Are Gains in Black Homeownership History?" Urban Institute (urban.org); "Table 11. Infant Mortality Rates, by Race: United States, Selected Years 1950–2015," *Health, United States, 2016—Individual Charts and Tables*, Centers for Disease Control and Prevention (cdc.gov); "Table 15. Life Expectancy at Birth, at Age 65, and at Age 75, by Sex, Race, and Hispanic Origin: United States, Selected Years 1900–2015," *Health, United States, 2016—Individual Charts and Tables*, Centers for Disease Control and Prevention (cdc.gov); Kris Warner, unpublished tabulations of incarcerated population data, using Bureau of Justice Statistics and U.S. Census Bureau data.

Article 5.6

INEQUALITY IN THE WORLD

BY ARTHUR MacEWAN
November/December 2014

> Dear Dr. Dollar:
> *I had thought that neoliberal globalization was making the world more un-equal. But recently I have seen claims that the distribution of income in the world has become more equal. Is this true?*
> —Evan Swinerton, Brookline, Mass.

The answer to these questions depends on what you mean by "in the world." In many countries in the world—including most of the high-income countries and the most populous lower-income countries—the distribution of income has become more unequal. If we look at the income differences among countries, however, the situation has become more equal because per capita income has generally increased more rapidly in lower-income countries than in higher-income countries—though with important exceptions. And if we look at income distribution among all the people in the world—accounting for inequality both within and between countries—it seems that in recent decades the very high degree of inequality has remained about the same. (Before proceeding, please see the warning in the box below.)

Distribution *Within* Countries

Take a look at Figures 1 and 2, which show the changes in the distribution of income within selected countries, several high-income and several low- or middle-income,

---

Warning!

There are many problems in determining the extent of income inequality. The results can differ depending on which measure of inequality we use. Also, there are data difficulties. While some of these difficulties arise from poor reporting, plenty arise from the complexity of the issues. Also, different countries collect income data in different ways and do so in different years. With one exception (explained below), I will not detail the difficulties here, but readers should keep in mind that such difficulties exist.

How we compare incomes in different countries, where relative prices differ, currencies differ, and exchange rates (e.g., the number of Mexican pesos it takes to buy a dollar) often do not tell us accurately the buying power of income in different countries. The income data here are reported in terms of purchasing power parity (PPP) and reported in relation to the U.S. dollar. Comparing incomes in different countries using the PPP method gives us a comparison of the real buying power of income in the different countries. Calculating PPP data is complex and not precise, but the PPP figures are the best we have.

FIGURE 1: INCOME RATIO, TOP 10% TO BOTTOM 10%, SELECTED HIGH-INCOME COUNTRIES

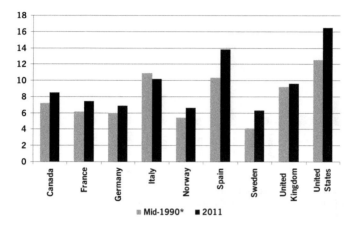

Source: OECD. *For the U.K. the figure is for 1999; for Spain the figure is for 2004; for France the figure is for 1996. For all others the earlier figures are for 1995. The later U.S. figure is for 2012.

over roughly the last two decades. The measure of income distribution used in these graphs is the ratio of the total income of the highest-income tenth of the population to the total income of the lowest-income tenth of the population.

The first thing that stands out in Figure 1 is that the U.S. income distribution is substantially more unequal than those of any of the other countries. Also, the absolute increase by this measure of inequality is greatest in the United States. However, with the sole exception of Italy, all the countries in Figure 1 experienced *rising income inequality.*

Things are different in Figure 2, which includes the 10 most populous lower-income countries (ten of the twelve most populous countries in the world, the United States and Japan being the other two). The degree of inequality is quite high in some of the countries in the graph. Brazil is the extreme case. However, Brazil and most of the other countries in Figure 2 experienced a *reduction of inequality* in this period—though several are still highly unequal. The most populous countries in Figure 2—China, India, and Indonesia—though, experienced rising inequality. These countries are the first, second, and fourth most populous countries in the world (with the United States third).

The data in Figures 1 and 2 illustrate the widespread rise of income inequality *within* countries, especially among high-income countries. Among lower-income countries, the picture is mixed. Although Brazil remains highly unequal, the reduction of inequality in Brazil is important because it has been achieved, at least in part, by policies directed at reducing poverty. Brazil's redistributive policies represent a trend in many Latin American countries—a backlash against the neoliberal policies of preceding decades.

FIGURE 2: INCOME RATIO, TOP 10% TO BOTTOM 10%, MOST POPULOUS LOW- AND MIDDLE-INCOME COUNTRIES

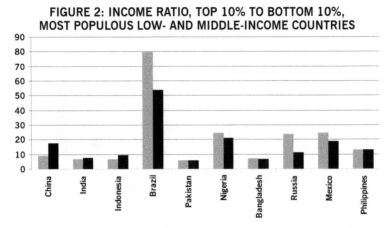

Source: World Bank. *Note:* These countries along with the United States and Japan are the twelve most populous countries in the world. The combined population of these ten accounts for 55% of the world's population in 2014.

FIGURE 3: PER CAPITA GDP, MOST POPULOUS LOW- AND MIDDLE-INCOME COUNTRIES, AS PERCENTAGE OF U.S. GDP (PPP)

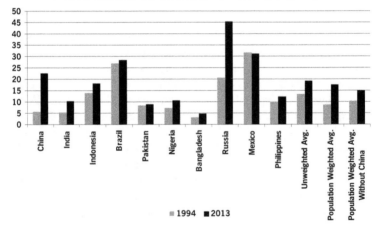

Source: World Bank.

Distribution *Among* Countries

Figure 3 illustrates what has been happening to income distribution *among* countries and indicates that the situation has become more equal because, in general, lower-income countries have grown more rapidly during the last two decades than have higher-income countries. For 1994 and 2013, the two columns in Figure 3 show Gross Domestic Product (GDP) per capita in the ten most populous low- and middle-income countries (listed by population) compared to GDP per capita in the United States. The comparison is in terms of purchasing power parity (PPP).

For nine of these ten countries—Mexico is the exception—GDP per capita rose more rapidly than in the United States. Taken as a group and using an average weighted by population, these ten countries in 1994 had an average GDP per capita 9% of that in the United States, but by 2013 this figure had risen to 17%. The basic result is not due simply to the remarkably rapid economic growth in China. When China is removed from the group, the weighted average still increases over this time period, from 10% to 15%. (This general phenomenon is certainly not a universal phenomenon; several very low-income countries have fallen further and further behind.)

So, if countries are our units of observation, Figure 3 illustrates how things have become more equal since the early 1990s. Going back further in time, comparing countries' incomes weighted by population shows inequality dropping pretty much continuously since 1960, and especially sharply since the early 1990s. But if the average is not weighted by population—thus removing the dominance of China, India, and some other very populous countries—the situation among countries only started to become more equal from 2000. Nonetheless, many low-income countries have been left behind in this period, most notably several countries of Africa. The dominant trend is not the exclusive trend.

Global Distribution Among People

To obtain a truly global estimate of the distribution of income, it is necessary to compare the incomes of people (or families or households) in the world. Availability of data (as well as other data problems) makes such an estimate rough, but useful nonetheless. Branko Milanovic, perhaps the leading expert on these issues, has shown that, from the mid-1980s to 2011, global inequality remained roughly constant, with a slight decline toward the end of this period—likely explained by the greater slowdown of high-income countries compared to low-income countries in the Great Recession. The relative stability of income distribution would seem to result from a rough balance between the reduction of inequality among countries (Figure 3) and the rise of inequality within countries (Figure 1 and the most populous countries of Figure 2).

Milanovic's estimate uses the Gini coefficient, a standard measure of income inequality. The Gini takes account of incomes of the whole population, unlike the measure used in Figures 1 and 2, which focuses on extremes. The Gini can vary from 0 (everyone has the same income) to 1 (all the income goes to one person). For income distribution in almost all countries, the Gini ranges from about 0.27 (Norway) to about 0.65 (South Africa).

For the global population, over the period of Milanovic's estimates, the Gini varies around 0.70—a higher figure, showing a more unequal distribution, than for any single country. However, if inequality were measured by a comparison of extremes, it is likely that inequality would be rising. There remains a large share of the world's population that continues to live in extreme poverty, while incomes at the very top have sky-rocketed in recent years. But whether the measure is the Gini or a comparison of extremes, the distribution among people in the world is very unequal.

What Matters?

Each of these measures of income inequality "in the world" matters in one way or another. For example, to understand political conflicts within countries, the changes in the distribution within countries is probably most important. To understand how the changing structures of the global economy have affected people's lives in various parts of the world, it is useful to consider all of these measures. And to understand the dynamics of international politics, the measures that focus on inequalities among countries are probably paramount.

The measurements show both some positive and negative changes in the world. On the one hand, the rapid growth of several low-income and middle-income countries has, in spite of the high (and sometimes rising) level of inequality in these countries, pulled many people out of abject poverty. On the other hand, we know that rising inequality within a country tends to undermine social cohesion and generate stress at virtually all levels of society—with damaging effects on health, education, the natural environment, and crime. Even in this era of increased globalization, it is in the national context that inequality has the primary impact on people's behavior and how they judge their well-being.

And no matter how we look at the situation, the world has long been and remains a very unequal place. ❑

Sources: Branko Milanovic, *Worlds Apart: Measuring International and Global Inequality*, Princeton University Press, 2005; Branko Milanovic, *Global Income Inequality by the Numbers: in History and Now—An Overview*, The World Bank, Development Research Group, Poverty and Inequality Team, November 2012; Christoph Lakner and Branko Milanovic, *Global Income Distribution: From the Fall of the Berlin Wall to the Great Recession*, The World Bank, Development Research Group, Poverty and Inequality Team, December 2013, WPS6719; Richard Wilkinson and Kate Pickett, *The Spirit Level: Why Greater Equality Makes Societies Stronger*, Bloomsbury Press, 2009.

Article 5.7

WEALTH INEQUALITY AND WEALTH TAXATION
A Primer on Piketty

BY STEVEN PRESSMAN
May 2014

G reat works in economics address important issues head-on, adopt a broad per-spective, and change our views regarding how economies work. Make no mis-take about it: Thomas Piketty's *Capital in the Twenty-First Century* is a great work. As an added bonus, it is extremely well written (and translated).

Given decades of rising inequality and its negative consequences and public concern about a disappearing middle class, this book is particularly timely. It re-lies on a wide array of data, collected by the author, showing long-term trends in income and wealth distribution. It explains the causes of these trends and finishes by setting forth some bold policy solutions.

Still, the most important aspect of *Capital in the Twenty-First Century* is that it changes how we view the world. The following parallel might provide some his-torical perspective on the book, and help understand its importance and the emo-tional reaction it has elicited.

Thomas Robert Malthus became one of the most controversial figures in economics following the publication of his *Essay on Population* in 1798. De-spite much optimism at the time that ordinary people's lives could be improved, for Malthus poverty was inevitable due to the relationship between population growth and the growth of the food supply. His *Essay* argued (based on some em-pirical data) that population growth would outstrip food supply growth, result-ing in famine and misery.

Piketty can best be understood as a sort of modern-day Malthus. Both doubt-ing Thomases sought to refute popular beliefs that life could easily be improved for most people, both used simple growth rates to do this, and both were criticized for their pessimistic conclusions.

Optimism regarding the future distribution of income stems from the work of Nobel laureate Simon Kuznets. In the 1950s, Kuznets examined U.S. income-tax data and saw income inequality improving over several decades. According to the standard interpretation of his work, he hypothesized that as capitalist econo-mies develop, inequality first increases and then decreases. This message fit Amer-ica's economic experience during the post-war years and its geo-political needs during the Cold War. Most economists came to accept this message of hope.

But times have changed. Inequality is rising in the United States and other high-income capitalist countries. Piketty explains why economists got it wrong. He argues that greater equality between World War I and the 1960s was not part of some positive long-term trend; rather, it stemmed from a unique set of fac-tors—two wars (that destroyed much wealth), the very high marginal tax rates implemented to pay for these wars, plus a stock-market crash and Great Depres-sion. Starting in the 1970s or 1980s (dates differ by country) the moneyed class revolted and began to influence policy. Top income-tax rates fell; income and wealth inequality rose rapidly. As a result, we seem headed toward another Gilded Age, similar to the late 19th century, where the fabulously wealthy live charmed lives and everyone else struggles to survive.

Piketty, like Malthus, draws his dismal conclusion from the relationship between two growth rates. In Piketty's case, they are the rate of return to wealth or capital (r) and the growth rate of the economy (g). When r exceeds g, more money flows to those at the top and inequality increases; when r is less than g, more benefits of economic growth flow to workers, making income and wealth distribution more equal.

One great virtue of Piketty's book is that it explains why income inequality has grown of late. First, the ratio of wealth to GDP declined in Europe from 6:1 or 7:1 around World War I to 2:1 in the 1960s. It has since rebounded to nearly 6:1. The United States experienced a smaller decline, since its factories were not destroyed by the two wars, but has also experienced a growing wealth-to-GDP ratio of late. Second, r has averaged around 5% over long periods of time in many different countries, while g cannot be expected to grow by much more than 1%.

Together these results create a distribution problem, which may be easiest to comprehend in personal terms.

Suppose you receive a $200,000 inheritance (your wealth) and you make $100,000 a year. If your wealth grows at 5% per year and your wages grow by 1%, after 35 years (a typical working life) your wages would be around $140,000 and your wealth (assuming no spending down of this wealth) over $1 million. After several generations, around 100 years, your great grandchild would have labor income of $268,000 and have $25 million in capital assets. With a 5% return, their capital income ($1.25 million) would dwarf their labor income. If some income from wealth gets consumed, which is likely, this process just takes a little longer to work out. At some point income from wealth will far exceed income from labor.

The problem is that we don't all begin with equal amounts of capital. Some start with large inheritances; most people begin with nothing. As a result, the incomes of the haves grow much more rapidly than those of the have-nots—and wealth inequality soars.

Piketty's story is far superior to standard economic explanations of rising inequality, such as technological change and globalization. He rightly rejects these theories because they cannot explain national differences in rising inequality—technological change and globalization should have similar impacts on all developed nations.

Compiling the data to make this case has been a heroic endeavor. Piketty uses income tax returns to get data on the share of national income going to the top 10%, the top 1%, and the top 0.1% of households. Estate tax returns enable him to estimate wealth inequality. Substantial evidence supports Piketty's conclusion that income and wealth inequality have risen in the United States and elsewhere since the late 20th century.

Similar to Malthus's *Essay*, Piketty's *Capital* contains virtually no economic theory. It does not address what determines economic growth or the return to wealth. Its dismal conclusion stems from historic trends and Piketty's explanation of why high rates of return to wealth increase inequality.

So Where Do We Go From Here?

The last part of Piketty's book discusses how to deal with rising inequality. Piketty is skeptical that institutional policies such as raising the minimum wage, or more generous government spending programs, will help much. It is not that he opposes such efforts. Rather, he thinks they are inadequate when wealth is so unevenly distributed and grows so rapidly. Government spending programs can help, but they cannot increase labor income by 5% annually over the long run.

Tax policy is all that is left (no pun intended). Piketty favors a more progressive individual income tax, with a 70% top rate. Corporations, he argues, also need to be taxed based on where they pay wages so they cannot book profits to subsidiaries in low-tax countries.

These policies would reduce income inequality and slow down, but not reverse, the more pressing issue of greater wealth inequality. To deal with this latter problem, Piketty advocates an annual wealth tax, imposed at very low rates—one or two percent on wealth in excess of 1 million euros (around $1.1 million at mid-2015 exchange rates). And it must be a global tax, so that it cannot be escaped by moving wealth abroad.

Those on the right object to the tax rates that Piketty proposes as excessively high. The worst of these objections engage in name-calling, deeming anyone a socialist who proposes higher taxes for whatever reason. Almost as bad have been the objections that higher taxes would give the government more money to waste—as if businesses never, ever wasted money and consumers always spent their money cautiously and rationally (e.g., they would never buy homes or be able to obtain mortgages that they couldn't possibly afford to repay). The more thoughtful and reasonable objections from the right have focused on the bad incentives to work hard, earn money, accumulate wealth, and provide for one's children and grandchildren as a result of higher taxes.

Those on the left and toward the center of the political spectrum have been fairly consistent in maintaining that the main policy proposal of Piketty was impractical because a global wealth tax would never get enacted. After making this point, the next sentence of these critiques typically push other policies (invariably the personal favorites of those criticizing Piketty), which are just as unlikely to get enacted given the current political situation in the United States and elsewhere.

I find all these criticisms both disturbing and a little bit off the mark. But before looking at Piketty's wealth tax proposals in greater detail, it is worth examining what he has to say regarding monetary policy and fiscal policy, something which was not discussed in most of the prominent reviews of his book. Piketty downplays monetary policy in favor of fiscal policy. Monetary policy, he contends, cannot deal with the problem of rising inequality. In fact, he contends that we cannot know the impact of monetary policy on income and wealth distribution, although there is no argument for this. My gut instinct is that this is true, but I would have liked to see some data that supports this contention—say, looking at how income and wealth distribution vary based on interest rates. Such a study would make for a great thesis or doctoral dissertation, to say nothing about a nice professional paper.

Regarding fiscal policy, Piketty is fairly critical of government deficits. He spends a good deal of time focusing on the need to tax wealth so that we can repay existing government debt, but he fails to address the issue of whether government deficits and debt may be necessary at times. He also doesn't address the issue of whether government debt does any actual harm to overall macroeconomic performance. Rather, the focus is mainly (Surprise! Surprise! Surprise!) on the impact of debt on income distribution. Piketty's main point is that the large majority of government bonds created when the government goes into debt is owned by the very wealthy. They benefit greatly from government debt. With little risk, they receive positive returns on their money. This income generates part of their 5% rate of return on wealth or capital.

Unfortunately, the passages on fiscal policy and distribution are too brief. There are two key reasons I wish Piketty had written a good deal more on the relationship between fiscal policy and inequality. First, he argues throughout *Capital* that one main reason inequality declined from World War I through the 1950s was that there were high marginal tax rates on top incomes. This reduced the after-tax gains from owning wealth. Second, fiscal policy is central to Piketty's major policy proposals.

Writing more on fiscal policy and distribution would not have been all that difficult to do. Moreover, his entire case for changes in tax policy would have been considerably stronger had Piketty spent more time on this topic and then related it to the beginnings of the revolt of the rentiers in the United Kingdom and the United States, when Margaret Thatcher and Ronald Reagan were elected heads of government.

The story in both cases is rather similar and involved several policy changes. There was a sharp cut in government spending (that hurt the poor and middle class more than wealthy households, which can provide their own benefits) and a sharp cut in taxes focused at the top of the income distribution. Overall, the cuts in government expenditures were less than the tax cuts, and the government had to borrow money by selling bonds. Abstracting a little from the overall process, the Reagan and Thatcher governments gave large tax breaks to the wealthy, and then borrowed the money back from them to pay for the tax cuts. Everyone else got small tax cuts that were funded by cutting the government benefits they received. Or in slightly bolder and simpler terms, the Reagan and Thatcher governments decided to fund a good deal of government spending by borrowing money from the wealthy rather than taxing the wealthy.

As Piketty's data demonstrate, these changes led to sharply rising inequality in the UK and United States over the past several decades. And it is no wonder why this occurred. Those earning high incomes got to keep a lot more of their income. Yet they had to do something with all this additional money. It could not be kept under the mattress, earning nothing. Bank deposits were insured, but not for balances of the sort that the very wealthy possessed. The result could only be that all this additional disposable income fueled rising asset prices, which also primarily benefited the wealthy.

According to the gospel of "supply-side" economics, which was used to justify these policy changes, the whole process should have resulted in much greater economic growth and enormous tax collections by the government so that there would be no deficit. However, this claim ignored the "balanced budget multiplier" described by the great 20th-century U.S. economist Paul Samuelson. Samuelson showed that an equal cut in taxes and in government spending would slow economic growth or reduce GDP by an amount equal to the tax cut (or cut in government spending). The reason for this is very simple. A dollar less in government spending is a dollar less in spending while a dollar tax cut is not an additional dollar in spending since some of the added disposable income will be saved. Overall, this will reduce spending and economic growth. Yet ideology triumphed over economic knowledge. So, the U.S. and UK governments gave huge tax cuts to the wealthy, and then borrowed the money back from them in order to fund the tax cuts. Economic growth slowed as the balanced budget multiplier predicted it would. This made distributional matters even worse because it increased the gap between r and g—by lowering g.

One last thing is worth additional comment before getting to the issue of income and wealth taxes, especially since this has been one of the most frequent criticisms of Piketty. Many commentators complained that Piketty ignored alternative policies such as supporting unions and raising the minimum wage—but Piketty actually does discuss these policies. Chapter 9 of the book includes an extensive discussion of the minimum wage. The data Piketty presents and the written text both make it very clear that the distribution of wages has remained relatively equal in France because the French have continually increased the minimum wage and the French minimum wage is rather high compared to average wages. Piketty even discusses why this happened—French President Charles de Gaulle (in office 1958–1969) was worried about the crisis of May 1968 and used higher minimum wages to deal with a problem that was more cultural and social than economic. Moreover, Piketty clearly supports raising the minimum wage and even provides several justifications for doing so. So it is puzzling that so many people would criticize Piketty for not supporting higher minimum wages.

The real problem Piketty has with raising the minimum wage is not that it won't help equalize wage income, but that it won't deal with the problem of rising capital income in the long run. He is also skeptical that the minimum wage can be increased enough (5% per year in real terms) over the long haul without generating substantial unemployment. To try to make Piketty's point as simple and clear as possible, even if wages (and we can add rising union power here) were made completely equal across the board, inequality would be high and would continue to increase because of the immense wealth that is possessed by a few people.

It is wealth inequality for Piketty that is the main force driving the rise in inequality to under capitalism. A higher minimum wage can slow the process down. So can stronger unions. So, too, can government spending policies that equalize after-tax incomes, such as paid parental leave, child allowances, generous unemployment insurance programs, and a large and sturdy social safety net. These are all policies that Piketty, I imagine, would support. But the key insight of *Capital* is this: the driving force of inequality is that we start with great wealth inequality and the high returns to wealth make things worse over time. Policies that equalize income distribution will help a little, but they ignore the main problem.

Piketty argues, first, for a progressive income tax because this (along with inheritance taxes) is the only progressive form of taxation that governments have. Sales taxes or indirect taxes are regressive in nature and social-insurance taxes (for retirement and for unemployment) tend to be proportional or regressive. Again, Piketty does not make either a strong or forceful case for this policy. I wish he had put a little more emphasis on the fact that high marginal tax rates during the World War II years and in the decade or so after contributed to falling inequality in this era. Historically, he contends that high marginal income tax rates have led to lower (before-tax) inequality. It is in the data; it should have been stressed more in the policy section of the book.

Piketty also worries about current trends in individual income taxation. In particular, by exempting capital income from the income tax (or taxing it at lower rates) the income tax becomes regressive at the very top (because that is where they get most of their income) and tends to make the entire tax system regressive in developed countries. But, again, the big issue for Piketty is that progressive income taxes cannot solve the wealth inequality problem. Like progressive spending programs, a progressive income tax would help reduce income inequality, but it does not solve the problem that wealth inequality tends to rise because of the high returns to wealth—much of it, such as stocks and homes that are not sold, are not taxed at all.

In a couple of pages that were pretty much ignored in the reviews of *Capital*, Piketty calls for reforming corporate taxation. He proposes that corporate income taxes be assessed based on wages paid in different countries rather than on where in the world the multi-national firm declares its profits to come from (typically the country that has the lowest corporate income tax rate). This is not headline grabbing, and tax reform is never as exciting as proposing a new type of tax (this is why there are so many articles on the flat tax and the Tobin Tax and why reviews of *Capital* focused on the global wealth tax), but it is something that needs to receive serious consideration and should be pushed more.

Again, the fact that Piketty does not focus a lot of attention on this proposal probably stems from the fact that (like higher marginal income tax rates) it will affect income distribution but not wealth distribution. When corporations pay higher taxes to governments there is less profit to distribute to the owners as dividends. This will reduce current incomes. However, higher corporate income taxes also reduce future profits after-taxes, which should affect the value of corporate stock. This will lower the price of shares of stock. Since it is mainly the very wealthy who own large amounts of stock, and whose wealth portfolios contain a higher percentage of stock compared to middle-income households, this policy should have significant and substantial effect on wealth inequality.

Piketty and the Global Tax on Wealth

At last, we come to Piketty's main policy conclusion, his claim that the way to keep more and more income from going to those at the very top of the distribution is a global wealth tax. The tax needs to be global in order to keep wealth from moving to tax havens where it is not subject to the tax. Piketty also wants to keep the tax rate low (1-2%) in order to mitigate negative disincentives. His particular plan is that net assets worth between 1 million euros ($1.1 million) and 5 million euros ($5.5 million) be taxed at 1% and net assets worth more than 5 million euros be taxed at 2%. The goal in all this, Piketty makes clear, is not to raise money for social programs but to tame the inequality that inevitably results under capitalism.

Piketty provides several different arguments for his progressive and global wealth tax.

First, he resorts to an appeal to authority. He invokes the 1918 American Economic Association Presidential address by Irving Fisher, in which Fisher worried about the fact that only 2% of the U.S. population owned more than 50% of the nation's wealth while two-thirds of the population had no net wealth. Fisher then went on to suggest a steeply progressive wealth tax to remedy this situation.

Second, Piketty argues that the rewards going to the very top are not justified by traditional economic arguments (that they depend on the marginal productivity of the worker). Instead, Piketty makes the case that CEO pay is due to luck to a large degree and that a bargaining model fits the data better than marginal productivity theory. He argues that when the government takes a very large chunk of any extra income, it is not worth it for a CEO to bargain with a compensation committee or shareholders to get higher pay. And he points to empirical evidence that high marginal tax rates keep down CEO pay while not hurting the economic performance of the firm.

Finally there is the main argument—that a global wealth tax is the only way to limit the growth of wealth accumulation and a return to 19th-century levels of inequality. Or, this is the only way we can avoid the negative economic, social, and political consequences of great inequality. A tax on income will not achieve this end because much income is tied up in stocks and bonds and real estate that generally do not get taxed. The gains from these investments are taxed when assets are sold. This allows the gains to accumulate at the top and to keep doing so. Only a wealth tax can stop this process.

Of this I am rather skeptical. There are well-known problems with wealth taxation, including how to value assets that aren't regularly traded and liquidity issues for those with little cash assets. In addition, cash (and many other assets) are relatively easy to hide from tax authorities. I also worry about the consequences of letting every government in the world have access to everyone's wealth tax returns, which would be required with a global wealth tax. Last, but not least, past historical attempts to tax wealth (such as the infamous UK window tax) were universally detested, led to undesirable consequences (people bricked up their windows), and were soon abolished.

On the other hand, I find Piketty's other solutions are more promising—a strengthened corporate income tax, a more progressive individual income tax, and greater use of estate and inheritance taxes. We have substantial knowledge and experience with these forms of taxation. The high tax rates on corporate and individual incomes during most of the 20th century kept inequality from rising. And as argued above, higher income taxes on the returns to wealth will reduce wealth and wealth inequality. Moreover, substantial estate and inheritance taxes can break up large wealth holdings. One of the most important achievements of *Capital* is its demonstration that wealth inequality and income inequality are closely related. By controlling either one, we will be able to control the other one. ❑

Chapter 6

FISCAL POLICY, DEFICITS, AND AUSTERITY

INTRODUCTION

Most textbooks, at least to the extent that they are influenced by Keynesian economics, depict a macroeconomy stabilized by government intervention. They look at ways the government can use fiscal policy—government spending and taxation—to bolster a flagging economy. Today's economy, yet to recover fully from the worst economic crisis since the Great Depression, is still flagging.

What is the role of fiscal policy in this context? As the crisis worsened in the fall of 2008, the federal government increased spending and cut taxes. The fiscal stimulus, however, was both tilted too far toward tax cuts (which give the economy a smaller boost per dollar than spending increases) and just not large enough. It was enough to prevent a repeat of the Great Depression, but not enough to ignite the rapid economic growth necessary to put those who lost their jobs quickly back to work.

In the wake of the 2008 downturn, the federal budget went far into the red. While the increased spending played a role, it was mainly the collapse of the economy and the Bush administration's tax cuts and war spending that pushed up the deficit. The surge in government deficits and debt, however, somehow became the focus of macroeconomic policy debates in the United States, despite the persistence of historically high unemployment. The articles in this chapter contest the orthodox view that short-term deficit reduction should be a high priority, arguing that fiscal stimulus is necessary to tackle the stagnant growth and slow recovery of employment in the wake of the Great Recession.

In Article 6.1, economist Marty Wolfson debunks the widespread myth, parroted by mainstream politicians and media commentators, that government spending cannot create jobs. He sees this as part of a conservative ideological campaign to prevent government from doing just that. Government spending, he argues, need not be wasteful, and in fact is not necessarily less valuable than private spending. The government, he concludes, can and should be creating jobs.

Alejandro Reuss (Article 6.2) takes a close look at what Keynes actually had to say about the efficacy of fiscal policy in his most famous book, *The General Theory of Employment, Interest, and Money*. Keynes was a strong advocate of fiscal policy, especially government spending, as a response to business-cycle downturns. Reuss explains how Keynes challenged the "Treasury view" that government spending could not get the economy going because it would "crowd out" private investment, the same argument conservatives have invoked against fiscal stimulus policies today.

John Miller (Article 6.3) takes a hard look at the pro-rich, trickle-down Trump/ GOP Tax cut that was enacted into law in December 2017. Its benefits for the rich abound: a lower top income tax rate, higher exemptions for the alternative income tax and the estate tax, and a massive cut in the corporate tax rate. Nonetheless, Miller argues that there is little reason to expect that these handouts to the rich will produce an economic boom. The U.S. economy has grown its fastest with higher, not lower, top income tax rates, and other than a few token bonuses lower taxes for corporations have not led to higher wages for workers.

In March 2018, the state of New York enacted a work-around that will inoculate its residents against the limit on the deductibility of state and local states imposed by the Trump/GOP tax cut. In Article 6.4, Dean Baker explains how the New York tax change works, and why it helps to counteract what the Trump/GOP tax cut would do to erode the state's ability to provide important services. The plan turns around enacting a state payroll tax paid by employers (not subject to limit on the deductibility of state and local taxes) that lowers the gross income of employees but leaves their after-tax income unchanged.

In the next article, Evita Nolka takes us to Greece, where unemployment remains at stratospheric levels (Article 6.5). She describes not only the obvious economic costs of unemployment—loss of incomes and production—but also the human toll for young people seeing the primes of their lives fritter away, looking at a bleak future, and sometimes feeling compelled to leave their country in search of better opportunities. To be sure, disillusionment and cynicism about the political system are high, but Nolka also shows the resilient spirit of Greeks who are still fighting for economic change that will benefit the majority.

José A. Laguarta Ramírez's article about Puerto Rico's debt crisis (Article 6.6) points to its roots in colonialism. Subordinate to the U.S. government politically and to U.S. corporations economically, Puerto Rico is now mired in "odious debt"—neither incurred freely by its people nor used for their benefit. Meanwhile, legislation passed by the U.S. government will impose harsh austerity and an undemocratic "oversight" board. Laguarta Ramírez suggests that the solution to the crisis lies in the direction of repudiating the debt, which in turn points in the direction of political independence.

Finally, economist James M. Cypher investigates the forces that make the Pentagon and military spending resistant to change and budget cuts (Article 6.7). Cypher recounts how military contract after military contract has maximized costs, subsidizing the development of new technologies. On top of that, an "Industrial-Military-Congressional Juggernaut" is now in place that perpetuates military spending and operates with little presidential oversight. Finally, the Trump administration has embraced the need to "modernize" the U.S. military, a move that is likely to drive up military spending by 1% to 2% of GDP.

Discussion Questions

1. (Article 6.1) What are the main arguments made by opponents of government "stimulus" spending? How does Wolfson refute each of these points?

2. (Article 6.2) Why did Keynes think that the dollar-for-dollar crowding-out argument (the "Treasury view") was mistaken? And how might Keynes respond to the arguments conservatives leveled against fiscal stimulus policies during the Great Recession?

3. (Article 6.3) What evidence does Miller present to support his argument that the pro-rich Trump/GOP tax cut is unlikely to boost economic growth or to raise wages?

4. (Article 6.4) How does the state of New York's plan to enact a payroll tax on employers benefit the residents of the New York and improve the state's ability to sustain its tax base?

5. (Article 6.5) What are the costs of mass unemployment, according to Nolka, besides the loss of incomes and production? What does she suggest, as an alternative to current "austerity" policies?

6. (Article 6.6.) In what ways, according to Laguarta Ramírez, is Puerto Rico's debt crisis a result of its colonial status?

7. (Article 6.7) Why, according to Cypher, is it unlikely that Trump will drain the Pentagon swamp?

Article 6.1

THE IDEOLOGICAL ATTACK ON JOB CREATION
Responding to Anti-Government Arguments

BY MARTY WOLFSON
May/June 2012

> "Government doesn't create jobs. It's the private sector that creates jobs."
> —presidential candidate Mitt Romney, speaking at Wofford College,
> Spartenburg, S.C., January 18, 2012

It is jarring to hear pundits say that the government can't create jobs. It is even more jarring to hear the same refrain from someone whose job was created by the government! Perhaps Mr. Romney has forgotten, or would like to forget, that he used to have a government job as governor of Massachusetts.

But surely those currently on the government payroll have not forgotten, like the chairman of the House Republican Policy Committee, Rep. Tom Price (R-Ga.). He used the same talking points, "The government doesn't create jobs. It's the private sector that creates jobs," speaking on MSNBC's "Andrea Mitchell Reports" last June.

Rep. Price apparently thinks he doesn't have a real job, but what about teachers, firefighters, police officers, and school cafeteria workers? And what about the 2 to 4.8 million jobs—in both the public and private sectors—the U.S. Congressional Budget Office estimated were created by the 2009 U.S. economic stimulus package?

The "government doesn't create jobs" mantra is part of a coordinated right-wing campaign to *prevent* the government from creating jobs and promoting the interests of working families, and to instead encourage a shift in the distribution of income towards the wealthy. It is supported by ideologically motivated arguments and theories from conservative economists and anti-government think tanks. In what follows, these arguments are addressed and criticized, in the hopes of clearing away some of the confusion undermining a vigorous government program to put people back to work.

The Argument That Government Spending Can't Increase Jobs

A Senior Fellow at the Cato Institute says the idea that government spending can create jobs "has a rather glaring logical fallacy. It overlooks the fact that, in the real world, government can't inject money into the economy without first taking money out of the economy." This argument is wrong for several reasons.

First, the government *can* inject money into the economy. It does so whenever it finances its spending by selling bonds to the Federal Reserve. In this case, money is created by the Federal Reserve when it buys the bonds. It creates a reserve account on its books; money is thus created without any reduction in money elsewhere in the economy.

Alternatively, the government can finance its spending by taxes or by selling bonds to the public. This is the case envisioned by the Cato analysis. The argument is that the money spent by the government is exactly balanced by a reduction in money in the pockets of taxpayers of bond buyers. However, if the taxpayers' or the bond buyers' money would otherwise have been saved and not spent, then there is a net injection into the economy of funds that can put people to work.

The argument made by the Cato Institute is actually a variation of another theory, known as "crowding out." In this theory, government spending creates competition for real resources that "crowds out," or displaces, private investment; private companies are unable to obtain the workers and capital they need for investment, so that any jobs due to government spending are offset by a decrease of jobs in the private sector.

This theory is valid only when there is full employment because there would be no idle resources, labor or capital, to put to use. In that case, though, neither the government nor the private sector would be able to create net new jobs. In contrast, in a situation of unemployment, it is precisely because the government can access otherwise idle resources that it can create jobs.

And, of course, that is exactly the situation we are in. As of March, the official unemployment rate stood at 8.2 %. Adjusted for underemployment, e.g., by counting those discouraged workers who have dropped out of the labor force and those workers who are working part-time but would like to work full-time, the more accurate unemployment rate was 14.5%.

The Argument That Cutting Government Spending Creates Jobs

Consistent with anti-government ideology, conservative economics asserts not only that government spending can't create jobs, but also that cutting government spending creates jobs. Here's how the argument goes: less government spending will reduce the government deficit; smaller deficits will increase the confidence of businesses that will invest more and in that way create more jobs. According to John B. Taylor, an economist affiliated with Stanford's conservative Hoover Institution, "Basic economic models in which incentives and expectations of future policy matter show that a credible plan to reduce gradually the deficit will increase economic growth and reduce unemployment by removing uncertainty and lowering the chances of large tax increases in the future." (Interestingly, an analysis by economist Robert Pollin of the Political Economy Research Institute at the University of Massachusetts-Amherst finds that Taylor's empirical model concludes that the stimulus bill was ineffective—but only because it included too much in tax cuts as opposed to direct government spending.)

This assertion is based more on wishful thinking than empirical validity, and has been criticized by Paul Krugman as depending on belief in a "confidence fairy." But it is not just liberal economists like Krugman who are critical of this theory. A confidential report prepared for clients by the investment bank Goldman Sachs concluded that a $61 billion cut in government spending from a bill passed by the House of Representatives in February 2011 (but not enacted into law) would lead to a decline in economic growth of 2%. And economist Mark Zandi, formerly an advisor to Republican presidential candidate John McCain, concluded that this $61 billion reduction in government spending could result in the loss of 700,000 jobs by 2012.

Ben Bernanke, chairman of the Board of Governors of the Federal Reserve System, stated that "the cost to the recovery [of steep reductions in government outlays now] would outweigh the benefits in terms of fiscal discipline." Even the International Monetary Fund, in its semiannual report on the world economic outlook, concluded that "the idea that fiscal austerity triggers faster growth in the short term finds little support in the data."

Also, in a review of studies and historical experience about the relationship between budget-cutting and economic growth, economists Arjun Jayadev and Mike Konczal concluded that countries historically did not cut government spending and deficits in a slump and that there is no basis to conclude that doing so now, "under the conditions the United States currently faces, would improve the country's prospects."

The Argument That Private Spending Is Always Better than Public Spending

Another way that right-wing economics tries to discredit the idea that the government can create jobs is to assert that private spending is always to be preferred to public spending. There are several rationalizations for this view.

One is that private spending is more efficient than public spending. This ideological refrain has been repeated consistently, and gained a following, over the past thirty years. But repetition does not make it correct. Of course, the proponents of this argument can point to examples of government mismanagement, such as that following Hurricane Katrina. However, government bungling and inefficiency by an administration that did not believe in government does not prove the point. A much more grievous example of inefficiency and misallocation of resources is the housing speculation and financial manipulation—and eventual collapse that brought us to the current recession—due to a deregulated private financial system. Yet for free-market ideologues, this somehow does not discredit the private sector.

Some people think that economists have "proven" that "free" markets are efficient. The only thing that has been proven, however, is that you can arrive at any conclusion if your assumptions are extreme enough. And the assumptions that form the basis for the free-market theory are indeed extreme, if not totally unrealistic and impossible. For example: orthodox free-market economics assumes perfectly competitive markets; perfect information; no situations, like pollution, in which private decision-makers do not take account of the societal effects of their actions; even full employment. But none of these assumptions hold true in the real world. Also, the distribution of income is irrelevant to the conclusions of this theory. The distribution of income is simply taken as given, so that the results of the theory are consistent with a relatively equal distribution of income as well as a very unequal distribution. As economist Joseph Stiglitz has said, "Today, there is no respectable intellectual support for the proposition that markets, by themselves, lead to efficient, let alone equitable outcomes."

A second reason for supposing that private spending is to be preferred to public spending is the notion that public spending is less worthwhile than private spending. This means, for many people, reducing government spending as much as possible. For example, Grover Norquist, founder and president of Americans for Tax Reform and author of the anti-tax pledge signed by many members of Congress, said that he wanted to "shrink [the government] down to the size where we can drown it in the bathtub." The anti-tax, anti-spending crusade has in many cases been successful in reducing government budgets, on the national as well as the local level. This has resulted in a significant decrease in government services. Although some people are attracted to the view that government spending should always be reduced, they probably at the same time don't want to drive on roads and bridges that aren't repaired and they probably want fire trucks to arrive if their house is on fire. Perhaps, too, they wouldn't automatically prefer twelve kinds of toothpaste to schools, parks, and libraries.

The Argument That Government Spending Is Wasteful

Another argument contends that public spending is wasteful. Discussions of government accounts generally do not take account of public investment, so all public spending is essentially treated as consumption. As such, it is considered unproductive and wasteful by those who wish to disparage government spending. In other words, the government budget does not make a distinction between long-term investments and other spending as corporate budgets do.

One implication of treating all government spending as consumption is the notion that the federal government should maintain a balanced budget. To put this in accounting terms, on this view government accounts are considered to only have an income statement (which shows current revenues and current expenditures), not a balance sheet (which shows assets and liabilities).

Corporations, in contrast, maintain balance sheets. They don't balance their budgets in the way that the budget hawks want the government to do. Private investment in plant and equipment, for example, is accounted for on the asset side of the balance sheet; borrowing to finance this investment is accounted for on the liability side. Interest on the debt is accounted for on the income statement, and it is only the interest, not the outstanding debt balance, that has to be covered by current revenues. The assumption behind this accounting is that borrowing to finance productive investment will generate the revenue to pay off the borrowing.

In other words, corporations borrow on a regular basis to finance investment. So they only attempt to balance their current expenditures and revenues and not their capital budget.

Much confusion about private and public spending, and also about budget deficits, could be avoided if discussion focused on a federal government balance sheet. In that way, current spending that needs to be balanced with current revenue could be separated from long-term investments that will increase the productivity of the American economy. Such investments, in areas like infrastructure and education, can increase future economic growth and income, and thus generate more tax revenue to pay off the debt. Just like a private company's investments, they are legitimately financed by borrowing.

Government Can Indeed Create Jobs

The main point, though, is this: whether financed by borrowing or taxes, whether consumption or investment, government spending that increases the demand for goods and services in the economy is not wasteful. It has the ability to employ underutilized resources and create jobs.

Ultimately, a job is a job, whether created by the private or public sector. A job has the potential to enable workers to support themselves and their families in dignity. We should not let ideological arguments keep us from using every available means to promote the basic human right of employment. ❏

Sources: Congressional Budget Office, "Estimated Impact of the American Recovery and Reinvestment Act on Employment and Economic Output From April 2010 Through June 2010," August 2010; Daniel J. Mitchell, "The Fallacy That Government Creates Jobs," The Cato Institute, 2008; John B. Taylor, "Goldman Sachs Wrong About Impact of House Budget Proposal," Economics One blog, February 28, 2011; Paul Krugman, "Myths of austerity," *The New York Times*. July 1, 2010; Jonathan Karl, "Goldman Sachs: House Spending Cuts Will Hurt Economic Growth," The Note, 2011; Mark Zandi, "A federal shutdown could derail the recovery," Moody's Analytics, February 28, 2011; Pedro da Costa and Mark Felsenthal, "Bernanke warns against steep budget cuts," Reuters, February 9, 2011; International Monetary Fund, *World Economic Outlook: Recovery, Risk, and Rebalancing*, 2010; Arjun Jayadev and Mike Konczal, "When Is Austerity Right? In Boom, Not Bust," *Challenge*, November-December 2010, pp. 37-53; Joseph Stiglitz, Foreword, in Karl Polanyi, *The Great Transformation: The Political and Economic Origins of Our Times*, 2001; David Aschauer, "Is Public Expenditure Productive?" *Journal of Monetary Economics*, 1989, pp. 177-200; Robert Pollin, "US government deficits and debt amid the great recession: what the evidence shows, *Cambridge Journal of Economics*, 2012, 36, 161-187; Kelsey Merrick and Jim Horney, "Chairman Ryan Gets 62 Percent of His Huge Budget Cuts from Programs for Lower-income Americans," Center on Budget and Policy Priorities, March 23, 2012; Paul Ryan, The Path to Prosperity, March 20, 2012; Ethan Pollack, "Ryan's Budget Would Cost Jobs," The Economic Policy Institute, March 21, 2012.

Article 6.2

FISCAL POLICY AND "CROWDING OUT"

BY ALEJANDRO REUSS
May/June 2009

In response to the deepest recession in the United States since the Great Depression, the Obama administration proposed a large fiscal "stimulus" plan. (Fiscal policies involve government spending and taxation. A fiscal stimulus involves increases in government spending or tax cuts, or both.) The current stimulus plan, after some compromises between the Obama administration and Republicans in Congress, included both substantial tax cuts and increases in government spending. Together, they would increase the federal government deficit by over $700 billion.

A fiscal stimulus is a standard "Keynesian" response to a recession. The logic behind these policies is that recessions can be caused by insufficient total demand for goods and services. If saving (a "leakage" from demand) exceeds investment (an "injection" of demand), there will not be enough demand to buy all the goods and services that the economy is capable of producing at the "full employment" level. Some goods will go unsold, and firms will reduce output. They will cut jobs, cancel supply orders, and even close production facilities. The economy will spiral into a recession.

In standard Keynesian models, either tax cuts or increased government spending can increase total demand, and therefore total output and employment. An initial increase in spending (by either the government or the recipients of the tax cuts) results in new income for other individuals, who then go on to spend part (not all) of this income, which results in new income for still other individuals, and so on. Ultimately, this series of additions to income results in a total increase in GDP greater than the original increase in government spending or reduction in taxes. The increase in real GDP divided by the initial spending increase is called the "multiplier." The standard Keynesian view implies a multiplier greater than one.

The Conservative Critique

Conservative economists, whose intellectual heritage includes decades-old attempts to refute Keynesian theory, disagree with this view. They argue that government spending cannot possibly increase overall economic activity, and that the stimulus plan is therefore doomed to fail. This position is sometimes known as the "Treasury view" (because it mirrors the arguments of the British Treasury Department during the Great Depression) or the theory of "crowding out." The new government spending, these economists argue, "has to come from somewhere," either from higher taxes or increased government borrowing. Either way, the increase in government spending will come at the expense of private spending.

If the spending is financed by tax increases, conservative economists argue, this will reduce individuals' after-tax incomes and therefore reduce their spending. If it is financed through borrowing, the increased government demand for loans will drive up interest rates, and this will "crowd out" private investment. (Some private investment projects that would have been profitable at lower interest rates would not be profitable at the higher rates, and therefore would not be undertaken.) Extreme versions of this theory, known as "dollar-for-dollar" crowding out, argue that the decrease in private investment will exactly offset the increase in government spending, and there will be no change in the overall output of goods and services.

Government intervention is not only incapable of pulling the economy out of a recession, conservative economists argue, it is also unnecessary. If there is more saving than investment, the quantity of funds people are willing to loan out will exceed the quantity that people are willing to borrow at the current interest rate. The surplus of loanable funds will drive down the interest rate. People will save less (since the reward to saving is lower) and borrow more and invest more (since the cost of borrowing is lower), until the injection of investment and the leakage of saving are equal. In short, if insufficient demand ever caused a recession, the economy would quickly pull itself back to full employment without any need for government intervention.

Keynes' Rejoinder

Keynes agreed with the idea that saving equals investment. In his view, however, this is true not only when the economy is producing at its full-employment capacity, but also when it is producing at far less than its capacity. Keynes argued that the "classical" economists (as he called the conservative orthodoxy of his time) had an incorrect view of the relationship between interest rates and savings, and that this was at the heart of their errors about the possibility of prolonged recessions.

The classicals believed that as interest rates increased, savings would increase, and that as interest rates declined, savings would decline. Keynes agreed that this was true at "a given income," but that a change in the interest rate would also affect the amount investment and therefore the level of income. A higher interest rate, he argued, was associated with lower investment, lower incomes, and therefore lower saving; a lower interest rate, with higher investment, higher incomes, and therefore higher saving. (As people's incomes increase, they spend more *and* save more; as their incomes decline, they spend less *and* save less.) In Keynes' view, saving will equal investment whether investment and saving are both high (at or near the full employment level of output) or if investment and saving are both low (in a low-output, high-unemployment economy). In the latter case, Keynes believed, there was no guarantee that the economy would pull itself back to full employment.

Keynes was also well aware, long before his critics, that government borrowing could crowd out some private investment. In *The General Theory* itself, he noted that the effects of the government directly increasing employment on public works may include "increasing the rate of interest and so retarding investment in other directions." This does not imply, however, dollar-for-dollar crowding out. Keynes still believed, and the empirical evidence confirms, that under depression conditions an increase in government spending can result in an increase in total output larger than the initial spending increase (a multiplier greater than one).

Of Spending and Multipliers

In a January 2009 article in the *Wall Street Journal*, conservative economist Robert Barro declares, as a "plausible starting point," that the multiplier actually equals zero. That's what the dollar-for-dollar crowding-out theory means—an increase in government spending will be matched by equal decreases in private spending, and so will have zero effect on real GDP. When it comes to estimating the multiplier, based on historical data from 1943–1944, however, Barro finds that it is not zero, but 0.8.

First, contrary to Barro's intent, this is actually a disproof of dollar-for-dollar crowding out. It means that increased government spending brought about increased real GDP, though not by as much as the spending increase. It increased the production of public-sector goods by (much) more than it reduced the production of private-sector goods. Unless one views private-sector goods as intrinsically more valuable than public-sector goods, this is not an argument against government spending.

Second, Barro chose to base his study on two years at the height of the U.S. mobilization for World War II. When the economy is at or near full employment, the multiplier is bound to be small. If all resources are already being used, the only way to produce more of some kinds of goods (say, tanks and war planes) is to produce less of some others (say, civilian cars). Keynesian economists certainly understand this. Their point, however, is that government spending creates a large multiplier effect when the economy is languishing in a recession, not when it is already at full employment.

Economist Mark Zandi of Moody's Economy.com reports much higher multipliers for government spending. Zandi estimates multipliers between 1.3 and 1.6 for federal aid to states and for government infrastructure expenditures. The multipliers are even larger for government transfers (such as food stamps or unemployment compensation) to the hardest-hit, who are likely to spend all or almost all of their increase in income. Zandi estimates these multipliers at between 1.6 and 1.8. Tax cuts for high income individuals and corporations, who are less likely to spend their additional disposable income, have the lowest multipliers—between 0.3 and 0.4.

Why the *General* Theory?

The conservative case against standard Keynesian fiscal stimulus policy rests on the assumption that all of the economy's resources are already being used to the fullest. Keynes titled his most important work *The General Theory* because he thought that the orthodox economics of his time confined itself to this special case, the case of an economy at full employment. He did not believe that this was generally the case in capitalist economies, and he sought to develop a theory that explained this.

The argument conservatives make against government spending—"it has to come from somewhere"—is actually no less true for private investment. If dollar-for-dollar crowding out were true, therefore, it would be just as impossible for private investment to pull the economy out of a recession. This, of course, would be nonsense unless the economy was already at full employment (and an increase in one kind of production would have to come at the expense of some other kind of production).

If the economy were already operating at full capacity—imagine a situation in which all workers are employed, factories are humming with activity 24/7, and no unused resources would be available to expand production if demand increased—the argument that increased government spending could not increase overall economic output might be plausible. But that is manifestly not the current economic situation.

Real GDP declined at an annual rate of 6.3% in the fourth quarter of 2008. The official unemployment rate surged to 8.5%, the highest rate in 30 years, in March 2009. Over 15% of workers are unemployed, have given up looking for work, or can only find part-time work. Employment is plummeting by more than half a million workers each month. A theory that assumes the economy is already at full employment can neither help us understand how we got into this hole—or how we can get out. ❏

Sources: John Maynard Keynes, *The General Theory of Employment, Interest, and Money,* 1964; Associated Press, "Obama: Stimulus lets Americans claim destiny," Feb. 17, 2009; Paul Krugman, "A Dark Age of macroeconomics (wonkish)," Jan. 27, 2009 (krugman.blogs.nytimes.com); J. Bradford DeLong, "More 'Treasury View' Blogging," Feb. 5,2009 (delong.typepad.com); J. Bradford DeLong, "The Modern Revival of the 'Treasury View,'" Jan. 18, 2009 (delong.typepad. com); Robert J. Barro,"Government Spending is No Free Lunch," *Wall Street Journal,* Jan. 22, 2009 (wsj.com); Paul Krugman, "War and non-remembrance," Jan. 22, 2009 (krugman.blogs. nytimes.com); Paul Krugman, "Spending in wartime," Jan. 23, 2009 (krugman.blogs.nytimes. com); Mark Zandi, "The Economic Impact of a $750 Billion Fiscal Stimulus Package," Moody's Economy.com, March 26, 2009; Bureau of Labor Statistics, Alternative measures of labor underutilization; Bureau of Labor Statistics Payroll Employment.

Article 6.3

THE TRUMP/GOP TAX ACT
Update on the Massive Giveaway to the Rich

BY JOHN MILLER
January 2018

Judging by what's in the Tax Cut and Jobs Act, Donald Trump and the Republicans who pushed this disastrous bill through Congress in December must have thought American inequality wasn't severe enough.

As anticipated their act showers benefits on the best-off taxpayers. For the rest of us, it offers only meager tax reductions written in disappearing ink.

In 2018, the Tax Policy Center estimates, taxpayers with incomes of $1 million or more will get an average tax cut of $69,660, while those under $75,000 will get an average cut of $353. By 2027, 81% of the tax cuts will go to those taking in more than $1 million, while taxes on those making less than $75,000 will go up.

Bonanza for the Rich

The final version of tax act did not repeal the estate tax and the Alternative Minimum Tax (AMT) as some earlier versions had, but it nonetheless lavished tax cuts on the wealthy.

First, the act lowers the top income tax rate from 39.6% to 37%, benefiting taxpayers whose income exceeds $426,700.

Second, it increases the exemption for the alternative minimum income tax, which benefits nearly exclusively taxpayers with over $200,000 of income.

Third, it doubles the exemption for the estate tax to $11.2 million. This overwhelmingly benefits the top 10% of income earners, and especially the richest 0.1%—those with annual incomes in excess of $3.9 million.

The act does put a $10,000 cap on the state and local taxes you can deduct from your federal income tax, a provision that will hit wealthier taxpayers in high-tax states. Residents of those high-tax states often vote Democratic.

Business owners and corporate stockholders will be especially rewarded. The act slashes taxes on corporate profits from 35% to 21%. Most studies find that more than three-quarters of the benefits of lower corporate tax rates go to owners of capital, rather than their employees, and close to half of the benefits go to the richest 1% of taxpayers.

In the name of providing tax relief to small businesses, the act allows one-fifth of the first $315,000 of profits of pass-through businesses (which pay personal income taxes instead of corporate income taxes) to go untaxed. Over 80% of the benefits of this provision will go to the top 5% of taxpayers, including the Trump family, which owns more than 500 pass-through businesses.

Effects Cancel Out

Republicans were far stingier when it came to taxpayers with modest incomes, and most of tax cuts that will benefit lower and middle income people are set to expire in 2025.

The act did double the standard deduction—used by most low- and middle-income taxpayers—to $12,000 for individuals and $24,000 for married couples. But at the same time, it eliminates the $4,500 exemption for each taxpayer and each dependent. For a family of three, these lost exemptions will cancel out the doubling of the standard deduction.

The act doubles the child tax credit to $2,000. A family with two children and $100,000 of income will get the full $2,000 credit per child. But because the credit is only partially refundable, a family with two children and $24,000 of income will get a credit of just $1,400 per child, and families with lower incomes will receive even less—as little as $75 per child.

The bill also ends the itemized deduction for an employee's unreimbursed job expenses, including union dues.

On top of all that, the bill scraps the Affordable Care Act mandate for individuals to buy health insurance or pay a fine. As a result, a projected 13 million fewer people will have health insurance. Premiums will rise, for non-group plans, by "about 10 percent in most years" in the next decade, according to the Congressional Budget Office.

Expect No Boom

Tax cut supporters insist that this lopsided pro-rich law will create an explosion of economic growth that will create jobs and enrich us all. It's not happening.

Cutting taxes on the rich is not an engine of economic growth, as even the Congressional Research Service attests to. For Congressional Research Service economists Jane Gravelle and Donald Marples report that, "past changes in tax rates have had no large clear effects on economic growth,"

Cutting taxes on corporate profits is similarly unlikely to trickle down. After-tax corporate profits, when compared to gross domestic product, are already nearing record highs. In addition, corporations are unlikely to use their windfall to make the investments that will jump-start economic growth, create jobs, and raise wages. After all, if they're not investing now, it's not because of lack of funds. In 2016, according to Standard and Poor's, U.S. firms were already holding in the country $800 billion in cash and liquid assets, which they were unwilling to invest in long-term projects.

Seemingly intoxicated by their coming tax windfall, some corporations are handing out bonuses to their workers. Most prominently Walmart announced a one-time $1,000 bonus to its employees—but buried the fact that only workers who have been with the company for 20 years will get the full $1,000. The average Walmart worker is expected to get under $200. The bonuses will cost Walmart only 2.2% of the $18 billion it's likely to save over the next decade from the tax cut, leaving plenty to hand over to shareholders.

Hours later, Walmart revealed it was closing more than 60 of its Sam's Club stores and laying off thousands of workers.

Watch Out

On top of all that, this tax giveaway to the rich adds a whopping $1.8 trillion to the federal budget deficit, according to the Congressional Budget Office. Republican lawmakers are already bemoaning the ballooning deficit they've created and saying they'll have to cut Social Security, Medicare, Medicaid, and public services to close the budget gap.

That's a one-two punch that we need to make sure doesn't connect. ❑

Article 6.4

NEW YORK STATE'S BIG MIDDLE FINGER TO THE REPUBLICAN TAX PLAN

BY DEAN BAKER
April 2018, Center for Economic and Policy Research

Last month New York State gave a big middle finger to Donald Trump and the Republican Congress. It included measures in its budget bill that will allow people in the state to get around the new tax law's limit on the deductibility of state and local taxes. This could save the state's ability to maintain and extend its level of public services.

A provision in the Republican tax overhaul bill limits the amount of state and local taxes (SALT) that could be deducted from federal income tax to $10,000. In a relatively high-tax state like New York, many families have state and local taxes that far exceed this amount. The capping of the SALT deduction is a Republican effort at the federal level to deny states the revenue they would need to maintain and extend current levels of public services. This is why the workarounds designed by Gov. Andrew Cuomo's administration are a big deal.

While the people who will be affected by this cap are mostly higher-income families, its impact would be felt statewide. New York has a relatively progressive income tax, with the highest income families facing an 8.2% income tax rate.

While it is a safe bet that people never like to pay taxes, the deduction against federal taxes made the state income tax less costly, especially for high-income people. With a top federal income tax rate of 39.6%, the SALT deduction effectively meant that the federal government was reimbursing 40 cents of every dollar that high-income people paid in state and local taxes. This meant that the top New York tax rate of 8.2%, was really a tax rate of 5% (60.4% of 8.2%), after factoring in the deduction on federal taxes.

By limiting the SALT deduction, the Republican tax bill changes this arithmetic. Higher income families will now pay 100 cents on the dollar of any additional taxes imposed by state and local governments. This restriction was explicitly included in the bill to make it more difficult for states like New York to maintain a high level of social services.

Republican congressional lawmakers assumed that limiting the deduction would make high-income people more resistant to any future tax increases and may even cause them to push for tax rollbacks. In a context where progressive change is unlikely to come out of Washington in the foreseeable future, measures like extending healthcare coverage, affordable child care and free college are most likely to advance at the state level. New York's work around is leading the way for other states that will be penalized by the tax law.

While there are two distinct measures in the state's budget for getting around the SALT limit, the more important measure replaces a portion of the state income tax with an employer-side payroll tax. Under this plan, an employer would pay a 5%

payroll tax to the government, similar to the employer-side payroll tax they pay now at the state level for workers' compensation and unemployment insurance and at the federal level for Social Security and Medicare.

Economists typically expect that an employer-side payroll tax will come out of wages. They don't care whether they pay wages to the worker or taxes to the government. This means that if an employer paid a 5% payroll tax on a worker's $200,000 salary, this amount ($10,000) would come out of the workers' paycheck. Instead of $200,000 a year, this worker would get $190,000 a year.

If you're wondering why a worker would ever want to see their pay cut by $10,000, you have to look more closely. When the worker was being paid $200,000, she had to pay $10,000 in taxes to New York State. Now she is only earning $190,000, but doesn't owe any money in taxes to New York State. This means that her pay, net of state taxes, is exactly the same.

What's more, she is better off now when it comes to federal taxes. Instead of being taxed on $200,000, she will only pay federal taxes on $190,000. Since this person would likely be in the 32% bracket, this tax shift would save her $3,200 on her federal taxes. And, as a neat twist, she will get these tax savings even if she doesn't itemize on her federal returns.

While it might have been desirable to make this tax switch mandatory, New York's law is voluntary for employers for political reasons. Several commentators have claimed that few employers are likely to take advantage of this switch because it is too complicated.

A factor suggesting that the switch will be widely adopted is the popularity of Flexible Savings Accounts (FSA). These accounts allow workers to put aside pre-tax dollars to cover medical bills, effectively saving the income and payroll taxes they would otherwise pay on this money.

There is a considerable amount of paperwork involved in documenting expenses for FSAs. Also, money that is not spent at the end of the year is lost. Furthermore, relatively low caps mean the potential savings are limited, typically to a few hundred dollars a year.

Nonetheless, FSAs are very popular. By comparison, the payroll tax shift requires just a one-time adjustment by the employer (like the one they just did for the new tax law). The potential gains are far larger with the employer-side payroll tax; as noted in the example here, the worker could save $3,200 a year on her federal taxes.

For this reason, it is likely that the employer-side payroll tax device will catch on quickly, even though it is not mandatory. It would be great if other liberal states adopted similar workarounds to preserve most of the SALT deduction for their residents.

If that were to be the case, we would get a situation where the only people who lose the benefit of the SALT deduction would be higher-income people living in Republican states. Now that would be a great product of the Republican tax bill. ❏

Article 6.5

THE HUMAN TOLL OF GREEK AUSTERITY

BY EVITA NOLKA
March/April 2016

Giannis and Lena, both in their early 30s and with MBA degrees, consider themselves lucky to be employed. Living in Thessaloniki, Greece's second largest city, located in the heart of Macedonia, Giannis is a merchandise buyer at a company that imports household items. Lena works in the export department of a pasta-producing enterprise.

"Every Greek family is experiencing the crisis their own way," Lena tells me. "Unemployment, wage and pension cuts, taxes, and increases in prices of basic goods have caused despair to millions of people."

Giannis shares a bit more. His family's income has taken a real hit. His father's wages have been reduced by one third and his mother got laid off three years ago. She used to work at a ready-made garments factory that went bankrupt soon after. For a year and a half, she hasn't been paid and she is still claiming the money she is owed.

Like so many others, Giannis had been unemployed for years. There was nothing he could do other than hope to get accepted at one of the five-month temporary work programs in the country funded by the European Union (EU). "You're being deprived of the opportunity to work during the most productive years of your life," Giannis tells me as he explains the psychological burden of unemployment. "There's a feeling that you're standing still even though the whole world keeps moving and after a while you feel numb. You accept that's how things are and you are unable to get out of the rut."

Sticking with Austerity

For six years now, Greece has lived under unprecedented austerity policies demanded by its lenders and accepted by a succession of governments. The social and political reality created by austerity was demonstrated sharply by two events on the same day in October 2015.

First, Eurostat, the European statistical service, released a report on poverty and social exclusion in Greece. The report showed that, in 2014, 22.1% of the Greek population lived in conditions of poverty, 21.5% were severely materially deprived, and 17.2% lived in families with very low work intensity. (Economists define "work intensity" as the total number of months that all working-age household members have worked as a percentage of the total number of months they theoretically could have worked. Households under 20% are considered to have "very low" work intensity.) Altogether, 36% of the population faced one or more of these terrible conditions. That figure was 7.9 percentage points higher than in 2008.

Second, the Greek parliament approved a new piece of legislation imposing further austerity measures as demanded by its creditors—primarily the EU and the International Monetary Fund (IMF)—to meet the terms of Greece's most recent (third) bailout agreement. The new package involves cutting public spending by 14.32 billion euros, while raising taxes by 14.09 billion euros, over the next five years. The measures will primarily affect privately owned businesses, homeowners, and employees close to retirement.

Austerity policies were first adopted in 2010 as a "solution" to the economic crisis that erupted in 2009–10. Severe cuts in public spending, deep reductions in wages and pensions, enormous tax increases, and a stripping back of labor protections were imposed—ostensibly—to stabilize the economy and gain the confidence of financial markets. In practice, the measures have plunged the Greek economy into a prolonged recession that has led to the disastrous results outlined by Eurostat. Unfortunately, the current Greek government, formed by the left-wing SYRIZA party, appears determined to keep the country on the same path.

The Crushing Burden of Unemployment

In the course of the recession, the Greek economy has shrunk by more than 25%. At present, more than one out of four workers is unemployed (one out of two among the nation's youth), and more than one million jobs have disappeared. The prospects for improvement, given the austerity policies imposed under the third bailout agreement, are dim at best. "No legislation can guarantee even the most basic labor rights," Lena says in describing the way employers have used the specter of unemployment to further reduce wages. "It's no wonder," she adds, "that so many well-educated young people choose to leave the country."

Since the unemployment rate for people with higher education is nearly 20%—the highest in the world—more than 200,000 young Greeks have left the country in search of better opportunities abroad. I discussed Greece's brain drain with Victoria, 18, a first-year electrical and computer engineering student at the University of Thessaly. "Don't be mistaken," she says, "all those young people that seek a better life abroad care deeply for Greece and won't hesitate to return once things have improved." Victoria herself is already considering leaving Greece once she finishes her studies. Who can blame her? She is highly unlikely to find a job in her field after graduation.

Collapse of Production

Austerity policies have also led the country's productive sector to near collapse, with industrial production in 2015 down by a staggering 35% compared to its level in 2008. Industrial production currently represents less than 10% of Greece's GDP, an exceptionally low level historically for the country, as well as for the eurozone today.

To be sure, the deindustrialization of the Greek economy started a lot earlier, in the early 1980s. The country's new development model, after its integration into the European Community and the emerging Single Market, systematically favored the tertiary (services) sector and ignored the primary (agriculture, mining, etc.) and secondary (manufacturing) sectors. Greek industries, accustomed to the heavy protectionist measures of the post-war period and poorly prepared for the requirements of market integration and the liberalization of trade, failed to adapt. The massive influx of European funds to the tertiary sector (mainly tourism) shaped a services-centered economy (the services sector contributes over 80% to the country's GDP), while weakening the country's competitiveness and contributing decisively to the dismantling of its industrial base.

Things got immeasurably worse after 2009. During the recession, about 250,000 small and medium-sized enterprises closed down. Many more have been forced to the verge of closure due to reduced revenues and increased financial obligations to social security funds, tax offices, and banks. Thousands of small business owners have opted to relocate to neighboring Balkan countries, which offer lower labor costs and corporate tax breaks.

"Reality has shown that the austerity measures applied across Europe are not the most effective response to the crisis," says Costas, a civil engineer from Patra, Greece's third largest city, in the southern region of the Peloponnese. Costas is 45 years old and a former member of SYRIZA, the current governing party. "No other country in the eurozone has had to impose such far-reaching austerity programs," he says, "and I just don't see how Greek society can sustain the burden of yet another bailout."

The policy is simply not working, even on its own terms. After five years of austerity and three bailout agreements, Greece's national debt of 320 billion euros is right where it was in 2010. But its debt-to-GDP ratio has shot up to 175% (compared to 150% in 2010), and the European Commission projects that it will rise to 200% in 2016. The country's destroyed economy will never be able to repay this huge volume of debt.

SYRIZA U-Turn, Popular Disillusionment

Originally elected in January 2015 on a vehement anti-austerity platform, Greek Prime Minister Alexis Tsipras subsequently made a complete U-turn. Ignoring the popular outcry against austerity, loudly expressed in a referendum on July 5, he has given in to the creditors' demands. In August, SYRIZA and the creditors signed a new bailout agreement, including not only another round of austerity measures but also neocolonial restrictions on Greece's national sovereignty. No legislation related to the objectives of the bailout, however minor, can be taken by Greece's political institutions without the prior approval of its creditors. The creditors thus have the right to monitor the Greek government and to wield veto power over virtually all policy measures in Greece.

And yet, on September 20, Tsipras won a new election, again forming a government. The result seemed to vindicate his capitulation. It appears that Greek voters, confronted with a narrative presenting the new agreement as inescapable, opted to give the governing party a second chance. "This wasn't a vote of hope," says Costas, the civil engineer from Patra, "but a vote for the 'lesser evil' within the limits of a 'nothing can really change' mentality."

Costas is even convinced that if there were another general election soon, the governing party would still emerge victorious. Greek voters appear to think that there is no credible alternative to austerity. "Ever since the PM marginalized any voices in SYRIZA that tried to show a different way and declared there was no alternative," he says, "Greek society, having lost its morale, has come to accept its fate."

Defeat and Apathy

To fully understand the popular mood, one must look at the abstention rates in the recent election. Turnout plummeted, with a record-high abstention rate of 45%. In addition, blank ballots reached an extraordinary 2.5%. The message is quite clear:

The Greek people's disappointment has led to a massive rejection of the political process altogether. Victoria tells me that most of her friends either cast a blank ballot or didn't bother to vote at all since "they didn't believe any of the existing political parties could actually make a difference."

The low turnout was not an isolated incident. During the past few years, social unrest and frustration over the austerity measures have given rise to widespread discontent and large-scale demonstrations. But the decline of the struggle as unemployment began to bite and, especially, SYRIZA's betrayal of popular hopes have led to a wholesale rejection of politics by broad layers of the population. The sense of defeat and indifference is pronounced among workers, and especially the young.

"Wishful thinking," says Costas about SYRIZA's hopes to overturn austerity by creating a domino effect in the countries of the European periphery. The balance of power has proven not that easy to change and now people feel that Greece is being punished for daring to question Europe's neoliberal policies.

European Union officials have categorically ruled out any possibility of a debt write-down. Restructuring in the form of a lengthening of maturity or perhaps a lowering of interest rates is still on the table, but it would have very debatable long-term results. Greece would probably be given more time to get back on its feet, but this would not eliminate short-term financing problems. Besides, even though Greek aid loans are very long-term (over thirty years) and interest rates have already been lowered several times (lower than 1%), the country's national debt is still considered unsustainable.

As for the SYRIZA government's current promise to implement a "parallel" social program that would ease the burden of harsh new austerity policies on poorer Greeks, it has already been forced to withdraw the intended bill following severe objections by the country's creditors. Many of the proposed measures lacked required budget-impact estimates. There were also concerns about the program's compatibility with the conditions of the third bailout agreement. "Parallel" programs running alongside austerity measures are not what the EU has in mind, nor would they be possible to implement within the strict framework of the latest bailout.

The Prospect of Change

The only real question for Greece at the moment is: Could there be an alternative path?

Not everyone has given in to despondency and apathy. In a school building in central Athens, I meet Georgia, a young teacher and mother of three, who offers extra classes to underprivileged students free of charge. "People would take to the streets because they hoped they could make an actual difference," she says. "Now it is clear that our hopes were false." Nonetheless, she tells me, the economic crisis has made her more politically aware. She now chooses to spend much of her time and energy in political and social movements and social solidarity structures, where she can actually feel useful.

Popular Unity, a new political front including SYRIZA's left wing, which split from the party by refusing to accept the new bailout, has so far offered the only coherent argument about how Greece could adopt an anti-bailout strategy. Its radical program includes the introduction of a new national currency, a deep national debt write-off, a lifting of austerity measures, and a restructuring of the productive sector

---

ENKLO: Life, Death—and Rebirth?

A case in point of Greece's manufacturing decline is provided by United Textiles (ENKLO), a 140-year-old company operating in Central Macedonia and Thrace with a strong presence in international markets, a skilled workforce, advanced technology, and excellent product quality. The company closed down in 2009, sinking under a debt burden of 350 million euros due mostly to poor management decisions and the expansion of its business activities beyond the textiles industry.

Ever since its shutdown, the laid-off workers, unable to find other jobs and refusing to accept that the company would never operate again, have been maintaining the equipment and guarding the buildings in order to prevent theft. "We are here night and day to make sure that the machines remain unharmed," says Petros, who has worked as an electrician for 25 years.

Instead of the scheduled liquidation of the company's property, the workers now propose its revival by converting its debts into stockholders' equity, taking advantage of the country's bankruptcy code. It is an ambitious business plan that aspires to utilize the existing equipment and the invaluable expertise of the workers.

No public funds are needed to re-start production. All that's required is a government intervention that would settle any legal complications that may arise. With the government's support, Petros argues, the company could operate the very next day.

---

and the welfare state. However, Popular Unity has so far failed to convince Greek voters, and did not gain parliamentary representation in the last elections.

Social injustice has spurred new modes of resistance far from political parties and trade unions. As the state becomes ever more hostile to the Greek people, many choose to self-organize by forming neighborhood assemblies and solidarity networks that support basic human rights, organizing micro-economies without middle-men, and setting up "solidarity clinics" providing free healthcare.

This is a period of reflection and finding alternative forms of resistance that could potentially be the basis for something new to emerge in the future. All hope is not yet lost that Greece may regain some economic stability and find a development policy in the interest of its people. "People feel exhausted, defeated and betrayed," says Georgia, "but many refuse to give up." ❑

Sources: Eurostat news release 181/2015 (ec.europa.eu/eurostat/documents); Eurostat dataset (ec. europa.eu/eurostat), "Youth unemployment rate," "Long-term unemployment rate," "Production in industry—manufacturing," "Production in industry—total (excluding construction)," "Production in industry—annual data, percentage change," "General government gross debt—annual data"; "Young, gifted and Greek: Generation G—the world's biggest brain drain," *The Guardian* (theguardian.com); C. Pitelis & N. Antonakis (2003), "Manufacturing and competitiveness: the case of Greece," *Journal of Economic Studies*, Vol. 30, Issue 5, pp. 535—547; H. Louri and I. Pepelasis Minoglou (2002), "A hesitant evolution: industrialisation and de-industrialisation in Greece over the long run", *Journal of European Economic Studies*, Vol. 31, No. 2, pp. 321-348; M. Nence, "Greek entrepreneurship after crisis—investment abroad, the easiest solution" (pecob.eu); Kathimerini, "Crisis wipes out a quarter of Greece's SMEs" (ekathimerini.com); September 2015 official election results (ekloges.ypes.gr)..

Article 6.6

PUERTO RICO'S COLONIAL DEBT
"Compromise" protects vulture funds, not Puerto Rico.

BY JOSÉ A. LAGUARTA RAMÍREZ
JULY/AUGUST 2016

At least 23 of the 49 people killed in the mass shooting that took place at Pulse nightclub in Orlando on June 12, 2016 were born in Puerto Rico. While the horrendous hate crime targeted LGBT people of all ethnicities, the large proportion of island-born casualties is not surprising, as the central Florida city has become a preferred destination of Puerto Rican migrants over the past two decades. Steadily growing since the onset of the island's current "fiscal" crisis in 2006, yearly out-migration from Puerto Rico now surpasses that of the 1950s. The island's total population has begun to decline for the first time in its history.

Nearly a third of the island-born victims of the Orlando massacre were 25 or younger, most of them students employed in services or retail. This is the population group that will be hit hardest when the ironically named Puerto Rico Oversight, Management, and Economic Stability Act (PROMESA) comes into effect. Among its other "promises" for working-class Puerto Ricans, PROMESA will cut the minimum wage in Puerto Rico for those under 25, from the current federally mandated $7.25 to $4.25 per hour, and scale back the federal nutritional assistance program on the island. Purportedly aimed at "job-creation," these measures will likely intensify the outflow of able-bodied "low-skilled" workers. Ongoing out-migration has already decimated the number of available healthcare and other professionals on the island. Puerto Rico's 2013 median household income of $19,183 was barely half that of Mississippi, the poorest U.S. state (at $37,479), despite a cost of living that rivals that of most major cities in the United States. Inequality on the island is also greater than in any of the states.

The U.S. House of Representatives approved PROMESA on the evening of June 9, following a strong endorsement by President Barack Obama. The bill, which would also impose an unelected and unaccountable federal oversight board and allow court-supervised restructuring of part of the island's $73 billion debt, now awaits consideration by the Senate. Its advocates hope the president can sign PROMESA into law before July 1, when $1.9 billion's worth of Puerto Rico general obligation bonds will come due. Unlike those issued by public utility corporations and certain autonomous agencies, general obligation bonds, under Puerto Rico's colonial constitution, must be repaid before any further public spending for the following fiscal year is authorized. Puerto Rico's government has partially defaulted three times within the past year, but not on general obligation bonds. Puerto Rico is not the only place, under the global regime of austerity capitalism, to face predatory creditors and the imposition of unelected rulers—as illustrated by cases like Argentina, Greece, and postindustrial U.S. cities such as Flint, Mich.—but its century-old colonial status has made it particularly vulnerable and defenseless.

The House vote followed a concerted, carefully timed media push by the Democratic establishment, on the premise that "despite its flaws" PROMESA represents a bipartisan compromise that is, in Obama's words, "far superior to the status quo." Among similar statements, a *New York Times* editorial on May 31 claimed that PROMESA "offers the island its best chance of survival." However, following the bill's approval, Republican House Speaker Paul Ryan tweeted in almost identical terms that PROMESA is "the best chance," but for something quite different—"for American taxpayers to be protected from a bailout of Puerto Rico." The threat of a taxpayer-funded "bailout" (which has never been on the table) has been deployed in anonymous scare ads, probably financed by high-risk/yield-seeking "vulture funds" that hold Puerto Rican bonds and so oppose PROMESA's mild restructuring provisions.

PROMESA's oversight board, which will be staffed by San Juan and Washington insiders with the bondholders' best interests at heart, is sure to continue to impose draconian austerity measures that have already slashed much-needed social services. (Former Puerto Rico governor Luis Fortuño, a Republican who enacted legislation laying off up to 30,000 public employees in order to appease credit rating agencies, has been mentioned as a likely appointee.) Democratic support for the bill was forthcoming despite the fact that neither the oversight provisions nor those reducing the minimum wage were removed.

Most U.S. observers reduce Puerto Rico's debt crisis to a result of "mismanagement" by its local administrators. (A Google search of the terms "Puerto Rico," "debt," and "mismanagement" yields pieces articulating this narrative from Bloomberg, CNN, *USA Today*, the *National Review*, and the Huffington Post, among others, within the top 10 hits.) This view conveniently erases the historical and structural roots of the crisis.

U.S. troops occupied Puerto Rico in 1898 and the Supreme Court quickly declared it an "unincorporated territory" subject to the authority of the U.S. Congress and federal courts system, without voting representation in Congress. Although U.S. citizenship was extended to individuals in 1917, and a local constitution was authorized and adopted in 1952 (not without significant amendments by Congress), the juridical fact of colonialism has remained unaltered, as reiterated by the Court on the very day of the House vote on PROMESA. (See Puerto Rico v. Sánchez Valle, a criminal case on double jeopardy, in which the Court reminds Puerto Rico's local government that unlike states, it is not legally considered a "sovereign" separate from Congress.) In the mid-1970s, Puerto Rico's comparative advantage as the only low-wage tax haven with direct access to the U.S. market waned. Washington's solution to the colony's economic stagnation was Section 936 of the Internal Revenue Code, which granted federal tax exemptions to U.S. corporations on products made in Puerto Rico, in addition to local tax breaks in place since the 1940s. The local government, in turn, pursued massive debt-fueled investment in infrastructure, whose use by these corporations it heavily subsidized. The resulting debt addiction spiraled out of control in the 1990s, fed by easy credit, and exacerbated after Congress began a ten-year phase out of Section 936 in 1996. Meanwhile, profits continue to leave the island to the tune of $30 billion annually.

In international law, the term for debt incurred by colonial, corrupt, or authoritarian regimes is "odious debt." A prominent example of its application was the cancellation of Cuba's colonial debt when that country achieved its independence from Spain, following the so-called Spanish-American War of 1898. The U.S. government's argument at the time, which Spain never formally accepted but most of Cuba's creditors eventually did, was that the debt was incurred neitherwith the consent of the Cuban people nor to their benefit. Although odious debt is a grey area of international law, with sufficient political resolve Puerto Rico's leadership could use it to bolster a claim to refuse payment. In 2008, Ecuador invoked the doctrine as part of a largely successful audit and partial default. Such a course would necessarily put Puerto Rico on a collision course with colonialism, as it would need to refuse to recognize any resulting lawsuits in U.S. courts.

This is precisely the type of outcome that PROMESA is designed to prevent. It is one which Puerto Rico's current administrators have proven entirely unwilling to pursue. Yet it is a path that is not alien to U.S. political history: one of the grievances that led to the thirteen colonies' Declaration of Independence was the imposition of new taxes—largely to pay debts incurred by Britain in the Seven Years' War. An independent Puerto Rico, released of an illegitimate debt burden incurred to profit U.S. corporations, could better focus on serving the needs of its poor and working-class majority. A movement capable of leading such a process has yet to materialize, but with U.S. statehood farther away than ever and housing and labor markets in migrant destinations becoming increasingly saturated, the matter is far from decided.

As living conditions on the island continue to deteriorate under PROMESA (and they surely will), young Puerto Rican students and workers will continue to flood those places where family connections, climate, the price of airfare, and job opportunities pull them. Not all will be targeted for physical violence because of their multiple identities, as the Orlando victims were. Their fate, however, will continue to be a haunting reminder of the ways in which invisible forces pattern seemingly random events in the lives of individuals and communities. ❑

Article 6.7

MILITARY SPENDING IN THE SWAMPLAND
What Now, What Next?

BY JAMES M. CYPHER
March/April 2017; updated June 2018

On September 11, 1941, the U.S. War Department commenced construction of its new headquarters, the Pentagon: With each of its five sides running the length of three football fields, encompassing four million square feet of work space, it remains even today the world's largest office building. Placing it where President Roosevelt wanted meant that the edifice would be constructed on the Potomac River's flood plain, largely over a swamp in an area known as Hell's Bottom, requiring the sinking of 41,192 pilings—approximately one piling for each person to be housed in the Pentagon—to keep the giant, fortified edifice from sliding into the swamp.

President Trump has repeatedly boasted of his intentions to drain the Pentagon swamp—as one commentator put it, "taking down the Military-Industrial Complex one tweet at a time"—emphasizing the need to alter the long-known propensity of the U.S. Department of Defense (DoD) for coddling military contractors and facilitating the cozy, "revolving door" employment opportunities provided for high-ranking retired military officials. During the 2016 presidential campaign, he committed his administration "to conducting a full audit of the Pentagon" to eliminate duplicate personnel and to uncover profligate contracting procedures.

But is there reason to expect that the increasingly secret, increasingly remote, increasingly unanalyzed National Security State—the Pentagon's "State within the State"—will experience a major reconfiguration? This is the deeply embedded State which exercises its "relative autonomy" through the coordination of the National Security Council (NSC), the chairman of the Joint Chiefs of Staff, and the 17 intelligence agencies which define and project global U.S. military power. The Trump administration will operate the NSC in an unprecedented manner, with the President's top political advisor, "alt-right" militarist Stephen Bannon, as a voting member of the key Principals Committee of the Council. [Note: The once-important role played by Bannon at the NSC ended with his dismissal in April 2017. —*Eds.*] The Principals Committee exercises sweeping powers over the nature and scope of U.S. foreign policy decisions by framing and recommending stratagems to the President. That the Industrial-Military-Congressional Juggernaut (IMCJ)—which constitutes the institutional base on which the National Security State was erected—could be slowed or redirected by the incoming presidential administration defies credibility. If anything, there is every reason to anticipate that in the Pentagon's lucrative and murky wetlands, wherein the giant "prime" military contractors and their subcontractors dwell, the swamp will increase in depth and opacity.

Plumbing the Depths

Like so many of the details surrounding the IMCJ, the annual total number of contracting firms cannot be accurately determined. The fact that a single "multiple awards" contract—issued by the Navy on June 20, 2016—went to 608 firms indicates that a very large number of U.S. corporations are directly tied to the IMCJ. The total number of U.S. corporations feeding at the Pentagon trough—directly or indirectly—is unknown, because the DoD does not track the thousands of subcontractor firms. The Defense Contract Management Agency stated that in 2014 they were supervising over 20,000 direct (or "prime") contractors, meaning that the total number of firms involved could easily be around 60,000. Notably, there are military contractor "enclaves," such as San Diego, Calif., where $45 billion in military spending in 2016 functioned, according to economist Lynn Reaser, as the "most important and largest economic catalyst," accounting for 20% of the regional economy. Yet a review of the daily contracts issued by the DoD clearly demonstrates that contracts were spread across almost all of the United States in 2016.

In the 1970s and early 1980s, a steady stream of research focused on how the IMCJ functioned, and for whom. In the post-9/11 era of constant war, critical scrutiny of the IMCJ (save the occasional revealing broadside) has waned. A culture increasingly marked by militarism—the glorification of or unconscious deference to all things military—has created a new ideological climate wherein an analytical critique of U.S. military power projection and the economic and structural role of the National Security State is most unwelcome. Even when it does occur, it is largely overlooked.

However, once in a while some outsized travesty perpetuated by the IMCJ briefly draws critical attention. Over the past 15 years, the $400 billion F-35 fighter plane contract has become the standard reference point used by critical observers, including many on the left, to illustrate the IMCJ's affinity for cost overruns. In December 2016, then-president-elect Trump unexpectedly disparaged the F-35 contract and, in February 2017, he wrangled a promise from its contractor, Lockheed Martin Corporation, to push the price down from an astronomical $102 million per plane to a merely elephantine $94.6 million.

More broadly, the Pentagon's Command, Control, Communications, Computers, Intelligence, Surveillance and Reconnaissance (C4ISR) programs have historically overrun their scheduled costs by 67%, space programs by 89%, and drone programs by 109%. Meanwhile, the Lockheed Corporation has spread F-35 production activities through 35 U.S. states, claiming that the vast project now maintains, directly and indirectly, 146,000 jobs. Even if the administration cuts back a bit on the rate of price increases for the planes, this will be no more than a Presidential showman tactic—the small sums saved will be redirected toward other programs.

The Secret $100 Billion B-21 Raider

More important at this juncture, in terms of public policy, are the contractors' current marketing tactics. Combined with the military doctrines and strategic policies pursued by the National Security State, they set the present and future course of the

Pentagon steamroller. For one example, there is the case of the forthcoming B-21 Raider, a follow-on contract to the B-2 stealth bomber.

The stealthy, drone-toting, missile-laden, long-range B-21 Raider nuclear bomber project was quietly announced by the Pentagon on October 27, 2015: Virginia-based Northrop Grumman Corporation received the "prime" contract award—with an estimated full-development price of $100 billion (including all support systems) according to the Senate Arms Services Committee chairman. Meanwhile, the anticipated delivery date (rumored to be 2025), as well as the quantity (thought to be 100, but maybe 150), both remain unknown to U.S. citizens.

More than a year later, little if anything is known regarding this fantastic artifact except that steps toward development and production had been initiated by several subcontractors, including Janiki Industries near Seattle—a location represented by members of important military-related subcommittees in the Senate and House. Likewise, production or engineering has begun in several other states or congressional districts represented by powerful members of the armed services committees: major subcontractors in these states/districts include Orbital ATK (Ohio), BAE Systems (New Hampshire), Pratt & Whitney (Connecticut), GKN Aerospace (Missouri), Rockwell Collins (Iowa), and Spirit Aerosystems (Kansas). For Northrop Grumman, the B-21 contract is particularly attractive because the company will orchestrate the complex web of first-, second-, and third-tier subcontractors while holding a "cost plus" (instead of a fixed-price or competitive-bid) contract with the Pentagon for the initial development phase. (See box.) This is business as usual.

Military contracting is essentially a "cost maximizing" undertaking. The Pentagon is fundamentally disinterested in controlling procurement and maintenance costs, since they are a "quality maximizing" institution with the ability (generally) to pay any price for cutting-edge performance. Fat profits on the initial Pentagon contract are not necessarily the major inducement for contractors. With the tax-

---

Profit Pyramiding

"Cost plus" means, in the first instance, that "profit pyramiding" will be rampant: the pyramiding process allows the third tier contractors to pass their profits through as "costs" to the second tier, while the second tier contractors do the same, on up to the "prime" contractor on the B-21 (Northrop Grumman). Thus, should the Pentagon agree to a "reasonable" profit margin of perhaps 5% over cost on widget X, which is an input to widget Y, which is an input to widget Z, Northrop can then turn around and incorporate all three widgets into its costs (including the subcontractors' profits at each stage), finally tacking on its own approved markup of 5%. Ignoring the impact of all-but-inevitable cost overruns, a "modest" approved profit margin of 5% on the $100 billion contract will not amount to $5 billion, but rather to $15 to 20 billion.

The difference between the acknowledged rate of profit which Northrop Grumman will show and the *actual rate* (which will include all that gleaned by the subcontractors) will be obscured by the Pentagon, never to be known by the U.S. taxpayers—who have long been conditioned to accept the Industry-Pentagon precept that the idea of "war profiteering" is a crank fantasy. Consider, finally, that "profit"—according to the standard economics textbook explanation—is the "reward" for the risks that successful competing firms must face. By definition, "cost-plus" contract have no risks; rather, the contractor is rewarded for all so-called "reasonable" cost allowances, however conjured.

payers funding all the learning involved in the mastery of new engineering, design, and production processes, the "prime" contractor frequently can count on a big "after-market" for weapons systems in terms of foreign arms sales and rich licensing agreements. Potentially even more important are the long-term benefits arising from the technological advancements, sometimes yielding patents and innovation breakthroughs. Prohibitive research and development costs are frequently offloaded onto the Pentagon while the contractors reap a cornucopia of technological spinoffs.

As recently documented by Marianna Mazzucato in *The Entrepreneurial State* and by Linda Weiss in *America Inc.? Innovation and Enterprise in the National Security State*, military/government contracts have been instrumental in covering much of the developmental costs for major technologies giving rise to the computer, the semiconductor, biotechnology, and nanotechnology. The world's largest tech company in 2016, Apple, soared because it "mastered designing and engineering technologies that were first developed and funded by the U.S. government and military," notes Mazzucato. The same has been true for key technologies such as the satellite, the global positioning system (GPS), artificial intelligence, and robotics.

The estimated value of the B-21 contract is not overwhelmingly large by the standards of the IMCJ—the giant F-35 fighter aircraft contract is currently anticipated to ring out at $400 billion. The B-21 may not be exactly "representative," but it is close. Large contracts are routinely granted to only a handful of giant military contracting corportations: Northrop Grumman, the number two military contractor in fiscal year 2014, received $5.76 billion from its direct sales to the Pentagon. (The company is also an important subcontractor in the F-35 program.) While the B-21 bomber will puportedly have an astonishing range of military capabilities, it is not conceived as a stand-alone project. Rather, it will apparently require an "escort" fighter plane, under the Penetrating Counter-Air (PCA) Program. This vaguely described "power projection aircraft," or "sixth generation" war plane, would have long range (intercontinental) capabilities and would be highly manuverable. As currently conceived, then, the B-21 Raider would come with a "long tail" of accompanying multi-billion dollar "escort" warplane contracts.

Trump and the IMCJ

These two new, technology-loaded aircraft programs would form the core of the current "modernization" wave for the U.S. Air Force. Prior to President Trump's election, widespread concern was voiced throughout the IMCJ as to where sufficient funds could be found to push these two programs forward—along with several others designed for the various branches of the military/space services. In September 2016, only a year after the B-21 program was announced, the Air Force Secretary called into question the viability of this weapons-modernization program, declaring that funding for Air Force personnel needs would have to come first. It therefore followed, given what were then considered lasting budgetary constraints, that President Obama's weapons-modernization programs would have to be postponed, cut, or abandoned in deference to the payroll requirements of the DoD's nearly three million military and civilian employees.

But then November's presidential-election results changed the equation. Like many before him, Trump apparently wants "more bang for the buck" (high weapon capacity at low per unit cost). But, more importantly, he also stands for "more bucks for more and bigger bangs" (widescale weapons modernization programs) which will most likely mean the largest surge in military spending since President Reagan's program to "Rearm America." Under President Trump, the first target of the forthcoming arms buildup will be the elimination of the so-called congressional "sequestration" program that has largely capped major increases in military expenditures since 2013. The sequestration program mandated roughly a $500 billion cut in planned military expenditures over a decade, excluding the military's payroll. Even so, the basic military budget for fiscal year (FY) 2013 (October 1, 2012-September 31, 2013) was never cut by the mandated amount of $55 billion, as fast-shuffle adjustments and accounting subterfuges brought the programmed reductions down to just over $30 billion. By FY 2014, the Pentagon was skating through a loophole befitting its customary style via a special "war funding" slush fund known as Overseas Contigency Operations (OCO) expenditures. By doing so, the actual "base" military budget (for weapons procurement, research and development, maintenance, and operations) plus the OCO budget was reduced by little more than 0.5% from planned Pentagon spending prior to the sequester program.

Nonetheless, the IMCJ wanted to push military spending up at a rapid rate to support the vast costs of modernization—something that basically could not be done under the terms of the sequestration deal. (That leaves social programs as the only target for deficit hawks' spending cuts.) Fear of the deficit, and the ever-building government debt that it caused, had largely put the kibosh on plans to boost military outlays until candidate Trump emerged at the head of the pack in the election race. Republican congressional leaders will now implement Trump's September 2016 call "to fully eliminate the defense sequester."

The Obama Administration tried to maintain effective parity in growth between the military and non-military portions of the budget. Now, the military's floodgates are swinging open once again, providing hundreds of billions of dollars in new contracts for the IMCJ over the next four years. In late January 2017, Trump issued a "Presidential Memorandum—Rebuilding the US Armed Forces," which announced a forthcoming budget amendment for military readiness for FY 2017 (thereby probably jettsoning the sequestration program) as well as issuing a carte blanche mandate to the Secretary of Defense, to prepare a "plan of action" within 30 days. This plan will be the basis for the Secretary's Readiness Review, to be implimented before FY 2019. The Memorandum also authorized a new National Defense Strategy—a sweeping document used to define the strategic military goals and priorities of the United States—also to be prepared by the Secretary of Defense. This was followed by the President's commitment to "one of the greatest military buildups in U.S. history" in late Feburary and the announcement that the FY 2018 military budget would rise by more than 9%. Here is a summary of the personnel, policies, and programs the Trump Administration now plan to deploy:

1. A battle-tested, jingoistic, self-confident array of former generals—exuding more than a whiff of Prussian military swagger—will occupy the

key leadership positions in the National Security State, once historically reserved for civilian leaders: these include the appointment of Generals James Mattis as Secretary of Defense, H.R. McMaster as the National Security Advisor, Keith Kellogg as the NSC's Chief of Staff, and John Kelly to head the Department of Homeland Security, the third largest cabinet department. Holding a military history Ph.D. degree from the University of North Carolina, counterinsurgency expert McMaster (known as the "Inconoclastic General") seeks to expunge the Vietnam Syndrome. Arising from the U.S.'s prolonged (1954–1975) Southeast Asian military debacle, the term encapsulates the profound reluctance of the U.S. citizenry to send military personnel into deadly combat, and to only support engagement-at-a-distance by sanctioning a minimal fighting force backed by a maximum level of advanced military technologies—such as "network-centric warfare" operations. Based on his interpretation of the Vietnam War and experience in the Iraq military campaigns, McMaster strongly advocates prioritizing unfiltered military expertise (rather than the views of civilian advisors mesmerized by "shock and awe" visions of technocratic warfighting) in the guidance and execution of U.S. Grand Strategy—the coordination and deployment of all national resources in pursuit of U.S. hegemony via "power projection."

2. President Obama, upon signing his last (FY 2017) National Defense Authorization Act in December 2016, opened a path to greatly extend the arms race in space by authorizing the Pentagon to begin research, development, testing, and evaluation (RDTE) for a space-based missile system. A 2012 report by the National Academy of Sciences concluded that a minimal space-based weapons system would cost at least $200 billion to build and necessitate hundreds of billions to operate. Operation would likely require establishment of a new Unified Combat Commander in Chief's (CINCs) mission area for Space. Currently there are six area Combat Commands, such as the new U.S. Africa Command and the U.S. Central Command (covering the Middle East).

3. A massive build-up of ships deployed by the U.S. Navy—from 272 to 350—will cost an estimated $120 billion (excluding cost overruns). This is considered the largest single expenditure of the anticipated Trump build-up and would constitute a major national jobs creation program to revitalize an infrastructure of naval construction shipyards, depots, and auxilary facilities. The Navy is charged with sustaining its presence in 18 maritime regions where, ostensibly, the U.S. has "critical national interests."

4. An increase of 90,000 active duty military personnel for the U.S. Army will require a 20% increase in the Army's budget, or about $118 billion over the next four years, using current per soldier costs as the basis of the calculation.

5. An increase of 300 fighter aircraft (now including the "escort fighter" plane for the B-21 Raider nuclear bomber) over the current baseline of 900. The U.S. Air Force budget would have to leap upward, considering that a "generic" F-35 fighter currently may cost about $150 million. Even at half that price, the 300 new aircraft would cost $22.5 billion (once again excluding cost overruns). On top of this amount would be the estimated $100 billion to develop the B-21 Raider. And, of course, all planes come with massive support costs: operating costs per hour routinely reach $58,000.

Simply summing the costs of the items mentioned above reveals potential new outlays of $560.5 billion, or over $140 billion per year over a four year period. Contract delays and funding debates might conceivably hold this to a $70 billion per year jump in the *base* (or discretionary) military budget: This would translate into a 13.4% increase over FY 2017—which would be mandated through congressional special appropriations at President Trump's urging.

Larger annual *base budget* outlays necessitate more spending for retirement funds (including healthcare) as well as for Veterans Affairs. With interest rates almost sure to rise, and with President Trump using deficits to finance the forthcoming arms buildup, the share of the national debt attributable to national security spending will rise, as will annual interest payments.

The Bottom Line

For 2017, based on President Obama's last military budget, *total U.S. military related spending* (including the special warfighting account known as the Overseas Contingency Opertions budget, nuclear bomb building, retirement and Veterans outlays, International Affairs, Homeland Security, and interest payments attributable to past military expenditures) will be $1.04 *trillion* in FY 2017, or more than 5% of current GDP, according to the January-March 2016 *Defense Monitor*.

But this calculates only the direct effects of military spending: The indirect or "induced" effects of secondary and tertiary rounds of spending, using the calculating methods adopted by the San Diego regional economic impact study, suggest that, pre-Trumpland, about 8% of U.S. GDP is dependent in some way on the Pentagon-financed programs, past or present. Adding in direct foreign arms sales of $40 billion per year (which would not exist without the comparative adavantage created by Pentagon largesse) would modestly raise these estimates.

President Trump's administration could easily push up total military spending (including all direct and indirect effects) by 1 or 2% of GDP, *excluding warfighting scenarios*. Unfortunately, new high-cost warfighting scenarios are extremely likely: The leadership positions of the National Security State are now held by a troika of warlords. Living under the sway of "military metaphysics," these "crackpot realists" (to use the terminology of sociologist C. Wright Mills) back warfighting programs across the Middle East and North and Central Africa. As Mills noted in 1958: "In crackpot realism, a highflying moral rhetoric is joined with an opportunist crawling among a great scatter of unfocused fears and demands. ... The official expectation of war also enables men to solve the prob-

How Has It Turned Out?

Trump's rhetoric about swamp-draining convinced a lot of people—including some on the left—that he was committed to non-interventionism, even as he called for the bombing of three nations and the continued occupation of another during his campaign. But James Cypher's prediction that the national security state "swamp will increase in depth and opacity" under Trump appears to be right on the mark.

Trump's hawkish national security team has gotten even more hawkish. Secretary of State Rex Tillerson and National Security Advisor H.R. McMaster were replaced by Mike Pompeo and John Bolton, respectively. Both are determined to rip up the Iran nuclear deal, a decision that will not only bring the United States and Iran closer to war, but continue to harm Iranian civilians (particularly the Iranian poor) and inhibit the potential for Iranians to spur independent change within Iran.

Even tepid promises by Trump to reduce the costs of individual weapons have gone by the wayside. Though Trump claimed he got Lockheed Martin to reduce the costs of their F-35 fighter plane contract by $8 billion, plans to expedite the construction of the plane have led to a variety of defects that will make the finished planes "less reliable [and] more costly… to maintain" for the future.

The problem goes far deeper than just Trump, or even the GOP. Seventy-three Democrats in the House and 36 Democrats in the Senate voted in support of the "Bipartisan Budget Act of 2018," otherwise known as H.R. 1892, which allotted an $80 billion increase in military spending in 2018, and $85 billion in 2019. Still, pundits continue to parrot the idea that the government is revenue-constrained to justify austerity, even though there always seems to be enough money for defense spending. There is an important lesson in this: Trump's militarism is bad not because it is attached to higher deficit spending, but because it targets the world's most vulnerable people and diverts real resources that could be used to create a more peaceful, equitable world.

—*Sean Keith, June 2018*

lems of the economic cycles without resort to political policies that are distastful to many politicians."

Going forward into Trumpland, instead of draining the Pentagon's swamp the available evidence suggests that U.S. society is headed down the military drain as "defense needs" starve out the few skeletal social programs that have survived decades of neoliberal attack. ❑

Sources: C. Wright Mills, *The Causes of World War Three* (Simon and Schuster, 1958); Dan Graizer, "Senators Vote to Keep Bomber Price Secret," *The Defense Monitor,* July-August 2016; Dave Majumdar, "Lockheed Martin, General Dynamics, Northrop Grumman, Boeing and Raytheon: America's 5 Top Defense Contractors," *The National Interest,* Nov. 10, 2016 (nationalinterest. org); David Williams, "President Obama signs defense bill that could spur new space-based arms race," *Los Angeles Times,* Dec. 23, 2016 (latimes.com); Defense Contract Management Agency, "Director, Defense Contract Management Agency," 2014 (dcma.mil); Linda Weiss, *America Inc.? Innovation and Enterprise in the National Security State* (Cornell University Press, 2014); Mandy Smithberger, "Pentagon's 2017 Budget was Mardi Gras for Defense Contractors," *Defense Monitor,* January-March 2016; Marianna Mazzucato, *The Entrepreneurial State* (Anthem Press, 2013); Michael Shear, et.al., "Trump Joining List of Critics of Fighter Jet," *New York Times,* Dec. 13, 2016; Northrup-Grumman Corporation, "Announcement of Long-range Strike Bomber Contract Award," Oct. 27, 2015 (northropgrumman.com); San Diego Military Advisory Council,

"Press conference & luncheon attended by Mayor Kevin Faulconer, California Governor's Military Council, military commanders & defense industry leaders," 2016 (sdmac.org); Sidney Freedberg, "Bow Wave Time Bomb: B-21, Ohio Replacement Costs Likely To Grow," *Breaking Defense*, Aug. 4, 2016 (breakingdefense.com); Steve Vogel, "The Battle of Arlington: How the Pentagon Got Built," *Washington Post*, April 26, 1999 (washingtonpost.com); U.S. Department of Defense, "Contracts Press Operations Release No: CR-124-16" (defense.gov); President Trump, "Presidential Memorandum-Rebuilding U.S. Armed Forces" (whitehouse.gov); H.R. McMaster, "Kicking the Vietnam Syndrome," Hoover Daily Report, Feb. 17, 2003 (hoover.org).H.R. McMaster, "The Human Element: When Gadgetry Becomes Strategy," *World Affairs*, Winter 2009 (worldaffairsjournal.org).

Chapter 7

MONEY AND MONETARY POLICY

INTRODUCTION

I n October 2008, former Federal Reserve Chair Alan Greenspan confessed before
Congress that he had "made a mistake in presuming that banks ... were capable
of protecting their own shareholders," and that the financial crisis had left him "in
a state of shocked disbelief."

His successor, Ben Bernanke—given the unenviable task of pulling the economy's fat out of the fire—arguably did help to avert a complete economic meltdown.
The Federal Reserve (usually known as "the Fed") undertook limited steps to resolve
the nearly intractable mortgage debt crisis and to put in place the measures that
might prevent another financial crash. Still, working people fared no better under
Bernanke than they had under Greenspan.

Even before the financial crisis, Greenspan worried that, under his tenure, inequality had worsened to levels that threatened our democratic institutions, and
that the unprecedented level of U.S. reliance on foreign borrowing had become unsustainable. Bernanke acknowledged the seriousness of both problems as well, but
seemed just as incapable as his predecessor of seriously addressing them. In 2014,
he was succeeded as Fed chair by economist Janet Yellen, formerly the Chair of
the Council of Economic Advisers (under Bill Clinton) and Vice Chair of the Fed
(2010–2014). Jerome Powell, who was appointed by President Trump, succeeded
Yellen in February 2018. Economic stagnation, slow job growth, and severe inequality remain the order of the day.

Why should it matter who chairs the Federal Reserve? The Fed is charged with
using monetary policy to keep inflation in check and provide liquidity to keep the
economy going (or bolster a flagging economy). The Fed is supposed to use its three
tools—the reserve requirement, the discount rate, and open-market operations—to
manipulate banking activity, control the money supply, and direct the economy to
everyone's benefit.

It all sounds very technical and value-free. But what the Fed really does is
serve those who hold financial assets. So when it comes to making monetary policy, the Fed puts the interests of bondholders first, well before those of workers
or job seekers. Investors look to the Fed to protect the value of their stocks and

bonds by keeping inflation low—and if that means keeping a lid on employment growth, so be it.

To begin the chapter, three articles take us through the basics of money and the monetary system. We use money every day, but usually do not stop to think about how money is defined, how it has evolved historically, or how it is created today. Economist Doug Orr explains in everyday language what money is and how the Fed attempts to control the money supply (Article 7.1). In a related article, Robert Hockett provides a comprehensive introduction to Modern Monetary Theory, or MMT, which incorporates Keynes's "quantity theory of money" and shows us what a "curious commodity" money truly is (Article 7.2). Then, Arthur MacEwan explains how a "fractional reserve banking" system works, and whether or not it is at the root of our current economic troubles (Article 7.3).

Next, Gerald Friedman confirms that, in a "liquidity trap," monetary policy is bound to fail (Article 7.4). This was evident during Great Recession, when the Federal Reserve attempted to increase the money supply through open-market operations only to generate an explosion in excess reserves held by U.S. commercial banks. The Fed can do little to get the economy going using conventional monetary policy if banks won't make loans.

Next, in his article on the Federal Reserve's interest-rate hike (Article 7.5), Marty Wolfson explains that the Fed is planning on paying banks billions of dollars in interest even though it doesn't really have to. The Fed's conduct of monetary policy is channeled through private banks and beholden to their interests. What's more, its decision-makers see it as their sacred mission to act as protectors and benefactors of high finance.

The final two articles of the chapter step back to take a broader view of monetary policy historically.

Gerald Epstein analyzes the transition, over the last few decades, toward "inflation targeting"—central bank policies prioritizing the achievement of very low inflation above all other policy goals—in high-income and developing economies alike (Article 7.6). He considers, too, alternative goals that central banks have pursued in the past, and could again in the future, like full employment and economic development.

To round out the chapter, Alejandro Reuss (Article 7.7) looks at the key arguments made by John Maynard Keynes, in *The General Theory of Employment, Interest, and Money*, on the limitations of monetary policy as a tool for reviving economies mired in depression conditions. Reuss applies lessons from Keynes' work to current problems in the U.S. economy.

Discussion Questions

1. (Article 7.1) What are the mechanisms the Fed uses to "control" the creation of money by the banking system? Why, according to Orr, is the Fed's control over the creation of money "limited"?

2. (Article 7.2) Compare and contrast Doug Orr's article on money (7.1) with Robert Hockett's (7.2). What new elements does Keynes add to the theory of money?

3. (Article 7.3) What is "fractional reserve banking"? Do banks "create money out of thin air"? In what ways, according to MacEwan, do U.S. economic problems go deeper than the monetary system?

4. (Article 7.4) Why does Friedman, like others before him, liken monetary policy to "pushing on a string"? What evidence does Friedman offer to show that this analogy is an apt description of monetary policy today?

5. (Article 7.5) Does it make sense for the Fed to pay banks interest for their reserves, so that they will not lend at interest rates that are too low? Why or why not?

6. (Article 7.6) Why have central banks moved from prioritizing goals like full employment and economic development to championing very low inflation? Do you agree with Epstein that it would be better if central banks abandoned single-minded "inflation targeting" in favor of a broader set of macroeconomic goals?

7. (Article 7.7) What, according to Keynes, were the key limitations of monetary policy, as a response to an economic downturn? If these were well described many decades ago, why did governments rely on monetary policy in responding to the Great Recession?

Article 7.1

WHAT IS MONEY?

BY DOUG ORR
November/December 1993; revised October 2010

We all use money every day. Yet many people do not know what money actually is. There are many myths about money, including the idea that the government "prints" all of it and that it has some intrinsic value. But actually, money is less a matter of value, and more a matter of faith.

Money is sometimes called the universal commodity, because it can be traded for all other commodities. But for this to happen, everyone in society must believe that money will be accepted. If people stop believing that it will be accepted, the existing money ceases to be money. Recently in Poland, people stopped accepting the zloty, and used vodka as money instead.

In addition to facilitating exchanges, money allows us to "store" value from one point in time to another. If you sell your car today for $4,000, you probably won't buy that amount of other products today. Rather, you store the value as money, probably in a bank, until you want to use it.

The "things" that get used as money have changed over time, and "modern" people often chuckle when they hear about some of them. The Romans used salt (from which we get the word "salary"), South Sea Islanders used shark's teeth, and several societies actually used cows. The "Three Wise Men" brought gold, frankincense, and myrrh, each of which was money in different regions at the time.

If money does not exist, or is in short supply, it will be created. In POW camps, where guards specifically outlaw its existence, prisoners use cigarettes instead. In the American colonies, the British attempted to limit the supply of British pounds, because they knew that by limiting the supply of money, they could hamper the development of independent markets in the colonies. Today, the United States uses a similar policy, through the International Monetary Fund, in dealing with Latin America.

To overcome this problem, the colonists began to use tobacco leaves as money. This helped the colonies to develop, but it also allowed the holders of large plots of land to grow their own money! When the colonies gained independence, the new government decreed gold to be money, rather than tobacco, much to the dismay of Southern plantation owners. Now, rather than growing money, farmers had to find or buy it.

To aid the use of gold as money, banks would test its purity, put it in storage, and give the depositor paper certificates of ownership. These certificates, "paper money," could then be used in place of the gold itself. Since any bank could store gold and issue certificates, by the beginning of the Civil War, over 7,000 different types of "paper money" were in circulation in the United States, none of it printed by the government.

While paper money is easier to use than gold, it is still risky to carry around large amounts of cash. It is safer to store the paper in a bank and simply sign over its ownership to make a purchase. We sign over the ownership of our money by writing a check. Checking account money became popular when, in an unsuccessful attempt to control the amount of money created by banks, the government outlawed the printing of paper money by private banks in 1864.

How Banks Create Money

Banks are central to understanding money, because in addition to storing it, they help to create it. Bankers realize that not everyone will withdraw their money at the same time, so they loan out much of the money that has been deposited. It is from the interest on these loans that banks get their profits, and through these loans the banking system creates new money.

If you deposit $100 cash in your checking account at Chase Manhattan Bank, you still have $100 in money to use, because checks are also accepted as money. Chase must set aside some of this cash as "reserves," in case you or other depositors decide to withdraw money as cash. Current regulations issued by the Federal Reserve Bank (the Fed) require banks to set aside an average of three cents out of each dollar. So Chase can make a loan of $97, based on your deposit. Chase does not make loans by handing out cash but instead by putting $97 in the checking account of the person, say Emily, taking out the loan. So from your initial deposit of $100 in cash, the economy now has $197 in checking account money.

The borrower, Emily, pays $97 for some product or service by check, and the seller, say Ace Computers, deposits the money in its checking account. The total amount of checking account money is still $197, but its location and ownership have changed. If Ace Computer's account is at Citibank, $97 in cash is transferred from Chase to Citibank. This leaves just $3 in cash reserves at Chase to cover your original deposit. However, Citibank now has $97 in "new" cash on hand, so it sets aside three cents on the dollar ($2.91) and loans out the rest, $94.09, as new checking account money. Through this process, every dollar of "reserves" yields many dollars in total money.

If you think this is just a shell game and there is only $100 in "real" money, you still don't understand money. Anything that is accepted as payment for a transaction is "real" money. Cash is no more real than checking account money. In fact, most car rental companies will not accept cash as payment for a car, so for them, cash is not money!

As of June 2010, there was $883 billion of U.S. currency, i.e. "paper money," in existence. However, somewhere between 50% to 70% of it is held outside the United States by foreign banks and individuals. U.S. $100 bills are the preferred currency of choice used to facilitate illegal international transactions, such as the drug trade. The vast majority of all money actually in use in the United States is not cash, but rather checking account money. This type of money, $1,590 billion, was created by private banks, and was not "printed" by anyone. In fact, this money exists only as electronic "bits" in banks' computers. (The less "modern" South Sea Islanders could have quite a chuckle about that!)

The amount of money that banks can create is limited by the total amount of reserves, and by the fraction of each deposit that must be held as reserves. Prior to

1914, bankers themselves decided what fraction of deposits to hold as reserves. Since then, this fraction has been set by the main banking regulator, the Fed.

Until 1934, gold was held as reserves, but the supply of gold was unstable, growing rapidly during the California and Alaska "gold rushes," and very slowly at other times. As a result, at times more money was created than the economy needed, and at other times not enough money could be created. Starting in 1934, the U.S. government decided that gold would no longer be used as reserves. Cash, now printed by the Fed, could no longer be redeemed for gold, and cash itself became the reserve asset.

Banks, fearing robberies, do not hold all of their cash reserves in their own vaults. Rather, they store it in an account at a regional Fed bank. These accounts count as reserves. What banks do hold in their vaults is their other assets, such as Treasury bonds and corporate bonds.

The Fed and Bank Reserves

The only role of the government in creating money is indirectly through the Fed, which is controlled by neither the Congress nor the executive branch. If the Fed wants to expand the money supply, it must increase bank reserves. To do this, the Fed buys Treasury bonds from a bank, and pays with a check drawn on the Fed itself. By depositing the check in its reserve account at the Fed, the bank now has more reserves, so the bank can now make more loans and create new checking account money.

By controlling the amount of reserves, the Fed attempts to control the size of the money supply. But as recent history has shown, this control is limited. During the late 1970s, the Fed tried to limit the amount of money banks could create by reducing reserves, but banks simply created new forms of money, just like the POW camp prisoners and colonial farmers. In 1979, there was only one form of checking account money. Today, there are many, with odd names such as NOWs, ATSs, repos, and money market deposit accounts. If there is a profit to be made creating money, banks will find a way.

In 2010, we have the opposite problem. The Fed is trying to expand the money supply, but banks are refusing to create new money. In good times, banks hold as few reserves as possible, so they can profit from making loans. In times of crisis, banks fear that we will lose faith in the commercial banking system and all try to take out our "money" as cash. Since there is far more electronic money than cash, this is impossible. But if the bank cannot give us our money in the form we want it, the bank fails and ceases to exist. Since the start of 2007, over 300 banks, with assets totally more than $637 billion, have failed.

Since all banks fear they will be next, they want as many reserves as possible. Excess reserves are any reserves above those required by the Fed. During the 1990s, these averaged about $1 billion for the entire banking system. During the crisis of 2001, they spiked to the then unheard of level of $19 billion. As of June 2010, excess reserves in the banking system were $1,035 billion! This is the classic case of trying to push on a string. The Fed can create reserves, but only banks can create money and they are not yet willing to make any new loans.

These amorphous forms of money function only because we believe they will function, which is why the continued stability of the banking system is so critical. While it is true that the bailout of the banking system was not handled very well, and that many people who created the crisis are still profiting from it, the bailout was a necessary evil. In a modern market economy, banks create the money, and no market economy can function without its money. Money only exists if we believe in it, so we have to maintain the faith. To maintain the faith we need more democratic control over money creation, which can only come if regulation of the financial system is greatly expanded. ❏

Sources: Money supply: Federal Reserve Board, www.federalreserve.gov/releases/h6/current/; excess reserves: St. Louis Federal Reserve Bank, research.stlouisfed.org/fred2/series/EXCRESNS; bank failures: Federal Deposit Insurance Corporation (FDIC), www.fdic.gov/bank/individual/failed/banklist.html.

Article 7.2

MODERN MONEY
A Legal, Functional, and Historical Primer on Modern Monetary Theory

BY ROBERT HOCKETT
MARCH/APRIL 2018

Something remarkable has happened since the financial dramas of 2008–2009. A once-ignored, even deliberately marginalized school of thought within the discipline of monetary economics has moved steadily from obscurity to prominence. Its name recognition has grown to the point that its *name*—"Modern Money Theory" (a.k.a. "Modern Monetary Theory," or "MMT")—now likely rings more bells in lay public consciousness than any other school of monetary thinking, perhaps even of macroeconomic thinking.

Exponents of MMT now regularly appear at academic conferences and in policy debates. They figure frequently on television news programs and podcasts. One architect of MMT—Stephanie Kelton—even served as chief economist for the Democratic Minority Staff of the Senate Budget Committee in the years preceding the 2016 elections, and as chief economic advisor to Senator Bernie Sanders in his barnstorming bid for the Democratic presidential nomination.

Though I am not myself an MMT theorist, my approach to money, the financial system, and the macro-economy as a legal and financial theorist/practitioner is in broad sympathy with MMT. And as it happens, MMT lends itself nicely to exposition by people with legal and practical financial knowledge. For unlike some "classical" approaches to monetary and financial subjects, its practitioners understand from the get-go our money's—and with it, finance's—deep roots in our laws and our institutions.

"Capital," Contortion, and Therapy

The best way to begin an exposition of what MMT is might be by reference to what it is not. MMT aims to correct a mistake on which much of the classical macroeconomic and monetary theory of the past appears to have been founded. This is the error of falsely assimilating resources to legal claims upon resources, and falsely assimilating sovereign units of political organization to units that buy under the jurisdiction of such sovereigns. Conflating these things tends to generate cognitive mash-ups that vitiate theory and policy nostrum alike.

MMT cures macro and monetary economics of the vast tangle of conceptual contortions that have historically proceeded from its founding fallacies. How did past orthodoxy fall into its fallacies, exactly? In a word, "capital." There's a regrettable equivocation both in popular usage and in the use of the word by classical economists. Sometimes the word designates what would better be specified as "physical capital," or what I'll call "resources." Other times it designates what would better be specified as "financial capital," or what I'll call "claims upon resources."

It's easiest to trace the procession of errors that stem from the "capital" confla-tion by walking through a just-so story that many people seem to take as founda-tional. In this story, there are "two kinds of people in this world." On the one hand are "surplus units"—people who've saved money or accumulated resources over time. On the other hand are "deficit units"—people who have need of saved money or accumulated surplus but don't have it. Financial institutions and markets, we are then told, spring up as "middle men" to enable these units to find one another. They broker contracts between parties for the use of "scarce capital" at a price—interest, equity appreciation, or some other form of compensation. I call this "the intermedi-ated scarce private capital myth."

Among the "deficit units" in our story is something that classical orthodoxy calls "the government." Government "doesn't produce anything," in the classical story, nor can it sell equity stakes in itself. So it has nothing to sell to earn money. It therefore has only two means of funding its operations. It must either borrow or "take" from the surplus units, which we know as taxation.

If the government borrows too much, we are told, it will grow less creditworthy, will "crowd out" private producers who also need access to scarce private capital, or both. And if the government taxes too much, then it will again crowd out private investment, and might be ousted by angry citizens who launch "tax revolts." Either way then, "government" is at the mercy of "surplus units" who have accumulated "scarce capital" that the government needs to operate.

It's not hard to see how this picture prompts certain policy admonitions we hear all the time. References to "skittish capital" and "bond vigilantes," particularly in connection with alleged government overspending, channel the myth. So do com-plaints about taxes, and assurances by George Bush and Grover Norquist that "it's your money" when they demand "tax relief." And so, of course, do cries that we're "burdening our grandchildren with debt," or that "the government will go broke," or that the Fed, as Sarah Palin once charged, is "debasing the currency" when it ac-commodates fiscal expansion by purchasing Treasury bonds in open-market mon-etary operations.

But all of this is a howler. The foundational pictures upon which this story rests—the equivocation about "capital" and the intermediated scarce private capital myth—are erroneous.

Resources, Claims, and Credit

To see why, we must attain clarity about the relations among resources, claims upon resources, and credit. Once we do, we'll see that the classical economists' conflation of sovereign political units with families and firms corresponds to its conflation of re-sources with claims upon resources—and to a false separation of credit and money.

Let's begin with a family or firm that takes part in an exchange economy. Adult family members purchase homes, vehicles, education, and so on. They sell services of various kinds—often all lumped together as "labor"—to earn what is needed to purchase these things. Firms act in similar fashion. They purchase "inputs" to what they produce, and use the proceeds of sales of what they produce both to pay for those inputs and to yield surplus above inputs, or profits.

In most of these cases, households and firms engage in exchange via some medium of exchange. This medium is often called "money," which can be thought of as a claim upon what it's exchanged for. Its status as legal tender makes it a legal claim upon what it buys—a claim upon resources. But money is more than a present-moment claim, or a medium of immediate exchange. It also works as an inter-temporal claim, a medium of exchange between present and future, or what economists call a "store of value." What classical economists historically over-looked is that the inter-temporal aspect of money is rooted in its relation to credit, which stems from the Latin word credere ("to believe"). Money bridges time be-cause credit bridges time—the "belief" involved in extensions of credit is belief in the future, belief that the one who is credited will live up to her obligations.

Often a household or firm does not yet possess enough money to purchase what it needs. And often it's not possible to earn such money without first selling something that one needs money to make or supply in the first place. (Hence the old adage, "it takes money to make money.") I might have to purchase a car, for ex-ample, in order to take a new high-paying job far from home. But I also might lack the money to purchase the car until I have already worked at the job for a while and been paid. The same holds for firms, which typically need money to buy what they use to produce what they sell for money.

My starting the job and my buying the car in this story are a bit like those men at the doorway who keep saying "after you." The two men—the old comic strip characters Alphonse and Gaston—never pass through the doorway *even though each has the capacity to walk through the door*. What constrains them? What we might call the *structure of their social relation*—in this case, the fact that each feels compelled to wait for the other to walk through the door before himself walking through the door. It is their convention—their "after you" convention—that blocks their way. We're faced with a situation, then, in which there is no basic capacity-constraint, no salient resource-constraint, but a significant institutional constraint.

Most societies with exchange economies develop institutions to deal with this Alphonse/Gaston problem. In many societies we call these "financial" institutions, like banks. They enable more exchange to take place across space by enabling ex-change across time. And in so doing, they make possible more productive activity across time. (Here is the source of what some heterodox economists, including John Maynard Keynes, have called "the monetary theory of production.") They allow "advances" now on what is expected to be "realized" later.

None of this would be possible unless resources and claims upon resources were two different things. The money you borrow is a claim upon current resources that you can then use to produce more future resources. And while material capacities or resources must of course be pre-accumulated to be used, claims upon such resources need not be pre-accumulated. They can be *generated*.

Credit, Money, and Credit-Money

Money is not simply associated with credit. In an important sense, money is credit. Its function as circulating credit is part of what enables money to function as an inter-temporal claim—a "store of value"—in the first place.

How can that be? To begin to appreciate how, take out a dollar bill from your pocket. Across the top, you'll see the inscription, "Federal Reserve Note." What do you suppose "Note" means here? It isn't a "mental note," or a missive, but we call a promissory note.

A promissory note represents a legally enforceable commitment—a contractual promise. The promisor undertakes to do something in future. The promisee undertakes to trust the promisor—to believe her when she says she will do what she's promised to do. The promisee "credits" the promisor with whatever he puts at risk of the promisor's possibly breaching the promise. In so doing, the promisee becomes a creditor, the promisor a debtor. The creditor holds an asset, the debtor owes a liability. The promissory note signifies both the issuer's liability and the holder's asset. Promissory notes in scenarios like this one function as means of payment—a medium of exchange.

But what is the Fed promising? The great heterodox economist Hyman Minsky once memorably said anyone can issue a currency; the trick is to get it accepted. Private promissory notes can serve as methods of payment from one party to other parties who know and trust her but are unlikely to be accepted in payment by parties who don't know or trust her. They can function as private money, but not public money. If something is to circulate widely as a mode of payment, then, it must be a sort of promissory note everyone recognizes and trusts, that everyone will accept in payment as a form of money. That note in the United States is the Fed note, and in any other jurisdiction is that jurisdiction's own central bank or monetary authority's notes.

When you borrow money, then, you hand a bank your own promissory note in exchange for Fed promissory notes (or for a check or deposit denominated in note units). You transform narrowly accepted notes into widely accepted notes, private money into public money. It's still all about promises—about credit and debt, asset and liability. All that varies is *whose* credit, *whose* debt, or *whose* asset, *whose* liability.

One way of thinking of private banking institutions, then, is as outsourced credit-checking offices of the Fed, and hence of all Americans, whose central bank the Fed is. Private lending banks, which in theory have better access to information about the creditworthiness of those who live near them, do the credit-checking for us and our Fed. In so doing, they decide whose private promissory notes will be temporarily tradable for the public promissory notes—the Fed notes—that banks dispense. They thereby help the Fed turn private money into public money. And in so doing they provide credit in the form of money, which enables the wide use of current resources to produce future resources. In other words, they finance—or at any rate are meant to finance—*productive activity*.

"Precious Metals," "Paper Promises," and Money's History

There was a very brief time during which Federal Reserve notes were "backed up" by gold. They could in this sense be thought of as something like "claim checks" on gold. Some view this fact—which was true for only a very brief span of the Fed's 105-year history—as indicating that inscriptions like "Federal Reserve Note" now are vestigial, a bit like the human tailbone. But that is a mistake. What people who argue this fail to grasp is that gold itself was like paper when it first came to be used as a medium of exchange. Gold is no more "inherently" monetary than paper.

In the ancient Near East, early civilizations were heavily dependent on agriculture. Because crop yields were subject to mercurial nature, it became common practice to store grain during fat years to provide for lean years. Grain storage of this sort was not left to the wisdom of individuals alone. It was a state function, much as old-age insurance in the form of Social Security is today. Growers were required to make "grain deposits" into a community pool, the requirement operating as a kind of countercyclical tax or mandatory social insurance premium.

When you "deposited" your grain per this requirement, the authority who received your deposit gave you a token or "receipt" that indicated that you had made your required deposit. In time, these tokens began circulating as currencies. It is not hard to see why. Suppose that your neighbor has land that yields a bumper crop, while your land is more barren, but you're a good toolmaker. In such case there are gains to be had from letting your neighbor "deposit" extra grain at the grain-store, collect extra receipts for having done so, and then give you those extra receipts in return for your making her tools. That way you both get to do what you're best at, and both of you are able to produce more in aggregate and prove that your grain obligation has been satisfied.

Implicit in the practice of giving a receipt for the grain deposit is a commitment by the grain-gathering authority to recognize receipts as verification that required grain deposit have been made. Once this commitment is in place, the "receipt" will acquire the characteristics of a claim. It is a claim to the authority's recognizing the receipt-bearer as one who has already "paid his taxes." And, once those lean years commence, it is a claim to some grain from the grain store. Once tax receipts become "vertical claim checks" against the taxing authority, it is only a matter of time before they begin circulating as "horizontal claims" among those who need them for "vertical" purposes. All people need them, and so all people accept them as—not only for grain, but also tools and much else. These are public liabilities that function and circulate as private assets, so everyone uses and accepts them.

You can see here how the Federal Reserve notes might function as claims on or liabilities of the federal government even as they circulate as claims or as assets among citizens. Think of the Treasury Department as the grain-gathering authority, and of the Fed as the claim check issuing authority. These are two organs of one government—*our* government. And the one organ recognizes only the receipts issued by the other in payment of taxes.

But what about gold? How did that ever come into the picture? And why did the Fed ever have anything to do with it?

The important thing about claim checks was never their material form, but the fact that they reliably represented claims. In the ancient Near East, clay tokens stamped with the grain authority's seal were a convenient form. (That seal was the progenitor of the later "Federal Reserve Note" inscription.) Later, as civilization advanced through the Mediterranean, Anatolia, Persia, India, China, and beyond, new material representations of the same kind of claim came along. One that became widespread for a time was the so-called "precious metal" coin. It is of course commonplace nowadays to think of metals like gold, silver, platinum and others as somehow inherently precious, and thus "natural" stores of monetary value. But the truth seems to be the reverse—these metals became precious largely because they came to be used widely as material representations of money claims.

Why did that happen? The answer seems to be that the comparative softness and malleability of these metals, combined with their resistance to corrosion, made them easy to stamp durable official images and code words upon. Precious-metal coins thus became dominant money-forms throughout the ancient world. This continued into the medieval period, with only the taxers and issuers—monarchs, feudal lords, and so on—and their images changing. As cities with increasingly differentiated economies began growing at the margins of feudal manors, however, coins and big blocks of metal called "bullion" became increasingly inconvenient as money forms. For one thing, they were heavy. This problem grew worse during times of inflation, when more metal was needed for the same purchasing power. For another thing, lugging metal signaled to brigands that you were fat prey. So people began "depositing" their metals with metalsmiths, who had "safes," for safe-keeping. The smiths issued paper claim checks—or "notes"—representing claims on deposited metals.

Once such "claim check" issuance spread, it didn't take long for people to discover that using the paper in payment, rather than going back to get gold and then carrying it to transaction sites, could save time and effort. It also didn't take long for the metalsmiths to discover a new opportunity their claim checks afforded: Once their claim checks began circulating as paper currency, they could issue such checks to themselves at no cost and then buy things. They also could issue them for lending at interest. As long as the checks were not issued too far in excess of the coins and bullion in store, there was no danger in doing this, and there was much to be gained.

In time this line of work became much more lucrative than metalsmithing. The benches on which metalsmiths did their smithing— "banca," as they are called in Italy, where this practice developed—gave their name to what we now call "banking." And the practice of issuing more notes than one had coins and bullion became known as "fractional reserve banking." The metal money tokens were a "reserve," which represented a mere fraction of total note issuance.

This practice of issuing more notes than they had coins made banking profitable, socially useful, and risky. It was profitable because note-issuers got something for nothing—they received "seignorage," so-called because the first issuers who enjoyed this privilege were monarchs or manorial lords (Old French, *seignors*) themselves. It was socially useful because it allowed for an "elastic currency"—a currency whose supply could be grown both to accommodate growing transaction activity and to finance growing productive activity. (Recall our Alphonse and Gaston story above.) And it was risky—both for the banker and for society—because the elastic currency could be "over-stretched," issued too far in excess of the metal that "backed" it.

As a result, much of bank regulation in olden days took the form of reserve regulation. But there was no inherent need for required reserves to be metals. The only reason for this was because such metals were stamped by the sovereign as "legal tender," good for the discharge of "all obligations public and private." In other words, just as the paper memorialized promises, so did the metal. The only difference was that the *paper* memorialized *private bank* promises, while the *metal* memorialized *public authorities'* promises (which generally were "worth" more thanks to the power of sovereigns).

In time, public authorities began memorializing their promises with paper as well—with both sovereign bonds and sovereign currencies. Gold was used mainly for cross-border, cross-jurisdiction transactions for much of the 17th, 18th, and early 19th centuries. Periodically, and especially in the mid-19th century, some jurisdictions would reintroduce gold as "reserve money" in order to signal to their populations and one another that they would not over-issue currency, as sometimes happened during rough patches like revolutions and wars. The U.S. Fed was established during this later period, and so for a brief while it shared in "the gold standard" with other nations' central banks.

But not long after the Fed's founding, the Bank of England abandoned metallic standards, and the Fed followed shortly thereafter. There is no metal constraint at all. The only "natural" constraint on a private bank is what loans can be made profitably; and the only "natural" constraint on a central bank—the Fed—is essentially the same: how much credit-money can be privately generated and publicly accommodated as Fed-recognized loans before the credit-money supply's growth rate grows too rapid for "real," materially productive growth to keep pace and avoid inflation.

Constraint, Balance, and Health

This latter is a key point for MMT advocates. It is their answer to "gold bugs," to classical economists, and to the intermediated scarce private capital myth itself. There is no "natural" limit on how much credit can be generated, or how much money can be issued. Even required reserve ratios calculated in relation to gold were not "natural," since the ratio itself could always be changed by fiat. The gold standard itself, in other words, just like the first sovereign gold coin, was a sovereign promise.

The only "natural" limit on credit-money issuance, then, is nature itself. MMT advocates call this the "resource constraint." But what they mean by "resource" here isn't just natural resources like land, water, or air. They mean aggregate material resources, produced and unproduced, including what can realistically be produced over a given time interval. The credit-money supply must be able to grow at a rate that allows for this resource stock to grow through the productive activity of those who need claims upon current such resources—money—in order to produce future resources. There must be enough money, in other words—enough circulating resource-claims—to accommodate people like me in my car-and-job story above.

It is possible, of course, for there to be less than the optimal quantum of money in circulation. But it is also possible for there to be more than this optimal money supply. If those promises that are money proliferate more rapidly than our aggregate capacity to fulfill them through real productive activity, then we will have over-promised, over-committed. We will have issued more promissory notes than can realistically be redeemed.

In such case the promises will lose value, possibly becoming worth less, as the old adage has it, "than the paper they're printed on." This is what we call "inflation." And it is the real constraint upon sovereign spending and "borrowing," not the gold supply or even the current resource supply. This is because financial capital (claims upon resources), unlike physical capital (resources), is not "scarce" or "intermediated," but *generated* by the Fed, the banking system through which it works, and the Treasury.

What, then, do bond issuances and taxes do, if they do not "fund" the government as orthodoxy has it? Selling bonds and levying taxes takes privately held money out of circulation. Often it's helpful to do this when our government is itself spending, because if we don't there's a risk of inflation. But sometimes there's also no need to do this—e.g., during a downturn or debt-deflation, when not inflation but its opposite is the salient danger. In such cases public spending supplements inadequate private spending, and need not be "funded"—i.e., accompanied by contractionary measures like taxing and bond-selling—at all.

Any tax lawyer will tell you that this is what the Internal Revenue Code is for—it's for altering the volume and/or the allocation of money flows, not for "raising money." And anyone at the New York Fed trading desk, who buys or sells Treasuries every morning in pursuit of Fed "open-market operations," will tell you that Treasury securities are for providing the markets with "safe assets" and for buying and selling to alter the money supply, not for "borrowing money." It's a shame that so many classical economists, who evidently needn't know how the actual tax code and bond markets work, have historically not listened to those lawyers and traders.

We can now see, in any event, the error of classical orthodoxy in bold relief. It is wrong to conflate resources with claims upon resources, because claims can be generated in excess of current resources as long as doing so prompts the production of additional resources. It is wrong to conflate sovereigns with households and firms, because sovereigns can issue claims upon everything—public money—while households and firms can issue claims only upon themselves—private money. And it is wrong to believe all capital is "scarce, private, and intermediated," because this too is to conflate resources with claims upon resources—and to forget moneys are claims to performance of promises.

Once we see all of this, we see that classical orthodoxy was and is superstition, rooted in distant spells cast by stamped shiny metals, traditions that treat debts as sins (some languages actually use the same word for both), and mystical conflations of signs with things signified. Currency and coin are not money; they represent money. Debt is not sin; it is worthiness of credit—credibility. And metals are neither inherently precious nor "basic." Credible, publicly endorsed promises are the basis of money. They are what banks give you public money for. This is what MMT and its allies want you to see. ❏

Sources: Irving Fisher, *Booms and Depressions* (1932); David Graeber, *Debt: The First 5000 Years* (2011); Michael Hudson, *Debt and Economic Renewal in the Ancient Near East* (2002); John Maynard Keynes, *A Tract on Monetary Reform* (1924); John Maynard Keynes, *A Treatise on Money* (1930); Georg Friedrich Knapp, *The State Theory of Money* (1905); Hyman Minsky, *Can "It" Happen Again?* (1982); Hyman Minsky, *Stabilizing an Unstable Economy* (1986); Joseph Schumpeter, *The Theory of Economic Development* (1934); L. Randall Wray, *Credit and State Theories of Money: The Contributions of A. Mitchell Innes* (2004); L. Randall Wray, *Modern Money Theory: A Primer on Macroeconomics for Sovereign Monetary Systems* (2012).

Article 7.3

SHOULD WE BLAME "FRACTIONAL RESERVE" BANKING?

BY ARTHUR MacEWAN
May/June 2013

> Dear Dr. Dollar:
> *I have seen various arguments (on the Internet, for example) that a prime cause of our economic problems (inequality, crises, mass unemployment, the immense power of the banks, etc.) is our monetary system. In particular, that it is a "fractional reserve system," in which "money is created out of thin air." Could you comment?*
>
> —Mike Smith, New York, NY

The last several years, when banks and the whole financial system have been at the core of economic disruption, could easily lead one to see the monetary system as central to our economic problems.

Keep in mind, however, that we have had essentially the same monetary system for decades, the Federal Reserve has existed for a hundred years, and the "fractional reserve" system existed before the Fed. During these earlier eras, including periods when we relied on the gold standard as the basis of our monetary system, we have had depressions, inflation, severe inequality, and excessive power in the hands of finance and large corporations generally. We have also had some relatively good times—periods of stable economic growth, less economic inequality, lower unemployment, and less power and profits for the banks. So, whatever is wrong with our monetary system (and there are certainly things wrong), the explanation of our economic problems must be more complex.

But what is the fractional reserve system? Basically, it is the system by which banks keep as reserves only a fraction of the amount of deposits that their customers have with the banks. Banks can do this because at any time their customers will demand only a fraction of those total obligations. When, for example, you deposit $100 in the bank, the bank will loan out to someone else perhaps $90 of that $100. This $90 is new money that the bank has created. The person or business taking this loan then deposits the $90 in another account with the bank or another bank, allowing a new loan of $81 to be generated by the banking system; the remaining $9 (10% of the deposit) will be kept as reserves. And so on.

By this process, if people are willing to take out the loans, the banks can create an additional $900 of money based on an original deposit of $100. This is sometimes called "creating money out of thin air." In fact, it is creating money on the basis of 10% reserves.

If banks were left to their own devices, competition would create pressure to push down the reserve ratio—they could, for example, make twice the amount of loans were they to reduce their reserves from 10% to 5% of obligations. However, the Federal Reserve has a great deal of authority over what the banks can do. It sets the reserve ratio. Banks cannot simply lower the amount of reserves to make more loans. (The actual reserve ratio varies depending on type of obligation; 10% is just an example that makes calculations easy.) Most frequently, the Fed affects the supply of money by buying bonds from the banks, thus increasing the banks' reserves (and enabling them to lend more), or selling bonds to the banks, thus reducing the banks' reserves.

That's the formal way it works. Although critics of a fractional reserve system claim it "debases the currency" (i.e., leads to inflation), it does not automatically allow the banks to create more and more money without limits, which could indeed generate severe inflation. The U.S. economy has experienced mild inflation for most of the last century (averaging 3.2% annually), but fractional reserve banking is not generally associated with high "runaway" inflation. Ironically, in light of the claims of the critics, the Fed has often followed policies that work in exactly the opposite direction—restricting the banks' ability to create money, thus restricting the loans they can make, and restraining economic growth and employment. (After all, neither banks nor other large corporations like severe inflation.)

But of course the formal way the system works is not the whole story. The banks themselves and other big firms have a great deal of influence over what the Fed does. So the Fed usually regulates the banks with a very light hand. In the Great Recession, in particular, the Fed (along with the U.S. Treasury) provided the banks with funds to meet their obligations when many of those banks would have otherwise failed. In this respect, the way the Fed works is not so different from the way the government works in general—money has a great deal of influence over policy.

It would be nice if our economic problems were so simple that they could be solved by some reorganization of our monetary system. But the problems are bigger and deeper. ❑

Article 7.4

PUSHING ON STRINGS

*The explosion of U.S. banks' excess reserves since 2008
illustrates the dramatic failure of monetary policy.*

BY GERALD FRIEDMAN
May/June 2009; updated June 2018

Monetary policy is not working. Since the economic crisis began in July 2007, the Federal Reserve has dramatically cut interest rates and pumped out over a trillion dollars, increasing the money supply by over 15% in less than two years. These vast sums have failed to revive the economy because the banks have been hoarding liquidity rather than lending.

The Federal Reserve requires that banks hold money on reserve to back up deposits and other bank liabilities. In the past, beyond these required reserves, banks would hold very small amounts of excess reserves, holdings that they minimized because reserves earn very little or no interest. Between the 1950s and September 2008, U.S. banks held over $5 billion in total excess reserves only once, after the September 11 attacks. This changed with the collapse of Lehman Brothers. Beginning with less than $2 billion in August 2008, excess reserves soared to $60 billion in September and then to $559 billion in November before peaking at $798 billion in January 2009. (They had dropped to $644 billion by the time this article was written.)

This explosion of excess reserves represents a signal change in bank policy that threatens the effectiveness of monetary policy in the current economic crisis. Aware of their own financial vulnerability, even insolvency, frightened bank managers

BANK EXCESS RESERVES SINCE 1999

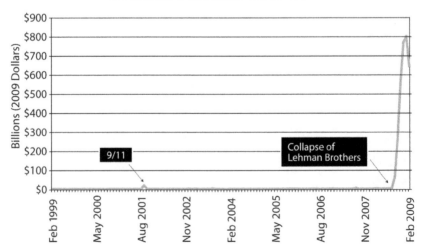

Source: "Excess Reserves of Depository Institutions," Federal Reserve Bank of St. Louis, research.stlouisfed.org.

responded to the collapse of major investment houses like Lehman Brothers by grabbing and hoarding all the cash that they could get. At the same time, a general loss of confidence and spreading economic collapse persuaded banks that there are few to whom they could lend with confidence that the loans would be repaid. Clearly, our banks have decided that they need, or at least want, the money more than consumers and productive businesses do.

Banks could have been investing this money by lending to businesses needing liquidity to buy material inputs or pay workers. Had they done so, monetarist economists would be shouting from the rooftops, or at least in the university halls, about how monetary policy prevented another Great Depression. Instead, even the *Wall Street Journal* is proclaiming that "We're All Keynesians Again" because monetary policy has failed. Monetary authorities, the *Journal* explains, can create money but they cannot force banks to lend or to invest it in productive activities. The Federal Reserve confronts a reality shown in the graph above: it can't "push on a string," as Fed Chair Marriner Eccles famously put it in testimony before Congress in 1935, in the depths of the Great Depression.

If the banks won't lend, then we need more than monetary policy to get out of the current crisis. No bailout, no TARP program, can revive the economy if banks hoard all the cash they receive. The Obama stimulus was an appropriate response to the failure of string-pushing. But much more government stimulus will be needed to solve a crisis this large, and we will need programs to move liquidity from bank vaults to businesses and consumers. It may be time to stop waiting on the banks, and to start telling them what to do with our money.

Update, June 2018

Ten years after the onset of the Great Recession, sometimes called the Lesser Depression, we can better appreciate the limits of monetary policy in stimulating a depressed economy. Four years after the 2008 crash, the Federal Reserve pushed money into the economy in hopes of stimulating investment. While not a complete failure, the Fed's monetary policy did little to stimulate the economy, with investment demand in particular continuing to lag in what has been the slowest economic recovery since World War II. The failure of monetary policy, not only in the United States but in Japan and Europe as well, has led even many orthodox economists, notably Paul Krugman and Larry Summers, to warn that the United States has entered a period of "secular stagnation" where the rate of return has fallen so low that the interest rate cannot drop to a level where capitalists can profit from new investment. With the return on investment this slow, the economy has fallen into what John Maynard Keynes, and Krugman, call a "liquidity trap," a situation where there is so little demand for investment that further increases in the money supply will simply go into idle cash reserves rather than new economic activity. In such a situation, monetary authorities can do little but "push on strings" because only active fiscal policy can provide economic stimulus by substituting government spending for failing private investment. Inadequate fiscal stimulus in the United States and, even more, in Europe accounts for the slow economic recovery from the Lesser Depression despite active monetary stimulus. ❏

Article 7.5

THE FED RAISES INTEREST RATES ... BY PAYING THE BANKS

BY MARTY WOLFSON

January/February 2016

The business and financial press has been abuzz with speculation about when the Federal Reserve would begin raising interest rates. After the meeting of its Federal Open Market Committee (FOMC) on December 15-16, the Fed ended the suspense by announcing that it was raising its target federal funds rate by a quarter of a percentage point (to a range of 0.25 to 0.50%). Flying under the radar, though, was the Fed's use of a dramatically different method of raising interest rates. The new method involves paying billions of dollars to banks, primarily by paying interest on banks' reserves held at the Fed. The payments will reduce the amount of money that the Fed remits to the Treasury and, ultimately, to taxpayers.

Why Is the Fed Paying the Banks?

This new method is best understood when viewed in the context of the recent financial crisis. The collapse of the housing bubble in 2007 threatened both the financial system and the broader economy. The Federal Reserve began a campaign of aggressively reducing interest rates, lowering the interest rate that it controls, the federal funds rate, from its peak of 5.25% in September 2007 to just 2% in April 2008. The federal funds rate is an interest rate that banks pay when borrowing from other banks. Lower costs for the banks in turn lead to lower interest rates for business and consumer borrowing, thus encouraging greater spending, output, and employment.

In making these changes to the federal funds rate, the Fed used its classic method of changing the level of bank reserves. (See sidebar.) It is this method that the Fed jettisoned when it announced its new procedures.

After the failure of Lehman Brothers in September 2008, financial markets became unsettled and many of the traditional funding sources for financial institutions dried up. Into this void stepped the Federal Reserve, which dramatically increased its lending and other interventions to help the banks. In the process, it pumped money into the banking system and expanded bank reserves, significantly beyond the level of reserves necessary to maintain its target for the federal funds rate.

On October 1, 2008, the Federal Reserve began to pay interest on bank reserves. Then-Fed Chair Ben Bernanke, in his recent memoir, gave this reason for the change: "The concern in 2008 was that emergency lending would lead short-term interest rates to fall below our federal funds target and thereby cause us to lose control of monetary policy."

In other words, without paying interest on reserves, banks would have so many excess reserves that did not earn any interest, and be so eager to gain at least some return on them, that the Fed would be unable to prevent them from lending at rates below the Fed's target for the federal funds rate (2% at that time). By paying interest on reserves, the Fed would eliminate banks' incentive to lend at rates below those it was receiving from the Fed.

This, however, is a curious explanation. The Fed dropped its target federal funds rate by 0.5% on October 8, 2008, and then by another 0.5% on October 29. On December 16, it lowered its target all the way to zero (a band of 0 to 0.25%), where it has stayed for seven years. Why was it concerned about the federal funds rate falling below its target rate when it was in the process of dropping its target rate to zero?

Moreover, in October 2008 the economy was moving into free fall. Real gross domestic product (GDP) fell at an annual rate of 8.2% in the fourth quarter of 2008 and unemployment was increasing rapidly. The Fed explained that it reduced the federal funds rate to zero "in order to provide stimulus to household and business spending and so support economic recovery." So why was the Fed giving the banks an incentive to keep their excess reserves at the Fed rather than lend them out?

The Fed's action can perhaps be understood by examining how it interprets its objectives. In addition to its mandates affecting employment and inflation, the Fed is also responsible for promoting financial stability. For the Fed, this means easing panic in financial markets, but also protecting the viability and profitability of the banks, especially those judged to be systemically important.

Promoting financial stability in the fall of 2008 meant the necessary step of intervening aggressively to prevent the collapse of the global financial system. But the Fed also interpreted it to mean bailing out large banks, even if the process did not sufficiently curtail the banks' power and risky practices. And it meant paying interest on reserves. Such payments directly boosted bank profitability, even if they may have come at the expense of the broader economy.

The Classic Method of Affecting Interest Rates: Change the Level of Bank Reserves

Banks are required to hold cash in proportion to the amount of their deposits. This cash is termed bank reserves. (Currently, the reserve requirement is 10% of the total amount deposited in checking accounts.) Banks hold some of this cash in their vaults in order to meet requests for withdrawals, but typically much of it is held as deposits with the Fed.

Some banks hold more reserves than they need to satisfy reserve requirements, but some find themselves with a deficit. Those banks needing reserves typically borrow them from banks with a surplus. The interest rate that banks charge to lend their reserves to other banks is called the federal funds rate.

When the Fed wants to lower the federal funds rate, as it did in 2007-08, it buys government securities and writes a check to the seller. When the seller deposits the check in a bank, the bank sends the check to the Fed, which then credits the bank with more reserves. A greater amount of reserves in the banking system reduces the need for borrowing to meet reserve requirements, and the federal funds rate falls.

Likewise, when the Fed wants to increase the federal funds rate, it sells government securities. The buyer gives a check to the Fed written on the buyer's bank, and the Fed reduces the amount of reserves the bank has on deposit with the Fed. The bank, now short of reserves, seeks to borrow them from other banks and is willing to pay an increased federal funds rate in order to do so.

The reserves not needed to meet reserve requirements are called excess reserves. Up to 2008, the Fed did not pay any interest on excess reserves. To earn interest, banks lent out the cash to businesses and consumers and thereby encouraged greater spending. In this way, excess reserves were usually kept relatively low.

The Implications of Quantitative Easing

With the federal funds rate at zero, the Federal Reserve began its program of "quantitative easing." This involved buying longer-term assets, U.S. Treasury securities as well as mortgage-backed securities. The Fed's stated objective was to reduce long-term interest rates so as to stimulate spending in housing and business investment.

There were three stages of quantitative easing, and interest rates did indeed fall. But, again, the Fed also had its eye on the banks. After the financial crisis, the demand for mortgage-backed securities fell, since massive numbers of mortgages were in default and payments on the securities were therefore down. As demand fell, the prices of the mortgage-backed securities plummeted. Many of the banks held large quantities of these securities. By purchasing so many of them, the Fed supported their prices and increased their value on the banks' balance sheets.

As a result of its quantitative easing programs, the Fed dramatically expanded its holding of assets. At the end of 2008, it owned less than half a trillion dollars in Treasury securities and no mortgage-backed securities. By November 2015, it held $2.5 trillion in Treasuries and $1.8 trillion in mortgage-backed securities. Because buying all these securities meant that the Fed's checks became reserves for the banks, and because the banks were paid for keeping these reserves with the Fed, excess reserves ballooned to $2.5 trillion.

The Fed's announcement on December 16 that it is raising its target for the federal funds rate does bring to the fore Bernanke's concern in 2008: how to increase the federal funds rate when there are so many excess reserves. The Fed ruled out any largescale reduction of excess reserves when it also announced on December 16 that it would not be reducing its large holdings of securities. By not selling securities, the Fed would not be accepting checks from bank accounts and thus not reducing the reserves the banks hold on deposit with the Fed.

The Fed's solution, instead, is to double down and increase the payment of interest on bank reserves. It announced that it will begin paying interest on reserves at 0.5%. This procedure won't reduce reserves, but will give banks an incentive not to make loans at interest rates below the amount they can get from the Fed.

However, this will not totally solve the Fed's problem. Even when it was paying the banks 0.25% interest on reserves, the effective federal funds rate (the rate at which reserves at the Fed were actually being traded) was below 0.25%. This is why the Fed adopted a range for the federal funds rate of -0.25%.

The reason the Fed could not keep the federal funds rate at 0.25% was because financial institutions other than banks participate in the federal funds market. In particular, government-sponsored enterprises (GSEs) like Fannie Mae, Freddie Mac, and the Federal Home Loan Banks are allowed to keep funds at the Fed but are not paid interest on them. In recent years the Home Loan Banks have become the main lender in the federal funds market. (They were established during the Depression to lend to savings and loan associations to support housing, but now lend mainly to banks.)

The Home Loan Banks were able to lend federal funds at interest rates below 0.25% and still make a profit. In turn, banks were able to take the borrowed funds and deposit them with the Fed at 0.25%, making a profit as well.

So when the Fed on December 16 established a range of 0.25-0.50% for the federal funds rate, it also announced a new procedure designed to keep the federal funds rate from falling below 0.25%. The new procedure is to conduct overnight reverse repurchase agreements (ON RRP) with the Home Loan Banks (as well as with banks, other GSEs, and money market mutual funds, which are important lenders in short-term markets).

ON RRP is an imposing-sounding term, but reflects a relatively simple process: the Fed sells government securities to the financial institutions on one day and then buys them back the next. The financial institutions are essentially making an overnight loan to the Fed, with the securities as collateral.

But here's the point: the money the Fed pays to buy back the securities is not only a repayment of the original loan. It also includes an interest payment. And the Fed plans to pay interest at 0.25%, the bottom of its target for the fed funds rate, thus giving the Home Loan Banks an incentive not to lend at less than 0.25%. Although it plans to use ON RRP as a secondary tool to its main focus of paying interest on bank reserves, it anticipates that both of these tools will keep the fed funds rate within its target range of 0.25-0.5%.

It seems that the Fed has backed itself into a corner, where the only way to raise the federal funds rate is to increase its payments to financial institutions. With reserves held at the Fed equal to $2.6 trillion, even a 0.5% payment to the banks would cost $13 billion. And, of course, including the expense of the ON RRP program and increasing the fed funds rate in the future would add even more to the cost.

To add insult to injury, 25 minutes after the Fed's announcement on December 16, Wells Fargo Bank reported that it is raising its prime rate (an interest rate tied to business and consumer loans) by 0.25% but not the rates it pays to depositors. Later in the day other large banks, including JP Morgan Chase and Bank of America, made similar declarations.

Is There an Alternative?

Could the Fed, instead, choose not to pay interest to the banks and other financial institutions? This would have the effect of reducing excess reserves, but it would also mean that the Fed would have to delay raising interest rates.

That would, in fact, be a good policy decision. Although the unemployment rate is 5.0%, inflation is still below the Fed's 2% target. In the late 1990s, under then-Chair Alan Greenspan, the Fed allowed unemployment to fall below 4% without an appreciable increase in inflation. If the Fed waits, it could see how far excess reserves would fall without the payment of interest on reserves and how far the unemployment rate would fall without pushing inflation above 2%.

But what if a growing economy and a falling rate of unemployment edged the inflation rate past 2%, say, to 3 or 4%? The top 1% of the income distribution would not like inflation to eat away at their accumulated wealth. However, during times of very low unemployment the demand for workers can be strong enough to push money wages up faster than prices, so workers without a job and those who haven't seen a raise in many years would probably not be unhappy.

Under current Chair Janet Yellen, the Federal Reserve has shown a genuine concern about unemployment, but it is still trapped in its assumptions: There is a "maximum feasible" level of employment. Above that level (or below the corresponding rate of unemployment) inflation will exceed its 2% target. The conclusion from these assumptions is that the Fed should raise interest rates to prevent employment from exceeding the "maximum feasible" level.

Instead, the Fed should adopt a real full-employment target: a job for everyone who wants to work. It should adopt a "minimum feasible" target for inflation: the lowest possible rate compatible with full employment. We need a policy perspective in which economic justice for workers is a higher priority than paying the banks. ❏

Article 7.6

INFLATION TARGETING AND NEOLIBERALISM

BY GERALD EPSTEIN

May 2016

*I*n recent decades, central banks in both high-income ("developed") and lower-income ("developing") countries have turned increasingly towards "inflation targeting" monetary policy—the emphasis on very low inflation, to the exclusion of other policy objectives. In this interview, Gerald Epstein, a professor of economics at UMass-Amherst and a founding co-director of the Political Economy Research Institute (PERI) explains the causes behind the rise of inflation targeting, its effects in practice, and possible alternative approaches. —Eds.

Dollars & Sense: When we talk about central banks and monetary policy, what precisely is meant by the phrase "inflation targeting"? And how does that differ from other kinds of objectives that central banks might have?

Gerald Epstein: Inflation targeting is a relatively new but very widespread approach to central bank policy. It means that the central bank should target a rate of inflation—sometimes it's a range, not one particular number, but a pretty narrow range—and that should be its only target. It should use its instruments—usually a short-term interest rate—to achieve that target and it should avoid using monetary policy to do anything else.

So what are some of the other things that central banks have done besides try to meet an inflation target? Well, the United States Federal Reserve, for example, has a mandate to reach two targets—the so-called "dual mandate"—one is a stable price level, which is the same as an inflation target, and the other is high employment. So this is a dual mandate. After the financial crisis there's a third presumption, that the Federal Reserve will look at financial stability as well. Other central banks historically have tried to promote exports by targeting a cheap exchange rate. Some people have accused the Chinese government of doing this but many other developing countries have targeted an exchange rate to keep an undervalued exchange rate and promote exports. Other countries have tried to promote broad-based development by supporting government policy. So there's a whole range of targets that, historically, central banks have used.

D&S: Has inflation targeting gone hand-in-hand not only with prioritizing price stability over other kinds of objectives, but also an emphasis on very low rates of inflation?

GE: That's right. In practice, what inflation-targeting advocates have argued for is an extremely low rate of inflation. For example, the European Central Bank has a 2% target, or to keep inflation in fact just below 2%, and typically what is called for is inflation in the low single digits. In developing countries, targets have ranged from 4% to 8%. So these are targets for inflation that are very low compared to broad historical experience. These days, very low inflation and indeed the threat of deflation in some countries have raised all kinds of issues about this inflation targeting approach.

I see this as part of a whole neoliberal approach to central banking. That is, the idea that the economy is inherently stable, it will inherently reach full employment and stable economic growth on its own, and so the only thing that the macro policymakers have to worry about is keeping a low inflation rate and everything else will take care of itself. Of course, as we've seen, this whole neoliberal approach to macroeconomic policy is badly mistaken.

D&S: Why have we seen inflation targeting become more prevalent in monetary policy making, both in high-income and lower-income countries, in recent years? What are the key arguments that are made by advocates of inflation targeting in favor of that approach? And what might be some underlying political and economic causes, even apart from those arguments?

GE: It's been a real revolution in central bank policy and, as I said earlier, it's in my view part and parcel of the whole neoliberal trend in macroeconomic policy. The essential thing underlying this, in my view, is to try to reduce the power of government and social forces that might exercise some power within the political economy—workers and peasants and others—and put the power primarily in the hands of those dominating in the markets. That's often the financial system, the banks, but also other elites.

The idea of neoliberal economists and policymakers is that you don't want the government getting too involved in macroeconomic policy. You don't want them promoting too much employment because that might lead to a raise in wages and, in turn, to a reduction in the profit share of the national income. So, sure, this might increase inflation, but inflation is not really the key issue here. The problem, in their view, is letting the central bank support other kinds of policies that are going to enhance the power of workers, people who work in agricultural areas, and even sometimes manufacturing interests. Instead, they want to put power in the hands of those who dominate the markets, often the financial elites.

That is, of course, not what the advocates of inflation targeting say publicly. What the advocates say is, "Look, inflation is harmful. We've got to keep a low and stable rate of inflation in order to promote economic growth." They build on the neoclassical, New Keynesian, or even New Classical approaches to macroeconomic policy that say the market economy is stable in and of itself, so government intervention can only mess things up. So there's only one thing left to do—there's only one thing on the "to do" list for macroeconomic policy—and that is to keep a stable inflation rate, so let's assign the central bank to do that and not to do anything else, and the capitalist economy will take care of itself.

This approach, I think, really has contributed to enormous financial instability. Notice that this inflation targeting targets commodity inflation. But what about asset bubbles, that is, asset inflation? There's no attempt to reduce asset bubbles like we had in subprime or in real estate bubbles in various countries. That is another kind of inflation that could have been targeted.

Of course, we know that the capitalist economy does not achieve full employment on its own. So why not target higher employment? In South Africa, for example, they have unemployment rates of 25 or 26%. They have an inflation-targeting regime to keep inflation in the low single digits, rather than targeting employment. It makes no sense at all.

The other argument that inflation-targeting advocates make is a government failure argument. Even if you concede that the economy won't do perfectly on its own, any time the government gets involved in the market economy they just mess it up. So, they argue, let's just have a minimalist kind of government intervention and at least the government will do no harm. I think this is a common argument as well. But as we know, there have been many successful government interventions in South Korea and China and elsewhere where governments working with a financial system and other actors in the economy have played a crucial role in economic development. The government-failure arguments, I think, have now been shown to be pretty fallacious. Olivier Blanchard, who was the chief economist at the IMF said we had this beautiful illusion that all we needed is one target, that is low inflation, and one interest rate, that is a short-term interest rate, and everything would be OK. Well, after the crisis, we now know that we need multiple targets and we need multiple tools to achieve our goals.

D&S: Hasn't it been a central concern on the part of elites in capitalist countries, at least in those where there is representative government, that the majority could impose its will and force policymakers to prioritize full employment and wage growth (as opposed to, say, "sound money")? Has the transition toward inflation targeting been accompanied by institutional changes to "wall off" monetary policy from those kinds of popular pressures?

GE: Yeah, I think that's a very important point here. Inflation targeting ideas have also been often accompanied by the idea that central banks should be "independent"—that is, independent from the government. I think you'll find that these two things go hand-in-hand.

If you look at the whole list of central bank rules that the International Monetary Fund (IMF) and others have advocated for developing countries, the argument goes like this: You want to have an independent central bank. Well, what should this independent central-bank do? It should target inflation. Well, isn't this anti-democratic? No, what we're really saying is that central bankers should have instrument independence, that is, the ability to decide how they'll achieve their target. The government should set the target, but what should target be? Well, the consensus is that the target should be a low rate of inflation. So that's a nice little package designed to prevent the central bank from doing such things as helping to finance government infrastructure investment or government deficits. It's designed to prevent the central bank from keeping interest rates "too low," which might actually contribute to more rapid economic growth or more productivity growth, but might lead to somewhat higher inflation.

Where do they get this low inflation rate from? There's no economic evidence, in fact—and there have been lots of studies—to demonstrate that an inflation rate in the low single digits is optimal for economic growth in most countries, certainly not in developing countries. Some early studies—and this has been replicated many times—have suggested that inflation rates of up to 15%, even 20%, as long as they're relatively steady, don't harm economic growth. They might even contribute to it. So this is a kind of strait-jacket that these forces are trying to put the central bank in, in order to prevent them from making policies in the interest of a broader part of the economy. And it's just one plank in the macroeconomic neoliberal straitjacket. The other plank, of course, is no fiscal deficits. So you limit what government can do—no fiscal deficits or low fiscal deficits—you limit what the central bank can do—only target low inflation—and you've pretty much made it impossible for the government to engage in macroeconomic policy that's going to have a broad-based supportive effect on the economy.

D&S: What is the record of inflation targeting policy in practice, in terms of economic outcomes we can actually observe, in both developing and so-called developed countries?

GE: The first thing to realize, I think, is that inflation-targeting approaches have been devastating in the reaction to the financial crisis of 2007–2008, particularly in Europe. There you had, an extreme case where the European Central Bank (ECB) mandate was to target inflation—period—and nothing else. And indeed to keep inflation in the low single digits, less than 2%. And what this did—along with other rules, other problems in Europe, not just this—was give the ECB the cover to do very little in terms of fighting the crisis when it hit, to in fact raise interest rates within the first year after the crisis hit. And it took the ECB several years before it finally realized the disaster that had befallen Europe and, when Mario Draghi finally came in as president of the ECB in 2011, to do whatever it takes to keep the euro going. It took a break from this kind of orthodoxy for them to begin to turn around Europe. (As we can now see Europe is still in terrible shape.)

Second, the single-minded focus on inflation in Europe and in other countries made them ignore the financial bubble, the asset bubbles that were occurring. Central bankers said, "Well, you know, that's not my department. I'll just worry about commodity inflation. I won't worry about other kinds of inflation because that's not my mandate." They had this tunnel vision, not seeing what else was going on around them in the economy.

In developing countries, there's pretty strong evidence that real interest rates have been higher than they would have been otherwise. There's some evidence that economic growth is lower in a number of developing countries than it would have been otherwise, because real interest rates have been so high. And there is some evidence that this has contributed to a redistribution of income towards the rentiers, that is, to the bankers and the financiers, and away from others because real interest rates have been so high and inflation has been relatively low. Most of the evidence suggests that it has had a negative consequence for working people and others in developing countries as well.

In the end, the negative impacts have been mitigated to some extent by the fact that a lot of central banks, in developing countries particularly, claim to be following a very strict inflation-targeting regime but in fact they've been "cheating." Almost all of them target exchange rates to some extent because they know they can't let their exchange rates get too overvalued or otherwise that is going to hurt their exports and cause other problems. They've been fiddling with the inflation data, or exactly what kind of inflation target they use, etc. In some ways it's a bit of a ruse. For developing countries, it's saying to the IMF, "OK, we're doing what you're telling us." Saying to the global financial markets, to the global investors, "OK we're doing this orthodox thing, but (wink wink) if we really did this all the time in a strict way it would be suicide so we're not going to really do this completely." So they're finally is a recognition, I think, that inflation targeting is a very destructive practice.

D&S: In your view, then, what would be a preferable approach to central bank policy—what priorities should central banks have and how should they go about achieving these aims?

GE: Central banks should be free and open, in conjunction with their governments, to identify the key problems facing their own countries, the key obstacles to social and economic development, and developing tools and targets that are appropriate to dealing with those problems. And these are going to differ from country to country. So, for example, in South Africa, my colleague Bob Pollin, James Heintz, Leonce Ndikumana, and I did a study a number of years ago: We proposed an employment-targeting regime for the central bank. The Reserve Bank of South Africa, in conjunction with the government of South Africa, would develop a set of policies and tools—such as credit allocation policies, subsidized credit, lower interest rates, capital controls to keep the capital in the country, more expansionary and targeted fiscal policy—so that monetary policy and fiscal policy would work hand-in-hand to lower the massively high unemployment rate in South Africa. That's an example of an alternative structure for monetary policy and one that has worked for other developing countries. So, for example, in South Korea in the 1950s, 1960s, and 1970s, the central bank supported the government's industrial policy—by lending to development banks that would lend to export industries, by subsidizing credit for export industries, and they would do this as part of the government plan to develop the economy. I call this developmental central banking, that is, central banking that in combination with the government is oriented to developing the country using a variety of tools—interest rates, credit allocation tools, etc.

Not all countries would do the same thing. It not only depends on the country, but also on the problems of the historical conjuncture. So take the United States for example. Right now we do have for the Federal Reserve a dual mandate, which some Republicans are trying to get rid of, for high employment and stable prices. But the financial intermediation system is broken because of what happened in the crisis. Interest rates are down to zero but banks aren't lending to the real economy. People aren't able to borrow from banks for small businesses and so forth. The Federal Reserve, through quantitative easing, bought a lot of financial assets but it's probably time for the Fed to develop new tools, to give direct credit to small businesses, for infrastructure development, etc.

It is the case now, with the crisis and with negative interest rates, or very low interest rates, central banks are being much more experimental trying to develop new tools, new approaches. But they're all doing it under the guise of inflation targeting. European central bankers were doing all these wild monetary experiments, but their goal was really just to get inflation up to 2%. In fact, what's happening is that this inflation targeting is no longer the guiding post for central banks. They need to have much broader sets of tools and targets to get out of this terrible slump that most of these economies are in. ❑

Article 7.7

KEYNES AND THE LIMITS OF MONETARY POLICY

BY ALEJANDRO REUSS

April 2009

As the United States has plunged into financial crisis and the deepest recession since the Great Depression, the U.S. Federal Reserve (the "Fed") has pursued an aggressively "expansionary" monetary policy. Monetary policy refers to government policies affecting the money supply or interest rates. Expansionary monetary policy is aimed at increasing the money supply or lowering interest rates. The idea is that, by lowering interest rates, the government can stimulate investment (such as firms' purchases of new equipment and construction of new plant). Projects that would not be profitable for a company if it had to borrow at a higher interest rate could be profitable if borrowing were less costly. Fed policymakers hope, then, that lower interest rates will encourage investment and bring about renewed economic growth.

The main interest rate the Fed targets is the "federal funds rate," the interest rate that banks charge each other for overnight loans. For all of 2006 and 2007, the federal funds rate stood at over 4%. In the course of 2008, as the financial crisis and recession grew deeper, the Fed moved aggressively to cut interest rates. By the end of the year, the federal funds rate was 0.0-0.25%, where it remains today. Even with the federal funds rate basically at zero, however, the economy has spiraled deeper into recession. GDP shrank at an annual rate of 6.2% in the fourth quarter of 2008 and the official unemployment rate climbed to 8.5% by March 2009.

Are Interest Rates Coming Down?

Firms and consumers cannot borrow at the federal funds rate. Then why does the Fed try to bring down the federal funds rate when it wants to stimulate economic activity? Fed policymakers hope that by pulling down very short-term interest rates that do not directly affect firms and consumers, they can indirectly pull down longer-term interest rates that are important to firms and consumers.

Interest rates on 30-year fixed-rate mortgages have declined, reaching historic lows under 5% in March 2009. The low mortgage rates, however, may be deceptive. Mortgage lenders have generally tightened lending standards, and the low rates are only available to borrowers that banks consider very safe. Other borrowers may pay rates several percentage points higher, or be unable to borrow at all. Meanwhile, banks have raised credit-card interest rates and dramatically tightened borrowing limits.

Key corporate interest rates have not come down as the Fed hoped. Moody's AAA bond rate, an index of the interest rates on long-term bonds for low-risk corporate borrowers, was about the same in March 2009 as in January 2008 (about 5.3%). Moody's Baa bond rate, the equivalent index or higher-risk corporate borrowers, has gone from about 6.5% in January 2008 to over 8% in March 2009. The spreads between these rates and the federal funds rate have increased dramatically as the federal funds rate has fallen.

That would come as no surprise to John Maynard Keynes. Keynes argued, in *The General Theory of Employment, Interest, and Money* (1936), that during boom periods the general estimation of risk by both lenders and borrowers is "apt to become unusually and imprudently low." Lenders loan out money freely, even recklessly, accepting a low rate of interest relative to the risk involved. During crisis periods, on the other hand, lenders often become much more risk-averse, parting with their money less freely, and insisting on a higher rate of interest in exchange for the risk of not being paid back. This is sometimes known as the "flight to liquidity" or "flight to safety." Keynes' analysis suggests that during economic crises the interest rates on assets that are considered very safe—like government bonds—are apt to go down, since people are looking to avoid losses and willing to accept a low rate of return to do so. But the interest rates on riskier assets may go up. A rise in the interest rates that firms or consumers pay would tend to deepen—rather than correct—an economic downturn.

Can't the Fed Do More?

If interest rates are not low enough to turn the economy around, then why doesn't the Fed increase the money supply some more—until interest rates *are* low enough? The answer is that nominal interest rates can reach a lower bound below which they cannot decline further. (The "nominal" interest rate, in contrast to the "real" interest rate, does not account for changes in the purchasing power of the dollar due to inflation.) This lower bound can be greater than 0%, but cannot be lower than 0%. The federal funds rate is now about 0%. When interest rates reach this lower limit, the economy is commonly described as being caught in a "liquidity trap."

People hold their wealth in the form of bonds rather than money because they can earn interest on bonds. For example, you may be able to buy a bond for $100 that promises a payment of $110 in one year. That gives you a 10% annual interest rate (you loaned the bond issuer $100 for a year, and at the end of the year get your $100 back plus $10 interest). That is the incentive to buy the bond instead of just holding money.

Suppose the Fed wants to lower interest rates to stimulate spending. It offers to buy government bonds (previously sold to the public) at a higher price, driving down the interest rate. For instance, the Fed might offer $110 for bonds that promise $110 in one year. If you were to buy such a bond at the new price of $110, you would receive the same amount of money back a year later. The interest rate on that bond is now 0%. The idea of the policy is that banks will sell their government bonds to the Fed at the new higher price, take the money and buy other bonds (such as those issued by corporations), driving up their price and lowering the interest rate on those bonds.

Imagine that the Fed, however, decided that an interest rate of 0% was not low enough, and decided instead to pay banks $120 for bonds that promise $110 in a year. The banks would gladly sell their bonds, so the money supply would increase. But they would not loan out the money they received at a negative interest rate (paying consumers or firms to borrow from them). They would be better off just keeping the money in their vaults. In other words, once the interest rate reaches 0%, there is nothing more that the government can do with conventional expansionary monetary policy. That is the liquidity trap—any extra liquidity (money) the Fed makes available gets trapped, instead of being loaned out.

Monetary Policy and Interest Rates Today

Economic journalists and commentators have inaccurately described "interest rates" as being at or near 0% these days. The federal funds rate has hit rock bottom, but other interest rates clearly have not. Keynes was acutely aware that, when monetary authorities limit themselves to buying short-term securities, the "effect may ... be mainly confined to the very short-term rate of interest and have but little reaction on the much more important long-term rates of interest."

In a famous passage in *The General Theory,* Keynes notes the possibility that "after the rate of interest has fallen to a certain level ... almost everyone prefers cash to holding a debt which yields so low a rate of interest." This passage is often taken to be Keynes' description of the liquidity trap. He goes on to say that he did not know of any case when this had actually happened and notes that it is not likely to happen "owing to the unwillingness of most monetary authorities to deal boldly in debts of long term." It is clear from this passage that Keynes was not describing merely a situation in which certain short-term interest rates targeted by the government (such as the federal funds rate) were pushed to their lower limits, but rather one in which all interest rates hit rock bottom—a different situation from what is commonly referred to as a "liquidity trap" today.

Keynes viewed monetary policymakers' focus on certain short-run interest rates not as an inherent limitation in monetary policy, but as a limitation in the ways monetary policy was conventionally practiced. He notes that governments did not usually buy long-term bonds and drive down long-term interest rates, but that there was no reason they could not. In March, the Fed actually began to do just that, buying billions in long-term government securities in an attempt to bring down long-term rates. The 10-year Treasury bond rate dropped dramatically (from about 3% to 2.5%) the day the purchases began. It has increased somewhat since then, but remains lower than it was before November 2008.

Any attempt to revive private investment by manipulating interest rates, however, faces at least two additional barriers:

First, the interest rates consumers and firms pay do not move in lockstep with interest rates on government securities, either short-term or long-term. The contrast between short-term and long-term bonds is not the same as the difference between relatively safe government bonds and riskier corporate bonds or consumer loans. As we have seen, interest rates on corporate bonds have failed to decline, even as rates on long-term government bonds have declined. Banks' consumer lending standards, likewise, have tightened even as the Fed has driven down interest rates on government bonds.

Second, economic activity simply may not change dramatically in response to changes in interest rates, especially during a recession. Expectations of future sales and profits are extremely negative, so firms are dramatically slashing payrolls and investment spending. Total employment has decreased by over half a million people for each of five consecutive months from November 2008 to March 2009. Non-residential fixed investment decreased by over 20% in the last quarter of 2008; investment in nonresidential structures by nearly 10%. Firms have inventories they cannot sell, are laying off workers, and are producing below their existing productive capacity. Most of them are not going to make large investments in new plant and equipment under such conditions.

For these reasons, Keynesian economists have advocated a very large fiscal stimulus. Fiscal policy, in contrast to monetary policy, involves government spending and taxation. A fiscal stimulus program involves increases in government spending or reductions in taxes. Keynesian economists, believing that monetary policy is not adequate to pull the economy out of its current crisis, have argued especially for a dramatic increase in government spending as the surest way to revive overall spending, production, and employment. ❑

Sources: John Maynard Keynes, *The General Theory of Employment, Interest, and Money*, First Harvest/Harcourt, 1964; The Federal Reserve Bank, Intended federal funds rate, Change and level, 1990 to present; Bureau of Economic Analysis, News Release: Gross Domestic Product (GDP) and Corporate Profits, March 26, 2009; Bureau of Labor Statistics, Table A-12, Alternative measures of labor underutilization; Luke Mullins, "Banks Tighten Mortgage Lending Standards," *U.S. News and World Report*, Feb. 2, 2009; Jeannine Aversa and Alan Zibel, "Mortgage rates down, but standards remain high," Associated Press, Press-Telegram (Long Beach, CA), March 19, 2009; Bob Tedeschi, "Mortgages: 'Cashing Out' is Now Harder," *New York Times*, March 19, 2009; Kathy Chu, "Changing credit card terms squeeze consumers," *USA Today*, Dec. 16, 2008; Jane J. Kim, "BofA to Boost Rates on Cards With Balances," *Wall Street Journal*, April 9, 2009; Federal Reserve Bank of St. Louis, Moody's Seasoned Aaa Corporate Bond Yield; Federal Reserve Bank of St. Louis, Moody's Seasoned Baa Corporate Bond Yield; Paul Krugman (blog), "Spreads," Jan. 19, 2009; Jon Hilsenrath, "Fed in Bond-Buying Binge to Spur Growth," *Wall Street Journal*, March 19, 2009; Paul Krugman (blog), "Return of depression economics," March 4, 2009; Federal Reserve Bank of St. Louis, Ten-Year Treasury Constant Maturity Rate; Bureau of Labor Statistics, Payroll Employment; Bureau of Economic Analysis, News Release: Gross Domestic Product (GDP) and Corporate Profits, March 26, 2009.

Chapter 8

SAVINGS, INVESTMENT, AND FINANCE

INTRODUCTION

In the orderly world of neoclassical macroeconomics, capital markets—governed by all-powerful interest rates—work seamlessly to assure that saving is matched by investment, fueling growth in the private economy, which in turn guarantees full employment. Should the flow of saving exceed the uptake of investment, falling interest rates automatically solve the problem.

In the real world, economies are far messier than neoclassical macroeconomics suggests. Keynes argued that there is no neat connection, or "nexus," between savings and investment in a modern financial economy. Savings often sit, hoarded and uninvested. And interest rates, no matter how low, seldom coax reluctant investors to lay out their money in a weak economy. In the Keynesian world, economies regularly suffer from investment shortfalls that lead to recessions and cost workers their jobs.

Ramaa Vasudevan provides a primer on the increased importance of financial markets, financial institutions, and financial elites in today's economy and its governing institutions. The fact that failed financial corporations have received massive bailouts, for Vasudevan, only underlines the power they wield in the era of "financialization" (Article 8.1).

Gerald Epstein (Article 8.2) discusses not only the dramatic growth in the size of the financial sector, but also the transformation from regulated "boring" banking to deregulated "roaring" banking. Epstein argues that the current system has ill-served the economy and society, and calls for regulation of private finance and development of alternative financial institutions as two parts of the needed solution.

Next, Arthur MacEwan (Article 8.3) tackles the issue of stock "buybacks" by corporations, which have grown dramatically in recent years. Stock buybacks serve several purposes for corporations, such as reducing the number of outstanding shares of stock (and so pushing up the company's earnings per share), boosting the stock price, and funneling income to top executives (whose compensation is tied to the stock price). There is little evidence, however, that stock buybacks fuel productive investment or "trickle down" to workers.

Alejandro Reuss (Article 8.4) looks back at economist John Maynard Keynes' understanding of financial instability, especially financial "bubbles"—a major problem in the U.S. economy. Reuss argues that bubbles have been a key driver of demand in the U.S. economy in recent decades, and so it will require deeper changes than just financial regulation to solve this problem.

Robert Pollin reviews the insights of post-Keynesian economist Hyman Minsky on the tendency toward excessive financial risk-taking during economic booms (Article 8.5). Minsky offers us a hypothesis of endogenous instability within financial markets. Minsky pointed to government regulation as a necessary substitute for the discipline of the market (which reins in risk-taking only through ruinous financial crashes).

Nina Eichacker explains how the boom-and-bust cycle of capitalist economies has been adrenalized by the deregulation of finance (Article 8.6). As Eichacker argues in her study of Iceland's financial collapse, no country has the institutional capacity to cope with the instability inherent in a deregulated and "supercharged" financial system.

The final essay comes from Dean Baker. Its title, "Ten Years After the Financial Crisis, Our Elites Have Learned Nothing" (Article 8.7), suggests that there is a well-compensated amnesia among bankers and policymakers as to the causes of the Great Recession. They appear to be racing to repeat their mistakes.

Discussion Questions

1. (Article 8.1) What is "financialization"? How does it manifest itself in today's economy? How did it contribute to the recent financial crisis?

2. (Article 8.2) "Roaring" sounds better than "boring." Why does Epstein believe that "boring" banking is better than "roaring" banking?

3. (Article 8.3) What are stock "buybacks," and what, in MacEwan's view, are their economic consequences?

4. (Article 8.4) Some economists argue that financial market instability is the result of "irrational" investor behavior. Did Keynes agree?

5. (Article 8.5) Why do financial companies tend to engage in excessive risk-taking during economic booms? If financial crashes are too harmful to tolerate, and bailouts (to prevent or contain a crash) only encourage further risky behavior, what are the alternatives?

6. (Article 8.6) Why did government, business media, and international institutions all profess that Iceland's financial deregulation posed little threat to the country's economic stability? Was this a simple "mistake," or was there more to it than that?

7. (Article 8.7) Dean Baker is particularly interested in the "zero money down or less" aspect of the subprime mortgages that were bundled into collateralized debt obligations. Why is a high rate of such mortgages a red flag about a coming crisis? What is a "NINJA" loan?

Article 8.1

FINANCIALIZATION: A PRIMER

BY RAMAA VASUDEVAN
November/December 2008

Y ou don't have to be an investor dabbling in the stock market to feel the power of finance. Finance pervades the lives of ordinary people in many ways, from student loans and credit card debt to mortgages and pension plans.

And its size and impact are only getting bigger. Consider a few measures:

- U.S. credit market debt—all debt of private households, businesses, and government combined—rose from about 1.6 times the nation's GDP in 1973 to over 3.5 times GDP by 2007.
- The profits of the financial sector represented 14% of total corporate profits in 1981; by 2001-02 this figure had risen to nearly 50%.

These are only a few of the indicators of what many commentators have labeled the "financialization" of the economy—a process University of Massachusetts economist Gerald Epstein succinctly defines as "the increasing importance of financial markets, financial motives, financial institutions, and financial elites in the operation of the economy and its governing institutions."

In recent years, this phenomenon has drawn increasing attention. In his latest book, pundit Kevin Phillips writes about the growing divergence between the real (productive) and financial economies, describing how the explosion of trading in myriad new financial instruments played a role in polarizing the U.S. economy. On the left, political economists Harry Magdoff and Paul Sweezy had over many years pointed to the growing role of finance in the operations of capitalism; they viewed the trend as a reflection of the rising economic and political power of "rentiers"—those whose earnings come from financial activities and from forms of income arising from ownership claims (such as interest, rent, dividends, or capital gains) rather than from actual production.

From Finance to Financialization

The financial system is supposed to serve a range of functions in the broader economy. Banks and other financial institutions mop up savings, then allocate that capital, according to mainstream theory, to where it can most productively be used. For households and corporations, the credit markets facilitate greatly increased borrowing, which should foster investment in capital goods like buildings and machinery, in turn leading to expanded production. Finance, in other words, is supposed to facilitate the growth of the "real" economy—the part that produces useful goods (like bicycles) and services (like medical care).

In recent decades, finance has undergone massive changes in both size and shape. The basic mechanism of financialization is the transformation of future streams of income (from profits, dividends, or interest payments) into a tradable asset like a stock or a bond. For example, the future earnings of corporations are transmuted into equity stocks that are bought and sold in the capital market. Likewise, a loan, which involves certain fixed interest payments over its duration, gets a new life when it is converted into marketable bonds. And multiple loans, bundled together then "sliced and diced" into novel kinds of bonds ("collateralized debt obligations"), take on a new existence as investment vehicles that bear an extremely complex and opaque relationship to the original loans.

The process of financialization has not made finance more effective at fulfilling what conventional economic theory views as its core function. Corporations are not turning to the stock market as a source of finance for their investments, and their borrowing in the bond markets is often not for the purpose of productive investment either. Since the 1980s, corporations have actually spent more money buying back their own stock than they have taken in by selling newly issued stock. The granting of stock options to top executives gives them a direct incentive to have the corporation buy back its own shares—often using borrowed money to do so—in order to hike up the share price and allow them to turn a profit on the sale of their personal shares. More broadly, instead of fostering investment, financialization reorients managerial incentives toward chasing short-term returns through financial trading and speculation so as to generate ballooning earnings, lest their companies face falling stock prices and the threat of hostile takeover.

What is more, the workings of these markets tend to act like an upper during booms, when euphoric investors chase the promise of quick bucks. During downturns these same mechanisms work like downers, turning euphoria into panic as investors flee. Financial innovations like collateralized debt obligations were supposed to "lubricate" the economy by spreading risk, but instead they tend to heighten volatility, leading to amplified cycles of boom and bust. In the current crisis, the innovation of mortgage-backed securities fueled the housing bubble and encouraged enormous risk-taking, creating the conditions for the chain reaction of bank (and other financial institution) failures that may be far from over.

Financialization and Power

The arena of finance can at times appear to be merely a casino—albeit a huge one—where everyone gets to place her bets and ride her luck. But the financial system carries a far deeper significance for people's lives. Financial assets and liabilities represent claims on ownership and property; they embody the social relations of an economy at a particular time in history. In this sense, the recent process of financialization implies the increasing political and economic power of a particular segment of the capitalist class: rentiers. Accelerating financial transactions and the profusion of financial techniques have fuelled an extraordinary enrichment of this elite.

This enrichment arises in different ways. Financial transactions facilitate the reallocation of capital to high-return ventures. In the ensuing shake-up, some sectors of capital profit at the expense of other sectors. More important, the capitalist class as a whole is able to force a persistent redistribution in its favor, deploying its newly expanded wealth to bring about changes in the political-economy that channel even more wealth its way.

The structural changes that paved the way for financialization involved the squashing of working-class aspirations during the Reagan-Thatcher years; the defeats of the miners' strike in England and of the air traffic controllers' (PATCO) strike in the United States were perhaps the most symbolic instances of this process. At the same time, these and other governments increasingly embraced the twin policy mantras of fighting inflation and deregulating markets in place of creating full employment and raising wages. Corporations pushed through legislation to dismantle the financial regulations that inhibited their profitmaking strategies.

Financialization has gathered momentum amid greater inequality. In the United States, the top 1% of the population received 14.0% of the national after-tax income in 2004, nearly double its 7.5% share in 1979. In the same period the share of the bottom fifth fell from 6.8% to 4.9%.

And yet U.S. consumption demand has been sustained despite rising inequality and a squeeze on real wages for the majority of households. Here is the other side of the financialization coin: a massive expansion of consumer credit has played an important role in easing the constraints on consumer spending by filling the gap created by stagnant or declining real wages. The credit card debt of the average U.S. family increased by 53% through the 1990s. About 67% of low-income families with incomes less than $10,000 faced credit card debt, and the debt of this group saw the largest increase—a 184% rise, compared to a 28% increase for families with incomes above $100,000. Offered more and more credit as a privatized means of addressing wage stagnation, then, eventually, burdened by debt and on the edge of insolvency, the working poor and the middle class are less likely to organize as a political force to challenge the dominance of finance. In this sense, financialization becomes a means of social coercion that erodes working-class solidarity.

As the structures created by financial engineering unravel, the current economic crisis is revealing the cracks in this edifice. But even as a growing number of U.S. families are losing their homes and jobs in the wake of the subprime meltdown, the financial companies at the heart of the crisis have been handed massive bailouts and their top executives have pocketed huge pay-outs despite their role in abetting the meltdown—a stark sign of the power structures and interests at stake in this era of financialization. ❏

Sources: Robin Blackburn, "Finance and the Fourth Dimension," *New Left Review* 39 May-June 2006; Robert Brenner, "New Boom or Bubble," *New Left Review* 25 Jan-Feb 2004; Tamara Draut and Javier Silva, "Borrowing to make ends meet," *Demos*, Sept 2003; Gerald Epstein, "Introduction" in G. Epstein, ed., *Financialization and the World Economy*, 2006; John Bellamy Foster, "The Financialization of Capitalism," *Monthly Review*, April 2007; Gretta Krippner, "The financialization of the US economy," *Socio-Economic Review* 3, Feb. 2005; Thomas Palley, "Financialization : What it is and why it matters," Political Economy Research Institute Working Paper #153, November 2007; A. Sherman and Arin Dine, "New CBO data shows inequality continues to widen," Center for Budget Priorities, Jan. 23, 2007; Kevin Phillips, *Bad Money: Reckless Finance, Failed Politics, and the Global Crisis of American Capitalism*, 2008.

Article 8.2

FROM "BORING" BANKING TO "ROARING" BANKING
How the financial sector grew out of control, and how we can change it.

AN INTERVIEW WITH GERALD EPSTEIN
May/June 2015

Gerald Epstein *is a professor of economics and a founding co-director of the Political Economy Research Institute (PERI) at the University of Massachusetts-Amherst. He has written extensively about U.S. and global finance and recently delivered the Distinguished Faculty Lecture at UMass-Amherst titled "When Big is Too Big: Do the Financial System's Social Benefits Justify Its Size?" In April, he sat down with* Dollars & Sense *co-editor Alejandro Reuss to discuss major themes in his current research—the dramatic growth in the financial sector, the transformation from regulated "boring" banking to deregulated "roaring" banking, the ways the current system has ill-served the economy and society, and the need for regulation of private finance and development of alternative financial institutions.*

Dollars & Sense: What should we be looking at as indicators that the financial sector has grown much larger in this most recent era, compared to what it used to be?

Gerald Epstein: There are a number of different indicators and dimensions to this. The size of the financial sector itself is one dimension. If you look at the profit share of banks and other financial institutions, you'll see that in the early postwar period, up until the early 1980s, they took down about 15% of all corporate profits in the United States. Just before the crisis, in 2006, they took down 40% of all profits, which is pretty astonishing.

Another measure of size is total financial assets as a percentage of gross domestic product. If you look at the postwar period, it's pretty constant from 1945 to 1981, with the ratio of financial assets to the size of the economy—of GDP—at about four to one. But starting in 1981, it started climbing. By 2007, total financial assets were ten times the size of GDP. If you look at almost any metric about the overall size of the financial sector—credit-to-GDP ratios, debt-to-GDP ratios, etc.—you see this massive increase starting around 1981, going up to a peak just before the financial crisis, in 2006.

Two more, related, dimensions are the sizes of the biggest financial firms and the concentration of the industry. For example, the share of total securities-industry assets held by the top five investment banks was 65% in 2007. The share of the total deposits held by the top seven commercial banks went from roughly 20% in the early postwar period to over 50%. If you look at derivatives trading, you find that the top five investment banks control about 97% of that. So there's a massive concentration in the financial system, and that hasn't declined—in some ways, it's gotten ten worse—since the financial crisis.

D&S: Could you describe the qualitative changes in financial institution behavior in this same era, and the origins of these changes? When we hear that year 1981, we immediately think of deregulation. Is it just deregulation, or is there more to it than that?

GE: We can roughly think about two periods of banking and finance in the post-World War II era. Coming out of the Great Depression, when there was a lot of financial regulation, the Glass-Steagall Act separated investment from commercial banking, there were rules governing the issuing of complex and risky securities, rules for different kinds of financial institutions in terms of what kinds of assets they could hold. Savings and loans could mostly focus on housing, commercial banks primarily on business loans, investment banks couldn't take deposits and mostly engaged in underwriting and those kinds of activities. There were interest-rate ceilings, high capital requirements, leverage requirements. During this period, most of the activity of banks, commercial banks particularly, was in terms of taking in deposits and making individual loans—business loans, mortgages, real-estate loans. Many people call this the age of "boring banking." It was also called the age of "3-6-3" banking—bankers paid 3% interest, lent out at 6%, and got to the golf course by 3:00 in the afternoon.

Then starting in the late 1970s and early 1980s, their activities really changed, partly as a result of financial deregulation, partly as a result of increased competition from other kinds of financial institutions. Relatively unregulated banks could pay depositors higher interest rates, could charge higher interest rates on their loans, and could engage in new kinds of financial innovation—such as securitization, which is placing a bunch of loans into a bundle, such as an asset-backed security or mortgage-backed security, and selling these things off. "Boring banking" could no longer compete, so instead of engaging in one-to-one lending, they started engaging in more activities with the capital markets—bundling up or securitizing loans, selling them off, using derivatives to hedge risks but also to make bets. They kind of became like hedge funds in the sense of doing a lot of trading, buying and selling a lot of derivatives, engaging with the securities and capital markets. But they still had the government guarantees like they were banks.

D&S: How does finance measure up, during this most recent era of deregulated finance, against the key claims that are made about its socially constructive role?

GE: If you look at the textbook description of the positive roles that finance plays, basically it comes down to six things: channel savings to productive investment, provide mechanisms for households to save for retirement, help businesses and households reduce risk, provide stable and flexible liquidity, provide an efficient payments mechanism, and come up with new financial innovations, that will make it cheaper, simpler, and better to do all these other five things. If you go through the way finance operated in the period of "roaring" banking, one can raise questions about the productive role of banking in all of these dimensions.

Taking the first role, channeling finance to productive investment, in the early postwar period, nonfinancial corporations on average got about 15-20% of their funding for productive investment from outside sources, from banks and from the capital markets. For the rest, they used retained earnings. In the latter period, after around 1980 or so, this was cut more or less in half—to 7–10%. So finance didn't really provide a huge percentage of funds for nonfinancial corporate investment in the age of roaring banking. So you have this paradoxical situation where the income going to finance grew significantly while the real contribution to providing funding for investment went down. During the 1960s, finance got about 40 cents for every dollar they gave to nonfinancial corporations for investment. By the 2000s, it was up to 66 cents.

What was finance doing instead? As Juan Montecino, Iren Levina, and I point out in a paper we wrote, they started lending to each other, instead of to the real economy or nonfinancial corporations. So we looked at intra-financial sector lending as a share of total lending from 1950 to 2010 and we found that, from 1950 up to around 1980 or so, they were only doing about 10% of total lending to each other. Just before the crisis in 2008 or so, they were doing almost 30% of all lending to each other. This lending to each other really was a way of providing finance for derivatives trading and other kinds of betting, rather than financing real investment.

The second role is providing mechanisms for households to save for retirement. There are a lot of studies that show that banks didn't do a very good job in the period of roaring banking. Part of the problem is that the savings vehicles that finance provides for households come at a very high cost. If you put your money in a mutual fund, say, with Fidelity or one of these other companies, oftentimes the fees that you have to pay are very high, and the returns that you get aren't any better—sometimes worse—than if you put your money in a broad portfolio of stocks, like the S&P 500 or something like that. There are a lot of studies that show that the returns that you get from putting your money in these active funds is more than 2% less than if you just put it into a broad stock portfolio. Well, this 2% is going directly to the company, to Fidelity and the people who work for them, so it's a way that finance is overcharging.

The way in which finance has failed in helping households save for retirement is even more stark if you realize that, for most households in the United States, most of the wealth that people have is in their homes. If you think about what the financial sector did to people's savings in their houses in that period, it's a pretty dismal record—especially for African American and Hispanic and other minority households, much more so than for white households. Already, African Americans' wealth

---

How the Banks Broke Out of Regulations

D&S: You talk about banks that had been comfortably and profitably engaging in highly regulated "boring" activities coming under competitive pressure. How much of this coming from new players and how much is it the banks themselves finding those niches to evade the regulations that existed at the time?

GE: It's both, for sure. I can't really tell you about the relative weights of those two factors, but certainly both are going on. So for example, one of the key restrictions that commercial banks were working under was the "Regulation Q ceiling." There were limits on what they could pay for deposits. In the late 1960s and 1970s, when inflation began taking off, savers were finding that the real interest rates they were getting from their deposits with banks were turning negative, banks couldn't raise the interest rates they paid to keep depositors. And these aren't small savers. We're talking about big corporations and wealthy people. Financial institutions were able to find niches outside the regulations, particularly money market mutual funds and other innovations. Fidelity Investments, for example, was

is just a fraction of white wealth, and most of their wealth was in their houses. The financial crisis of 2006-2007 pretty much wiped out a large percentage of African American wealth during this period. So clearly, roaring banking didn't do much to help households save for retirement.

The third role is to reduce risk. You just need to look at the kinds of financial products that banks were selling under the guise of reducing risk—like credit default swaps, mortgage-backed securities, asset-backed securities, etc. These products lost enormous amounts of value during the financial crisis, and would have lost almost all of their value if the government hadn't bailed them out. The financial sector was a source of enormous risk, rather than a source of reducing risk.

The same can be easily said of the fourth function, providing stable and flexible liquidity. If you look at the housing bubble and the tremendous run-up in asset prices provided by the tremendous increase in liquidity from the financial sector—through asset-backed securities, subprime lending, and so forth—you realize that it was not stable. It was actually what led to the asset bubble and crash. So private banking does not provide stable or flexible liquidity. In the end, in 2008, the Federal Reserve had to come in and provide enormous amounts of liquidity to the system to keep it from melting down entirely.

For the fifth role, to provide an efficient payments mechanism, we see a similar kind of thing. The only thing that kept the payments system operating after the financial crisis was the enormous amounts of liquidity that the Federal Reserve flooded into the financial system. Moreover, if anyone has ever tried to transfer money from one bank to another, or overseas, you realize that our payments mechanism—even in normal times—is very inefficient. Banks can hold onto your funds for two or three or four days before making them available to you, when you try to transfer from one bank to another, just as a way of extracting more money from households. Both in abnormal times and in normal times, the payments mechanism in the period of roaring banking is very poor.

---

able to create a checking account based on a money market mutual fund. They could start offering much higher interest rates.

But the banks themselves also found out ways of breaking out of this, primarily through the Eurodollar market that developed in the mid-1960s. Citibank, Bank of America, and all these other banks were able to develop these same kinds of financial products overseas, where they weren't subject to the same kinds of restrictions. Of course, it wasn't really overseas, it was just accounting changes on their books. One set of accounts was the Eurodollar market and another set of accounts was domestic, but they were all really in the same place, in New York or wherever. They were able to develop these kinds of new products and able to keep their commercial customers and others by setting up in the Eurodollar market rather than in New York.

Citibank was one of the examples of a bank that started pushing the envelope in various ways, to set up these accounts in the United States. The Federal Reserve essentially looked the other way—gave them an administrative pass—in the late 1970s. This just started opening up a floodgate. So it was a combination of new players coming in and developing these kinds of things and the old players figuring out ways around restrictions, primarily by booking all of this in overseas accounts.

Finally, that brings us to banking innovations. Paul Volcker famously told a group of bankers in 2009 that the only financial innovation that he could see in the last 20 years that had been at all efficient was the ATM. There's no evidence that financial innovations have led to more economic growth. Jim Crotty and I did a literature survey that showed that at the minimum 30-40% of financial innovations over the last 20 years or so are used at least to some extent, if not largely, to evade regulations or to evade taxes—that is, to shift around pieces of the pie from the public to the banks, rather than to increase the size of the pie.

In short, roaring banking has done a pretty dismal job of providing any of these functions that the textbook case says finance should provide.

D&S: Of course, bubbles burst and exacerbate the severity of downturns. One of the amazing things about the aftermath of the recent crisis has been the apparent imperviousness of the financial sector to serious reform—especially in contrast to the Great Crash of 1929 and the Great Depression. How do you make sense of that?

GE: You have to use a political economy approach to understand the sources of political support for finance. I call these multilayered sources of support the "bankers' club."

The lead group in the bankers' club is the bankers themselves, and the politicians that they're able to buy off with financial contributions and so forth. Their ability to do that, of course, has become much greater with changes in the campaign finance reform laws and Citizens United and so forth, so it makes it much easier for the banks to throw enormous amounts of money at politicians and prevent significant reform. This is true for both parties, for the Republicans and for the Democrats. We know how important finance was to Bill Clinton's political coalition in raising money. That's been true for Democrats for many years, not just Republicans.

The bankers have a lot of other support as well. Historically, the Federal Reserve has been one of the main orchestrators of the bankers' club. You can clearly see that in the role that Timothy Geithner played—when he was at the New York Fed, and then after he became Treasury Secretary under Obama—in fighting tooth-and-nail against any significant reform. He was one of the main figures in the opposition to tough reform through the Dodd-Frank Act. The Federal Reserve, through many mechanisms—the "revolving door" mechanism, the fact that they regulate banks, and so on—is a very strong member of the bankers' club.

A perhaps surprising group in the bankers' club has been many economists, especially academic economists who work on finance. Some of them take quite a bit of money from financial firms as consulting fees or are on the boards of directors of financial firms. Jessica Carrick-Hagenbarth and I studied this, looking at a group of 19 well-known academic economists who were working with two groups, the Pew Charitable Trusts Financial Reform Project and the Squam Lake Working Group on Financial Regulation, on financial reform issues. And they were coming up with financial reforms that, while some of them were OK, a lot really lacked teeth. We found that many of them, if not most of them, had some kind of association with financial firms, but were not disclosing this when they would write their academic papers speak on the radio or on TV or give testimony.

An important source of power of the bankers' club is that bankers can threaten to fail if we don't bail them out. They can threaten to leave—to move to London, Frankfurt, Hong Kong, or Shanghai—if we don't give them what they want. So this threat is the ultimate "club" that the bankers hold over our heads, and they use that all the time in the fight over financial reform.

On top of that, there's an important member of the bankers' club that in the 1930s wasn't a member—nonfinancial corporations. This time around, if you look at the fight over Dodd-Frank, you find very little opposition to banks from other members of the capitalist class. They were either silent or supported the banks. This is a big contrast to the 1930s when a lot of industrial firms did not support the banks, and in fact joined with FDR on financial regulation. Why is this? Why didn't we see more opposition from other capitalists to what the banks had done? After all, what the banks did led to this massive recession and hurt profits, at least initially, created all sorts of problems for nonfinancial corporations—and yet they supported the banks. Part of the answer may be that nonfinancial corporations have now become financialized themselves. The CEOs of these corporations get a lot of their incomes and wealth through stock options and other kinds of financial activities. Some nonfinancial firms have large financial components themselves. GE, for example, is now spinning off its financial subsidiary, GE Capital. But for many years it was getting quite a lot of income from GE Capital. And it's not just GE but also many other large nonfinancial corporations.

So there was a united front among the capitalists to oppose strong financial reform. Finance had plenty of money to buy off politicians. And while there was strong and valiant effort on the part of Americans for Financial Reform, Better Markets, some academic economists who were opposing what the banks did, and important roles played by Elizabeth Warren and some other senators—it just wasn't enough, given this united front of capitalists, the money machine, and the academic economists who were giving legitimacy to what the banks were doing.

D&S: That brings us to the question of a reform agenda for now. We've heard a lot about the need for re-regulation of finance, with an eye toward the restoration of the boring banking of the 1950s–1970s. The other question is whether the functions of finance require capitalist banks at all, even within a capitalist economy. Could all the functions of finance be done better by public and cooperative financial institutions, rather than private capitalist banks?

GE: The way I've been thinking about it is that we need both—that they're complements to each other. Short of complete overthrow of capitalism, and having a totally socialist economy, which is unlikely to happen in the immediate future, what I think we should argue for is both re-regulation of private finance and a much stronger push for what I call "banks without bankers." We need to have re-regulation of private finance as long as it continues to exist, for two reasons.

First, as we've seen—and as John Maynard Keynes and Hyman Minsky and others argued—private finance can create a lot of problems if it's not regulated. As Keynes put it, when "enterprise is a bubble on a whirlpool of speculation," we're in big trouble. You have to bring private finance under control so that it can't continue

Did the U.S. Economy Rely on a Financial "Bubble Machine"?

D&S: What would you think of the characterization that—within the context of U.S. capitalism becoming reliant on asset bubbles for achieving anything close to full-employment output—finance played the role of being the "bubble machine"? So, finance as an essential cog of a bigger dysfunctional system.

GE: My colleague Robert Pollin wrote a great book about this called *Contours of Descent*, about the Clinton administration and its role in creating this bubble machine. One of the impacts of all this roaring banking and this "pro-cyclical" liquidity creation—massive liquidity on the way up and then withdrawal of liquidity on the way down—was that it did have a huge levitating effect on wealth and, through this wealth effect, led to significant consumption particularly among the wealthy. And that helped to propel the economy forward in the 1990s.

Sometimes, people talk about this as if capitalism needed this to survive and that's why it's happened that way. I don't like that type of thinking methodologically. The question is: What is the counterfactual? What would have happened if the bubble machine weren't operating? Would the economy have slid into a long period of stagnation, or would there have been economic and political forces that would have generated a much healthier type of growth? These are things that we can't know, though which are certainly worth asking. But the characterization that bubbles had that kind of effect—of generating these booms, particularly during the Clinton years—is certainly correct.

to generate these massive bubbles and then crashes, which create enormous problems for workers and for households all over the world.

Second, as long as there's private finance out there and the bankers are making enormous profits and incomes, not only does that generate a worsening of the income distribution—it's an engine for inequality—it also makes it hard to have a stable and productive public financial sector. If you have public or cooperative banks, and you have people running those institutions and they think of themselves as financiers or bankers, and they realize that they could jump ship and work for the private financial sector and make five, ten, fifteen, twenty times what they're making in the public interest, this can be extremely tempting. Or it can get them to reorient the activities that they engage in to make them more profitable and look more like private banks. This is what happened to a number of public financial institutions around the world in the run-in up to the financial crisis. The first financial institution that really got into trouble, or one of the first, was a Landesbank, a regional provincial public bank in Germany that was supposed to be making boring banking investments, but instead was making roaring banking investments, because they wanted to keep up with the private financial institutions.

You can't let there be too big a gap between the activities and the incomes and pay between the public sector and the private sector if the public sector is going to do the job it needs to do. Of course, you can have a gap, and it can be somewhat large, but it can't get as big as it got in the 2000s. So for both of those reasons I do think that we do need to control private finance.

But in order to break up the bankers' club and to provide the real kind of finance that society needs, we do need to promote more cooperative finance and public finance. How do you do that? Well, there are a bunch of different ways. For example, there's the State Bank of North Dakota, and there are a number of organizations that are trying to promote state banks in other states. I know there's been an organization in Massachusetts, for example, that's been trying to do this. There are credit unions all over the country, so building the credit unions by having a national credit union bank to support them. These are all things that should be done.

The government should stop subsidizing the "too big to fail" banks by bailing them out. This lowers the cost of funds for these banks, allows them to grow larger and squeeze out cooperative and other kinds of community banks. So the government should end too big to fail as a way to make more room for these other kinds of public and cooperative banks. The Federal Reserve could serve as a backstop for these types of banks, by agreeing to act as a lender of last resort, to let them use their securities as collateral for borrowing. So there are all different kinds of ways that the government could support the creation or expansion of these sorts of institutions.

I think that's necessary for us to get out of the trap that we're in. ❏

Article 8.3

STOCK BUYBACKS: ANY POSITIVE OUTCOME?

BY ARTHUR MacEWAN
November/December 2016; updated June 2018

> Dear Dr. Dollar:
> *When a corporation buys back some of its own stock, is there any positive*
> *outcome (for the economy) other than making upper management richer?*
> — Julia Willebrand, New York, N.Y.

In early 2018, shortly after Congress and the President enacted sweeping new tax legislation, the Apple corporation said it would use $100 billion of its gains from the new tax laws to buy back shares of its own stock. Apple is not new to the buyback game, but this 2018 action takes it to a new high. Exxon, which before Apple held the top buyback position, was spending *only* $20 billion per year on buybacks before 2015.

According to research by the Morgan Stanley bank, corporations expect to spend 43% of their tax cut gains on buybacks. They expect that another 26% will go to paying down debt and to mergers and acquisitions, whereas capital spending would account for 17%. Only 13% would go to wage increases. (The extent to which wages will be increased by investment is an open question; but new investment is a relatively small share of firms' tax change gains.) Yet although buybacks are a major part of the tax change story in 2018, they are not a new phenomenon.

Usually we think of firms issuing—i.e., selling—shares of stock to raise money for their investments. However, firms can also buy back those shares, which are shares of ownership in the firms. In recent years, buy-backs have become a big deal. In the decade 2006 to 2015, U.S. nonfinancial corporations' total net equity issues—new share issues minus shares taken off the market through buybacks and merger-and-acquisition deals—averaged negative $416 billion per year.

These buybacks, this reversal of the conventional view of how firms operate, do not generate a positive outcome for the economy. That is, these buybacks do not lead to economic growth or other changes that would benefit those of us who neither manage a company nor hold large amounts of its stock—just about everybody. Certainly, a firm's executives can gain through buybacks. As can some shareholders, both the ones who sell their shares in the buyback and the ones who, continuing to hold the company's stock, may see its value rise.

A driving force in the buyback game is that it generally serves to raise the incomes of companies' top executives. They are gaming the system to raise their own incomes. Yet, top executives have always wanted more income, and buybacks were relatively insignificant until the mid-1980s. So why have stock buybacks become so substantial in more recent years?

In a 2014 article in the *Harvard Business Review*, William Lazonick, a professor at the University of Massachusetts Lowell emphasizes two new developments. The first is Wall Street's increasing focus on earnings per share (EPS) as a princi-

TOP 5 INDIVIDUAL FIRMS AND TOTAL OF TOP 50 FIRMS WITH LARGEST AMOUNT SPENT ON BUYBACKS IN THE 2006-2015 DECADE

	Spending on buybacks (millions of dollars)	Spending on buybacks as percentage of net income
ExxonMobil	$206,253	59.2%
Microsoft	$123,640	71.1%
IBM	$119,497	88.8%
Apple	$103,468	45.5%
Proctor & Gamble	$72,487	69.2%
Top 50	$3,739,442	59.8%

pal means to evaluate the well-being of a firm. EPS is the amount of net earnings (i.e., profits after taxes) divided by the total number of shares of stock outstanding, usually calculated for a three-month period. A firm's spending on buybacks is not counted as an operating expense and therefore does not affect net earnings, but the buybacks do reduce the number of shares outstanding. So the buybacks increase EPS.

Focusing on EPS means focusing on the immediate or short-run performance of a firm, and it tells little about the firm's long-run prospects. Furthermore, the firm's long-run prospects can be harmed by the buybacks, since, though not counted as an operating expense, the buyback expenditure reduces the firm's retained earnings that are the financial foundation for investing in productive capabilities.

Associated with this EPS emphasis is that the salaries of top executives are often tied to their firms' EPS. Moreover, executives are often paid in company stock. By buying back a firm's stock (i.e., raising demand for the stock), executives are able to lift the stock price, even if only temporarily. So buybacks and the consequent increase in a firm's EPS are a way that top executives can game the system all the way to the bank.

The second factor that Lazonick points to in explaining the change is that in 1982, the Securities and Exchange Commission (SEC) instituted Rule 10b-18 of the Securities Exchange Act, which greatly facilitated stock buybacks without meaningful regulation. Lazonick points out: "In essence, Rule 10b-18 legalized stock market manipulation [by a firm] through open market purchases." (An "open market" purchase is the purchase of a company's stock in the securities market or, if the purchase is directly between the buyer and seller, at the securities market price.)

There is also a third factor, which helps explain the surge of buybacks in the most recent years—namely the poor performance of the U.S. economy. In a slow-growth economy, the opportunities to profit from productive investment are limited, which raises the relative appeal of gaming the system through buybacks and other means. Yet, devoting funds to buybacks and abandoning productive investment contributes to the economy's poor performance.

During the decade ending in 2015, large firms with familiar names dominated in terms of the amount spent on buybacks (as shown in the table). ExxonMobil led, spending $206.3 billion on buybacks during this period, amounting to nearly 60% of its net income (profits after taxes). Then came Microsoft and IBM, with the latter's spending on buybacks amounting to 89% of its net income. For the top fifty firms in terms of amount spent on buybacks, the total spending was $3.7 trillion in the years 2006-2015, an amount equal to 60% of their total net income over that period. In more recent years, as noted above, Apple has become the leader of the pack.

In a 2016 paper, which supplies additional data and analysis of buybacks, Lazonick sums up the phenomenon: "Given the importance of these corporations to the operations and performance of the economy, it is fair to say that the 21st century U.S. industrial economy has become a 'buyback economy.'"

Of course, there are those who claim that buybacks are good for the economy. In a rather trite attack on Lazonick's *Harvard Business Review* article, Greg Satell in a *Forbes* article claims that buybacks can put more of their "excess cash" in the hands of investors who will be able "to create new value." One wonders: If so many major firms themselves cannot find, or choose not to find, productive investments "to create new value," why will those who sell stock back to the firms make productive investments? Most likely, they too will use the funds to game the system, entering into the grand casino we call "Wall Street." ❑

Sources: William Lazonick, "How Stock Buybacks Make Americans Vulnerable to Globalization," AIR Working Paper #16-0301, March 2016 (theairnet.org); William Lazonick, "Profits without Prosperity," *Harvard Business Review*, September 2014 (hbr.org); Greg Satell, "Why Stock Buybacks Are Good For The Economy And The Country," *Forbes*, May 9, 2015 (forbes.com); Steven Rattner, "Testimony Before the House Ways and Means Committee," May 16, 2018 (waysandmeans.house.gov); Jack Nicas, "Apple Says It Will Buy Back $100 Billion in Stock," *The New York Times*, May 1, 2018 (nytimes.com).

Article 8.4

BUBBLE BUBBLE, TOIL AND TROUBLE
Keynes and Financial Instability

BY ALEJANDRO REUSS
October 2013

In recent years, the United States has experienced major "bubbles"—increases in asset prices fueled by nothing more than the expectation that in the future others will be willing to pay even more—in the stock market and in real-estate markets. The S&P Composite Index, a broad index of stock prices, stood at less than 850 in early 2003, after the "dot.com" crash. By 2007, it had ballooned to over 1500. The real-estate bubble saw the Case-Shiller 20-City Housing Price Index, the main index of U.S. housing prices, more than double from 100 at the beginning of 2000 to over 206 in the middle of 2006. Both have crashed since then. The Case-Shiller Index fell to less than 150 by January 2008. The S&P lost about half its value, down to a little more than 750, between its 2007 peak and March 2009.

Sources of Market Volatility

In the words of former Federal Reserve chair Alan Greenspan, a wave of "irrational exuberance" fueled the stock market boom. It is easy to believe that daredevil risk-taking, an unreasoning faith that prices will keep rising and rising, and possibly testosterone intoxication, are responsible for asset "bubbles." That may not be entirely false, but we chalk up bubbles exclusively to irrational behavior at the peril of ignoring the element of individual rationality in joining into a bubble and fueling its growth. In *The General Theory*, Keynes argued that financial-market instability, in particular, was due not merely to some "wrong-headed propensity" on the part of the individuals involved, but to the organization of financial markets themselves.

Conventional economic theory of asset markets is dominated by the "efficient markets hypothesis." Proponents of this view argue that the price of a financial asset at any given moment reflects all the available information about its true value (e.g., stock prices at any given moment reflect all the available information about the value of a company, or real-estate prices about the value of those properties). When new information becomes available, either about a particular asset or about the national or world economy, this causes market participants to revalue the asset, and the price goes up or down accordingly. If it were possible to know now that a stock's price would, say, go up to a specific level the next day, people would buy it now in anticipation of the rise, bidding up the price today. We would not have to wait until tomorrow to get to the new, higher price. In this view, stock prices reflect the real values of the assets being traded, so far as the available information allows, and price fluctuations on the stock market and other asset markets originate from outside the markets themselves.

Critics of the efficient markets hypothesis have argued that it underestimates the instability generated within asset markets. Price fluctuations are caused not only by newly available information, but by market participants' reactions to previous price fluctuations and prediction of how other participants will react to those fluctuations. Market participants are concerned, in Keynes' view, not with correctly ascertaining the long-term value of an asset, but primarily with guessing what others will be willing to pay for it in the short-run. They buy and sell, Keynes argued, not on the basis of "what an investment is really worth to [someone] who buys it 'for keeps'," but on the basis of "what the market will value it at ... three months or a year hence."

Keynes' Beauty Contest

In *The General Theory*, Keynes famously compared financial markets to a strange sort of beauty pageant run by London newspapers in his time. The papers published an array of photos, and readers could enter a contest in which the winner was the reader who guessed which faces would be chosen by the most other readers. (Keynes was not commenting, one way or another, about the existence of these or other "beauty contests." In fact, he was not focused on this as a contest between the women pictured, but as a contest between the readers doing the guessing.) As Keynes pointed out, it would not do to simply choose the photo that one found most attractive, for one's own tastes might not match those of other entrants. Neither, however, should one choose the photo that one thought other entrants would find most attractive (for they would not themselves be choosing the one they found most attractive). Each entrant would, rather, be trying to guess what other entrants would guess about which photos most other entrants would choose.

In the same way, participants in the stock market, Keynes argued, did not generally attempt to estimate the likely returns from a company's investments (often referred to these days as its "fundamentals"), but to "guess better than the crowd how the crowd will behave." If other market participants are, for whatever reason, buying a particular kind of asset and driving up its price, rational participants would decide to buy as well (to benefit from the short-run increase in prices) as long as they expected that the price would continue to rise.

This makes sense, from the standpoint of an individual buyer, even if the buyer, in some sense, knows better—that is, believes that the company in question has bad long-term prospects, that "the market" has overpriced the stock, that other buyers are acting unwisely, and so on. For example, you may not think that Springfield Nuclear Power is a very well-run company, but as long as you think other people are (unwisely) going to buy its stock, pushing up the stock price, it makes sense for you to buy the stock and profit from these future price increases. As more people buy in to take advantage of a crowd-induced rise in prices, of course, they further fuel the growth of the bubble. These price increases, in turn, may induce still others to buy the stock in anticipation of further increases, and so on.

This process can dramatically unhitch the price of an asset from its "fundamentals," at least for a time. To show that the price of a stock, of houses, or of some other asset has grown out of all due proportion, however, we must have some basis for estimating the "correct" value. For stocks, one comparison is the "price-earnings (P/E) ratio" (the ratio of the stock price to the corporation's profits, on which stocks ultimately are a claim). For housing, one can use a ratio between housing prices and "owner's equivalent rent" (how much it would cost to rent a similar house), or the "price-rent ratio." By these measures,

U.S. stocks and housing have been grossly overvalued during the bubbles of recent years. Economist Robert Shiller, a leading authority on asset bubbles, notes that price-earnings ratios in the mid 20s are above historical norms. In 2007, the P/E ratio peaked over 27. (It had peaked at over 44 in late 1999, during the dot.com bubble.) The price-rent ratio, likewise, went way above historical norms in 2007. The national average for the 15 preceding years was less than 17. In mid 2007, it was nearly 23.

Bubbles and the Real Economy

Some people will profit in any bubble. But bubbles do not go on forever. Some end with a fizzle (prices stop rising, and inflation gradually erodes the value of the asset); others, with a dramatic crash, as in the U.S. stock market and housing markets did in 2008. As a bubble bursts, however, the price may not simply return to the "right" level. Instead, market participants may believe that price declines now mean that prices are likely to continue to fall in the future (in effect, this is a bubble in reverse, known as a "panic selloff"). As the price of an asset declines, more and more people sell to avoid getting stuck with it, fueling a further decline, and so on. Falling asset prices may, in short, overshoot the mark in the other direction.

Keynes was concerned that the "daily revaluations of the Stock Exchange ... inevitably exert a decisive influence of the rate of current investment"—that fluctuations in stock prices affect real economic activity. Rising stock prices, which make it possible for a company to raise capital cheaply by issuing new shares, have the same effects as falling interest rates. Some investment projects, which would be unprofitable if the cost of capital were greater, will be undertaken. Plummeting stock prices, on the other hand, are like increasing interest rates. They make it more expensive for companies to raise capital, and may therefore result in decreased real investment.

The collapse of the stock and housing bubbles reverberated on real economic activity in at least two more ways.

First, people's consumption spending is affected not only by their current incomes, but also their wealth (the value of the assets they own, minus their debts, at any given time). As people's wealth increases, they spend more freely; if their wealth decreases, they curtail their spending. This is known as the "wealth effect." Keynes described this phenomenon in *The General Theory*, writing that the "consumption of the wealth-owning class may be extremely susceptible to unforeseen changes in the money-value of its wealth." The stock-market and real-estate bubbles certainly fueled increased consumption. Many people simply spent more freely because they felt financially secure. Some borrowed against the rising values of their homes, often for consumption spending. As the values of these assets have plummeted, people have cut back dramatically on spending.

Second, the collapse of the housing market detonated a major financial crisis. Banks had bet heavily on the continued rise in real-estate prices. They extended mortgage loans indiscriminately. They bought enormous amounts of mortgage-backed securities (which pay returns to their owners based on payments made on an underlying set of mortgages). When real-estate prices plummeted and mortgage defaults skyrocketed, banks were left holding assets that were plummeting in value and were basically unsellable. Many curtailed their lending dramatically, trying to build their cash reserves as a guard against bankruptcy. The resulting tightening of credit made it difficult for consumers and firms to borrow, further dragging down spending and contributing to the deepening recession.

Is Regulation the Answer?

In the parts of *The General Theory* focused on financial instability, Keynes argued that the speculative short-term speculative buying and selling of securities disconnected financial markets from any real evaluation of the long-term prospects of different investments. While this was, in Keynes' view, harmless enough if the speculation existed on the surface on a "steady stream of enterprise," it could be very harmful if enterprise became the surface on top of a "whirlpool of speculation."

It's easy to see the relevance of this analysis to the current economic crisis. From the 1940s to the 1970s, banks, insurance companies, and other financial institutions were highly regulated, and financial crises were relatively rare. Since the deregulation of finance, in the 1980s, the nonregulation of ever-more-exotic financial securities, and the creation of a vast world of "shadow banking," they have become much more frequent. Enterprise (that is, the real economy) seems to have been dragged down, as Keynes foresaw, into the whirlpool.

The chain-reaction of excessive financial risk-taking, the eruption of the financial crisis, and the deepest recession since the 1930s has resulted in calls for renewed financial regulation. As of yet, only partial and inadequate measures have been adopted, and the largest banks are flying higher than ever. Even if there were robust new financial regulation, however, that would not solve the problems that cause the Great Recession in the first place—since these problems went way beyond just excessive financial speculation or risk-taking.

Economic growth in capitalist economies depends on growing demand for goods and services to match the growing productive capacity of an economy. From the late 1940s to the early 1970s, the rate of productivity growth was matched by the rate of real wage growth. Ordinary workers, then, largely created the demand for the goods that they were producing in ever-greater abundance. Since then, however, real wage growth has stagnated, while productivity and total output have kept right on rising. The demand for these goods and services had to come from somewhere. In part, it came from the wealthy who, enjoying a growing share of the total income, spent more. In part, it came from working families that made up for stagnant wages with more hours of paid work (especially by women) and more and more debt. In large measure, though, it also came from bubbles! Remember, growing asset prices encourage people to spend more. Unsustainable asset bubbles are not just a way that the U.S. economy has *failed* over the last few decades—they are a way that it has *worked*.

This way of structuring a capitalist economy, however, is prone to periodic crises that inflict an enormous human toll. Creating an economy that does not depend on the next bubble, however, requires much more than just an overlay of financial regulation. ❑

Sources: John Maynard Keynes, *The General Theory of Employment, Interest, and Money* (Harcourt, 1964); S&P/Case-Shiller Home Price Indices; "Stock Market Winners Get Big Payoff—In Testosterone," *Scientific American*, April 21, 2008 (scientificamerican.com); Robert Shiller, Online Data; Robert Shiller, *Irrational Exuberance*, 2nd ed. (Princeton University Press, 2000).

Article 8.5

WE'RE ALL MINSKYITES NOW

BY ROBERT POLLIN
October 2008; The Nation

As the most severe financial crisis since the 1930s Depression has unfolded over the past eighteen months, the ideas of the late economist Hyman Minsky have suddenly come into fashion. In the summer of 2007, the *Wall Street Journal* ran a front-page article describing the emerging crisis as the financial market's "Minsky moment." His ideas have since been featured in the *Financial Times*, *BusinessWeek* and *The New Yorker*, among many other outlets. Minsky, who spent most of his academic career at Washington University in St. Louis and remained professionally active until his death, in 1996, deserves the recognition. He was his generation's most insightful analyst of financial markets and the causes of financial crises.

Even so, most mainstream economists have shunned his work because it emerged out of a dissident left Keynesian tradition known in economists' circles as post-Keynesianism. Minsky's writings, and the post-Keynesian tradition more generally, are highly critical of free-market capitalism and its defenders in the economics profession—among them Milton Friedman and other Nobel Prize-winning economists who for a generation have claimed to "prove," usually through elaborate mathematical models, that unregulated markets are inherently rational, stable and fair. For Friedmanites, regulations are harmful most of the time.

Minsky, by contrast, explained throughout his voluminous writings that unregulated markets will always produce instability and crises. He alternately termed his approach "the financial instability hypothesis" and "the Wall Street paradigm."

For Minsky, the key to understanding financial instability is to trace the shifts that occur in investors' psychology as the economy moves out of a period of crisis and recession (or depression) and into a phase of rising profits and growth. Coming out of a crisis, investors will tend to be cautious, since many of them will have been clobbered during the just-ended recession. For example, they will hold large cash reserves as a cushion to protect against future crises.

But as the economy emerges from its slump and profits rise, investors' expectations become increasingly positive. They become eager to pursue risky ideas such as securitized subprime mortgage loans. They also become more willing to let their cash reserves dwindle, since idle cash earns no profits, while purchasing speculative vehicles like subprime mortgage securities that can produce returns of 10% or higher.

But these moves also mean that investors are weakening their defenses against the next downturn. This is why, in Minsky's view, economic upswings, proceeding without regulations, inevitably encourage speculative excesses in which financial bubbles emerge. Minsky explained that in an unregulated environment, the only way to stop bubbles is to let them burst. Financial markets then fall into a crisis, and a recession or depression ensues.

Here we reach one of Minsky's crucial insights—that financial crises and recessions actually serve a purpose in the operations of a free-market economy, even while they wreak havoc with people's lives, including those of tens of millions of innocents who never invest a dime on Wall Street. Minsky's point is that without crises, a free-market economy has no way of discouraging investors' natural proclivities toward ever greater risks in pursuit of ever higher profits.

However, in the wake of the calamitous Great Depression, Keynesian econo-mists tried to design measures that could supplant financial crises as the system's "natural" regulator. This was the context in which the post–World War II system of big-government capitalism was created. The package included two basic elements: regulations designed to limit speculation and channel financial resources into so-cially useful investments, such as single-family housing; and government bailout operations to prevent 1930s-style depressions when crises broke out anyway.

Minsky argues that the system of regulations and the bailout operations were largely successful. That is why from the end of World War II to the mid-1970s, markets here and abroad were much more stable than in any previous historical period. But even during the New Deal years, financial market titans were fighting vehemently to eliminate, or at least defang, the regulations. By the 1970s, almost all politicians—Democrats and Republi-cans alike—had become compliant. The regulations were initially weakened, then abol-ished altogether, under the strong guidance of, among others, Federal Reserve chair Alan Greenspan, Sen. Phil Gramm (R-TX), and Clinton Treasury Secretary Robert Rubin.

For Minsky, the consequences were predictable. Consider the scorecard over the twenty years before the current disaster: a stock market crash in 1987; the savings-and-loan crisis and bailout in 1989-90; the "emerging markets" crisis of 1997-98—which brought down, among others, Long-Term Capital Management, the super-hedge fund led by two Nobel laureates specializing in finance—and the bursting of the dot-com market bubble in 2001. Each of these crises could easily have produced a 1930s-style collapse in the absence of full-scale government bailout operations.

Here we come to another of Minsky's major insights—that in the absence of a com-plementary regulatory system, the effectiveness of bailouts will diminish over time. This is because bailouts, just like financial crises, are double-edged. They prevent depressions, but they also limit the costs to speculators of their financial excesses. As soon as the next economic expansion begins gathering strength, speculators will therefore pursue profit opportunities more or less as they had during the previous cycle. This is the pattern that has brought us to our current situation—a massive global crisis, being countered by an equally massive bailout of thus far limited effectiveness.

Minsky's Wall Street paradigm did not address all the afflictions of free-market capitalism. In particular, his model neglects the problems that arise from the vast dispar-ities of income, wealth and power that are just as endemic to free-market capitalism as are its tendencies toward financial instability, even though he fully recognized that these problems exist. Yet Minsky's approach still provides the most powerful lens for under-standing the roots of financial instability and developing an effective regulatory system.

Minsky understood that his advocacy of comprehensive financial regulations made no sense whatsoever within the prevailing professional orthodoxy of free-market cheerleading. In his 1986 magnum opus, *Stabilizing an Unstable Economy*, he conclud-ed that "the policy failures since the mid-1960s are related to the banality of orthodox economic analysis.... Only an economics that is critical of capitalism can be a guide to successful policy for capitalism." ❏

Article 8.6

LESSONS FROM ICELAND'S FINANCIAL CRISIS

BY NINA EICHACKER
March/April 2016

In a span of just three days in 2008—between October 7 and October 9—Iceland's three largest banks, Landsbanki, Glitnir, and Kaupthing, all failed. The banks' debts amounted to over 15 times Iceland's GDP at the time. Iceland residents, British and Dutch account holders, bank shareholders, and, soon, the rest of the world learned that those banks were completely insolvent, and that the Icelandic government could not afford to bail them out (at an estimated price tag of $300 billion).

Following these events, the people of Iceland began the "Kitchenware Revolution," gathering in front of parliament while banging pots and pans. They successfully demanded the resignation of the ruling right-wing Independence Party, which had implemented the financial deregulation that had led to the implosion of Iceland's financial system. In addition, they laid the groundwork for the rejection in a national referendum of the next government's plan to pay loan guarantees, for one of the country's three big banks, to the governments of the UK and the Netherlands. In December 2008, the Icelandic government created the Special Inquiry Commission, which produced an exhaustive report of the causes and consequences of the financial crisis. The government authorized a special prosecutor to investigate and bring charges against guilty parties—including prominent political figures such as the former minister of finance, financial figures including the president and CEO of Glitnir, the president and chairman of Kaupthing, and the president and managing director of Landsbanki.

The crisis, years in the making, was a consequence of the Icelandic government's rapid deregulation and privatization of Iceland's banking system back in the 1990s and early 2000s, and of the banks' embrace of large-scale and risk-heavy investment banking. With little or no supervision, and relying on the widespread belief globally in the integrity of Iceland's government and financial system, bankers got away with murder—until the fall of the U.S. investment bank Lehman Brothers in 2008, after which Iceland's banks could no longer rely on cheap and easy credit from U.S. investment banks.

Foreseeable, But Not Foreseen

Policymakers, academics, and business reporters should have seen it coming. By 2006, Icelandic banking and economic data described an overheating financial sector and overall economy. Foreign banks' lending to Iceland increased from just over 50% of Icelandic GDP in 1999 to nearly 80% in 2003 to over 400% in 2007. Icelandic credit intermediation—the share of loans held by financial corporations compared to borrowing by non-financial firms, the general government, households, and non-profits—also increased in this period, from 64% in 2004 to 80% in 2007. This trend of a rapidly growing financial sector relative to the "real" sector of the economy was by no means unique to Iceland, but the scale was. Financial firms' debt rose from less than four times Iceland's GDP in 2003, to over nine times in 2007, to over 15 times in 2008. The net negative financial worth of Iceland's financial corporations rose from 4% of GDP in 2003, to 147% in 2007, to 649% in 2008.

Economist Anne Sibert and finance expert Gudrun Johnsen have written about "love-letters"—debt securities issued by Icelandic banks and then used as collateral for borrowing from other Icelandic banks, the Central Bank of Iceland, and even the European Central Bank. Icelandic banks' developed this fraudulent practice as they found it more difficult to borrow in global capital markets from 2006 onward. Economist and former banking regulator William K. Black has argued that the rapid acceleration of the banks' debts just before the collapse of Iceland's banking system was the result, not of desperate attempts to resurrect the banks, but of fraud: bank officers were trying to loot as much money as possible while they still could. In the years that Icelandic banks engaged in these practices, Frederic Mishkin (Columbia University), Richard Portes (London Business School), and Fridrik Baldursson (Reykjavik University) all wrote reports celebrating the integrity of the Icelandic financial system.

Perhaps as a consequence of these reports, top Icelandic officials, like the then prime minister and head of the central bank, were still surprised by the onset of the country's financial crisis, as were reporters with major media outlets like the *New York Times*, *Fortune*, and *BusinessWeek*. Top economists who had promoted the Icelandic strategy of financial deregulation, like Arthur Laffer (formerly economic advisor in the Reagan administration), Mishkin, Portes, and Baldursson were quiet in the immediate aftermath.

These events point to the dominance of neoliberal theories about the necessity of financial deregulation, and an assumption that a northern European country would have the institutional sophistication to avoid financial crises like those observed in developing countries that had rapidly deregulated. Neoclassical economists with outsize faith in the efficiency of financial markets and integrity of the Icelandic state believed that little could go wrong in Iceland—the crisis in October of 2008 proved otherwise. A wider understanding of the theories of John Maynard Keynes and Hyman Minsky (see Reuss, p. 227, and Pollin, p. 251) would have helped policymakers and other observers foresee Iceland's crisis, and to prevent future such episodes. Keynes and Minsky understood—as Icelandic government officials, academic economists, and the financial press did not—that financial actors will engage in risky behavior in the pursuit of profits, making financial crises inevitable in the absence of regulation to prevent such behavior. Governments therefore must regulate financial sectors for the greater economic good.

Underproduction of Criticism, Overproduction of Praise

The lack of financial-market transparency was one integral reason that Iceland's crisis went unforeseen. Organizations that could have reported on the conditions of the Icelandic financial marketplace and the state of the Icelandic economy simply did not. The Icelandic state threatened to defund public institutions and agencies that published reports contradicting the narrative of a robust financial infrastructure and growth.

Iceland's Chamber of Commerce paid economists, like Columbia University's Mishkin, hundreds of thousands of dollars to write favorable reports—including one titled "Financial Stability in Iceland"—about the country's financial sector and overall economic growth prospects. Mishkin would later become infamous, in the documentary "Inside Job," for that report and for changing its title to "Financial Instability in Iceland" on his curriculum vitae after Iceland's collapse.

The Icelandic news media consistently underpublicized reports critical of the Icelandic financial sector, while publishing many stories that praised Iceland's big three banks. Iceland's center-right party historically had large ownership stakes in several Icelandic media companies; the shared interest of Iceland's right and center-right parties in promoting the financial sector explains some of the media's lack of coverage of financial malfeasance.

Another cause of this disparity was the cross-ownership of media-company shares by Icelandic financial actors and institutions, and financial-corporation shares by Icelandic media institutions. The chair of the board of directors of Baugur Group, a large stakeholder in Kaupthing Bank, also owned 365—parent company of *Frettabladid*, Iceland's largest-circulation daily newspaper—as well as DV, another large media company. Björgólfur Guðmundsson, the former majority owner and chairman of Landsbanki, acquired Arvakur, the company that publishes *Morgunbladid*, the other major Icelandic newspaper, only to sell in 2009 after declaring bankruptcy. The interconnectedness of these industries created conflicts of interest for all involved.

Credit-rating agencies, meanwhile, also contributed to the notion that Iceland's financial markets were safer than they were. The sub-prime mortgage crisis of 2007 revealed a host of problems with how the three largest global credit-rating agencies—Moody's, Standard & Poor's, and Fitch—operate. It used to be that parties interested in investing in a particular class of assets paid for reports evaluating their riskiness. Since the 1970s, however, the setup as shifted, to one in which institutions issuing securities paid for ratings. This gave the agencies an incentive to rate securities as safer than they were. In other words, it created huge conflicts of interest.

In 2007, Fitch, the smallest of the big three rating agencies, downgraded Iceland's credit rating on the basis of its overextension. But Moody's, one of the two bigger agencies, upgraded it, on the premise that Iceland was so financially leveraged that its central bank would, as the lender of last resort, bail out the big three banks. This move paradoxically increased broad confidence in Icelandic financial stability, despite the fact that the rationale for the improved rating was the excessive leverage of Iceland's financial sector. This further lulled international investors and retail banking customers into trusting Icelandic financial actors with their money and spurred still greater leverage and risky behavior. The feedback effects increased the scale of the financial system relative to the Icelandic economy as a whole, placed more and more actors throughout Iceland at risk in the likely event of failure, and increased the severity of the imminent collapse of Iceland's financial system.

In short, the underproduction of criticism and the overproduction of praise for Iceland's banks skewed public understanding of the country's financial sector.

Governments and International Institutions

The Icelandic Central Bank's decision to change from stability-promoting to inflation-targeting monetary policy led to rising interest rates, precipitous increases in capital inflows, and asset bubbles in the housing market.

Prior to the early 1990s, the Icelandic Central Bank had pursued economic stability above all else. It charged very low interest rates in order to promote lending to local banks, and to hedge against possible bank failures at the local level. Bank employees at all levels were compensated in ways that would not encourage risky behavior.

The shift to inflation-targeting monetary policy resulted in a rapid increase in Icelandic interest rates. Inflation targeting is designed to prevent an increase in the price level, typically through high interest rates, which make it more difficult for banks and other institutions to borrow. High interest rates, however, attracted capital flows from investors in the United States and Western Europe, two financial markets with low interest rates in the early 2000s. This, in turn, had the perverse consequence of raising the value of the Icelandic krona relative to other global currencies. As the krona grew stronger, Iceland's exports fell and its imports rose, leading to a large trade deficit. The financial inflows also provided Icelandic bankers with a ready source of funding for financial speculation. The government's promotion of non-financial firms' and households' purchase of shares in the banks created perverse incentives for them to raise share prices, and increased the scope of losses in the event of the banks' failure. Bank employees now had motivation to boost share prices by whatever means; households with little understanding of the activities of the banking sector would be increasingly vulnerable to the fate of the banks' performance.

Global financial institutions, meanwhile, seemed to forget that Argentina and Chile had liberalized their financial markets in the 1970s and 1980s with bad results: banks became more risk-taking, without becoming more efficient. Argentina's Central Bank offered guarantees on bank deposits, which encouraged more capital inflows. Though Chile's government initially stated that it would not insure deposits, its Central Bank ultimately guaranteed them after several panics early in the liberalization process. The big banks that had been privatized in the 1970s had to be re-nationalized during the crisis of the early 1980s, despite the "free market" views of the University of Chicago economists (or "Chicago Boys") who made economic policy for Chile's military dictatorship.

Foreign governments' economic and political pressure for governments and central banks to insure their investments guaranteed what economists call "moral hazard" problems: if businesses and banks trust that a government will bail them out in times of crisis, they will likely engage in riskier behavior, since they will profit more in the event of success, and not pay as much (or perhaps not pay anything) in the event of failure. Private financial institutions around the world, but particularly in Europe, trusted in Iceland's supposedly robust financial governance, despite Iceland's short history of financial liberalization. Many followed the advice of economists like Mishkin and Portes, who argued that Iceland should not be assumed to have the same financial risks as developing economies, despite the newness of its supercharged financial system. Outside investors' continued willingness to lend to Iceland increased the leveraged state of Icelandic banks and the scope of the eventual financial crisis.

Heading Off the Next Crisis

Iceland's crisis reveals the inherent instability created by rapid financialization. When a country deregulates banks, encourages international capital inflows, and promotes wide-scale acquisition of those financial institutions' securities (by households, non-financial firms, government, and other banks), financial firms appear to be artificially profitable. Conflicts of interest develop that weaken the stability of the financial sector and the economy as a whole.

Mainstream economists failed to recognize this. However, this was well understood by heterodox figures like Keynes and Minsky, who argued that financial systems without adequate regulatory apparatuses are inherently prone to crisis. A number of current scholars, absorbing the lessons of Keynes and Minsky, argued that Iceland's financial sector was due for a collapse given the changes that had occurred in banking practices and economic orientation of the country. These processes increased Icelandic instability and the costs of the inevitable crisis.

Irrational exuberance and moral hazard overcame the ample evidence that Iceland was dangerously over-leveraged. Investors had access to data demonstrating the risks of investing in Iceland's financial system and economy, yet turned headlong into the storm. National and international unwillingness to compare Iceland's policy actions and history to that of developing economies like Argentina and Chile reflected the faulty assumption that Icelandic institutions were ready for the job of supervising a radically transformed financial sector. The Icelandic government's repression of data demonstrating instability, and the Icelandic media's unwillingness to publish unflattering stories, gave the lie to the notion that western European states' financial institutions and governments were robust enough for highly liberalized financial sectors.

Iceland's crisis demonstrates the need for the radically different policies: States and social movements must promote widespread financial literacy, so that ordinary people are aware of changes in the financial landscape and better able to protect themselves. If it is to be undertaken, financial deregulation, like cigarette packages, should come with large and impossible-to-miss warnings about its inherent dangers. These warnings should alert the public to the risks of purchasing large shares in globally active banks or other under-regulated financial products, and should warn less sophisticated financial intermediaries like pension funds about the riskiness of different financial assets. In Iceland, as in the United States, the financial system's default setting was to push households into excessive risk-taking; a public counterweight that prioritizes stability over risk would be valuable. "Nudges" encouraging safer approaches to personal wealth management—like insured deposits, defined-benefit retirement plans, and manageable mortgage loans—would still allow financially savvy or risk-loving individuals to engage in riskier transactions, while protecting the broader public. Stability-minded monetary policy is another means to ensuring greater financial and economic well-being. Greater regulatory vigilance against the excesses of financialization and shadow banking, too, would benefit most.

More broadly, given Iceland's experiences and those of other countries before it, states should reject financial deregulation and finance-led growth strategies. The costs of financialization, in the presence of moral hazard and irrational exuberance, expand rapidly in the absence of meaningful oversight. Iceland's experience illustrates this to the rest of the world. The country's policy responses to the crisis—starting with a systematic inquiry and prosecution of guilty bankers—also provide a worthy model for the world. Other countries would be wise to follow its example: The renationalization of banks that could have bankrupted the Icelandic government and central bank, implementation of capital controls (regulations on international capital flows) to stabilize an out-of-control financial system, and enforcement of new financial regulations to protect banks, firms, and households from the consequences of another financial bubble. ❑

Sources: Robert Aliber, "Monetary Turbulence and the Icelandic Economy," in Robert Aliber and Gylfi Zoega, eds., *Preludes to the Icelandic Financial Crisis* (Palgrave MacMillan, 2011); Anna Andersen, "The Watchdog That Didn't Bark," Reykjavik Grapevine, October 2010 (grapevine.is); Daniel Chartier, *The End of Iceland's Innocence: The Image of Iceland in the Foreign Media During the Financial Crisis* (University of Ottawa Press, 2011); V. Corbo and J. De Melo, "Lessons from the Southern Cone Policy Reforms." *The World Bank Research Observer,* 2(2), 1987; Jon Danielsson and Gylfi Zoega, "The Collapse of a Country," Working Paper 09:03, Institute of Economic Studies (hhi.hi.is); C. Diaz-Alejandro, "Good-Bye Financial Repression, Hello Financial Crash." *Journal of Development Economics,* 19(1), 1985; Gudrun Johnsen, Bringing Down the Banking System (Palgrave MacMillan, 2014); John Maynard Keynes, "National Self-Sufficiency," *The Yale Review* 22, 1933; Charles Kindleberger and Robert Aliber, *Manias, Panics, and Crashes: A History of Financial Crises* (Wiley, 2005); E. G. Mendoza and M.E. Terrones, *An Anatomy of Credit Booms and Their Demise* (No. w18379), National Bureau of Economic Research, 2012 (nber.org); Hyman Minsky, *Stabilizing An Unstable Economy* (McGraw-Hill, 2008); Hyman Minsky, "The Financial Instability Hypothesis," The Levy Institute, Working Paper No. 74, May 1992 (levyinstitute.org); Hyman Minsky, *Can 'It' Happen Again? Essays on Instability and Finance* (M.E. Sharpe, Inc., 1982); Frederic Mishkin and Tryggvi Herbertsson, "Financial Stability in Iceland," Iceland Chamber of Commerce Publication, 2006 (vi.is); F. S. Mishkin, *Inflation Targeting in Emerging Market Countries* (No. w7618), National Bureau of Economic Research (nber.org); D. Rodrik, "Growth Strategies," in P. Aghion and S.N. Durlauf, eds., *Handbook of Economic Growth*, Volume 1 (Elsevier, 2005); Throstur Sigurjonsson, "Privatization and Deregulation: A Chronology of Events," in Robert Aliber and Gylfi Zoega, eds., *Preludes to the Icelandic Financial Crisis* (Palgrave Macmillan, 2011); Robert Wade, "Iceland as Icarus," *Challenge* 52, 2009; Robert Wade and Silla Sigurgeirsdottir, "Lessons from Iceland," *New Left Review* 65, 2010; Robert Wade and Silla Sigurgeirsdottir, "Iceland's Rise, Fall, Stabilization, and Beyond," *Cambridge Journal of Economics* 36, 2011; Gylfi Zoega, "A Spending Spree," in Robert Aliber and Gylfi Zoega, eds., *Preludes to the Icelandic Financial Crisis* (Palgrave Macmillan, 2011).

Article 8.7

TEN YEARS AFTER FINANCIAL CRISIS, OUR ELITES HAVE LEARNED NOTHING

BY DEAN BAKER
August 2017, Center for Economic and Policy Research

Last week, I heard BBC announce the 10th anniversary of the beginning of the financial crisis. This is dated to the decision by the French bank BNP Paribas to prohibit withdrawals from two hedge funds that were heavily invested in subprime mortgage backed securities. According to BBC, this was when lending began to freeze and house prices began to fall.

The problem with BBC's story is that house prices had already been falling for more than a year. While the nationwide decline was still relatively modest, around 4%, the drop in many of the most active markets was more than 10%.

This was the reason that the mortgage-backed securities in the Paribas hedge funds had plunged in value. When people bought homes with zero or near zero down, and the price dropped by 10% (and was falling rapidly), the mortgages suddenly did not look like very good investments.

While some people may try to make good on a mortgage that exceeded the value of their home, many others would simply walk away. This was especially likely when the mortgage was an adjustable-rate mortgage that was due to reset to a much higher interest rate in the next year or two.

This timing matters because the financial crisis was first and foremost the story of the housing bubble. If mortgage debt had not been tied to an asset that was hugely over-valued, there would not have been a crisis shaking the financial system. This is true even if we recognize the corruption of the financial sector and the number of people who were dealing in complex financial instruments they did not understand.

It is understandable that economists and economic reporters would like to turn attention away from the housing bubble since it was easy to see for anyone paying attention at the time. The country had an unprecedented nationwide run-up in house prices, as house sale prices rose far faster than the overall rate of inflation across most of the country. This was a break with the usual pattern where nationwide house prices just tracked inflation.

This should have set off alarm bells, not only because the run-up was extraordinary, but because there was no remotely corresponding change in rents. The rental indexes barely outpaced the rate of inflation in these years. Also, even as house sale prices were going through the roof, the vacancy rate for housing was reaching record levels.

The fact that houses were being purchased with dubious loans was also hardly a secret. It was common to refer to "NINJA" loans, which stood for "no income, no job, and no assets." Banks were happy to make loans to anyone who would take them since they knew they could resell these loans almost immediately in the secondary market.

A survey by the National Association of Realtors found that 43% of first-time buyers in 2005 had a down payment of zero or less on their mortgage. The "or less" refers to the fact that some homebuyers actually borrowed more than the sale price in order to get money to cover closing costs, renovations or moving expenses.

The housing bubble was also the story of the Great Recession. The housing bubble was driving the economy in the years leading up to the crash. Soaring house prices lead to an unprecedented boom in construction, which peaked at just under 6.5% of GDP. This would be more than $1.2 trillion annually in today's economy. After the crash, the glut of housing led construction to fall to less than 2% of GDP. Anyone have a quick way to fill a demand gap of $800 billion a year?

But it was actually worse than this. Soaring house prices led to an unprecedented consumption boom as people spent against the bubble generated equity in their homes. When prices came back down to Earth and the equity disappeared, people cut back their spending accordingly. We lost the equivalent of more than $500 billion in annual demand due to the fall in consumption in the wake of the crash.

In all, we were looking at a demand gap on the order of 7–8 percentage points of GDP, or $1.4 to $1.6 trillion in today's economy. The Obama stimulus, which was less than 2% of GDP in 2009 and 2010, was helpful, but nowhere near large enough, nor did it last long enough. The result was the slow and weak recovery that we have seen.

The economic disaster that cost millions of people their jobs and/or their homes, and forced tens of millions to accept lower wages, was 100% avoidable if the people responsible for making economic policy had been awake. Turning the story of the housing bubble into a story about the financial crisis is an effort to make issues that are quite simple seem very complicated.

This is a way to let those who are responsible off the hook, since, hey, it's complicated. And if they have to rewrite history to make the case, well that can be done. ❑

Chapter 9

THE GLOBAL ECONOMY

INTRODUCTION

When it comes to the global economy, most textbooks line up behind the "Washington Consensus"—a package of free-trade and financial-liberalization policies that the U.S. Treasury Department, the International Monetary Fund (IMF), and the World Bank have prescribed for the world's developing economies. Mainstream textbook discussions of exchange rates, international trade, and economic-development policies almost always promote a market-dictated integration into the world economy. Outside the classroom, however, popular discontent with the Washington Consensus has spawned worldwide movements calling into question the myth of self-regulating markets on which these policies rest.

While the doctrines of free trade and international financial deregulation are seldom questioned in mainstream economics textbooks, both are scrutinized here. Economist Arthur MacEwan shows how industrialized economies developed by protecting their own manufacturing sectors—never preaching the "gospel of free trade" until they were highly developed. Today, he argues, mainstream economists and pundits prescribe free trade not because it's the best way for others to develop, but because it gives U.S. corporations free access to the world's markets and resources, which in turn strengthens the power of businesses against workers (Article 9.1).

Economist Thomas Palley examines how globalization has led to further divisions among workers (Article 9.2). Palley uses the hands of a clock to illustrate how the uneven effects of globalization foster divisions among workers and leave them isolated. That workers benefit as consumers when exploitative conditions allow them to buy cheap goods stands in the way of overcoming those divisions and isolation, making it difficult for them to undertake collective action that would improve the conditions of most workers.

MacEwan follows with an overview of the changing place of the dollar in the global economy—especially its "dominance" as the key currency in which international trade is conducted and reserves are held—over the span of over 70 years (Article 9.3). He describes three critical moments: The first, near the end of the Second World War, when the Bretton Woods conference clearly established the dollar as the most important world currency; the next, in early 1970s, when the "dollar crisis" led the United States to abandon the convertibility of dollars for gold at a fixed rate (the "gold standard"), yet the dollar remained the dominant currency. The third is happening right now, with the United States' dominant position in the global economy slipping, and the future role of the dollar unclear.

Over 20 years after the passage of the North American Free Trade Agreement (NAFTA), Dean Baker looks at its consequences for wage growth in the United States (Article 9.4). He argues that NAFTA—not incidentally, but deliberately—dragged down wages for U.S. workers. This is not because of any inherent fact that causes some to thrive and others to flounder in the global economy. Rather, Baker argues that the treaty, like other trade-and-investment treaties that followed, deliberately exposed some workers to global competition while other groups (with more political power) remained insulated from competition.

In Article 9.5, John Miller exposes just where the Trump tariffs go wrong, from their fixation with the U.S. trade deficit with individual countries, to a focus nearly exclusively on exports, to ignoring the effects of steel tariffs on U.S. industries that use steel as an input. Miller, however, argues the free-trade alternative to Trump's tariffs favored by the *Wall Street Journal* editors and most economists would do no more to improve the lot of those left behind by globalization than Trump's misguided policies. What is needed instead, according to Miller, are global trade policies that would reduce inequality and insecurity by imposing tariffs on goods produced under conditions that violate workers' rights or are environmentally destructive.

John Weeks takes us across the Atlantic, to the situation in the United Kingdom in the wake of the Brexit vote (Article 9.6). The result was fueled by a vile and mendacious xenophobia. It also, however, owed to the failure of "remain" proponents to make a case for what was good about the EU—protections for human rights and labor rights that restrain European capitalists. Always lukewarm toward the European project (except the supposed economic benefits), the Labour Party did little to combat the right-wing campaign against the "bureaucrats in Brussels." With the Brexit result irreversible in the short run, Weeks argues, the task at hand is to muster resistance to a new business offensive against human rights and workers' rights.

In the final article in this chapter, economist Jayati Ghosh argues that imperialism has not disappeared, but changed shape (Article 9.7). The direct military conquest and control of economic territory by the great powers has given way (at least some of the time) to control through multilateral agreements and international institutions. It may still mean the seizure of land, mines, or oil fields—but it also may mean privatization of public assets and services, or the extension of intellectual property rights to new realms. Where the "labor aristocracy" of the imperialist countries once shared in the bounty of empire, the new incarnation of empire as "globalization" has helped grind away the incomes and status they once enjoyed.

Discussion Questions

1. (Article 9.1) MacEwan claims that the "infant industry" argument for trade protection is much more widely applicable than standard theory suggests. To what countries and industries might it apply in today's world economy? Explain your answer.

2. (Article 9.1) "Free trade" policies, MacEwan argues, give business greater power relative to labor. Why is this so? Is this a good reason to oppose such policies?

3. (Article 9.2) How does Palley use the hands of a clock to illustrate the way the uneven effects of globalization increase divisions among workers?

4. (Article 9.3) What does it mean to say that the dollar is the "dominant" currency in the world? Why has this been the case for nearly three quarters of a century? Consider economic and political factors.

5. (Article 9.4) Baker reports that NAFTA has contributed to wage suppression and to lower prices on many goods. What is the net effect on income distribution within the United States? Could a trade agreement be structured in a different way, and result in different distributional outcomes?

6. (Article 9.5) Evaluate Miller's list of the problems with Trump's tariff policies and his list of the problems with free-trade policies. What's your sense of what would constitute a good trade policy?

7. (Article 9.6) According to Weeks, supporters of the campaign for the UK to remain in the EU failed to make a strong case for their position. What does Weeks see as the main advantages of continued EU membership? Does his assessment of the post-Brexit political fallout in the UK have any effect on those advantages?

8. (Article 9.7) According to Ghosh, imperialism has not disappeared, but changed shape. What have been the results of this change in shape on workers in the most powerful countries?

Article 9.1

THE GOSPEL OF FREE TRADE: THE NEW EVANGELISTS

BY ARTHUR MacEWAN
November 1991; updated June 2018

Note: This article, originally written in 1991 and updated in 2009, is followed by an afterword that takes into account the sharp changes in U.S. international economic policy that have developed under the Trump administration.

Free trade! With the zeal of Christian missionaries, for decades the U.S. government has been preaching, advocating, pushing, and coercing around the globe for "free trade."

As the economic crisis emerged in 2007 and 2008 and rapidly became a global crisis, it was apparent that something was very wrong with the way the world economy was organized. Not surprisingly, as unemployment rose sharply in the United States, there were calls for protecting jobs by limiting imports and for the government to "buy American" in its economic stimulus program. Similarly, in many other countries, as unemployment jumped upwards, pressure emerged for protection—and some actual steps were taken. Yet, free trade missionaries did not retreat; they continued to preach the same gospel.

The free-traders were probably correct in claiming that protectionist policies would do more harm than good as a means to stem the rising unemployment generated by the economic crisis. Significant acts of protectionism in one country would lead to retaliation—or at least copying—by other countries, reducing world trade. The resulting loss of jobs from reduced trade would most likely outweigh any gains from protection.

Yet the argument over international economic policies should not be confined simply to what should be done in a crisis. Nor should it simply deal with trade in goods and services. The free-traders have advocated their program as one for long-run economic growth and development, yet the evidence suggests that free trade is not a good economic development strategy. Furthermore, the free-traders preach the virtue of unrestricted global movement of finance as well as of goods and services. As it turns out, the free flow of finance has been a major factor in bringing about and spreading the economic crisis that began to appear in 2007—as well as earlier crises.

The Push

While the U.S. push for free trade goes back several decades, it has become more intense in recent years. In the 1990s, the U.S. government signed on to the North American Free Trade Agreement (NAFTA) and in 2005 established the Central American Free Trade Agreement (CAFTA). Both Republican and Democratic presidents, however, have pushed hard for a *global* free trade agenda. After the demise of the Soviet Union, U.S. advisers prescribed unfettered capitalism for Eastern and Central Europe, and ridiculed as unworkable any move toward a "third way." In low-income countries from Mexico to Malaysia, the prescription has been the same: open markets, deregulate business, don't restrict international investment, and let the free market flourish.

In the push for worldwide free trade, the World Trade Organization (WTO) has been the principal vehicle of change, establishing rules for commerce that assure markets are open and resources are available to those who can pay. And the International Monetary Fund (IMF) and World Bank, which provide loans to many governments, use their financial power to pressure countries around the world to accept the gospel and open their markets. In each of these international organizations, the United States—generally through the U.S. Treasury—plays a dominant role.

Of course, as with any gospel, the preachers often ignore their own sermons. While telling other countries to open their markets, the U.S. government continued, for instance, to limit imports of steel, cotton, sugar, textiles, and many other goods. But publicly at least, free-trade boosters insist that the path to true salvation—or economic expansion, which, in this day and age, seems to be the same thing—lies in opening our market to foreign goods. Get rid of trade barriers at home and abroad, allow business to go where it wants and do what it wants. We will all get rich.

Yet the history of the United States and other rich countries does not fit well with the free-trade gospel. Virtually all advanced capitalist countries found economic success through heavy government regulation of their international commerce, not in free trade. Likewise, a large role for government intervention has characterized those cases of rapid and sustained economic growth in recent decades—for example, Japan after World War II, South Korea in the 1970s through the 1990s, and China most recently.

Free trade does, however, have its uses. Highly developed nations can use free trade to extend their power and control of the world's wealth, and business can use it as a weapon against labor. Most important, free trade can limit efforts to redistribute income more equally, undermine social programs, and keep people from democratically controlling their economic lives.

A Day in the Park

At the beginning of the 19th century, Lowell, Massachusetts, became the premier site of the U.S. textile industry. Today, thanks to the Lowell National Historical Park, you can tour the huge mills, ride through the canals that redirected the Merrimack River's power to those mills, and learn the story of the textile workers, from the Yankee "mill girls" of the 1820s through the various waves of immigrant laborers who poured into the city over the next century.

During a day in the park, visitors get a graphic picture of the importance of 19th-century industry to the economic growth and prosperity of the United States. Lowell and the other mill towns of the era were centers of growth. They not only created a demand for Southern cotton, they also created a demand for new machinery, maintenance of old machinery, parts, dyes, *skills*, construction materials, construction machinery, *more skills*, equipment to move the raw materials and products, parts maintenance for that equipment, *and still more skills*. The mill towns also created markets—concentrated groups of wage earners who needed to buy products to sustain themselves. As centers of economic activity, Lowell and similar mill towns contributed to U.S. economic growth far beyond the value of the textiles they produced.

The U.S. textile industry emerged decades after the industrial revolution had spawned Britain's powerful textile industry. Nonetheless, it survived and prospered. British linens inundated markets throughout the world in the early 19th century, as the British navy nurtured free trade and kept ports open for commerce. In the United States, however, hostilities leading up to the War of 1812 and then a substantial tariff made British textiles relatively expensive. These limitations on trade allowed the Lowell mills to prosper, acting as a catalyst for other industries and helping to create the skilled work force at the center of U.S. economic expansion.

Beyond textiles, however, tariffs did not play a great role in the United States during the early 19th century. Southern planters had considerable power, and while they were willing to make some compromises, they opposed protecting manufacturing in general because that protection forced up the prices of the goods they purchased with their cotton revenues. The Civil War wiped out the planters' power to oppose protectionism, and from the 1860s through World War I, U.S. industry prospered behind considerable tariff barriers.

Different Countries, Similar Experiences

The story of the importance of protectionism in bringing economic growth has been repeated, with local variations, in other advanced capitalist countries. During the late 19th century, Germany entered the major league of international economic powers with substantial protection and government support for its industries. Likewise, in 19th-century France and Italy, national consolidation behind protectionist barriers was a key to economic development.

Britain—which entered the industrial era first—is often touted as the prime example of successful development without tariff protection. Yet, Britain embraced free trade only after its industrial base was well established; as in the U.S., the early and important textile industry was erected on a foundation of protectionism. In addition, Britain built its industry through the British navy and the expansion of empire, hardly prime ingredients in any recipe for free trade.

Japan provides an especially important case of successful government protection and support for industrial development. In the post–World War II era, when the Japanese established the foundations for their economic "miracle," the government rejected free trade and extensive foreign investment and instead promoted its national firms.

In the 1950s, for example, the government protected the country's fledgling auto firms from foreign competition. At first, quotas limited imports to $500,000 (in current dollars) each year; in the 1960s, prohibitively high tariffs replaced the quotas. Furthermore, the Japanese allowed foreign investment only insofar as it contributed to developing domestic industry. The government encouraged Japanese companies to import foreign technology, but required them to produce 90% of parts domestically within five years.

The Japanese also protected their computer industry. In the early 1970s, as the industry was developing, companies and individuals could only purchase a foreign machine if a suitable Japanese model was not available. IBM was allowed to produce within the country, but only when it licensed basic patents to Japanese firms. And IBM computers produced in Japan were treated as foreign-made machines.

In the 20th century, no other country matched Japan's economic success, as it moved in a few decades from a relative low-income country, through the devastation of war, to emerge as one of the world's economic leaders. Yet one looks back in vain to find a role for free trade in this success. The Japanese government provided an effective framework, support, and protection for the country's capitalist development.

Likewise, in many countries that have been late-comers to economic development, capitalism has generated high rates of economic growth where government involvement, and not free trade, played the central role. South Korea is a striking case. "Korea is an example of a country that grew very fast and yet violated the canons of conventional economic wisdom," writes Alice Amsden in *Asia's Next Giant: South Korea and Late Industrialization,* widely acclaimed as perhaps the most important analysis of the South Korean economic success. "In Korea, instead of the market mechanism allocating resources and guiding private entrepreneurship, the government made most of the pivotal investment decisions. Instead of firms operating in a competitive market structure, they each operated with an extraordinary degree of market control, protected from foreign competition."

Free trade, however, has had its impact in South Korea. In the 1990s, South Korea and other East Asian governments came under pressure from the U.S. government and the IMF to open their markets, including their financial markets. When they did so, the results were a veritable disaster. The East Asian financial crisis that began in 1997 was a major setback for the whole region, a major disruption of economic growth. After extremely rapid economic growth for three decades, with output expanding at 7% to 10% a year, South Korea's economy plummeted by 6.3% between 1997 and 1998.

Mexico and Its NAFTA Experience

While free trade in goods and services has its problems, which can be very serious, it is the free movement of capital, the opening of financial markets that has sharp, sudden impacts, sometimes wrecking havoc on national economies. Thus, virtually as soon as Mexico, the United States and Canada formed NAFTA at the beginning of 1994, Mexico was hit with a severe financial crisis. As the economy turned downward at the beginning of that year, capital rapidly left the country, greatly reducing the value of the Mexican peso. With this diminished value of the peso, the cost of servicing international debts and the costs of imports skyrocketed—and the downturn worsened.

Still, during the 1990s, before and after the financial crisis, free-traders extolled short periods of moderate economic growth in Mexico —3% to 4% per year—as evidence of success. Yet, compared to earlier years, Mexico's growth under free trade has been poor. From 1940 to 1990 (including the no-growth decade of the 1980s), when Mexico's market was highly protected and the state actively regulated economic affairs, output grew at an average annual rate of 5%.

Most important, Mexico's experience discredits the notion that free-market policies will improve living conditions for the masses of people in low-income countries. The Mexican government paved the way for free trade policies by reducing or eliminating social welfare programs, and for many Mexican workers wages declined sharply during the free trade era. The number of households living in poverty rose dramatically, with some 75% of Mexico's population below the poverty line at the beginning of the 21st century.

China and Its Impact

Part of Mexico's problem and its economy's relatively weak performance from the 1990s onward has been the full-scale entrance of China into the international economy. While the Mexican authorities thought they saw great possibilities in NAFTA with the full opening of the U.S. market to goods produced with low-wage Mexican labor, China (and other Asian countries) had even cheaper labor. As China also gained access to the U.S. market, Mexican expectations were dashed.

The Chinese economy has surely gained in terms of economic growth as it has engaged more and more with the world market, and the absolute levels of incomes of millions of people have risen a great deal. However, China's rapid economic growth has come with a high degree of income inequality. Before its era of rapid growth, China was viewed as a country with a relatively equal distribution of income. By the beginning of the new millennium, however, it was much more unequal than any of the other most populace Asian countries (India, Indonesia, Bangladesh, Pakistan), and more in line with the high-inequality countries of Latin America. Furthermore, with the inequality has come a great deal of social conflict. Tens of thousands of "incidents" of conflict involving violence are reported each year, and most recently there have been the major conflicts involving Tibetans and Ouigers.

In any case, the Chinese trade and growth success should not be confused with "free trade." Foundations for China's surge of economic growth were established through state-sponsored infrastructure development and the vast expansion of the country's educational system. Even today, while private business, including foreign business, appears to have been given free rein in China, the government still plays a controlling role—including a central role in affecting foreign economic relations.

A central aspect of the government's role in the county's foreign commerce has been in the realm of finance. As Chinese-produced goods have virtually flooded international markets, the government has controlled the uses of the earnings from these exports. Instead of simply allowing those earnings to be used by Chinese firms and citizens to buy imports, the government has to a large extent held those earnings as reserves. Using those reserves, China's central bank has been the largest purchaser of U.S. government bonds, in effect becoming a major financer of the U.S. government's budget deficit of recent years.

China's reserves have been one large element in creating a giant pool of financial assets in the world economy. This "pool" has also been built up as the doubling of oil prices following the U.S. invasion of Iraq put huge amounts of funds in the pockets of oil-exporting countries and firms and individuals connected to the oil industry. Yet slow growth of the U.S. economy and extremely low interest rates, resulting from the Federal Reserve Bank's efforts to encourage more growth, limited the returns that could be obtained on these funds. One of the consequences—through a complex set of connections—was the development of the U.S. housing bubble, as financial firms, searching for higher returns, pushed funds into more and more risky mortgage loans.

It was not simply free trade and the unrestricted flow of international finance that generated the housing bubble and subsequent crisis in the U.S. economy. However, the generally unstable global economy—both in terms of trade and finance—that has emerged in the free trade era was certainly a factor bringing about the crisis. Moreover, as is widely recognized, it was not only the U.S. economy and U.S. financial institutions that were affected. The free international flow of finance has meant that banking has become more and more a global industry. So as the U.S. banks got in trouble in 2007 and 2008, their maladies spread to many other parts of the world.

The Uses of Free Trade

While free trade is not the best economic growth or development policy and, especially through the free flow of finance, can precipitate financial crises, the largest and most powerful firms in many countries find it highly profitable. As Britain preached the loudest sermons for free trade in the early 19th century, when its own industry was already firmly established, so the United States—or at least many firms based in the United States—find it a profitable policy at the beginning of the 21st century. The Mexican experience provides an instructive illustration.

For U.S. firms, access to foreign markets is a high priority. Mexico may be relatively poor, but with a population of 105 million it provides a substantial market. Furthermore, Mexican labor is cheap relative to U.S. labor; and using modern production techniques, Mexican workers can be as productive as workers in the United States. For U.S. firms to obtain full access to the Mexican market, the United States has to open its borders to Mexican goods. Also, if U.S. firms are to take full advantage of cheap foreign labor and sell the goods produced abroad to U.S. consumers, the United States has to be open to imports.

On the other side of the border, wealthy Mexicans face a choice between advancing their interests through national development or advancing their interests through ties to U.S. firms and access to U.S. markets. For many years, they chose the former route. This led to some development of the Mexican economy but also—due to corruption and the massive power of the ruling party, the PRI—huge concentrations of wealth in the hands of a few small groups of firms and individuals. Eventually, these groups came into conflict with their own government over regulation and taxation. Having benefited from government largesse, they came to see their fortunes in greater freedom from government control and, particularly, in greater access to foreign markets and partnerships with large foreign companies. National development was a secondary concern when more involvement with international commerce would produce greater riches more quickly.

In addition, the old program of state-led development in Mexico ran into severe problems. These problems came to the surface in the 1980s with the international debt crisis. Owing huge amounts of money to foreign banks, the Mexican government was forced to respond to pressure from the IMF, the U.S. government, and large international banks which sought to deregulate Mexico's trade and investment. That pressure meshed with the pressure from Mexico's own richest elites, and the result was the move toward free trade and a greater opening of the Mexican economy to foreign investment.

Since the early 1990s, these changes for Mexico and the United States (as well as Canada) have been institutionalized in NAFTA. The U.S. government's agenda since then has been to spread free trade policies to all of the Americas through more regional agreements like CAFTA and ultimately through a Free Trade Area of the Americas. On a broader scale, the U.S. government works through the WTO, the IMF, and the World Bank to open markets and gain access to resources beyond the Western Hemisphere. In fact, while markets remain important everywhere, low-wage manufacturing is increasingly concentrated in Asia—especially China—instead of Mexico or Latin America.

The Chinese experience involves many of the same advantages for U.S. business as does the Mexican—a vast market, low wages, and an increasingly productive labor force. However, the Chinese government, although it has liberalized the economy a great deal compared to the pre-1985 era, has not abdicated its major role in the economy. For better (growth) and for worse (inequality and repression), the Chinese government has not embraced free trade.

Who Gains, Who Loses?

Of course, in the United States, Mexico, China and elsewhere, advocates of free trade claim that their policies are in everyone's interest. Free trade, they point out, will mean cheaper products for all. Consumers in the United States, who are mostly workers, will be richer because their wages will buy more. In Mexico and China, on the one hand, and in the United States, on the other hand, they argue that rising trade will create more jobs. If some workers lose their jobs because cheaper imported goods are available, export industries will produce new jobs.

In recent years this argument has taken on a new dimension with the larger entrance of India into the world economy and with the burgeoning there of jobs based in information technology—programming and call centers, for example. This "outsourcing" of service jobs has received a great deal of attention and concern in the United States. Yet free-traders have defended this development as good for the U.S. economy as well as for the Indian economy.

Such arguments obscure many of the most important issues in the free trade debate. Stated, as they usually are, as universal truths, these arguments are just plain silly. No one, for example, touring the Lowell National Historical Park could seriously argue that people in the United States would have been better off had there been no tariff on textiles. Yes, in 1820, they could have purchased textile goods more cheaply, but in the long run the result would have been less industrial advancement and a less wealthy nation. One could make the same point with the Japanese auto and computer industries, or indeed with numerous other examples from the last two centuries of capitalist development.

In the modern era, even though the United States already has a relatively developed economy with highly skilled workers, a freely open international economy does not serve the interests of most U.S. workers, though it will benefit large firms. U.S.

workers today are in competition with workers around the globe. Many different workers in many different places can produce the same goods and services. Thus, an international economy governed by the free trade agenda will tend to bring down wages for many U.S. workers. This phenomenon has certainly been one of the factors leading to the substantial rise of income inequality in the United States during recent decades.

The problem is not simply that of workers in a few industries—such as auto and steel, or call-centers and computer programming—where import competition is an obvious and immediate issue. A country's openness to the international economy affects the entire structure of earnings in that country. Free trade forces down the general level of wages across the board, even of those workers not directly affected by imports. The simple fact is that when companies can produce the same products in several different places, it is owners who gain because they can move their factories and funds around much more easily than workers can move themselves around. Capital is mobile; labor is much less mobile. Businesses, more than workers, gain from having a larger territory in which to roam.

Control Over Our Economic Lives

But the difficulties with free trade do not end with wages. In both low-income and high-income parts of the world, free trade is a weapon in the hands of business when it opposes any progressive social programs. Efforts to place environmental restrictions on firms are met with the threat of moving production abroad. Higher taxes to improve the schools? Business threatens to go elsewhere. Better health and safety regulations? The same response.

Some might argue that the losses from free trade for people in the United States will be balanced by gains for most people in poor countries—lower wages in the United States, but higher wages in Mexico and China. Free trade, then, would bring about international equality. Not likely. In fact, as pointed out above, free trade reforms in Mexico have helped force down wages and reduce social welfare programs, processes rationalized by efforts to make Mexican goods competitive on international markets. China, while not embracing free trade, has seen its full-scale entrance into global commerce accompanied by increasing inequality.

Gains for Mexican or Chinese workers, like those for U.S. workers, depend on their power in relation to business. Free trade or simply the imperative of international "competitiveness" are just as much weapons in the hands of firms operating in Mexico and China as they are for firms operating in the United States. The great mobility of capital is business's best trump card in dealing with labor and popular demands for social change—in the United States, Mexico, China and elsewhere.

None of this means that people should demand that their economies operate as fortresses, protected from all foreign economic incursions. There are great gains that can be obtained from international economic relations—when a nation manages those relations in the interests of the great majority of the people. Protectionism often simply supports narrow vested interests, corrupt officials, and wealthy industrialists. In rejecting free trade, we should move beyond traditional protectionism.

Yet, at this time, rejecting free trade is an essential first step. Free trade places the cards in the hands of business. More than ever, free trade would subject us to the "bottom line," or at least the bottom line as calculated by those who own and run large companies.

Afterword

The gospel of free trade remained the dominant policy outlook of business and political elites in the United States well into the 21st century. Both Democrats and Republicans in the White House and Congress pushed ahead with "free trade agreements." And they had wide support among economists. True, there was some opposition from the lower ranks of the Democratic Party, from unions, and from some businesses directly harmed by foreign competition. But this opposition had limited effect.

Then, in 2016, the chickens came home to roost. People who had been left behind by the economic changes of recent decades—wage stagnation and rising inequality, combined with the decline of manufacturing—had come to view their condition as being the result of the free trade or, more generally, "globalization." While their economic difficulties had multiple causes, "unfair" competition from China, Mexico, and elsewhere was readily identified and became the focus of their grievances.

In his ride to the White House, Donald Trump was able to combine this hostility to globalization with underlying racism and xenophobia. In his demagoguery, the United States was the victim in the world economy. And many people, some who really were the victims of the policies of free trade, bought the story. Trump promised to rip up NAFTA and withdraw from the Trans-Pacific Partnership (TPP) pursued by the Obama administration.

Upon taking office, Trump did abandon the TPP, and in 2018 it appears that NAFTA is on the verge of demise. More generally, as this update is being written in June 2018, the Trump administration has initiated a set of classical protectionist policies, imposing tariffs on many goods—not only from China, Mexico, and other low-wage countries, but also from Canada and the European Union.

While these actions appeal to his "base" and to workers and businesses that will directly benefit from a reduction in competition, the Trumpian counter to free trade will harm most workers and the U.S. economy generally. For example, jobs in the steel industry (a focus of the new tariffs) will increase somewhat, but more jobs will be lost in industries—particularly the auto industry—where higher prices for steel will yield production cutbacks. Also, as other countries impose retaliatory tariffs on U.S. exports, still more jobs in the United States will be lost. Most generally, the changes and unpredictability of the Trump administration's actions generate economic uncertainty, which is bad for business.

Few members of the political and business elites and few economists have voiced support for the reemergence of classical protectionism. For them, the gospel of free trade remains a gospel.

For most people, however, neither free trade nor classical protectionism is a reasonable way for the United States to engage with the global economy. There are other options. To develop these options, to build a progressive trade policy, it is useful to recognize that jobs are changing all the time due to several causes—international trade, but also technological change, and new wants and needs. It would not be useful to stop this change, but it is essential that in the process of these changes workers be protected. This means supporting meaningful and extensive retraining programs, job transfer programs, and ample funds for workers in transition. The goal should be to protect workers, which is not the same as protecting jobs.

Further, a progressive trade policy would take into account the conditions under which imported goods are produced—especially the impact on workers and on the environment. Restrictions would be placed on the import of goods produced under conditions where workers are denied basic human rights. Likewise, restrictions would be placed on the import of goods produced in an environmentally destructive manner. In both cases, the restrictions could be absolute or could be accomplished by tariffs that eliminated the cost advantages attained by abrogating labor rights and ignoring environmental concerns.

Engagement with the economies of the rest of the world can be quite valuable, both for narrow economic reasons and more broadly for many cultural, educational, and intellectual reasons. There is an important exception: international financial activity should be severely restricted because it removes a country's ability to control its own economy. But overall, a progressive policy is a policy of global engagement, not isolation. ❑

Article 9.2

THE GLOBALIZATION CLOCK

BY THOMAS PALLEY
May/June 2006

Political economy has historically been constructed around the divide between capital and labor, with firms and workers at odds over the division of the economic pie. Within this construct, labor is usually represented as a monolithic interest, yet the reality is that labor has always suffered from internal divisions—by race, by occupational status, and along many other fault lines. Neoliberal globalization has in many ways sharpened these divisions, which helps to explain why corporations have been winning and workers losing.

One of these fault lines divides workers from themselves: since workers are also consumers, they face a divide between the desire for higher wages and the desire for lower prices. Historically, this identity split has been exploited to divide union from nonunion workers, with anti-labor advocates accusing union workers of causing higher prices. Today, globalization is amplifying the divide between people's interests as workers and their interests as consumers through its promise of ever-lower prices.

Consider the debate over Walmart's low-road labor policies. While Walmart's low wages and skimpy benefits have recently faced scrutiny, even some liberal commentators argue that Walmart is actually good for low-wage workers because they gain more as consumers from its "low, low prices" than they lose as workers from its low wages. But this static, snapshot analysis fails to capture the full impact of globalization, past and future.

Globalization affects the economy unevenly, hitting some sectors first and others later. The process can be understood in terms of the hands of a clock. At one o'clock is the apparel sector; at two o'clock, the textile sector; at three, the steel sector; at six, the auto sector. Workers in the apparel sector are the first to have their jobs shifted to lower-wage venues; at the same time, though, all other workers get price reductions. Next, the process picks off textile sector workers at two o'clock. Meanwhile, workers from three o'clock onward get price cuts, as do the apparel workers at one o'clock. Each time the hands of the clock move, the workers taking the hit are isolated. In this fashion, globalization moves around the clock, with labor perennially divided.

Manufacturing was first to experience this process, but technological innovations associated with the Internet are putting service and knowledge workers in the firing line as well. Online business models are making even retail workers vulnerable—consider Amazon.com, for example, which has opened a customer support center and two technology development centers in India. Public-sector wages are also in play, at least indirectly, since falling wages mean falling tax revenues. The problem is that each time the hands on the globalization clock move forward, workers are divided: the majority is made slightly better off while the few are made much worse off.

Globalization also alters the historical divisions within capital, creating a new split between bigger internationalized firms and smaller firms that remain nationally centered. This division has been brought into sharp focus with the debate over the trade deficit and the overvalued dollar. In previous decades, manufacturing as a whole opposed running trade deficits and maintaining an overvalued dollar because of the adverse impact of increased imports. The one major business sector with a different view was retailing, which benefited from cheap imports.

However, the spread of multinational production and outsourcing has divided manufacturing in wealthy countries into two camps. In one camp are larger multinational corporations that have gone global and benefit from cheap imports; in the other are smaller businesses that remain nationally centered in terms of sales, production and input sourcing. Multinational corporations tend to support an overvalued dollar since this makes imports produced in their foreign factories cheaper. Conversely, domestic manufacturers are hurt by an overvalued dollar, which advantages import competition.

This division opens the possibility of a new alliance between labor and those manufacturers and businesses that remain nationally based—potentially a potent one, since there are approximately 7 million enterprises with sales of less than $10 million in the United States, versus only 200,000 with sales greater than $10 million. However, such an alliance will always be unstable as the inherent labor-capital conflict over income distribution can always reassert itself. Indeed, this pattern is already evident in the internal politics of the National Association of Manufacturers (NAM), whose members have been significantly divided regarding the overvalued dollar. As one way to address this division, the group is promoting a domestic "competitiveness" agenda aimed at weakening regulation, reducing corporate legal liability, and lowering employee benefit costs—an agenda designed to appeal to both camps, but at the expense of workers.

Solidarity has always been key to political and economic advance by working families, and it is key to mastering the politics of globalization. Developing a coherent story about the economics of neoliberal globalization around which working families can coalesce is a key ingredient for solidarity. So, too, is understanding how globalization divides labor. These narratives and analyses can help counter deep cultural proclivities to individualism, as well as other historic divides such as racism. However, as if this were not difficult enough, globalization creates additional challenges. National political solutions that worked in the past are not adequate to the task of controlling international competition. That means the solidarity bar is further raised, calling for international solidarity that supports new forms of international economic regulation. ❑

Article 9.3

DOLLAR DOMINANCE

BY ARTHUR MacEWAN
January/February 2015

> Dear Dr. Dollar:
> *What does it mean that the dollar is the "dominant" global currency? Why does this situation exist? And how does it matter?* —Anonymous

Suppose that, when you paid for things with checks, all the recipients of those checks believed that you were a very responsible person, that you would keep plenty of money in the bank to honor those checks. Moreover, not only did the check recipients believe in you, but people in general had this same opinion.

Under these circumstances, the people holding your checks wouldn't have to cash them in. Those checks could simply be used as money. The checks themselves would be acceptable in transactions among all those people who believed you were so responsible.

This situation would be nice for you because you could write plenty of checks and not worry about those checks being cashed in against your account. Extra buying power for you. At the same time, the people who used your checks as money would have an easier time with transactions, having your checks as a widely acceptable form of currency—i.e., they would have more "liquidity." Also, holding onto your checks—keeping them "in reserve"—would be a safe way for people to store money for when they needed it.

Fiction and Reality

To a large extent, this fictional situation with your checks is analogous to the real situation of the U.S. dollar in global commerce. With people and banks around the world using dollars and holding dollars, not "cashing them in" for U.S. goods, the United States— primarily its government and businesses—is able to spend more abroad without giving up so much in goods and services produced in the United States. Governments, businesses, and people around the world have more liquidity than they would otherwise, and they have more confidence than they would otherwise in the value of the currency (dollars) they are using and holding in reserve

Like you in the fictional scenario, the U.S. government in the real scenario is viewed as "responsible." An important part of the U.S. government being viewed as "responsible" is that it would keep the value of the dollar relatively stable—i.e., not much inflation (at least compared to other currencies). This organization of the global finance system, with the dollar in this special, or dominant, position has an interesting history—and some powerful implications.

Where Did This System Come From?

The crucial formal step in creating the dollar-dominated system came at the end of World War II, with the United States in an extremely strong economic position. Indeed, the high level of government spending on the war had brought the U.S. economy out of the Great Depression, while other high-income countries (and many low-income countries) had had their economies physically decimated by the war. Combined with this economic power, the United States had extreme military power. Thus, the era following World War II came to be called "The American Century" (Of course it was not really a full century, but let's not quibble.)

As the end of the war was coming into sight, in July 1944, representatives of the U.S. government and of 43 allied governments (over 700 delegates in all) met over three weeks at the Mt. Washington Hotel in Bretton Woods, N.H. The purpose of this conference was to set up the arrangements for the operation of the global economy in the postwar era. Although the Soviet Union and China were both represented at the Bretton Woods conference, in subsequent years they did not take part in the arrangements. (Today you can go to Bretton Woods and, at the entrance to the hotel's driveway, see the sign commemorating this conference, but you have to pay an entrance fee to actually get onto the hotel grounds.)

Unsurprisingly, given the relative economic and political power of the allied governments, the U.S. government basically dictated the conference outcomes, arrangements by which commerce among capitalist countries would be organized in the decades following World War II—the "Bretton Woods era." The central feature of these arrangements was that the dollar would be at the core of global commerce. Other countries' currencies would be "pegged" to the dollar, which meant that each government would set the value of its currency in terms of the dollar. For example, in 1949 the French franc was pegged at $0.37 and the British pound at $2.80. The dollar itself was set in relation to gold: $34 to the ounce. Other countries' banks could redeem their dollars for gold at this rate, but, as with your checks, they generally didn't do so. When the gold-redemption promise was terminated in 1971, it turned out not to make much difference—more on that in a moment.

Of course, economies change in relation to one another. In the postwar era, different rates of inflation and different rates of productivity growth meant that the values of the currencies in terms of the dollar had to be changed from time to time. For example, if France was running a trade deficit with the rest of the world (importing more than it was exporting), this meant that the value of its franc was too high in relation to the dollar—i.e., in terms of dollars, the cost of French goods was too high and France's exports would be low, while the cost for France of goods from elsewhere would be too low and France's imports would be high. Moreover, with French exports not paying for its imports, France would necessarily build up a foreign debt to pay for the excess imports.

One could look at this franc-dollar relationship another way: instead of the franc being too high, one could say that the dollar was too low. But the rules that were established at Bretton Woods excluded the dollar from having to adjust. In this example, it was the French who would have to adjust the value of their currency—i.e., France would have to devalue its currency. And, importantly, it would have to borrow to cover the foreign debt it had built up. The U.S. economy, on the other hand, was protected from the disruption that would have been caused by changing the value of the dollar.

The International Monetary Fund (IMF) was established at Bretton Woods to provide countries in this kind of situation with the loans they needed. The IMF provided these loans, but with various conditions—in particular that the county taking the loans would have to take steps to reorganize their economies, generally in ways that opened them to more foreign commerce, trade and investment.

While the IMF did play a role in European adjustments, its actions became especially important in lower-income countries, where it used its loan conditions to push countries towards a greater openness to international investment and trade—very much in the interests of multinational firms based in the richer countries. (The World Bank was also created at Bretton Woods, but its role is not a central part of the story here.)

Change Without Change

The Bretton Woods rules of the game worked fairly well for twenty-five years. In fact, from the perspective of the United States one might say they worked too well. While the Bretton Woods system promoted U.S. commerce, opening up trade and investment opportunities around the (capitalist) world, it also provided a stability in global affairs in which firms based elsewhere—in Japan and Europe—were able to also expand and ultimately challenge the dominant position of U.S firms.

A critical juncture in global commercial arrangements then came in 1971: the Bretton Woods system fell apart. A combination of heavy spending abroad by the U.S. government (on the Vietnam War), the economic challenge from other rich countries, and inflation in the United States led the U.S. government to drop its promise of redeeming dollars for gold. Yet, while the system fell apart, there was surprisingly little change in international trade and investment. The relative economic and military power of the United States, though not as extreme as it had been in the immediate post-World War II era, continued. And the perceived threat of the Soviet Union served as a glue, binding the world's major capitalist powers in Europe and Asia to the United States, and leading them to accept continued U.S. economic, as well as military, dominance.

After 1971, various new arrangements were put in place—for example, a system of partially managed "pegs" was established. Yet the dollar remained the central currency of global commerce. Prices of internationally traded goods—most importantly oil—continued to be set in dollars, and countries continued to hold their reserves in dollars.

Although 1971 marked the beginning of a new era in international financial arrangements, the dollar retained its dominant position. Regardless of the various economic problems in the United States, the dollar has remained both relatively stable and in sufficient supply to grease the wheels of international commerce. Indeed, an ironic example of the continuing role of the dollar came in the Great Recession that began in 2008. Even while the U.S. economy was in the doldrums, businesses and governments elsewhere in the world were buying U.S. government bonds—a principal means of holding their reserves in dollars—since they still considered these the safest assets available.

Power and a Symbol of Power

In years leading up to the Great Recession, China had entered the global for-profit economy and was exporting at a high rate, exceeding its imports. The Chinese government used the extra money that China was obtaining from its trade surplus to heavily invest in U.S. government bonds. That is, China built up extensive reserves in dollars. In effect, China was loaning money to the United States—loans which filled both the federal budget deficit and the U.S trade deficit. What many observers decried as a dangerous situation—We are becoming indebted to the Chinese! Horror!—in fact served both the U.S. and Chinese governments quite well.

The international role of the dollar is a symbol of U.S. power and is based on that power. At the same time, the dollar's role works to enhance that power, giving the U.S. government and U.S. business the liquidity needed for carrying out global operations—everything from wars to benign commerce.

There are problems with the system. The continued role of the dollar depends to a large extent on the avoidance of significant inflation in the United States. Yet restraints on inflation—e.g., the Federal Reserve raising interest rates—generally work against expanding employment. So maintaining the role of the dollar can come at the expense of most people in the country.

Also, there is always the risk of change. Just as the position of the dollar supports U.S. power in world affairs, if that position is undermined, U.S. power would suffer. In recent years, there has been some threat that other governments would challenge the dollar with their own currencies. China, in particular, has attempted to establish its own positon in world affairs, which, if successful, could ultimately undercut the dominance of the dollar. Indeed, the fear associated with China holding reserves in dollars (i.e., as U.S. government bonds) is to some extent based on concern about the potential implications of China shifting out of dollars (or threatening to do so). Yet, especially with the recent weakening of the Chinese economy, this particular challenge does not appear likely in the near future.

Over the last several decades, the role of the dollar in world affairs has become like the role of the English language. Both developed as a consequence of the extreme power of the United States. in the global economy, and both give advantages to the U.S. government, to U.S. firms, and to any individuals engaged in international activities. Most important, the roles of both the dollar and the English language have become thoroughly entrenched. Even as the power of the United States weakens, then, those roles are likely to continue for some time to come. ❑

Article 9.4

NAFTA: IT LOWERED WAGES, AS IT WAS SUPPOSED TO DO

BY DEAN BAKER

November 2013, New York Times

Given the trends in U.S. trade with Mexico over the last two decades, it is strange that there is much of a debate over NAFTA's impact on wages. At the time NAFTA was passed in 1993 the United States had a modest trade surplus with Mexico. In 2013 we are on a path to have a trade deficit of more than $50 billion. The $50 billion in lost output corresponds to roughly 0.3% of gross domestic product, assuming the same impact on employment, this would translate into more than 400,000 jobs. If each lost job would have led to half a job being created as a result of workers spending their wages, this would bring the total impact to 600,000 jobs.

Of course some of the shift from surplus to deficit might have occurred even without NAFTA, but it would be difficult to argue that NAFTA was not a major contributing factor. After all, one of the main purposes of the agreement was to make U.S. firms feel confident that they could locate operations in Mexico without having to fear that their factories could be nationalized or that Mexico would impose restrictions on repatriating profits. This encouraged firms to take advantage of lower cost labor in Mexico, and many did.

This can produce economic gains; they just don't go to ordinary workers. The lower cost of labor translates to some extent into lower prices and to some extent into higher corporate profits. The latter might be good news for shareholders and top management, but is not beneficial to most workers.

Lower prices are helpful to workers as consumers, but are not likely to offset the impact on wages. To see this point, imagine that NAFTA was about reducing the wages of doctors by eliminating the barriers that made it difficult for Mexican school children to train to U.S. standards and practice medicine in the United States.

If we got an additional 200,000 doctors from Mexico over the last 20 years then it would likely go far toward bringing the pay of doctors in the United States more in line with the pay of doctors in other wealthy countries. This would lead to tens of billions of years in savings in health care costs to patients and the government.

Even doctors would share in these savings, since they too would have to pay less for their healthcare. However no one would try to tell doctors that they were better off from this trade deal because of their reduced healthcare costs. The hit to their wages would have swamped the savings on their healthcare bill. This is the same story with ordinary workers and the impact of NAFTA.

NAFTA could have been structured to bring the pay of doctors and other highly paid professionals more in line with their pay in other wealthy countries by removing barriers. This would have produced substantial economic gains to the economy as a whole (it's the exact same model as economists use to show gains from the NAFTA we have), except these gains would be associated with a downward rather than an upward redistribution of income.

The doctors and their allies among the elite have been able to prevent such a deal from being considered by the politicians in Washington, American workers don't have that power. ❑

Article 9.5

BEYOND TRUMP'S TARIFFS AND TRADE WAR

BY JOHN MILLER
May/June 2018

> Mr. Trump raised the stakes late Thursday in his tariff showdown with Beijing, vowing to impose another $100 billion in tariffs on Chinese goods in light of its "unfair retaliation" after his initial $50 billion in tariffs. ...
>
> Then China popped off in return, saying it was ready to "forcefully" strike back if the new tariffs are imposed
>
> The basic economic problem with trade protectionism is that it is a political intervention that distorts markets. One political intervention leads to another, and the cumulative consequence is higher prices, less investment, and slower economic growth.
>
> —"Punishing America First" by the Editorial Board, *Wall Street Journal*, April 7, 2018.

The *Wall Street Journal* editors are right that President Trump's tariffs will undoubtedly harm the U.S. economy. Just how much will depend on whether his tariffs and trade bluster ignite a trade war. Not that it much worries Trump, who insists that trade wars "are easy to win." (See the box on the next page for an account of Trump's tariffs and trade threats.)

But that doesn't make the non-interventionist, free-market policies the *Wall Street Journal* editors are peddling a desirable alternative. Their hyper-globalization policies have not brought and will not bring economic relief to those who have been left behind and will instead continue to shower gains on financial elites.

The Trump Tariffs and the Triumph of Economic Illiteracy

The *Wall Street Journal* editors have complained that it is hard to discern the overall strategy to Trump trade policy, which seems to be backed up by little other than "nonsense trade economics." Economists of all stripes, advocates and critics of market-led globalization, agree.

To begin with, there's Trump's fixation with the U.S. trade deficit with China ($337 billion in 2017), when the United States trades with many other countries, too. Martin Wolf, the pro-globalization columnist at the *Financial Times*, the leading British business daily, likens worrying about running a trade deficit with one country to worrying about running a consistent trade deficit with your local supermarket (where you buy without selling). Your supermarket deficit is of no concern to you (or the supermarket) as long as you continue to pay your bills. Economist Joseph Stiglitz, a leading critic of corporate globalization, adds that even if tariffs reduced Chinese imports, they would not create jobs in the United States. Those tariffs would just increase prices for U.S. consumers and create jobs in Bangladesh, Vietnam, or any other country that steps in to replace the imports that had come from China.

The Trump Tariff Saga in a Nutshell

In February, the Trump administration imposed a 30% tariff on solar imports, an industry dominated by China. A month later, the Trump administration added a 30% tariff on steel and a 10% tariff on aluminum. After a multitude of country exemptions, several Asian countries and Russia are likely to be the only major importers subject to the tariffs. In April, China retaliated with tariffs on 128 U.S. products. Trump then announced 25% tariffs on another 1,300 Chinese products, about $50 billion of China's exports into the United States. In response, China threatened a 25% tariff on 106 U.S. exports (including soybeans, cars, and airplanes), to go in effect whenever the U.S. tariffs do. Then Trump vowed to impose another $100 billion in tariffs on Chinese goods because of China's "unfair retaliation" to his initial $50 billion in tariffs. That's when the *Wall Street Journal* editors chimed in with the editorial above.

Since then, Trump has angered Mexico and U.S. allies Canada and Europe by adding them to list of countries on which he will impose his steel and aluminum tariffs set to go into effect of July 1.

Each country has promised to retaliate by imposing tariffs of U.S. goods. Canada announced a list of tariffs it would impose on steel imports from the United States as well as 84 other U.S. products from yogurt to lawnmowers (both made in the swing state Wisconsin) to beer kegs to hair lacquers. The European Union would impose $3.4 billion of tariffs on U.S. imports including Harley Davidson motorcycles (manufactured in Wisconsin), bourbon whiskey (from Mitch McConnell's Kentucky), Levi's jeans, and a host of other U.S. imports. Mexico promises "dollar for dollar" tariffs on U.S. imports, targeting steel, pork, bourbon, motorboats, apples, potatoes, cranberries, and many other U.S. imports.

Finally, when the conference of G-7 nations held in early June ended in conflict, the threat of a trade war was yet closer to becoming a reality.

Then there's Trump's exports-only approach to trade policy. "Selling stuff [made in the United States] to foreigners is good, and buying stuff [that could have been made in the United States] from foreigners is bad," is conservative economist Robert Barro's best guess as to what constitutes Trump's theory of international trade. For Barro, Trump has things backward: "Imports are things we want," and "exports are the price we have to pay to get the imports." One doesn't have to accept Barro's vision of trade to acknowledge that any coherent trade theory needs to take into account the benefits of imports to consumers and producers as well as the production and employment effect of exports, and to recognize that running a trade deficit (imports that exceed exports) is not in and of itself a sign of a failed trade policy.

On top of that, Trump's tariffs are likely to cost U.S. manufacturers jobs, even without considering the debilitating effects of Chinese retaliatory tariffs. Take the 25% tariff that Trump imposed on imported steel. Steel tariffs might protect the jobs of workers in the steel industry, but they will damage industries and cost jobs in the many industries that use steel as an input. That includes the automobile sector, aerospace, heavy equipment, and construction, all of which will have to pay higher prices for steel. And the industries that use steel employ 80 times as many people as steel-producing industries, according to the estimates of economists Lydia Cox and Kadee Russ. While the United States might not get punished first, as the editors maintain, Trump's tariff policy does amount to a "stop or I'll shoot our economy in the foot strategy," as former Clinton Administration Treasury Secretary and Obama Administration economic advisor, Lawrence Summers, has put it.

Free-Trade Free Fall

The free-trade policies favored by the *Wall Street Journal* editors and traditional trade economists might be more disciplined than Trump's hodgepodge of tariffs, but they would do no less to serve the rich and do no more to improve the lot of those who have been left behind by globalization. In fact, a populist backlash against those policies helped to elect Trump president.

Honestly presented trade theory never promised a "win-win for everyone," as economist Paul Krugman puts it. Rather, traditional trade theory suggests that trade, rather than increase or decrease the number of jobs in a country, instead changes the mix of jobs. That in turn causes massive dislocation that leaves many behind, especially when they get little or no support from government. In his book *The Globalization Paradox*, economist Dani Rodrik finds that the primary effect of reducing tariffs in the United States would be to shift income from some groups to others, typically from those already hurt by globalization to those who are already benefitting. Rodrik calculates that in the case of the United States, for every $1 of overall gains, $50 of income gets shifted from one group to another. For typical working families, the $1 of overall gains is likely to be swamped by the fact that they are on the losing end of the $50 income shift.

On top of that, much of the gains from trade are diffuse, going to millions of consumers in the form of lower prices for cheap imports, while losses are highly concentrated, materializing in the form of lost jobs and the economic decline of towns and regions. An honest case for freer trade would require government to compensate those losers to ensure that everyone wins. But in the United States that compensation seldom, if ever, happens.

Even the net gains from free trade have been called into question. In their exhaustive empirical study of the major studies of trade policy and economic growth, Rodrik and fellow economist Francisco Rodriguez found "little evidence that open trade policies...are significantly associated with economic growth."

Historical evidence also casts doubt on the benefits of free trade. *New York Times* columnist Thomas Friedman once challenged the critics of globalization to name "a single country that has flourished, or upgraded its living or worker standards, without free trade and integration." The accurate answer is that every one of today's developed countries relied heavily on government policies that managed and controlled its involvement in international commerce during its rise to prowess. The world's first industrial power, Great Britain, advocated free trade only after protectionist policies helped 18th-century industries become well established. In the half century following the Civil War, the United States imposed tariffs on imports that averaged around 40%, a level higher than those imposed in virtually all of today's developing economies. During the second half of the 20th century, both Germany and Japan relied on managed trade, not free trade, to propel their rapid economic growth, as did South Korea and Taiwan during the 1960s and 1970s.

What Would Be Better?

A progressive policy would not turn away from trade but would engage the global economy with rules and policies that are more democratic and serve the interests of people across the globe. To begin with, a global commitment to sustained full employment would help workers escape jobs with dangerous working conditions that pay rock-bottom wages. It would also go a long way toward limiting transnational corporations' ability to pit the workers in one country against their employees in another country.

Nor should a progressive policy sweep away all tariffs. In his column last year ("What Would a Progressive Trade Policy Look Like?" *D&S*, July/August 2017), Arthur MacEwan made the case for two changes in U.S. international agreements that would use tariffs to reduce inequality and insecurity. First, goods produced under conditions where workers' basic rights to organize and to reasonable health and safety conditions are denied would not be given unfettered access to global markets. Second, goods whose production or use is environmentally destructive would likewise face trade restrictions.

Beyond those changes, with increased international trade comes the need for increased government intervention. Government must support people displaced by changes due to trade, from employment insurance funds to well-funded retraining programs to provisions for continuing medical care and pensions.

Those sorts of trade policies would help the majority of the world's people flourish economically. ❏

Sources: "Trump's China Tariffs," *Wall Street Journal* editorial, March 22, 2018; Joseph Stiglitz, "Trump's Trade Confusion," Project Syndicate, April 5, 2018; Martin Wolf, "The Folly of Donald Trump's Bilateralism in Global Trade," *Financial Times*, March 14, 2017; Robert Barro, "Trump and China Share a Bad Idea on Trade," *Wall Street Journal*, April 10, 2018; Bob Davis and Lingling Wei, "U.S. Set to Boost Pressure on China," *Wall Street Journal*, April 12, 2018; Lydia Cox and Kadee Russ, "Will Steel Tariffs put U.S. Jobs at Risk?" Econofact, February 26, 2018; Paul Krugman, "Oh, What a Trumpy Trade War!" *New York Times*, March 8, 2018; Larry Summers, "Tariffs Are a 'Stop or I'll Shoot Myself in the Foot' Policy," CNBC, April 6, 2018; Dani Rodrik, *The Globalization Paradox* (W.W. Norton, New York: 2011); John Miller, "The Misleading Case for Unmanaged Global Free Trade," Scholars Strategy Network, January 13, 2015.

Article 9.6

UNDERSTANDING BREXIT

A primer on the split tha has now been set into motion.

BY JOHN WEEKS
May/June 2017; updated June 2018

Within a year, two closely linked events transformed British politics. The first, a referendum on June 23, 2016, gave British voters the choice of whether to continue as part of the European Union. Fifty weeks later, the general election of June 2017 occurred as the direct result of that referendum. The outcome of the "Brexit" referendum came as a deep shock in Great Britain and across Europe. The implications of the second vote may prove even more transformative.

On that June day in 2016, 52% of those casting ballots voted to end British membership in the EU. Voters in England (population 53 million) and Wales (3.1 million) supported "Brexit" (about 53% voting to leave in both cases), while Northern Ireland (1.8 million) and Scotland (5.3 million) gave majorities for "Remain" (53% and a landslide 62%, respectively).

The results came on a high turnout of 72%, compared to 66% in the 2015 national election. Whether the outcome was "close" is a matter of opinion. Those in the losing camp think so, while the winners consider the outcome "decisive." Various hypotheses came forth to explain why a majority chose "Leave": national sovereignty (however defined), dislike of the EU, the revenge of globalization's "losers," and anti-immigration sentiment. While anger over the inequalities generated by globalization and fears of immigrants may have promoted many in the working class and middle class to vote for Brexit, this and other anti-EU motivations must be placed in the longer context of British relations with the continent.

British Governments' EU Ambiguity

At the end of World War II, British politicians and the public viewed the United Kingdom as among the winners of the war, and the continental countries the losers (with the obvious exception of Russia), either defeated and occupied by Nazi Germany or allies of the Nazis. When the governments of Germany, France, Italy, and the Benelux countries formed the European Coal and Steel Community (ECSC) in 1951, the Labour Government, by far the most progressive in UK history, declined to join, choosing instead to maintain a "special relationship" with the United States. While a committed anti-fascist during the 1930s and a progressive on domestic issues, Labour Prime Minister Clement Atlee was also pro-U.S. and anti-Soviet.

Twenty years later, the Conservative government of Edward Heath sought to join the ECSC's successor, the European Economic Community. Led by the trade unions, the vast majority of progressives opposed entry, rhetorically labeling the EEC a "capitalist club." However, in 1975 two-thirds of those voting supported joining the EEC, notwithstanding the infamous veto in 1967 of Britain's first attempt to join by French President Charles DeGaul.

Over the next 40 years, all British governments, Conservative and Labour, would vacillate in their approach to Europe and the EU (created by the 1993 Maastricht Treaty), ranging from lukewarm to overtly hostile. The xenophobic and chauvinistic right wing of the Conservative Party opposed the EU on principle. The Tory mainstream favored membership, but opposed the protection of worker rights and civil rights in the EU treaties (the so-called Social Chapter). The Labour government of Tony Blair signed onto the Social Chapter in 1997 but only half-heartedly, and it committed to a neoliberal "flexible" market domestically.

The EU treaties and legislation by the European Parliament facilitated and even accelerated many progressive reforms in the United Kingdom. The most important were LGBTQ rights and guarantees of employment rights such as paid vacations. However, for the last 20 years both the Conservative and Labour leadership emphasized the advantages of the single European market with rare mention of worker and civil rights. When the referendum campaign began, the mainstream of both major parties focused narrowly on the alleged economic advantages of EU membership. Only a minority of the electorate was aware of EU protection of citizen's rights.

The Ill-Fated Brexit Campaign

The anti-EU right wing campaigned by harping on the myth of a European superstate that would bring tyranny to Britain. They reinforced this with their trump card: the putative dangers of immigration. The free movement of labor within the EU stands out as the strongest anti-EU motivation. Pro-Brexit propaganda misrepresented intra-EU migration as equivalent to all immigration, shamelessly fanning fears of Islamic refugees. In contrast to the free movement of citizens guaranteed within the EU, migration from outside the union is severely restricted.

Yet in the months leading up to the referendum, debate over refugees from war-torn Syria dominated politics in the European Union. The issue became all the more explosive in the wake of the November 2015 terrorist attack in Paris. Had the UK vote occurred a year earlier, the anti-EU campaign would have found it much more difficult to whip up anti-immigrant hysteria, though a majority of voters might still have supported Brexit as an anti-globalization protest vote.

Leaving the EU may prove complex in procedure, but its meaning and consequences were no mystery. The major issues are 1) trade and investment flows after formally exiting the EU, 2) the status of citizens of EU countries who work in Britain, and 3) replacing the EU legal framework with domestic legislation. Despite receiving more publicity, the first two were considerably less problematic than the third. With regard to the first, both Britain and the EU have open capital markets that allow free flow of funds.

On trade, both the United Kingdom and the EU are subject to the rule prohibiting discrimination among trading partners. That implies that after Brexit is complete, British exporters and importers would face the same trade rules as any other WTO member. Anxieties about post-Brexit tariffs seem exaggerated given that the trade-weighted EU levy on imports is 2.3%. Further, the EU share of UK total goods trade has fallen for over a decade, to less than 50% in 2017.

The non-EU trade deficit is considerably smaller than that with EU countries both for goods and for services. Net foreign investment of all types into the UK has fallen consistently since the mid-2000s, more so from EU countries than the rest of the world. While post-Brexit goods trade will involve a transition in external commerce, predictions of disaster should be viewed as propaganda.

Before joining the then-EEC, no visas were required among Western European countries, an arrangement likely after Brexit. While the Brexit uncertainty forced upon EU citizens working in Britain by the Tory government is appalling, it would be astounding if a positive outcome were not achieved given the importance of those employees to the private and public sectors, and the large number of UK citizens working on the continent.

The core strategy of mainstream pro-EU groups was to represent Brexit as a disaster in the making. This strategy extends the counterproductive approach taken during the referendum campaign: that fear of the unknown would prove the most effective defense of EU membership. Stressing purely economic effects allows the pro-EU neoliberals to avoid discussion of the serious danger of Brexit: the loss of protection of civil rights and employment rights.

The consequences of leaving the EU were further obfuscated by the ubiquitous use of the adjectives "hard" and "soft." The message by Remain campaigners was clear: "hard Brexit" is "bad," verging on disastrous, and "soft Brexit" is "good" and the route of reason, with no Brexit best of all. "Hard Brexit" referred to a complete break with EU institutions, placing Britain into the category with the countries of the world that are neither EU members nor affiliates. The right-wingers inside and outside the Conservative Party favored this option. A group of far-right ideologues, Economists for Free Trade (formerly Economists for Brexit), provided the putative intellectual justification for a complete break. Their goal was to end legal constraints and regulations on British business set by EU environmental law, the employment rights protected in EU treaties, and civil and human rights enforced by the European Court of Justice. To be politically appealing, right-wing politicians packaged "hard Brexit" as the anti-immigration option. It should be more accurately named "hard-right Brexit."

A "soft Brexit" strategy sought to maintain association with as many EU institutions as possible consistent with the referendum outcome. Were it possible, the softest Brexit would have Britain become an associate rather than a member, and retain all the putative advantages of membership. However, political conditions in both Britain and among EU governments make the softest option difficult to achieve.

During 2017 and 2018, a joke circulating in the corridors of the EU held that the greatest uncertainty facing the British government was whether it could exit the EU while there was still a union to leave. More threatening than Brexit were the semi-authoritarian regimes in Hungary and Poland, far-right "euro-skeptic" governments elected in Austria (October 2017) and Italy (March 2018), and Catalonian separatism.

To non-Europeans the British exit from the EU might appear incomprehensible. Having opted out of the eurozone, a position it shares with Denmark, the British government and people need never fear the Brussels-imposed austerity policies that so devastated Greece. The opt out from the eurozone is reinforced by the Conservative government in 2014 being the only EU member to refuse to sign the dysfunctional Treaty on Coordination, Stability and Governance, which contained the enforcement progress for EU fiscal rules.

Brexit becomes comprehensible when one realizes that no British government has given strong support to membership other than as a trading arrangement. Complementary to this narrow approach to EU membership, Conservative governments consistently attacked the broader aspects of EU membership, while the Labour Party leadership largely ignored them as a political embarrassment. The impact of decades of attacks on the "bureaucrats in Brussels," repeated and successful demands from all UK governments for special treatment, and the 2003 condescending rejection of membership in the eurozone left public support for the EU shallow and volatile.

Law of Unintended Consequences

The Brexit vote brought mixed consequences for the British right. The defeat of the referendum creates the possibility of achieving the dream of much of the British corporate sector to escape the employment, environmental, and civil protections institutionalized in the EU treaties—a long-term goal of the right, dating back to Margaret Thatcher's war on the trade union movement and public-sector interventions in the 1980s. Exiting the EU offered the only way for a Conservative government to negate these rights without violating EU treaties. On the negative side, the loss of a Conservative parliamentary majority in June 2017 left the Tory right without the power to realize its deregulatory dream.

In both major national parties, the centrists suffered unmitigated disaster as a result of the referendum outcome. These centrists strongly supported remaining in the EU. The Labour centrists—the so-called Blairites—fervently opposed party leader Jeremy Corbyn and the radical change he sought for the Labour Party and the country. On June 23, 2016, those Labour centrists complacently assumed victory for the Remain campaign and looked forward to undermining the party leader and provoking his resignation. One year later, Brexit seems irreversible, and the social democrat they sought to undermine held increasingly firm control of the party. With no political home and the tide running against them, some of their prominent spokespersons have descended into despair.

Progressives who were deeply discontented with the political status quo in Britain nevertheless voted overwhelmingly in June 2016 to remain in the EU. A disparate group of left-of-center voters, Labour Party members, Scottish National Party supporters, Greens, and people not in parties endorsed the dream of a unified Europe, however flawed it was in practice.

Remain lost because the Leavers constructed a slightly larger coalition of nationalists on the basis of a more powerful narrative of xenophobia. A few progressives repelled by EU policies such as those involving Greece voted Leave, as did a very large number of people without fixed affiliation disgusted with austerity and its effect on them. However, pro-EU progressives will find it hard to deny that the referendum result they fought to prevent led to events beyond their most optimistic hopes: the fall of the Conservative David Cameron government and the stunning success of the Labour Party in the 2017 general election. The probability is great that the June 2016 referendum will in due course result in a UK government committed to social democracy, not neoliberalism.

The painful truth is that the vast majority of British households would be better off out of the European Union with a Labour government led by Jeremy Corbyn than in the European Union under the yoke of a Conservative government led by anyone. Had the 2016 referendum passed even by the narrowest majority, David Cameron would still reside in 10 Downing Street imposing fiscal austerity. The right wing of the Labour Party would still pose a constant threat to the party's progressive leader. At the very least a progressive should have a nuanced view of Brexit. It has been very long time since the law of unintended consequences rewarded us at all, much less so spectacularly. ❏

Sources: Andrew Walker, "The Tony Blair Years," BBC News, Aug. 28, 2003 (bbc.co.uk); Article 157, The Lisbon Treaty (lisbon-treaty.org); European Union Agency for Fundamental Rights, "LGBTI" (fra.europa.eu); Hannah Finselbach, "Trade in goods MRETS (all BOP: EU 2013): time series dataset," Office for National Statistics, April 7, 2017 (ons.gov.uk); Ian Traynor, Nicholas Watt, David Gow, and Patrick Wintour, "David Cameron blocks EU treaty with veto, casting Britain adrift from Europe," *The Guardian*, Dec. 9, 2011 (theguardian.com); Department for Business, Innovation & Skills and Nick Boles MP, "Trade Union Act Becomes Law," May 4, 2016 (gov.uk); John Weeks, "EU Charter of Fundamental Rights: Read it before you vote on 23 June," *Open Democracy UK*, June 19, 2016 (opendemocracy.net); John Weeks, "The Six-Pack: EU Mandate for Bad Economic Policy," *Social Europe*, April 6, 2016 (socialeurope.eu); Lisa O'Carroll and Caelainn Barr, "Half of young adults in the UK do not feel European, poll reveals," *The Guardian*, April 11, 2017 (theguardian.com); Matt Wrack and John Weeks, "The Weeks Update: Matt Rack, Head of Fire Brigades Union & John Weeks discuss the controversial Trade Union bill," 2016 (audioboom.com); "Parlemeter 2016," European Parliament (europarl.europa.eu); Sami Hamroush, "Foreign direct investment involving UK companies: Inward tables," Office for National Statistics, Dec. 2, 2016 (ons.gov.uk); Stuart Wier, "A 'Fresh Start' for Britain in Europe?" *Open Democracy UK*, Jan. 18, 2013 (opendemocracy.net); Tejvan Pettinger, "Gordon Brown's 5 Economic Test for Joining Euro," *Economics Help*, March 13, 2007 (economicshelp.org); "The European Convention on Human Rights," *Human Rights News, Views & Info*, (rightsinfo.org); "What does leaving the EU mean for trade?" Full Fact, June 28, 2016 (fullfact.org); World Trade Organization, "Principles of the Trading System" (wto.org).

Article 9.7

GLOBALIZATION AND THE END OF THE LABOR ARISTOCRACY

BY JAYATI GHOSH
March/April 2017

Twenty-first century imperialism has changed its form. In the 19th century and the first half of the 20th century, it was explicitly related to colonial control; in the second half of the 20th century it relied on a combination of geopolitical and economic control deriving from the clear dominance of the United States as the global hegemon and leader of the capitalist world (dealing with the potential threat from the Communist world). It now relies more and more on an international legal and regulatory architecture—fortified by various multilateral and bilateral agreements—to establish the power of capital over labor. This has involved a "grand bargain," no less potent for being implicit, between different segments of capital. Capitalist firms in the developing world gained some market access (typically intermediated by multinational capital) and, in return, large capital in highly developed countries got much greater protection and monopoly power, through tighter enforcement of intellectual property rights and greater investment protections.

These measures dramatically increased the bargaining power of capital relative to labor, globally and in every country. In the high-income countries, this eliminated the "labor aristocracy" first theorized by the German Marxist theorist Karl Kautsky in the early 20th century. The concept of the labor aristocracy derived from the idea that the developed capitalist countries, or the "core" of global capitalism, could extract superprofits from impoverished workers in the less developed "periphery." These surpluses could be used to reward workers in the core, relative to those in the periphery, and thereby achieve greater social and political stability in the core countries. This enabled northern capitalism to look like a win-win economic system for capital and labor (in the United States, labor relations between the late 1940s and the 1970s, for example, were widely termed a "capital-labor accord"). Today, the increased bargaining power of capital and the elimination of the labor aristocracy has delegitimized the capitalist system in the rich countries of the global North.

Increasing inequality, the decline in workers' incomes, the decline or absence of social protections, the rise of material insecurity, and a growing alienation from government have come to characterise societies in both developed and developing worlds. These sources of grievance have found political expression in a series of unexpected electoral outcomes (including the "Brexit" vote in the UK and the election of Trump in the United States). The decline of the labor aristocracy—really, its near collapse—has massive implications, as it undermines the social contract that made global capitalism so successful in the previous era. It was the very foundation of political stability and social cohesion within advanced capitalist countries, which is now breaking down, and will continue to break down without a drastic restructuring of the social and economic order. The political response to this decline has been expressed primarily in the rise of right-wing, xenophobic, sectarian, and reactionary political tendencies.

21st Century Imperialism

The early 21st century has been a weird time for imperialism. On the one hand, the phase of "hyper-imperialism"—with the United States as the sole capitalist superpower, free to use almost the entire world as its happy hunting ground—is over. Instead, the United States looks significantly weaker both economically and politically, and there is less willingness on the part of other countries (including former and current allies, as well as those that may eventually become rival powers) to accept its writ unconditionally. On the other hand, the imperial overreach that was so evident in the Gulf Wars and sundry other interventions, in the Middle East and around the world, continues despite the decreasing returns from such interventions. This continued through the Obama presidency, and it is still an open question whether the Trump presidency will lead to a dramatic reduction of this overreach ("isolationism") or merely a change in its direction.

The latter point is important, because there is little domestic political appetite in the United States for such imperial adventures, due to the high costs in terms of both government spending and the loss of lives of U.S. soldiers. The slogans that recently resonated with the U.S. electorate, such as that of "making America great again" were in that sense somewhat self-contradictory—looking towards an imagined past in which the American Dream could be fulfilled relatively easily (at least for some), without recognising that this was predicated upon the country's global hegemony and far-flung empire.

All this does not mean that there have been no changes in global economic and political power: there have been and will continue to be significant and even transformative changes. However, changes in the relative positions of different countries on the economic and geopolitical ladder do not mean that the basic imperialistic tendencies that drive the global system have disappeared—indeed, they may even become more intense as the struggle for economic territory becomes more acute.

This is particularly evident in the global spread of multinational corporations and their new methods of functioning, particularly with the geographic disintegration of production. Technological changes—advances in shipping and container technology that dramatically reduced transport times and costs, as well as the information technology revolution that enabled the breakdown of production into specific tasks that could be geographically separated—have been critical to this process. Together, they made possible the emergence of global value chains, which are typically dominated by large multinational corporations, but involve networks of both competing and cooperating firms. The giant corporations are not necessarily in direct control of all operations. Indeed, the ability to transfer direct control over production—as well as the associated risks—to lower ends of the value chain is an important element in increasing their profitability. This adds a greater intensity to the exploitation that can be unleashed by such global firms, because they are less dependent upon workers and resources in any one location, can use competition between suppliers to push down their prices and conditions of production, and are less burdened by national regulations that might reduce their market power.

This transformation has therefore given rise to what has been called the "Smiling Curve" of exchange values and profits. Value added and profits are concentrated in the pre-production (such as product design) and post-production (marketing and branding) phases of a value chain. These now provide immense economic rents to the global corporations that dominate them, due to the intellectual property monopolies these corporations enjoy. The case of Apple phones is now well known: The actual producers in China (both companies and workers) earn only about one-tenth of the final price of the good; the rest is taken by Apple for product design, marketing, and distribution. The producers of coffee beans across the developing world earn a tiny percentage of the price of coffee, in contrast to the high profits of a multinational chain like Starbucks. Small farmers and laborers growing cocoa beans earn next to nothing, compared to the leading sellers of chocolate, all of which are Northern companies. The economic rents associated with the pre- and post-production phases have been growing in recent years. Meanwhile, the production phase, from which workers and small producers mainly derive their incomes, is exposed to cutthroat competition between different production sites across the world, thanks to trade and investment liberalization. Therefore, incomes generated in this stage of the value chain are kept low.

The overall result is twofold. First, this has resulted in an increase in the supply of the "global" labor force (workers and small producers who are directly engaged in production of goods and services). Second, the power of corporations to capture rents—from control of knowledge, from oligopolistic/monopolistic market structures, or from the power of finance capital over state policy—has greatly increased. Overall, this has meant a dramatic increase in the bargaining power of capital relative to labor, which in turn has resulted in declining wage shares (as a percentage of national income) in both developed and developing countries.

Implications for Workers

These processes imply worsening material conditions, for most workers, in both the periphery and the core. Imperialism has generally weakened the capacity for autonomous development in the global South, and worsened economic conditions for workers and small producers there, so that is not altogether surprising. The growth of employment and wages in China is as a break from that pattern and an example of some benefits of global integration, at least for a subset of working people in the developing world. The beneficiaries, however, remain a minority of the workers in the global South. In other countries generally seen as "success stories" of globalization, like India, the economic realities for most people are much bleaker.

The more obvious—and potent—change that has resulted from this phase of global imperialism has been the decline of the labor aristocracy in the North. The opening of trade, and with it a global supply of labor, meant that imperialist-country capital was no longer as interested in maintaining a social contract with workers in the "home" country. Instead, it could use its greater bargaining power to push for ever-greater shares of national income everywhere it operated. This was further intensified by the greater power of mobile finance capital, which was also able to increase its share of income as well. In the advanced economies at the core of global capitalism, this process (which began in the United States in the 1990s) was greatly intensified during the global boom of the 2000s, when median workers' wages stagnated and even declined in the global North, even as per capita incomes soared. The increase in incomes, therefore, was captured by stockholders, corporate executives, financial rentiers, etc.

The political fallout of this has now become glaringly evident. Increasing inequality, stagnant real incomes of working people, and the increasing material fragility of daily life have all contributed to a deep dissatisfaction among ordinary

Poorer Than Our Parents?

A recent report from the McKinsey Global Institute, "Poorer than Their Parents? Flat or falling incomes in advanced economies" (July 2016) shows how the past decade has brought significantly worse economic outcomes for many people in the developed world.

Falling Incomes.

In 25 advanced economies, 65-70% of households (540-580 million people) "were in segments of the income distribution whose real incomes were flat or had fallen" between 2005 and 2014. By contrast, between 1993 and 2005, "less than 2 percent, or fewer than ten million people, experienced this phenomenon." In Italy, a whopping 97% of the population had stagnant or declining market incomes between 2005 and 2014. The equivalent figures were 81% for the United States and 70% for the United Kingdom. The worst affected were "young people with low educational attainment and women, single mothers in particular." Today's younger generation in the advanced countries is "literally at risk of ending up poorer than their parents," and in any case already faces much more insecure working conditions.

Shifting Income Shares

The McKinsey report noted that "from 1970 to 2014, with the exception of a spike during the 1973–74 oil crisis, the average wage share fell by 5 percentage points in the six countries studied in depth" (United States, United Kingdom, France, Italy, the Netherlands and Sweden); in the "most extreme case, the United Kingdom, by 13 percentage points." These declines occurred "despite rising productivity, suggesting a disconnect between productivity and incomes." Productivity gains were either grabbed by employers or passed on in the form of lower prices to maintain competitiveness.

Declining wage shares are widely seen as results of globalization and technological changes, but state policies and institutional relations in the labor market matter. According to the McKinsey report. "Swedish labor policies such as contracts that protect both wage rates and hours worked" resulted in ordinary workers receiving a larger share of income. Countries that have encouraged the growth of part-time and temporary contracts experienced bigger declines in wage shares. According to European Union data, more than 40% of EU workers between 15 and 25 years have insecure and low-paying contracts. The proportion is more than half for the 18 countries in the Eurozone, 58% in France, and 65% in Spain.

people in the rich countries. While even the poor among them are still far better off than the vast majority of people in the developing world, their own perceptions are quite different, and they increasingly see themselves as the victims of globalization. Decades of neoliberal economic policies have hollowed out communities in depressed areas and eliminated any attractive employment opportunities for youth. Ironically, in the United States this favored the political rise of Donald Trump, who is himself emblematic of the plutocracy.

Similar tendencies are also clearly evident in Europe. Rising anti-EU sentiment has been wrongly attributed only to policies allowing in more migrants. The hostile response to immigration is part of a broader dissatisfaction related to the design and operation of the EU. For years now, it has been clear that the EU has failed as an economic project. This stems from the very design of the economic integration—

The other side of the coin is the rising profit shares in many of these rich countries. In the United States, for example, "after-tax profits of U.S. firms measured as a share of the national income even exceeded the 10.1 percent level last reached in 1929."

Policy Matters

Government tax and transfer policies can change the final disposable income of households. Across the 25 countries studied in the McKinsey report, only 20–25% of the population experienced flat or falling disposable incomes. In the United States, government taxes and transfers turned a "decline in market incomes for 81 percent of all income segments ... into an increase in disposable income for nearly all households." Government policies to intervene in labor markets also make a difference. In Sweden, the government "intervened to preserve jobs, market incomes fell or were flat for only 20 percent, while disposable income advanced for almost everyone." In most of the countries examined in the study, government policies were not sufficient to prevent stagnant or declining incomes for a significant proportion of the population.

Effects on Attitudes

The deteriorating material reality is reflected in popular perceptions. A 2015 survey of British, French, and U.S. citizens confirmed this, as approximately 40% "felt that their economic positions had deteriorated." The people who felt worse-off, and those who did not expect the situation to improve for the next generation, "expressed negative opinions about trade and immigration." More than half of this group agreed with the statement, "The influx of foreign goods and services is leading to domestic job losses." They were twice as likely as other respondents to agree with the statement, "Legal immigrants are ruining the culture and cohesiveness in our society." The survey also found that "those who were not advancing and not hopeful about the future" were, in France, more likely to support political parties such as the far-right Front National and, in Britain, to support Brexit.

Source: McKinsey Global Institute, "Poorer than Their Parents?" July 2016 (mckinsey.com).

flawed, for example, in the enforcement of monetary integration without banking union or a fiscal federation that would have helped deal with imbalances between EU countries—as well as from the particular neoliberal economic policies that it has forced its members to pursue.

This has been especially evident in the adoption of austerity policies across the member countries, remarkably even among those that do not have large current-account or fiscal deficits. As a result, growth in the EU has been sclerotic at best since 2004, and even the so-called "recovery" after 2012 has been barely noticeable. Even this lackluster performance has been highly differentiated, with Germany emerging as the clear winner from the formation of the Eurozone. Even large economies like France, Italy, and Spain experienced deteriorating per capita incomes relative to Germany from 2009 onwards. This, combined with fears of German domination, probably added to the resentment of the EU that is now being expressed in both right-wing and left-wing movements across Europe. The EU's misguided emphasis on neoliberal policies and fiscal austerity packages has also contributed to the persistence of high rates of unemployment, which are higher than they were more than a decade ago. The "new normal" therefore shows little improvement from the period just after the Great Recession—the capitalist world economy may no longer be teetering on the edge of a cliff, but that is because it has instead sunk into a mire.

It is sad but not entirely surprising that the globalization of the workforce has not created a greater sense of international solidarity, but rather undermined it. Quite obviously, progressive solutions cannot be found within the existing dominant economic paradigm. But reversions to past ideals of socialism may not be all that effective either. Rather, this new situation requires new and more relevant economic models of socialism to be developed, if they are to capture the popular imagination. Such models must transcend the traditional socialist paradigm's emphasis on centralized government control over an undifferentiated mass of workers. They must incorporate more explicit emphasis on the rights and concerns of women, ethnic minorities, tribal communities, and other marginalised groups, as well as recognition of ecological constraints and the social necessity to respect nature. The fundamental premises of the socialist project, however, remain as valid as ever: The unequal, exploitative and oppressive nature of capitalism; the capacity of human beings to change society and thereby alter their own futures; and the necessity of collective organisation to do so. ❑

This is an excerpted version of an article that appeared in the March/April 2017 issue of Dollars & Sense *magazine. Portions of that article appeared in the author's earlier article, "The Creation of the New Imperialism: The Institutional Architecture," Monthly Review, July 2015.*

Chapter 10

RESISTANCE AND ALTERNATIVES

INTRODUCTION

Many of the articles in this book are about problems in the U.S. and global economies. Both the dominant economic ideologies and the ruling institutions, many authors argue, favor the wealthy and powerful and are stacked against workers, poor people, developing countries, and other less-powerful actors in the domestic and international economies. That is not, however, the whole story. Those who are getting a raw deal under existing arrangements are not merely passive victims. Some are standing up and resisting poverty, inequality, and enforced powerlessness. Some are fighting for changes in policies and institutions that would help shift the existing balance of power, and improve conditions of life for those at the "bottom," for a change. This chapter describes both resistance and alternatives to the current "neoliberal" economic orthodoxy, on the domestic U.S. and international scenes.

The first five articles in this chapter focus on the U.S. economy and its institutions.

To start, Arthur MacEwan points out that the burning problems in the U.S. economy—how to achieve sustainable growth and good jobs for all who want them—are not economic, but political (Article 10.1). That is, we have the resources we need to solve our problems, but they are not deployed correctly because powerful interests stand in the way.

Next, Robert Pollin criticizes the view that, in order to tackle the threat of climate change, we have to go to a no-growth or negative-growth economy (Article 10.2). Either of those outcomes, Pollin argues, would both be highly damaging economically and fail to reduce greenhouse-gas emissions enough. Instead, he proposes that we need to invest a significant portion of our growing economy to reducing our energy use and converting the energy sector to renewables.

Next, Gerald Friedman's "Progressives Need a Tax-Reform Agenda" (Article 10.3) offers us timely and concrete proposals for addressing the crisis of income inequality in this country with a fairer progressive system of taxation.

Dean Baker calls for a return to the regulations separating basic banking functions from speculation—rules that were put in place in the wake of the Great Crash in 1929 but abandoned at the urging of banks in the 1990s (Article 10.4).

Next, Robert Pollin makes the case for transforming the Fed into a democratically controlled investment bank that serves the interests of all of us (Article 10.5).

The next two articles address issues from around the world.

Arthur MacEwan (Article 10.6) takes on the thorny issue of how trade agreements can incorporate labor standards to improve conditions for workers in lower-income countries. MacEwan notes that barriers to exports from those countries, even those tied to labor standards, can harm workers by taking away employment opportunities. Activists pushing for international labor standards, in his view, should take their lead from the workers in the affected countries, and above all emphasize those workers' rights to organize for improved labor conditions.

Finally, Jawied Nawabi (Article 10.7) focuses on land reform and its importance to economic development. Part of the case for land reform, he notes, is "economic"—for example, small farms actually produce more output per acre than large landholdings. However, the crux of the case is not narrowly economic, but "sociopolitical." Land reform is so essential to economic development, Nawabi argues, because the power of large landlords stands in the way of needed development policies.

Discussion Questions

1. (Article 10.1) According to MacEwan, in what way are powerful vested interests standing in the way of needed reforms in the United States? How could this resistance ever be overcome?

2. (Article 10.2) If greenhouse gas emissions associated with human productive activity are the main cause of climate change, why does Pollin disagree with the prescription of a no-growth or negative-growth economy?

3. (Article 10.3) Gerald Friedman offers seven concrete suggestions for a progressive tax policy. What are they? What makes them "progressive"?

4. (Article 10.4) What was the Glass-Steagall Act and why does Dean Baker argue it should be revived?

5. (Article 10.5) What are the chief elements of Pollin's proposal to transform the Fed? How would the Fed's focus and decision-making change? Do you think the proposal would be effective?

6. (Article 10.6) Opponents of international labor standards argue that workers in very low-income countries just need jobs, and will only be hurt by well-intentioned efforts to raise wages or improve working conditions. How does MacEwan propose to avoid such unintended negative consequences?

7. (Article 10.7) Nawabi argues that land reform is important mainly for "sociopolitical" reasons—that it is necessary to break landlords' stranglehold on political power in order to adopt needed economic development policies. What is the ra-

tionale of this argument? Are there analogous arguments to be made for societies that are mostly urban and industrial, rather than rural and agricultural?

Article 10.1

WHAT WOULD FULL EMPLOYMENT COST?

BY ARTHUR MacEWAN
May/June 2015

> Dear Dr. Dollar:
> *What is the cost, the minimum budget the U.S. government could spend, to ensure everybody who wants a job can have one with decent pay and benefits? How could that be paid for?* —Brett O'Sullivan, Denver, Colo.

The barriers to change of this magnitude—creating good jobs for everyone—are not so much economic as political. We can imagine arrangements by which the economy could function well and would achieve full-employment, good jobs, and benefits. It is, however, hard in the present climate to think that steps in this direction would be politically possible (at least at the national level, though there are political possibilities in some states and localities).

There are things that could be done to move the economy in this direction without significant costs to society. Examples of steps that could improve pay and jobs without major government expenditures include raising the minimum wage and shortening the work week (e.g., requiring time-and-a-half pay for more than 30 hours of work per week). The former would improve workers' pay, and the latter would lead many employers to hire more workers to avoid the higher overtime rates. Also, the rules surrounding unionization could be improved; indeed, simple enforcement of existing rules (e.g., protecting workers trying to form a union) would be a significant step toward improving workers' opportunities.

Also, in terms of providing benefits, a major step forward would be the establishment of a single-payer ("Medicare for All") healthcare system, which would pay for itself by reducing the large overhead costs and profits of the private insurance companies while providing everyone with a prime benefit. Because a single-payer system would cost less than the current system, the payments (taxes) that the government would need would come from and be less than the current insurance premiums. The costs would go through the government, but there would be savings for society. Because this benefit would be for everyone, it would remove the problems that arise when healthcare is tied to employment.

Yet, full employment would also require government spending to stimulate job growth. While the economy operates as it has over the last several years, deficit spending is necessary to move us toward full employment. Especially in the current circumstances, with the economy far from full employment and with interest rates on U.S. government bonds extremely low, deficit spending would not impose large costs (i.e., the costs of paying the interest on the government borrowing to cover the deficit).

It is not hard to figure out what kinds of jobs should be created with government stimulus spending. Prime examples include environmental repair and preservation (including energy conservation), education and training, and infrastructure repair and extension (e.g., especially in public transportation).

Further, stimulus through deficit spending could be used be used for the government to directly create jobs. The quickest and most effective way to do this would be for the federal government to provide funds to the states to reverse the tens of thousands of layoffs of educational workers in the last few years. Also, there is an increasing need for workers in universal early childhood education, as has been instituted in New York City and a few states. Like expenditures on physical infrastructure, these expenditures on social infrastructure would have both short-run multiplier demand impacts and long-run impacts by raising productivity.

Such actions by the government would not require large tax increases, though higher taxes on people with very high incomes would help. Moreover, as the economy approached full employment, the bargaining power of workers would improve and unionization could be facilitated. As the economy moved back to full employment and incomes rose, taxes would increase without tax rate increases—thus preventing a continuing increase of the government debt.

There would certainly be objections to these sorts of changes. Defenders of the status quo would argue that stimulation of the economy would cause inflation and that raising the minimum wage and facilitating unionization would harm businesses' profits and lead them to cut back on investment (a "capital strike"). The inflation and cutbacks would, the argument goes, mean fewer jobs, and especially fewer good jobs.

With plenty of slack in the labor market, however, there is no reason to believe that government deficits would bring inflation, and as the economy approached full employment, deficit-based stimulus would no longer be needed. The real concerns of those opposed to stimulation of the economy are their opposition to the social programs that would probably grow with larger stimulation and their fear that the growth of those programs might ultimately lead to higher taxes on people with high incomes—prime defenders of the status quo.

As to the fear that business profits would suffer with the sorts of reforms proposed here, that would also be likely. Yet, weaker profits, while a real loss for those at the top, need not be bad for the rest of society. It is only necessary to look at the relatively recent period in our history when wages—including the minimum wage—were relatively higher, unions were stronger, and the distribution of income less unequal. Through the 1950s and into the early 1970s, these conditions were largely met, and the economy grew relatively strongly. There were many economic problems in those years (though not severe inflation) and many circumstances were different from today, but the experience of that period gives the lie to the claims that government stimulus, better working conditions, and greater economic equality would necessarily result in economic disaster.

These changes are blocked by the political power of business and the very wealthy—the infamous 1%—who employ specious arguments about inflation and the undermining of employment to protect their own interests. Changes that would move us toward more and better jobs would be good for most of us. But they would impose costs on those at the top, who raise the fearful specter of "drastic change of the economic system."

Yet, these changes that would meet the goal of more well-paying jobs with good benefits could be accomplished without some drastic system change or some large increase in the costs to society through greater government expenditures and taxation. Could we get more substantial improvements with greater change? Perhaps. But let's first recognize that, even within the profit system, things do not have to be as they are today. ❑

Article 10.2

HOW GROWTH CAN BE GREEN
Economic Growth, Clean Energy, and the Challenge of Climate Change

AN INTERVIEW with ROBERT POLLIN
November/December 2016

In a Gallup poll earlier this year, almost two-thirds of those polled said that global warming worried them "a great deal" or "a fair amount." Yet many are also worried that serious climate policy will require deep sacrifices—including big declines in production, incomes, and employment. In August, Robert Pollin, professor of economics and co-director of the Political Economy Research Institute (PERI) at UMass-Amherst, spoke with Dollars & Sense *co-editor Alejandro Reuss about these issues: Why "negative growth" is not a solution to climate change, why "green growth" is the best way to reduce greenhouse emissions, and how it can work in both high-income and low-income countries. —Eds.*

Dollars & Sense: You've argued in favor of "green growth" as a pathway for climate stabilization. That cuts against a conventional wisdom—both among advocates of serious action on climate policy and critics of such action—that greenhouse gas emissions reductions require a reduction in growth, no growth, or even negative growth. What's the basic case you make for green growth?

Robert Pollin: The argument for green growth is premised on the notion that, while an economy is growing, a given percentage of economic activity is devoted to the transformation of the energy sector—from fossil-fuel based energy to clean energy. According to my research, roughly speaking, if we look at about 1.5% of GDP per year—and I've done it for different countries, so it could be the United States, it could be Spain, it could be Brazil, it could be South Africa, or it could be the world as a whole—1.5% of GDP invested in clean energy—that is, clean renewable energy sources and energy efficiency—that I've costed this out and you could get to a global reduction in absolute CO_2 emissions on the order of 40% within twenty years, which is along the lines of the Intergovernmental Panel on Climate Change goals. That means that what you're doing is, as the economy is growing, you're taking part of economic activity and moving it from dirty activities to clean energy activity. So growth therefore becomes supportive of emissions and climate stabilization.

D&S: If the fruits of growth were heavily invested in projects to increase energy efficiency or develop sources of alternative "clean" energy (wind, water, solar), could a green growth approach actually achieve greater GHG emissions reductions than a hypothetical no-growth or de-growth alternative?

RP: If we're talking about a no-growth scenario, unless you're transforming the energy system you get no reduction in emissions. If you're at a flat level of economic activity, you get exactly the same level of emissions. If we cut GDP by 10%, and you keep the energy system the same, then emissions will go down by 10%, period. And a 10% emissions reduction is nowhere near what's required. On the other hand, reducing GDP by 10% would be the worst depression the world had ever experienced. GDP didn't go down by 10% during the 1930s. During the Great Recession of 2007–2008, global GDP went down by 2½%. So there's no way to get to a climate stabilization path just on the basis of cutting growth. If we want to go to zero growth, or we want to go to negative growth, we still have to transform the energy system, and the best way to transform the energy system is in a framework in which the economy is growing, because then you have a lot of opportunities and a lot of investment. You're creating more jobs. If you're trying to transform the energy system in a phase of no growth, you're imposing a depression, and who's going to be for that? Nobody, except the most fanatical environmentalists. But working people are going to see massive job loss, on a scale much greater than 2007–2009, greater than the 1930s. That has no political support and doesn't solve the problem anyway.

D&S: Is "green growth" a viable course of action for the developing world today? The high-income countries, including some that are now moving in the direction of greener energy, have mostly achieved high incomes through a carbon-intensive path. Can developing countries dramatically raise standards of living on the basis of a low-carbon-intensity path?

RP: Yeah, well the key is that the costs of delivering energy through clean renewable sources plus high efficiency are basically at parity now in developing countries, under average conditions. "Under average conditions" means that there is wide dispersion. It doesn't mean that in every single site if you put up a wind farm or install solar panels that the costs are going to be at parity with, say, the rich countries. But on average, if we believe the research that's out there, they are. And this also depends a lot on investments in high efficiency, because in developing countries the energy systems are very wasteful, so it's easy to get high returns from investing in raising efficiency standards. So actually the green growth path is even more effective in developing countries. I myself have written about it for India, for Brazil, for South Africa, for Indonesia. In a country like Indonesia or India—they expect to be high-growth countries, growing at 6, 7, or 8%—they can actually do that if they keep putting 1.5% of GDP so that their growth dividend moves into clean energy, and you start to see their emissions going down as a feature of economic growth itself.

D&S: What about the means of promoting investment in energy efficiency and alternative energy that you're talking about? You've written about the importance of a leading government role in promoting investment in those sectors. Are you skeptical that governments can just re-set the incentives to private actors—through a carbon tax or emissions permits system—and have that bring about the necessary investments?

RP: Well, we have to be skeptical, because it hasn't happened. And we have to be skeptical because there are obviously extremely powerful interests that are quite pleased with the profits that they're receiving from burning fossil fuels. That's a political question. On the other hand, as I said, on average the costs of renewable energy are close to parity or on parity with fossil fuel energy. Energy efficiency pays for itself, by definition. In fact, in the United States in 2007, under President George W. Bush, a law was passed that required the federal government to raise efficiency standards in all federal buildings by 30% as of the year 2015. Now, we didn't do it, but in the buildings that were retrofitted—there's a website and it shows it was saving the taxpayers hundreds of millions of dollars. So why isn't it happening? One, there's inertia. You do have to do the up-front investment. Two, there's opposition from the fossil fuel industry. So we have to struggle around those things, at the same time recognizing that achieving these kinds of growth projections for clean energy are quite feasible economically and are good for jobs. That's the other big barrier, this notion that you're going to hurt jobs if you're going to protect the environment. Well, you know, the thing that I've been focusing on for several years is that it's actually beneficial for employment to pursue the green growth path as opposed to maintaining the fossil fuel infrastructure. ❏

Article 10.3

PROGRESSIVES NEED A TAX-REFORM AGENDA

BY GERALD FRIEDMAN
January/February 2018

While slashing taxes for some of the country's most privileged, including Donald Trump and his family, the GOP's new tax act fails to address America's most pressing problems: rising inequality, the climate crisis, macroeconomic instability, and declining resources for needed public services in urban and rural America alike. But progressives should resist the temptation to simply attack the GOP giveaway to the ultra-rich. Instead, they should articulate their own tax plan, one that would fund needed services, promote stable growth, and compensate the unlucky, including the victims of globalization. We can have a tax system founded on coherent economic theory, a system that promotes fairness and economic efficiency by following three reasonable principles: all forms of income should be taxed equally, dangerous and destructive activities should be discouraged, and the distribution of income should reflect work rather than luck.

Ensure Fair Taxation of All Forms of Income

- *Tax all corporate profits regardless of where they are earned.* Whle keeping the corporate tax rate at 35%, eliminate the deferral of taxes on profits earned outside the United States. According to the Institute on Taxation and Economic Policy, corporations currently owe $700 billion in taxes on $2.6 trillion worth of profits, parked abroad in tax havens like the Cayman Islands.

- *Eliminate preference for unearned over earned income.* Since 1990, capital gains and some dividends are taxed at a lower rate than is earned income and wages. While workers pay payroll taxes for Social Security and Medicare, 25% income taxes on earnings above $37,651, and more on wage and sakary income above $91,150, capital gains income is taxed at 15% for most Americans, and no more than 20% for higher incomes. Eliminating this preferential treatment and taxing unearned income at the same rate as earned income would raise more than $100 billion a year in additional revenues.

- *Eliminate the tax preference for high-wage income.* The 12.4% retirement payroll tax that funds Social Security only applies to the first $118,500 of income, so about 6% of wage and salary earners only pay the tax on part of their earnings. Restoring the Social Security payroll tax for the richest 1%, those with wages and salaries above $300,000, would raise over $50 billion.

Promote Economic Efficiency

- *Restore the Financial Transactions Tax and implement a financial excise tax.* Until 1966, the United States, like 30 other countries including the United Kingdom, Singapore, and Switzerland, taxed financial transactions to discourage speculative financial activities that would distract from businesses' productive work. Taxing the giant banks would restore the economic balance, favoring the productive activities of Main Street over the financial shenanigans of Wall Street. A tax like this would raise more than $100 billion while increasing economic efficiency.
- *Reduce the deductibility of low wages and strengthen the penalty for companies that do not provide health insurance or pension benefits.* The public safety net, including SNAP and Medicaid, bear much of the burden when profitable companies pay low wages. *Forbes* estimated that in 2014 low-wage workers at Walmart received more than $6 billion in public assistance; Connecticut taxpayers in 2015 paid nearly $500 million in public assistance to employees of profitable businesses. Taxing low-wage employers would encourage higher wages while raising more than $14 billion in revenue.
- *Tax carbon emissions at $25/ton, to begin with, rising by $10/ton every year.* The build-up of carbon dioxide in the atmosphere from the burning of fossil fuels is already transforming the environment with devastating effects on crops, forests, and seaside communities. Charging for the damage done by burning carbon would slow global climate change and encourage the growth of energy-efficient and green industries. It would also raise nearly $100 billion a year at $25/ton and more at higher rates.

Reward Work Not Luck

- *Restore the 1980 estate tax (adjusted for inflation).* In 1980, the estate tax rate was 70% with an exemption (for gifts and estates) of about $1,000,000 in 2017 dollars. At this level of exemption, more than 97% of estates would go untaxed because the great majority of Americans are not fortunate enough to be born into families with such large estates. Revenue would increase by more than $50 billion, the great majority paid by a very small number of very lucky people.

While promoting healthy and stable economic growth, this program would generate more than $500 billion a year in additional revenue. If $400 billion of this revenue was devoted to eliminating income and payroll taxes for households with family income of under $75,000, then that would still leave $100 billion to spend on priorities like infrastructure and education. Instead of the Republicans' proposals designed to enrich a few, opponents can present a coherent program founded on principles of fairness. That is the tax reform that working Americans deserve.◻

Sources: "Fortune 500 Companies Hold a Record $2.6 Trillion Offshore," Institute on Taxation and Economic Policy, March 28, 2017 (itep.org); "The Tax Break-Down: Preferential Rates on Capital Gains," Committee for a Responsible Federal Budget, August 27, 2013 (crfb.org); Kathleen Romig, "Increasing Payroll Taxes Would Strengthen Social Security," Center on Budget and Policy Priorities, September 27, 2016 (cbpp.org); "The 2016 Annual Report of the Board of Trustees of the Federal Old-Age and Survivors Insurance and Federal Disability Insurance Trust Funds," Social Security Administration (ssa.gov); "Walmart on Tax Day: How Taxpayers Subsidize America's Biggest Employer and Richest Family," Americans for Tax Fairness, April 2014 (americansfortaxfairness.org); Daniel Kennedy, Stan McMillen, and Louise Simmons, "The Economic and Fiscal Impact of Connecticut's Proposed Statute to Recoup Costs Attributable to Low-Wage Employers," UCONN School of Social Work, May 18, 2015 (ssw.uconn.edu); "Options for Reducing the Deficit, 2017 to 2026," Congressional Budget Office, December 8, 2016 (cbo.gov); "Federal Estate and Gift Tax Rates, Exemptions, and Exclusions, 1916-2014," Tax Foundation, February 4, 2014 (taxfoundation.org); "The Distribution of Household Income and Federal Taxes, 2013," Congressional Budget Office (cbo.gov).

Article 10.4

GLASS-STEAGALL NOW
Because the banks own Washington.

BY DEAN BAKER
August 2013, Center for Economic and Policy Research

A bipartisan group of senators recently put forward a proposal for new Glass-Steagall legislation that would restore a strict separation between commercial banks and speculative trading. Anyone familiar with the ways of Washington knows that such legislation is badly needed. It is the only way to prevent the Wall Street gang from continuing to rip off the public and subjecting the rest of us to the risks of their speculation.

The idea of the original Glass-Steagall was to create two completely distinct types of banks. On the one hand there would be the standard commercial banks with which most of us are familiar. These are the banks where people have checking and savings accounts and where they might go to take out a mortgage or small business loan.

Because of the central role that commercial banks play in the day-to-day workings of the economy, the government established the Federal Deposit Insurance Corporation (FDIC) to guarantee the vast majority of accounts in full. The goal was to let people know that their money is safe in the bank.

Since the government guaranteed the money, people need never worry about racing to the bank to get their money before the bank vault is empty. As a result we have not seen the sort of old-fashioned bank-runs that were a mainstay of the pre-FDIC era.

The quid pro quo for having the government guarantee deposits was that commercial banks were supposed to restrict their loans to a limited number of relatively safe activities, such as mortgage loans, small business loans, car loans and other simple and standardized forms of credit. These restrictions are essential, because if customers know their money is guaranteed by the government, they won't care if their bank is taking enormous risks. The government must act to impose discipline on bank behavior that will not come from the market when deposits are insured.

By contrast, investment banks were set free to engage in whatever risky behavior they liked. Investment banks did not take deposits but rather raised money through issuing bonds or other forms of borrowing. In principle, their potential failure did not pose the same risk to the economy.

The ending of Glass-Steagall removed the separation between investment banks and commercial banks, raising the possibility that banks would make risky investments with government-guaranteed deposits. In principle, even after the ending of Glass-Steagall banks were supposed to keep a strict separation between their commercial banking and the risky bets taken by their investment banking divisions, but this depends on the ability of regulators to enforce this restriction.

The Volcker Rule provision in Dodd-Frank was an effort to re-establish a Glass-Steagall type separation but the industry is making Swiss cheese out of this regulation in the rule-writing process. Serious people cannot believe that this will keep the Wall Street banks from using their government-guaranteed deposits as a cushion to support their speculative game playing.

If anyone questions how this story is likely to play out in practice, we need only go back a few years to the financial crisis of 2008–2009. At that time, most of the major banks, Bank of America, Citigroup, Goldman Sachs and Morgan Stanley, almost surely would have failed without government support.

In fact, some of the top economic advisors in the Obama administration wanted to let them fail and have the government take them over, as the FDIC does all the time with insolvent banks. However Larry Summers managed to carry the day by arguing that such a move would be far too risky at a time when the financial markets were so unsettled. As a result, the big banks got their government money and were allowed to consolidate so that they are now bigger than ever.

This was primarily a problem of banks that are too big and too interconnected to fail, not just a problem of commercial banks merging with investment banks. But these mergers certainly help banks to reach too-big-to-fail status.

Some may argue that the crisis of 2008–2009 involved extraordinary circumstances. However when banks fail it is generally because the economy faces a crisis. They do not typically fail in good times. And it is a safe bet that there will always be a smart and belligerent Larry Summers on the scene aggressively arguing the case against anyone who wants to subject the banks to market discipline.

What is striking about the argument on re-instating Glass-Steagall is that there really is no downside. The banks argue that it will be inconvenient to separate their divisions, but companies sell off divisions all the time.

They also argue that foreign banks are not generally required to adhere to this sort of separation. This is in part true, but irrelevant.

Stronger regulations might lead us to do more business with foreign-owned banks since weaker regulations could give them some competitive edge. That should bother us as much as it does that we buy clothes and toys from Bangladesh and China.

If foreign governments want to subject themselves and their economies to greater risk as a result of bad financial regulation, that is not an argument for us to do the same. Are we anxious to be the next Iceland or Cyprus?

In short, the senators are on the right track pushing for a new Glass-Steagall. The public should hope that bankers' lobby doesn't derail their efforts. ❑

Article 10.5

TRANSFORMING THE FED

BY ROBERT POLLIN
November 1992

The U.S. financial system faces deep structural problems. Households, businesses, and the federal government are burdened by excessive debts. The economy favors short-term speculation over long-term investment. An unrepresentative and unresponsive elite has extensive control over the financial system. Moreover, the federal government is incapable of reversing these patterns through its existing tools, including fiscal, monetary, and financial regulatory policies.

I propose a dramatically different approach: transforming the Federal Reserve System (the "Fed") into a public investment bank. Such a bank would have substantial power to channel credit in ways that counter financial instability and support productive investment by private businesses. The Fed would use its powers to influence how and for what purposes banks, insurance companies, brokers, and other lenders loan money.

The U.S. government has used credit allocation policies, such as low-cost loans, loan guarantees, and home mortgage interest deductions, extensively and with success. Its primary accomplishment has been to create a home mortgage market that, for much of the period since World War II, provided non-wealthy households with unprecedented access to home ownership.

I propose increasing democratic control over the Federal Reserve's activities by decentralizing power to the 12 district Fed banks and instituting popular election of their boards of directors. This would create a mechanism for extending democracy throughout the financial system.

My proposal also offers a vehicle for progressives to address two separate but equally serious questions facing the U.S. economy:

- how to convert our industrial base out of military production and toward the development and adoption of environmentally benign production techniques; and
- how to increase opportunities for high wage, high productivity jobs in the United States. The U.S. needs such jobs to counteract the squeeze on wages from increasingly globalized labor and financial markets.

Transforming the Federal Reserve system into a public investment bank will help define an economic path toward democratic socialism in the United States.

My proposal has several strengths as a transitional program. It offers a mechanism for establishing democratic control over finance and investment—the area where capital's near-dictatorial power is most decisive. The program will also work within the United States' existing legal and institutional framework. We could implement parts of it immediately using existing federal agencies and with minimal demands on the federal budget.

At the same time, if an ascendant progressive movement put most of the program in place, this would represent a dramatic step toward creating a new economic system. Such a system would still give space to market interactions and the pursuit of greed, but would nevertheless strongly promote general well-being over business profits.

How the Fed Fails

At present the Federal Reserve focuses its efforts on managing short-term fluctuations of the economy, primarily by influencing interest rates. When it reduces rates, it seeks to increase borrowing and spending, and thereby stimulate economic growth and job opportunities. When the Fed perceives that wages and prices are rising too fast (a view not necessarily shared by working people), it tries to slow down borrowing and spending by raising interest rates.

This approach has clearly failed to address the structural problems plaguing the financial system. The Fed did nothing, for example, to prevent the collapse of the savings and loan industry. It stood by while highly speculative mergers, buyouts, and takeovers overwhelmed financial markets in the 1980s. It has failed to address the unprecedented levels of indebtedness and credit defaults of private corporations and households.

New Roles for the Fed

Under my proposal, the Federal Reserve would shift its focus from the short to the long term. It would provide more and cheaper credit to banks and other financiers who loan money to create productive assets and infrastructure—which promote high wage, high productivity jobs. The Fed would make credit more expensive for lenders that finance speculative activities such as the mergers, buyouts, and takeovers that dominated the 1980s.

The Fed would also give favorable credit terms to banks that finance decent affordable housing rather than luxury housing and speculative office buildings. It would make low-cost credit available for environmental research and development so the economy can begin the overdue transition to environmentally benign production. Cuts in military spending have idled many workers and productive resources, both of which could be put to work in such transformed industries.

Finally, the Fed would give preferential treatment to loans that finance investment in the United States rather than in foreign countries. This would help counter the trend of U.S. corporations to abandon the domestic economy in search of lower wages and taxes.

The first step in developing the Fed's new role would be for the public to determine which sectors of the economy should get preferential access to credit. One example, suggested above, is industrial conversion from military production to investment in renewable energy and conservation.

Once the public establishes its investment goals, the Fed will have to develop new policy tools and use its existing tools in new ways to accomplish them. I propose that a transformed Federal Reserve use two major methods:

- set variable cash ("asset reserve") requirements for all lenders, based on the social value of the activities the lenders are financing; and
- increase discretionary lending activity by the 12 district Federal Reserve banks.

Varying Banks' Cash Requirements

The Fed currently requires that banks and other financial institutions keep a certain amount of their assets available in cash reserves. Banks, for example, must carry three cents in cash for every dollar they hold in checking accounts. A bank cannot make interest-bearing loans on such "reserves." I propose that the Fed make this percent significantly lower for loans that finance preferred activities than for less desirable investment areas. Let's say the public decides that banks should allocate 10% of all credit to research and development of new environmental technologies, such as non-polluting autos and organic farming. Then financial institutions that have made 10% of their loans in environmental technologies would not have to hold any cash reserves against these loans. But if a bank made no loans in the environmental area, then it would have to hold 10% of its total assets in reserve. The profit motive would force banks to support environmental technologies without any direct expenditure from the federal budget.

All profit-driven firms will naturally want to avoid this reserve requirement. The Fed must therefore apply it uniformly to all businesses that profit through accepting deposits and making loans. These include banks, savings and loans, insurance companies, and investment brokerage houses. If the rules applied only to banks, for example, then banks could circumvent the rules by redefining themselves as another type of lending institution.

Loans to Banks That Do the Right Thing

The Federal Reserve has the authority now to favor some banks over others by making loans to them when they are short on cash. For the most part, however, the Fed has chosen not to exercise such discretionary power. Instead it aids all banks equally, through a complex mechanism known as open market operations, which increases total cash reserves in the banking system. The Fed could increase its discretionary lending to favored banks by changing its operating procedures without the federal government creating any new laws or institutions. Such discretionary lending would have several benefits.

First, to a much greater extent than at present, financial institutions would obtain reserves when they are lending for specific purposes. If a bank's priorities should move away from the established social priorities, the Fed could then either refuse to make more cash available to it, or charge a penalty interest rate, thereby discouraging the bank from making additional loans. The Fed, for example, could impose such obstacles on lenders that are financing mergers, takeovers, and buyouts.

In addition, the Fed could use this procedure to more effectively monitor and regulate financial institutions. Banks, in applying for loans, would have to submit to the Fed's scrutiny on a regular basis. The Fed could more closely link its regulation to banks' choices of which investments to finance.

Implementing this procedure will also increase the authority of the 12 district banks within the Federal Reserve system, since these banks approve the Fed's loans. Each district bank will have more authority to set lending rates and monitor bank compliance with regulations.

The district banks could then more effectively enforce measures such as the Community Reinvestment Act, which currently mandates that banks lend in their home communities. Banks that are committed to their communities and regions, such as the South Shore Bank in Chicago, could gain substantial support under this proposed procedure.

Other Credit Allocation Tools

The Fed can use other tools to shift credit to preferred industries, such as loan guarantees, interest rate subsidies, and government loans. In the past the U.S. government has used these techniques with substantial success. They now primarily support credit for housing, agriculture, and education. Indeed, as of 1991, these programs subsidized roughly one-third of all loans in the United States.

Jesse Jackson's 1988 Presidential platform suggested an innovative way of extending such policies. He proposed that public pension funds channel a portion of their money into a loan guarantee program, with the funds used to finance investments in low cost housing, education, and infrastructure.

There are disadvantages, however, to the government using loan guarantee programs and similar approaches rather than the Fed's employing asset reserve requirements and discretionary lending. Most important is that the former are more expensive and more difficult to administer. Both loan guarantees and direct government loans require the government to pay off the loans when borrowers default. Direct loans also mean substantial administrative costs. Interest subsidies on loans are direct costs to government even when the loans are paid back.

In contrast, with variable asset reserve requirements and discretionary lending policies, the Fed lowers the cost of favored activities, and raises the cost of unfavored ones, without imposing any burden on the government's budget.

Increasing Public Control

The Federal Reserve acts in relative isolation from the political process at present. The U.S. president appoints seven members of the Fed's Board of Governors for 14-year terms, and they are almost always closely tied to banking and big business. The boards of directors of the 12 district banks appoint their presidents, and these boards are also composed of influential bankers and business people within each of the districts.

The changes I propose will mean a major increase in the central bank's role as an economic planning agency for the nation. Unless we dramatically improve democratic control by the public over the Fed, voters will correctly interpret such efforts as an illegitimate grasp for more power by business interests.

Democratization should proceed through redistributing power downward to the 12 district banks. When the Federal Reserve System was formed in 1913, the principle behind creating district banks along with the headquarters in Washington was to disperse the central bank's authority. This remains a valuable idea, but the U.S. government has never seriously attempted it. Right now the district banks are highly undemocratic and have virtually no power.

One way to increase the district banks' power is to create additional seats for them on the Open Market Committee, which influences short-term interest rates by expanding or contracting the money supply.

A second method is to shift authority from the Washington headquarters to the districts. The Board of Governors would then be responsible for setting general guidelines, while the district banks would implement discretionary lending and enforcement of laws such as the Community Reinvestment Act.

The most direct way of democratizing the district banks would be to choose their boards in regular elections along with other local, regional, and state-wide officials. The boards would then choose the top levels of the banks' professional staffs and oversee the banks' activities.

Historical Precedents

Since World War II other capitalist countries have extensively employed the types of credit allocation policies proposed here. Japan, France, and South Korea are the outstanding success stories, though since the early 1980s globalization and deregulation of financial markets have weakened each of their credit policies. When operating at full strength, the Japanese and South Korean programs primarily supported large-scale export industries, such as steel, automobiles, and consumer electronics. France targeted its policies more broadly to coordinate Marshall Plan aid for the development of modern industrial corporations.

We can learn useful lessons from these experiences, not least that credit allocation policies do work when they are implemented well. But substantial differences exist between experiences elsewhere and the need for a public investment bank in the United States.

In these countries a range of other institutions besides the central bank were involved in credit allocation policies. These included their treasury departments and explicit planning agencies, such as the powerful Ministry of International Trade and Industry (MITI) in Japan. In contrast, I propose to centralize the planning effort at the Federal Reserve.

We could create a new planning institution to complement the work of the central bank. But transforming the existing central banking system rather than creating a new institution minimizes both start-up problems and the growth of bureaucracies.

A second and more fundamental difference between my proposal and the experiences in Japan, France, and South Korea is that their public investment institutions were accountable only to a business-oriented elite. This essentially dictatorial approach is antithetical to the goal of increasing democratic control of the financial system.

The challenge, then, is for the United States to implement effective credit allocation policies while broadening, not narrowing, democracy. Our success ultimately will depend on a vigorous political movement that can fuse two equally urgent, but potentially conflicting goals: economic democracy, and equitable and sustainable growth. If we can meet this challenge, it will represent a historic victory toward the construction of a democratic socialist future. ❑

Sources: Robert Pollin, "Transforming the Federal Reserve into a Public Investment Bank: Why it is Necessary; How it Should Be Done," in G. Epstein, G. Dymski and R. Pollin, eds., *Transforming the U.S. Financial System,* M.E. Sharpe, 1993.

Article 10.6

INTERNATIONAL LABOR STANDARDS

BY ARTHUR MacEWAN
September/October 2008

> Dear Dr. Dollar:
>
> *U.S. activists have pushed to get foreign trade agreements to include higher labor standards. But then you hear that developing countries don't want that because cheaper labor without a lot of rules and regulations is what's helping them to bring industries in and build their economies. Is there a way to reconcile these views? Or are the activists just blind to the real needs of the countries they supposedly want to help?* —Philip Bereaud, Swampscott, Mass.

In 1971, General Emilio Medici, the then-military dictator of Brazil, commented on economic conditions in his country with the infamous line: "The economy is doing fine, but the people aren't."

Like General Medici, the government officials of many low-income countries today see the well-being of their economies in terms of overall output and the profits of firms—those profits that keep bringing in new investment, new industries that "build their economies." It is these officials who typically get to speak for their countries. When someone says that these countries "want" this or that— or "don't want" this or that—it is usually because the countries' officials have expressed this position.

Do we know what the people in these countries want? The people who work in the new, rapidly growing industries, in the mines and fields, and in the small shops and market stalls of low-income countries? Certainly they want better conditions—more to eat, better housing, security for their children, improved health and safety. The officials claim that to obtain these better conditions, they must "build their economies." But just because "the economy is doing fine" does not mean that the people are doing fine.

In fact, in many low-income countries, economic expansion comes along with severe inequality. The people who do the work are not getting a reasonable share of the rising national income (and are sometimes worse off even in absolute terms). Brazil in the early 1970s was a prime example and, in spite of major political change, remains a highly unequal country. Today, in both India and China, as in several other countries, economic growth is coming with increasingly severe inequality.

Workers in these countries struggle to improve their positions. They form—or try to form—independent unions. They demand higher wages and better working conditions. They struggle for political rights. It seems obvious that we should support those struggles, just as we support parallel struggles of workers in our own country. The first principle in supporting workers' struggles, here or anywhere else, is supporting their right to struggle—the right, in particular, to form independent unions without fear of reprisal. Indeed, in the ongoing controversy over the U.S.-Colombia Free Trade Agreement, the assassination of trade union leaders has rightly been a major issue.

Just how we offer our support—in particular, how we incorporate that support into trade agreements—is a complicated question. Pressure from abroad can help, but applying it is a complex process. A ban on goods produced with child labor, for example, could harm the most impoverished families that depend on children's earnings, or could force some children into worse forms of work (e.g., prostitution). On the other hand, using trade agreements to pressure governments to allow unhindered union organizing efforts by workers seems perfectly legitimate. When workers are denied the right to organize, their work is just one step up from slavery. Trade agreements can also be used to support a set of basic health and safety rights for workers. (Indeed, it might be useful if a few countries refused to enter into trade agreements with the United States until we improve workers' basic organizing rights and health and safety conditions in our own country!)

There is no doubt that the pressures that come through trade sanctions (restricting or banning commerce with another country) or simply from denying free access to the U.S. market can do immediate harm to workers and the general populace of low-income countries. Any struggle for change can generate short-run costs, but the long-run gains—even the hope of those gains—can make those costs acceptable. Consider, for example, the Apartheid-era trade sanctions against South Africa. To the extent that those sanctions were effective, some South African workers were deprived of employment. Nonetheless, the sanctions were widely supported by mass organizations in South Africa. Or note that when workers in this country strike or advocate a boycott of their company in an effort to obtain better conditions, they both lose income and run the risk that their employer will close up shop.

Efforts by people in this country to use trade agreements to raise labor standards in other countries should, whenever possible, take their lead from workers in those countries. It is up to them to decide what costs are acceptable. There are times, however, when popular forces are denied even basic rights to struggle. The best thing we can do, then, is to push for those rights—particularly the right to organize independent unions—that help create the opportunity for workers in poor countries to choose what to fight for. ❑

Article 10.7

LAND REFORM
A Precondition for Sustainable Economic Development

BY JAWIED NAWABI
May/June 2015

> *It is in the agricultural sector that the battle for long-term economic development will be won or lost.* —*Gunnar Myrdal, economist and Nobel laureate*

The phrase "land reform" often conjures up memories, for those leaning right, of frightening extreme-left ideologies. On the progressive left, meanwhile, land reform is often treated as a passé topic.

With the advent of rising inequality, climate change, weak government institutions, failed states, terrorism, corruption, and a whole slew of other socio-economic problems—sown or exacerbated by three decades of neoliberal policies in the "developing world" (Global South)—it is high time we revisit the issue of land reform. We need to bring it back to the center of the discussion on sustainable economic development. Land reform is not political extremism; rather, it is a critical policy mechanism for the world to address issues of poverty, hunger, urban slums, and good governance.

What is "land reform"? It is usually defined as the redistribution of large land-holdings to smaller ones. Land is transferred from large landlords to those who have been working the land as tenants (such as sharecroppers) or paid agricultural workers, as well as dispossessed underemployed or unemployed urban workers who migrated from rural areas looking for employment and wound up living in urban slums. That is one model of land reform. Another model is redistribution in the form of rural communes or cooperative or collective farms. A combination of the two models is also possible.

Reemergence of Land Reform Movements

Despite the attempts by international institutions (like the IMF and World Bank) and oligarchic political elites in the global South to suppress land reform policies, there have been growing social movements pushing for land reform in the last two decades. Neoliberal "free trade" policies have exposed small farmers to devastating global competition (especially from giant mechanized industrial farms in the global North), leaving hundreds of millions of them dispossessed, and have forced them into the reserve army of impoverished unemployed or underemployed living in urban slums. From Brazil and Mexico to the Philippines and Zimbabwe, social movements for a more just and fair distribution of wealth—particularly land—are confronting these devastating consequences of neoliberalism.

Social protest has led even elite institutions such as the World Bank to acknowledge the issue. The Bank's *World Development Report 2008: Agriculture for Development*, at least rhetorically put agriculture and the productivity of small farmers "at the heart of a global agenda to reduce poverty."

Agriculture as a Technical Problem?

The central tendency of mainstream economic development theory since the 1940s and 1950s has been to view agriculture as a mere stepping stone towards industrialization. Economist Arthur W. Lewis' "dualist" model was particularly influential in casting agricultural labor in developing countries as redundant—with a "surplus" of workers adding little or nothing to agricultural production. This surplus labor force, Lewis argued, should be moved out of the agricultural sector—this would supposedly not reduce output—and into the industrial, which he viewed as the key sector of the economy.

Besides moving inefficient peasants out of the rural sector, mainstream development economists proposed to boost agricultural yields by consolidating small farms into large ones—supposedly to take advantages of economies of scale. Thus, instead of reducing land concentration, this would increase it, essentially accomplishing a reverse land reform. Such an industrial model of agriculture would use expensive capital equipment (imported from the global North), petroleum-based fertilizers, herbicides, and pesticides. Today's version of the model increasingly pushes the adoption of genetically modified seeds controlled by corporations like Monsanto.

During the 1960s and 1970s, this frame of thought led many international institutions (such as the World Bank, Asian Development Bank, etc.) and governments in the global South to embrace the "Green Revolution." The Green Revolution was essentially a plan to use "science and technology" to increase crop production in developing countries. The use of fertilizers, pesticides, and high-yield crop varieties was supposed to boost agricultural productivity, reduce rural poverty, solve problems of hunger and malnutrition, and thus avoid peasant movements and rural political instability. This was, as economists James M. Cypher and James L. Dietz put it, a "strategy wherein it was hoped that seed technologies could be substituted for missing land reform and for more radical 'red revolutions' of the socialist variety threatening to sweep across the globe at the time."

Viewing agricultural productivity as a purely technical problem, advocates of the Green Revolution did not aim to transform the structure of land inequality and landlord power. To take the case of India, the Green Revolution boosted agricultural yields, making the country technically self-sufficient in food production. However, the changes primarily benefited medium and large-sized landowners who used capital-intensive technologies, high-yielding monocrop seeds, and large inputs of fertilizers and pesticides. "Rural inequity worsened because of the growing prosperity of the large and medium farmers and the unchanged position of the landless and small farmers," concludes Indian scholar Siddharth Dube. "And because large farms use more capital and less labour per unit of produce than

Land Reform and Colonization

If we broaden the concept of land reform, the whole process of colonial settlement in North America, Central and South America, Australia, and New Zealand was one big land reform, appropriating the lands of indigenous peoples and distributing it to the European settlers. So land reform can be understood as a much more common experience of the "developed" world than it is usually thought of in the economic literature.

small farms, rural employment grew much less than it would have if land reform had taken place and the increase in production come from smaller farms."

The Economic and Socio-Political Cases for Land Reform

There are two broad arguments for the importance of land reform. The first is based on the widely observed inverse relationship between farm size and output per unit of land area: smaller farms produce more per acre of land than larger farms. Smaller land holdings are more productive and ecologically sustainable for a number of reasons:

1) Higher labor intensity. Small farmers use more labor per unit of land, which helps generate more output and more employment per unit.

2) Higher multiple cropping. They grow more crops per year on a given piece of land.

3) Higher intensity of cultivation. Small farmers leave a lower proportion of land fallow or uncultivated. In addition, they cultivate crops that are higher value-added per unit of land.

4) Lower negative environmental impacts. Small farms use fertilizers, pesticides, and other agrochemicals more sparingly than large farms. This reduces negative impacts of harmful chemicals on workers and neighbors. Small farmers, overall, have a greater incentive to employ environmentally sustainable techniques than large industrial ones.

While the economic case for land reform can be construed as a narrow technical argument on how best to boost agricultural productivity—which land-reform opponents could argue is unnecessary due to the advent of the Green Revolution—the socio-political argument is aimed against this kind of narrow technical thinking. The importance of a land reform is in changing the hierarchical structure of agrarian class relations while increasing productivity. The idea is to break the power of landlords, who keep peasants as a captive labor force in rural areas and act as a conservative political force at the local and national levels of the state.

The central mechanism by which landlords wield their power is through patron-client networks that give them control over local and regional government institutions. Landlords keep the poor majority dependent on them for jobs and access to land, while also using them as a captive power base for local elections (in countries where there are elections, such as India and Brazil). This way, they can block the development of state

Good Governance

The "good-governance functions" of the state are policies beneficial to the large majority of the population. Good-governance states exercise control over a certain territory, depend on a broad part of their population for revenue, and in turn provide the population with a wide range of public goods: the rule of law, transportation infrastructure (paved roads, extensive and affordable public transportation, etc.), public utilities (electricity, clean water, sewage systems), human services (health, education systems), and job security or at least temporary unemployment insurance.

programs providing public goods—like public roads, clinics, schools, water systems, etc.—for everyone. Instead, they perpetuate a more narrowly targeted development relying on private goods—fertilizer, pesticides, expensive high-yield seeds, privately controlled water wells, loans that put peasants in ever-deeper debt, etc. They provide, also, a form of private insurance system for those clients who exhibit proper loyalty, in contrast to social support systems available to all—which would reduce the peasants' vulnerability and the landlord's power. The consequence is that the state's good-governance capacities are distorted and corrupted, favoring the narrow interests of the landlords and the political elite that is connected to them (often by kinship).

Transformative sociopolitical land reform for developing countries is aimed at diminishing wealth inequalities in the initial stages of development and breaking the grip on power of the upper-class elite (including not only landlords but also big industrial, financial, and commercial capitalists generally allied with them). This democratization of society would make it possible to orient the state towards long-term national development policies which can create more conducive socioeconomic and sociopolitical conditions serving the population as a whole, and not just the elite.

The socioeconomic conditions would include a more egalitarian class structure in the rural sector, greater incentives for farmers to increase their productivity due to owning the land they work, greater farmer incomes allowing the farmers to send their children to school, better nutrition due to higher caloric intake, and greater small-farmer purchasing power leading to greater demand for the products of labor-intensive manufacturing. The sociopolitical democratization would mean the breaking of land-lord power, political stabilization resulting from the inclusion of the peasant masses in the political system, and democratization of decision making now liberated from landlord capture of local and national state bureaucracies.

Land Reform Is Not Enough

There have been many more failed land reforms than successful ones. Reforms have failed mainly because they have not been thorough enough in breaking the power of the landed elite, and in extending the role of the government in an inclusive development process. Across Latin America—in Mexico, Bolivia, Brazil, Chile, and Peru—land reforms have had partial success, but for the most part have not dislodged rural elites and their industrial counterparts from political dominance. This has contributed to an image of land reform, even among the progressive left, as a tried and failed policy. There are also examples of half-successful land reforms in South and East Asia—in India, the Philippines, Indonesia, and Thailand—where peasants did reap some benefits like reliable ownership titles, which allowed them to borrow on better terms, boosted crop yields, and reduced malnutrition, though without fundamentally altering the class structure.

On the other hand, successful land reforms were thorough, extensive, and swift. Key examples in the 20th century include Japan, Taiwan, South Korea, and China. Land in the first three countries was distributed as family-sized farms. (China initially had a collectivized land reform.) Looking at the Japanese and South Korean cases: In Japan in 1945, 45% of the peasants were landless tenants. By 1955, only

9% were tenants and even they benefited from much-strengthened protective laws. In pre-reform South Korea in 1944, the top 3% of landholders owned about 64% of the land, with an average holding of 26 hectares. By 1956, the top 6% owned just 18% of the land, with an average of about 2.6 hectares. Meanwhile, 51% of family farmers owned about 65% of the land, with an average holding of 1.1 hectares.

Nowhere in Latin America or Africa, nor elsewhere in Asia (except Kerala, India), did land reforms come so close to such equalization and radical reshaping of traditional social structures. The East Asian land reforms succeeded in bringing about the long-term national development policies by creating more conducive socioeconomic and sociopolitical conditions—breaking the existing power structure, allowing for the emergence of developmentally oriented states (as opposed to neoliberal models that saw state promotion of economic development as anachronistic and "inefficient"). Successful land reforms require follow up—supportive policies investing in rural infrastructure development (irrigation, electricity, roads, health clinics, schools), plus providing services such as clear and legitimate land records, micro-credit at reasonable rates of interest, and training for farmers in the newest skills for sustainable farming. Japan, Taiwan, South Korea, and arguably even China's development paths serve as examples of transformative land reforms in the last fifty years. What these countries achieved was remarkable growth with equity. ❑

CONTRIBUTORS

Dean Baker is co-director of the Center for Economic and Policy Research.

Peter Barnes, co-founder of Working Assets, is a senior fellow at the Tomales Bay Institute.

James M. Cypher is a *Dollars & Sense* Associate and a professor of economics in the Doctoral Program in Development Studies, Universidad Autónoma de Zacatecas (México).

Nina Eichacker is an assistant professor of economics at the University of Rhode Island and a member of the *Dollars & Sense* collective.

Gerald Epstein is a professor of economics and co-director of the Political Economy Research Institute (PERI) at the University of Massachusetts-Amherst.

Gerald Friedman is a professor of economics at the University of Massachusetts-Amherst.

Nancy Folbre is emeritus professor of economics at the University of Massachusetts-Amherst. She contributes regularly to the *New York Times* Economix blog.

Jayati Ghosh is a professor of economics at the Centre for Economic Study and Planning at Jawaharlal Nehru University.

Robert Hockett is a professor at Cornell University; senior counsel at Westwood Capital; a fellow at the Century Foundation, and former resident consultant at the Federal Reserve Bank of New York and at the International Monetary Fund.

Janelle Jones is an economic analyst at the Economic Policy Institute.

Sean Keith is an undergraduate studying history at Northeastern University and a *Dollars & Sense* intern.

José A. Laguarta Ramírez is a scholar-activist and educator born in San Juan, Puerto Rico and trained in anthropology, law, and comparative politics.

Arthur MacEwan, a *Dollars & Sense* Associate, is professor emeritus of economics at the University of Massachusetts-Boston.

John Miller is a *Dollars & Sense* collective member and a professor of economics at Wheaton College.

Jawied Nawabi is a professor of economics and sociology at CUNY Bronx Community College and a member of the *Dollars & Sense* collective.

Evita Nolka is a political theorist from Greece.

Doug Orr teaches economics at the City College of San Francisco.

Thomas Palley is an economist and the author of *Financialization: The Economics of Finance Capital Domination* (Palgrave Macmillan, 2013).

Robert Pollin teaches economics and is co-director of the Political Economy Research Institute at the University of Massachusetts-Amherst.

Steven Pressman is a professor of economics and finance at Monmouth University and the author of *Fifty Major Economists*.

Alejandro Reuss is a historian, economist, and former co-editor of *Dollars & Sense*.

Luis Rosero (co-editor of this book) is an assistant professor of economics at Framingham State University.

Jonathan Rowe was a fellow at the Tomales Bay Institute and a former contributing editor at the *Washington Monthly*. He died in March 2011.

John Schmitt is the vice president of the Economic Policy Institute.

Nick Serpe (co-editor of this book) is co-editor of *Dollars & Sense*.

Zoe Sherman is an assistant professor of economics at Merrimack College and a member of the *Dollars & Sense* collective.

Bryan Snyder (co-editor of this book) is a senior lecturer in economics at Bentley University.

Chris Sturr (co-editor of this book) is co-editor of *Dollars & Sense* and a lecturer on Social Studies at Harvard University.

William K. Tabb is professor emeritus of economics at Queens College and author of *The Restructuring of Capitalism in Our Time* (2012) and *Economic Governance in the Age of Globalization* (2004).

Chris Tilly, a *Dollars & Sense* Associate, is director of the Institute for Research on Labor and Employment and professor of urban planning, both at UCLA.

Ramaa Vasudevan is assistant professor of economics at Colorado State University and a former *Dollars & Sense* collective member.

John Weeks is an economist, one of the founders of the UK-based Economists for Rational Economic Policies, and part of the European Research Network on Social and Economic Policy.

Jeannette Wicks-Lim is an assistant research professor at the Political Economy Research Institute at the University of Massachusetts-Amherst.

Valerie Wilson is the director of the Economic Policy Institute's Program on Race, Ethnicity, and the Economy.

Marty Wolfson teaches economics at the University of Notre Dame and is a former economist with the Federal Reserve Board in Washington, D.C.